BEHIND THE THRONE

A DOMESTIC HISTORY OF THE ROYAL HOUSEHOLD

BY THE SAME AUTHOR

Historic Houses of the National Trust
Country Houses from the Air
Life in the English Country Cottage
Visions of Power: Ambition and Architecture
The Polite Tourist: A History of Country House Visiting
The Arts & Crafts House
The Art Deco House
His Invention So Fertile: A Life of Christopher Wren
By Permission of Heaven: The Story of the Great Fire of London
The Verneys: A True Story of Love, War and Madness in Seventeenth-Century England
Pirates of Barbary: Corsairs, Conquests and Captivity in the Seventeenth-Century Mediterranean
The Rainborowes: Pirates, Puritans and a Family's Quest for the Promised Land
The Long Weekend
The Great Fire of London

BEHIND THE THRONE

A DOMESTIC HISTORY OF THE ROYAL HOUSEHOLD

Adrian Tinniswood

JONATHAN CAPE

LONDON

1 3 5 7 9 10 8 6 4 2

Jonathan Cape, an imprint of Vintage Publishing,
20 Vauxhall Bridge Road,
London SW1V 2SA

Jonathan Cape is part of the Penguin Random House group of companies whose
addresses can be found at global.penguinrandomhouse.com.

First published by Jonathan Cape in 2018

penguin.co.uk/vintage

A CIP catalogue record for this book is available from the British Library

ISBN 9781910702826

Designed by Peter Ward
Printed and bound by Firmengruppe APPL, aprinta druck, Wemding, Germany

Penguin Random House is committed to a sustainable future for our
business, our readers and our planet. This book is made from
Forest Stewardship Council® certified paper.

Title page illustration: The Queen's Palace in St James's Park, depicted
by Thomas Rowlandson in 1809, before John Nash transformed it into
Buckingham Palace.

CONTENTS

The King's Breakfast

The King asked
The Queen, and
The Queen asked
The Dairymaid:
'Could we have some butter for
The Royal slice of bread?'
The Queen asked
The Dairymaid,
The Dairymaid
Said, 'Certainly,
I'll go and tell
The cow
Now
Before she goes to bed.'

The Dairymaid
She curtsied,
And went and told
The Alderney:
'Don't forget the butter for
The Royal slice of bread.'

The Alderney
Said sleepily:
'You'd better tell
His Majesty
That many people nowadays
Like marmalade
Instead.'

The Dairymaid
Said, 'Fancy!'
And went to
Her Majesty.
She curtsied to the Queen, and
She turned a little red:
'Excuse me,
Your Majesty,
For taking of
The liberty,
But marmalade is tasty, if
It's very
Thickly
Spread.'

The Queen said
'Oh!'
And went to
His Majesty:
'Talking of the butter for
The Royal slice of bread,
Many people
Think that
Marmalade
Is nicer.
Would you like to try a little
Marmalade
Instead?'

The King said,
'Bother!'
And then he said,
'Oh, deary me!'
The King sobbed, 'Oh, deary me!'
And went back to bed.
'Nobody,'
He whimpered,
'Could call me
A fussy man;
I *only* want
A little bit

Of butter for
My bread!'

The Queen said,
'There, there!'
And went to
The Dairymaid.
The Dairymaid
Said, 'There, there!'
And went to the shed.
The cow said,
'There, there!
I didn't really
Mean it;
Here's milk for his porringer
And butter for his bread.'

The Queen took
The butter
And brought it to
His Majesty;
The King said,
'Butter, eh?'
And bounced out of bed.
'Nobody,' he said,
As he kissed her
Tenderly,
'Nobody,' he said,
As he slid down
The banisters,
'Nobody,
My darling,
Could call me
A fussy man –
BUT

I do like a little bit of butter to my bread!'

A. A. Milne

For Susan and David

ACKNOWLEDGEMENTS

I HAVE HAD SO MUCH HELP in the writing of this book, from colleagues, from my students, from complete strangers who took the time on various social networks to answer my cries for help on some esoteric detail of court protocol. I am profoundly grateful to them all. I have enjoyed their company and benefitted from their wisdom; and if I have made mistakes, all I can say is that it is in spite of this army of friends, known and unknown, and not because of them.

Special thanks go to Patricia Lankester, who bravely read an early draft of the book and made many helpful suggestions; to Christopher Warwick, who shared his enormous knowledge of the royal family with characteristic kindness; to Sinéad Gallagher, Florence Gatten, Samantha Massey and Jennifer Scott, who in their different ways encouraged me and kept me sane.

Lastly, my thanks to Helen, without whom nothing would be possible.

Bath, May 2018

Black Books and Spangles

I<small>T WAS FIVE O'CLOCK</small> in the afternoon. General Sir Henry Lynedoch Gardiner realised with a jolt that he had made a terrible mistake.

A veteran of the Crimean War and the Indian Mutiny, Gardiner had served in the royal household for twenty-seven years. Now aged seventy-six, his memory was starting to fail him – rather a serious fault in Queen Victoria's senior equerry, whose job it was to smooth his sovereign's path through life. He was very defensive about it, lashing out at anyone who tried to remind him of his duties.

Whenever there was a big dinner at Windsor Castle, a Guards band entertained the Queen and her guests by playing on the terrace outside the dining room. To get there, they had to walk through the dining room itself, making sure they were at their places before the diners arrived. There was just such a dinner this evening: and Gardiner had forgotten to book the band. With less than four hours to go, the guardsmen were all at their camp in Windsor Great Park or, worse, out drinking in Windsor itself. There were no telephones and no cars. There was no way to contact them, no way to have them in place on the castle terrace by 8.45, when the Queen and her guests would sweep into the dining room, expecting music.

Gardiner decided he had no choice but to resign. He went to the junior equerry, a young Grenadier Guards officer named Fritz Ponsonby, and told him so. But Ponsonby reckoned the game was not yet lost. He sent a groom from the stables galloping off with a message for the officer commanding the regiment, begging him to gather the bandsmen together. He sent another to the superintendent of the stables at Windsor, ordering up three large wagonettes to bring the men to the castle as soon as they were assembled. Then, realising that if they were even slightly late they wouldn't be able to walk through to the terrace, he spoke to the head of the Windsor Castle fire brigade and persuaded him to have four ladders ready on the North Terrace. The bandsmen were going to have to scale the castle walls.

Just after 8.45 Queen Victoria and her guests entered the dining room. Fritz Ponsonby and General Gardiner brought up the rear, despondent as they realised there was no National Anthem wafting in through the windows from the terrace. But as the guests sat down, Ponsonby noticed shadowy figures clambering over the wall onto the terrace, lugging their instruments after them. Before Victoria had taken a mouthful of soup, the Guards band struck up an overture and the day was saved.

The next morning, Gardiner received a note from the Queen pointing out that the band should always play the National Anthem when she came in to dinner.

THIS BOOK IS ABOUT the private lives of royalty, from Elizabeth I, who ascended the throne of England in 1558, to Elizabeth II, who nearly four centuries later was proclaimed 'Queen Elizabeth the Second, by the Grace of God Queen of this Realm and of Her other Realms and Territories, Head of the Commonwealth, Defender of the Faith'. Not every one of the seventeen monarchs who bridged the years between receives an equal amount of attention: all sovereigns are interesting, but some are more interesting than others. Nor have I gone into any detail about the business of ruling, or the monarch's often complicated relationship with his or her ministers. Instead, I have focused on how the business of looking after royalty has changed (and in some respects, remained the same) over the past five centuries; how Fritz Ponsonby and his kind have helped to maintain the monarchy.

Kings and queens and their families were, and still are, entitled by virtue of their position to a certain level of comfort, a cocoon of support to make their lives a little easier. Sovereigns don't cook. They don't dress themselves, or pour themselves a drink, or make their own bed. If the stories are true, the future king of this realm and of his other realms and territories doesn't even squeeze his own tube of toothpaste; this task is given to one of his four valets, who applies toothpaste to the royal toothbrush from a crested silver dispenser.* Clarence House has formally denied the other famous 'pampered royal' legend, that each morning the Prince of Wales's staff would line up seven boiled eggs in ascending order of firmness, each one numbered according to cooking time, so that he could sample each and select the one which met his requirements.

In the twenty-first century, the size of Elizabeth II's household stands at around 1,200 employees, about the same as Charles II's household in

---

* And if it is true, it probably dates back to the time in 1990 when Prince Charles broke his right arm playing polo.

Preparations for a state
banquet in St George's
Hall, Windsor Castle.
Elizabeth II supervises as
the yeoman of the glass
and china pantry adjusts
the table settings.

the 1660s but an increase of one-third on the household of Elizabeth's great-great-grandmother Victoria, who had a staff of 921 salaried retainers. Some members of the current royal household are courtiers in the old-fashioned sense of the word, with ceremonial roles and titles which date back for centuries. Others – the Queen's private secretary and her communications secretary, for instance – are modern courtiers, providing advice and managing relations with government and people. Others still are support staff in a more domestic sense, cooking and cleaning and making the beds. The Prince of Wales, who keeps a separate establishment, employs over 160 full-time staff, most of whom are there to support the official duties and charitable activities of the Prince, the Duchess of Cornwall, and the Duke and Duchess of Cambridge and the Duke and Duchess of Sussex. Only twenty-six are described as personal, garden and farm staff.

Of course, rich people have always had entourages, small armies of secretaries and servants and sycophants. But for royalty, there is more to it. Kingship isn't a role to which one can aspire, like the presidency of the United States or the head of a social media empire. The rituals of royal care are there to separate the sovereign from the rest, to remind their subjects that they are not like other people, not even presidents and billionaire executives. If they were, if there was no difference between the prince and the pauper, then why shouldn't the pauper reign in the prince's place? Whether monarchs have ruled by repression or consensus, their lives were and still are a pattern of reminders that they are not like us. They are different.

IT HAS ALWAYS BEEN THAT WAY. When Henry VIII's servants made his bed each evening, they crossed themselves and kissed the spots where their hands had touched the sacred space. There were rules about how a servant should place the towel and napkin on the king's table ('no wrinkles'); about what Henry VIII's father, Henry VII, should wear at the traditional Twelfth Night festivities – a crown of gold set with sapphires, rubies, emeralds and pearls, which 'ought to be hallowed and no temporal man to touch it but only the king'.[1]

Those rules were set out for the instruction of newcomers to court life, and as a reminder for members of the royal household who might be inclined to forget what was due to their sovereign. Some household ordinances were simply lists of offices with pay and allowances, intended to help with budgeting. Others were meant to regulate behaviours. When Edward IV's seven-month-old son, also Edward, was created Prince of Wales in 1471, a set of 'Regulations for the Government of Prince Edward' was produced, setting out the infant prince's daily routine. It began soon after six o'clock in the morning, when his chaplains came into his bedchamber and said matins. After he was dressed, he went into his private chapel to hear mass. After breakfast he had lessons; then dinner at ten, or eleven if it was a fast day, where 'such noble stories as behoveth to a prince to understand' were read to him.[2] There were more lessons, and sports, in the afternoon. He was to be in bed by eight, and his attendants were urged to make him 'joyous and merry' at bedtime.[3]

The settings for these medieval displays of regal ritual varied enormously, from hunting lodges to castles to palaces. The kings and queens of England moved frequently. They liked to show themselves to their subjects as a demonstration of their power; they liked to hunt in different parts of their realm; they went in search of healthy air, avoiding plague and pestilence; and they went in search of provisions when supplies in the immediate neighbourhood ran low.

And they had plenty of royal houses to choose from. In the thirteenth century, Edward I owned around twenty houses. When Henry VII came to the throne in 1485 fourteen of those houses had been sold or given away or abandoned: the only ones left were Clarendon Palace in Wiltshire; Clipstone, a substantial hunting lodge in Nottinghamshire; Havering Palace to the east of London; Windsor Castle; Woodstock in Oxfordshire; and Westminster Palace, built by Edward the Confessor in the mid-eleventh century, at the same time as he established Westminster Abbey, and remodelled by the Norman and Angevin kings, most notably William Rufus, who in 1097–9 created in Westminster Hall the largest hall in England.

In addition to these six residences, medieval kings added and subtracted others as their fortunes rose and fell. Houses were given away, confiscated, abandoned. In some reigns, the number of royal houses amounted to twenty-five; in others, it fell to no more than nine or ten. Their interiors were a long way from the stark, stony survivals that we see as we wander round medieval houses today. Walls were often whitewashed and quarried – marked with lines, usually in red, to represent blocks – and those blocks were sometimes filled with painted decoration. Ceilings were covered with gold and silver spangles. Wainscoting in the form of vertical deal planking was popular in the royal palaces, and this was also painted, sometimes with quite elaborate 'histories' or allegorical scenes with deeply personal meanings. At Southampton Castle in 1182, Henry II, whose children were battling each other over the succession to the throne, ordered his chamber to be painted with a picture of an eagle being attacked by its offspring.

When Henry VIII came to the throne in 1509, his own architectural inheritance included a palace on the south bank of the Thames nine miles upstream from Westminster, at Sheen, renamed 'Richmond' by his father; and another new palace at Greenwich, also on the Thames and seven miles downstream. In 1512 a fire destroyed the residential part of the palace at Westminster. Rather than rebuild it, Henry VIII decided to leave what remained to serve as his administrative and legal headquarters, while he began a new palace at Bridewell on the edge of the old City of London. In the first two decades of his reign he acquired more houses, including Grafton in Northamptonshire and New Hall in Essex. But two acquisitions were by far the most important. The first came in 1527, when Henry's lord chancellor, Cardinal Thomas Wolsey, tried to stave off his

Members of the royal household pictured at Balmoral in 1920: from left to right, the king's telephonist, confectioner, court telegraphist, chef, court postmaster and a footman.

master's mounting displeasure over his failure to arrange the annulment of Henry's marriage to Catherine of Aragon by presenting him with the half-finished Hampton Court Palace on the Thames, twelve miles south-west of London; and then in 1529, Wolsey's fall enabled Henry to occupy the cardinal's town house, York Place, which sprawled along the Thames just yards from the old palace of Westminster. By 1532 Henry had renamed it Whitehall.

Henry VIII continued to accumulate houses at an extraordinary rate. Between 1531 and 1536 he built a large new house, St James's, on the site of an old leper hospital in Westminster. Various senior clerics were urged to follow Wolsey's example (or rather, to avoid following Wolsey's example) by handing over their houses to the King: Archbishop Cranmer gave up Mortlake in Surrey and Knole in Kent; the Bishop of Ely handed over Hatfield in Hertfordshire; the Bishop of Durham gave his episcopal house on the Strand. By the time of his death in 1547, Henry VIII owned over fifty houses – more than any other monarch before or since.[4]

The extent of the accommodation varied enormously, as did its configuration. But the principles remained the same, whether the sovereign was staying at a hunting lodge or a palace. By the fourteenth century the household had split into the Hall and the Chamber, both of which were departments rather than actual, architectural spaces. The Hall included quasi-public communal areas such as the physical hall, where most of the household ate, and service areas like the kitchens, larders and pantries. The Chamber, the king's private space (in so far as any space could be called private for a sovereign whose bowel movements took place in company), was his lodgings, a series of rooms and ante-rooms culminating in his bedchamber. As the Middle Ages wore on the sovereign took to eating in these rooms – usually in his bedchamber, which became a more public space in consequence, so that the bed was moved out into another room. By the end of the fifteenth century the Chamber had itself divided into the Great Chamber and the Privy Chamber, although the separate functions of each were by no means clear-cut. Henry VII ate sometimes in state in his hall; sometimes in his great chamber; and sometimes in his bedchamber, when his table was set up next to his bed.

We can see these separate departments in action in the most comprehensive medieval set of royal household ordinances to survive: the so-called *Liber niger domus regis angliae*, the Black Book of the household of Edward IV. Written sometime between 1467 and 1477, the Black Book was intended to address a problem which English and British sovereigns have grappled with for a thousand years: how to balance domestic economy with the proper display of regal grandeur. The role demands magnificence, and magnificence costs money.

The fifteenth-century judge Sir John Fortescue was one of the first to articulate the connection between wealth and kingship. Writing in the 1470s, Fortescue declared that 'it shall need that the king have such treasure, as he may make new buildings when he will, for his pleasure and magnificence; and as he may buy him rich clothes [and] rich furs'. A king needed money to buy hangings for his houses, vestments for his chapel, horses of great price for his stable. Without it, 'he lived then not like his estate, but rather in misery, and in more subjection than doth a private person'.[5]

Along with money, kingship required organisation. Those horses of great price in the royal stable didn't look after themselves. Chaplains were needed to wear the vestments and pray for the king's soul. Esquires of the body must be on hand to help him with his rich furs; once the new buildings were built for the king's pleasure and magnificence, they had to be populated with grooms and pages and yeomen and gentlemen ushers, who had to be fed by a small army of bakers and cooks and scullions, who had to be paid by an entire department of clerks in the counting house.

This system of household government was what the Black Book

set out to codify. It divided Edward IV's household into two parts: the *Domus Regie Magnificencie* and the *Domus Providencie*, which corresponded very roughly to the Chamber and the Hall, and less roughly to what later reigns would call 'above stairs' and 'below stairs'. The *Domus Providencie* dealt with the day-to-day practicalities of providing food and lighting and heat for a vast throng of servants. It was presided over by the lord steward, who enforced discipline and looked after the finances, heading the counting house or Board of Green Cloth, which was named after the cloth of green baize which customarily covered the board at which its officers sat. The officers who assisted him in this were the treasurer of the household, the comptroller, the cofferer and two clerks of the Green Cloth. But the lord steward's department also comprised the kitchens, the bakehouse, the buttery and pantry, the spicery and confectionery, the laundry and the woodyard, as well as the great hall where most household officers ate and the servants who waited on them. There is still a lord steward, a treasurer and a comptroller in Elizabeth II's household today, although the first is a ceremonial post – no one expects the lord steward to concern himself with budgets and recalcitrant staff any more – and the last two are purely political appointments, given to members of Parliament from whichever party is in government.

The chief officer of the *Domus Regie Magnificencie* was the lord chamberlain. He or his deputy was responsible for the royal apartments and the people who ministered to the king – his body servants, his waiting staff, his physicians and his chaplains, as well as the gentlemen ushers and yeomen ushers, the grooms and pages who looked after the more formal and more public areas of the king's lodgings. By Henry VIII's time, and possibly before it, the Chamber's two sub-departments, the Great Chamber and the Privy Chamber, were still technically in the charge of the lord chamberlain, but the Privy Chamber, the most intimate of the king's public spaces, was looked after by a small group of grooms of the chamber, headed by the groom of the stool. This officer originally had the task of supervising the sovereign's bowel movements, although from these unenviable beginnings he (or she, when the sovereign was female) eventually became one of the most powerful figures in the royal household, with the right to attend the king at all times. They were gatekeepers, controlling access to the king even when they weren't present at court, and mediating between him and other members of the household. The post was only discontinued when Victoria came to the throne in 1837.

In theory, everything about the workings of the royal household was

Members of Queen
Victoria's household,
including her dressers
and, standing in the
back row, two of her
detectives.

strictly controlled. Some of the sovereign's servants (and those servants'
own servants) were entitled to bouche of court – that is, they had food
and lodging, fuel to keep them warm and candles to light their way,
sometimes clothes or an allowance for clothes to help them do their
job. Lists of names set out who could receive bouche of court; who had
diet only with no lodgings at court; who had to fend for themselves.
Lists set down the wages due to each official, the number of servants an
officer could feed and lodge at the sovereign's expense. The porters were
empowered to prevent anyone 'of what estate, degree, or condition soever
he be' from slipping in extra servants to be fed at the king's expense. The
rights and responsibilities of each and every royal servant were clear.

In theory. In practice, for most of its history the royal household
gave an impression of barely controlled chaos. Additional servants were
always being smuggled into court, while those who were supposed to be
in attendance wandered off on business of their own. In Tudor times, pets
were smuggled in, as well: small spaniels were the only dogs allowed at
court, as pets for the queen and her women, but officers had a bad habit
of bringing their greyhounds and mastiffs into work, where they tripped
up the waiting men and bit each other and urinated all over the place.
Servants urinated all over the place, too: the Privy Council had to issue
an order banning urination in the precincts of the court, and big red

'No Pissing' crosses were painted on external walls. Household officers fought with each other and pilfered anything that wasn't nailed down: food, silver plate, candles, firewood and coal. They took locks from doors, stole the furniture, broke the windows.

Life in the royal household is a little more measured these days. The centuries that separate Elizabeth I from Elizabeth II have introduced different standards of behaviour – for both the sovereign and her household. The idea of monarchy has shifted, too. Nowadays Britain expects a sovereign who is both above the people and of the people, accountable yet unchangeable. But the crown still needs a support network of courtiers and officials and domestic servants, an interface with the public and a buffer to keep that public at bay. Life in the royal household, which is the subject of this book, could not be lived without them.

CHAPTER ONE

Progress

I T SEEMED SUCH A GOOD IDEA. A pleasant entertainment to amuse Queen Elizabeth I, a piece of community theatre for a Sunday afternoon in the summer of 1575.

The plan was simple. A bridal procession of townspeople would march two by two into the yard of Kenilworth Castle in Warwickshire, all dressed for the occasion and looking attractively pastoral. There would be rustic dancers and games and feats of arms beneath the Queen's window. Then the bride and groom would lead the procession back to town, and a second group would take over the castle yard and put on a play. It was an old piece, traditionally performed in nearby Coventry on the first Tuesday after Easter, Hock Tuesday – hence its title, *The Old Coventry Play of Hock-Tuesday*. It had been banned after the Reformation because of the general disorder and riot that went with it – the centrepiece was a great battle in which the Saxons massacred the Danes, and there were often casualties – and Coventry was determined to secure the Queen's permission for it to resume.

Everything started well. The rustic bridal procession arrived on time, led by 'all the lusty lads and bold bachelors of the parish', carrying branches of green broom tied on their left arms and staffs in their right hands.[1] Then came the bridegroom, wearing his father's tawny worsted jacket and a straw hat. He was followed by horsemen, Morris dancers, and a freckle-faced red-headed chap holding aloft the bride cup, which was festooned with broom and streamers of red and yellow buckram.[2] The bride brought up the rear, 'not very beautiful indeed, but ugly', according to an ungallant contemporary account.[3]

When everyone had gathered in the courtyard, the groom began the martial games by tilting at a quintain, a target which was set up to be attacked in a display of military prowess. The other men followed him, running at the target with their staves, in what was meant to be an orderly parade of military prowess for the Queen to admire from her chamber window.

Only, the youngsters' enthusiasm got the better of them. Some charged into the crowd of onlookers. Others fell over without doing

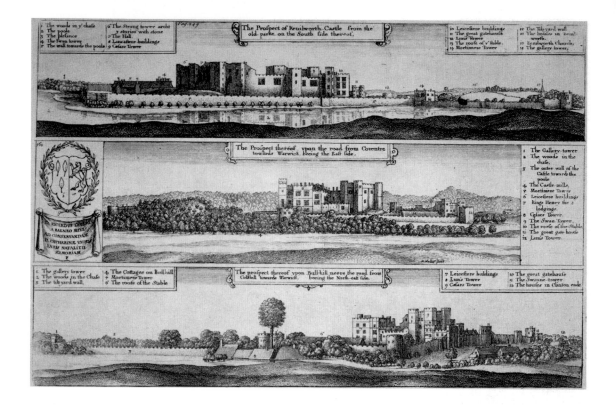

Three seventeenth-century prospects of Kenilworth Castle, by Wenceslaus Hollar. 'The lake, the lodge, the lord, are yours for to command,' Elizabeth I was told.

anything much at all. In a short time, everyone was ignoring the quintain and running at each other. The bride's dreams of dancing before royalty were dashed when Elizabeth decided she couldn't really see what was going on because of the 'great throng and unruliness of the people' and turned her attention to some more sophisticated dancing taking place inside her chamber.[4] And to cap it all, the troupe from Coventry arrived ahead of schedule and began their play, jostling for position with the bridal party. The afternoon descended into chaos and confusion. The bridal party was escorted from the castle in disgrace and the battle between Saxons and Danes was abandoned.

FORTUNATELY, THE BRIDAL GAMES and the Coventry play formed only a small part of the entertainments laid on for Elizabeth I. The Queen and her entourage had already been lodging at Kenilworth for more than a week, during which time her host, the Earl of Leicester, and his household had regaled her with 'excellent music of sundry sweet instruments', firework displays so loud and spectacular 'that the heavens

A sixteenth-century depiction of dancers at court, by an anonymous artist. It is traditionally said to show Elizabeth I and the Earl of Leicester.

thundered, the waters surged, the earth shook'; deer-hunting and bear-baiting; and feats of agility put on by an exceptionally nimble Italian acrobat.[5]

The tone for the royal visit was set when the Queen and her entourage first arrived. She was greeted by a fanfare from trumpeters stationed on the wall of the castle gatehouse. Then the Lady of the Lake floated across the waters of the moat on a movable island to welcome her in verse, ending 'Pass on, Madam, you need no longer stand, | The lake, the Lodge, the Lord, are yours for to command.'[6] After this pageant was ended, 'with a delectable harmony of hautboys, shawms, cornets and such other loud music', the Queen was led across a gravelled bridge lined with posts, each of which was crowned with different offerings, the gifts of the gods.[7] There were cages filled with curlews, bitterns, young herons and other birds, the gifts of Sylvanus, the god of fields, forests and woods; rare fruits, from Pomona, goddess of fruit; wheat, barley and oats from Ceres; grapes, white wine and claret from Bacchus; oysters, herring, salmon and other fish from Neptune; weapons and armour from Mars;

and finally, at the entrance to the castle, two branches of bay from which hung lutes, viols, shawms, cornets, flutes, recorders and harps, the presents of Phoebus, the god of music.

As the bridal games showed, royal entertainments didn't always go according to plan, and there were several more hiccups during Elizabeth's visit to Kenilworth. As she was returning to the castle from hunting one evening, a 'Savage Man' clad in ivy (George Gascoigne, a member of the Earl of Leicester's household) emerged from the woods and after making a pretty speech, broke his staff and threw it away in an extravagant gesture of submission and loyalty. Unfortunately, it nearly hit the Queen's horse on the head. The animal reared, and it was only the prompt action of her attendants which saved her from falling off.

During another of the Kenilworth entertainments, Henry Goldingham, also one of Leicester's men, lost his voice while playing the legendary Greek singer Arion, who was supposed to perform a song to Elizabeth while perched upon an artificial dolphin in the lake. 'He tears off his disguise', wrote an anonymous witness, 'and swears he was none of Arion not he, but e'en honest Harry Goldingham, which blunt discovery pleased the queen better, than if it had gone through in the right way.'[8]

More dramatic was the disaster that occurred at an entertainment produced for the Queen by Leicester's brother, the Earl of Warwick, during a previous royal progress into Warwickshire. In 1572 Elizabeth had spent a Saturday night in Warwick Castle as the earl's guest, and after supper on the Sunday he put on a spectacular martial display in Temple Fields, just in front of the castle. The centrepiece was an assault on a fortress of timber and canvas led by the Earl of Oxford, 'a lusty gentleman, with a lusty band of gentlemen'.[9] To add verisimilitude, the Earl of Warwick, who had been appointed by the Queen as master of the ordnance, overseeing the nation's defences and military supplies, arranged for real siege cannon and mortar-pieces to be sent up from the Tower of London, and besiegers and besieged – several hundred men in all – had a great time charging and yelling and setting off cannon and arquebuses, 'those in the fort shooting again and casting out divers fires terrible to those that have not been in like experiences'.[10]

The show turned out to be terrible to the townsfolk of Warwick, too. A cannon ball went straight through one house, leaving holes as big as a man's head front and back; while rockets landed in the middle of the town and set fire to four more houses, 'to the great peril or else great fear of the inhabitants'. It took the rest of the evening to bring the fires under control.

Robert Dudley, Earl
of Leicester, painted
by an unknown artist
around the time
of the Kenilworth
entertainment.

The reason for the 1575 Kenilworth entertainment, the best-documented and most spectacular of Elizabeth I's reign, was probably to persuade her that marriage to the Earl of Leicester was better for her and for the nation than a match with the French Duke of Alençon, who was being mooted as a potential husband. But it was also very much part of the Queen's summer routine. By the time she arrived at Kenilworth on 9 July she had already been on progress for nearly six weeks, and when she left on 27 July she would continue that progress for a further seventy-four days. In all, she was away from London for almost twenty weeks, touring nine counties. In that time, she made lengthy stays at two of her own houses, Grafton Regis in Northamptonshire, which had been acquired by her father in 1527, and Woodstock Manor, where she had been held prisoner in 1554 by her half-sister Mary Tudor.* Yet she also managed to visit forty-one of her subjects, sometimes staying for no more than a night, or even just a few hours, and occasionally for weeks on end, as she did at Kenilworth.

Elizabeth's 1575 progress was by far her most protracted, her entertainment at Kenilworth the most elaborate. But in the course of her 45-year reign she made no fewer than twenty-two summer progresses, and one brief winter foray into Kent. She went as far west as Bristol, where the local militia treated her to a mock battle between the forces of War and Peace, 'which martial experiment being very costly and chargeable (especially in gunpowder), the queen and nobility liked very well', according to a contemporary.[11] The northernmost county to receive her was Staffordshire, where she stayed a night at Stafford Castle on her great progress of 1575.

Wherever she went, her hosts vied with each other to shower her with gifts and lavish entertainments. Julius Caesar Adelmare, a judge of the Court of Admiralty and a man who was eager for preferment, gave his sovereign a gown embroidered with cloth of silver, a black mantle decorated with pure gold, a white taffeta hat adorned with flowers and 'a jewel of gold set therein with rubies and diamonds'.[12] The citizens of Southampton gave her cash – £40, to be exact. Lord Howard of Effingham, who had commanded the English fleet against the Spanish Armada in 1588, had a very nice dress to give his queen when she visited him at his house in Chelsea in 1602. Sadly for him, she took a fancy to a beautiful set of tapestries he had commissioned to celebrate the defeat of the Armada, so he had to give her those instead.

AND WHEN THE QUEEN TRAVELLED, so did her entire court. The master of horse was there for the entire length of her stay at Kenilworth in 1575, but then he was her host: the Earl of Leicester had served as her master of horse ever since Elizabeth's accession to the throne in November 1558. The lord chamberlain, the Earl of Sussex, was also there, at least for the early part of the royal visit: he then set off to Buxton to take the waters, his luggage going with him in three

* The Queen spent seventeen days at Grafton and five weeks at Woodstock. She also stopped off for a night at a third royal residence, Hatfield in Hertfordshire.

carts. The third great office of state, the lord stewardship, was currently vacant.

The Earl of Warwick, who had inadvertently set fire to the town of Warwick three years earlier, was present. Elizabeth's lord treasurer, Lord Burghley, was there for most of the visit. So were Sir Francis Knollys and Sir James Croft, respectively treasurer and comptroller of the household, and her two principal secretaries, Sir Thomas Smith and Sir Francis Walsingham.

Throughout Elizabeth's stay at Kenilworth – and indeed, throughout her progress through the Midland counties – these eight men, or various permutations of them, sat as her administrative advisers, her Privy Council, carrying out the day-to-day business of administering the nation's affairs. At various points on the progress other privy counsellors – there were sixteen at the time – would join them for a meeting or two, and most of the eight would absent themselves at one time or another. But essentially, the government of England – because that's what it was – travelled with the Queen. When the progress reached Lichfield, the Privy Council was ordering the sheriffs of Dorset, Southampton and Wiltshire to prepare for the defence of the Channel Islands against a possible French invasion, while at the same time authorising a French merchant to import quails, fruit and wine 'for her Majesty's use without paying of custom'.[13] At Worcester they met with a group of bishops to discuss the problem of recusants, those individuals, mainly Roman Catholic, who refused to attend Anglican services; and ordered justices on the Welsh Marches to levy a tax in order to pay for the repair of the stone bridge across the Severn at Upton.

These matters and hundreds more like them were the ordinary business of government. The fact that the court was on the move didn't mean they could be neglected, and the Privy Council sat no fewer than forty-eight times during the great progress of 1575, directing licences, commands and admonitions into every corner of the country.

The logistics of moving the Queen, her household, her court and her government around the country were formidable. As Elizabeth moved from country house to country house, she took with her an army of servants, the most senior of whom had servants of their own. Making travel arrangements for a group this large required careful planning. In advance of each progress an itinerary, called the geste, had to be worked out. This was the job of the lord chamberlain, who drew up an initial list of people and places to be visited on the route, with approximate dates. He also broke the news to the hosts.

From a host's point of view, a royal visit was a mixed blessing. It meant access to the Queen, an opportunity not only to demonstrate one's loyalty but also to petition for favours, grants, public office. The rewards of a successful royal visit could be considerable, as Lord Burghley noted in his famous letter to Sir Christopher Hatton in which he referred to the new houses both men were building with an eye to receiving their sovereign: 'God send us both long to enjoy her, for whom we both meant to exceed our purses in these.'[14]

The other side of the coin was the sheer cost involved in entertaining the sovereign and her entourage. When Elizabeth spent three nights at Harefield in Middlesex in the summer of 1602, Sir Thomas Egerton's expenses, which included everything from twenty-four lobsters and 624 chickens to 48,000 bricks used in building new ovens to feed the Queen and her retinue, came to a colossal £2,013 18s. 4d. When Sir Henry Lee heard in 1602 that the Queen was planning to visit him he wrote to her secretary of state, Sir Robert Cecil, to say that she couldn't come: he simply couldn't afford it. Even more inhospitable than Lee was the Earl of Lincoln, who, faced with the imminent arrival of the Queen's party at his house in Chelsea, simply made sure he was out. Worse, 'after a great knocking at both gates', the Queen could see some of Lincoln's servants peeping out from windows and looking over the walls.[15] The situation was so awkward that Lord Howard of Effingham and Sir Robert Cecil, who were accompanying the queen, stepped in and lied that Lincoln had been suddenly called away but had asked the pair of them to provide a dinner for her at his expense.

The procedure, once the route had been established, and assuming the Queen hadn't changed her mind (something she did quite often) and that her hosts weren't planning to run away or bolt their doors against her coming, was for an advance party of household officers to set off to check accommodation at the various private houses on the route. Few houses could take the numbers that a big royal visit involved, which might be anything up to 350; and some members of her retinue often had to be accommodated in tents or makeshift cabins or converted outbuildings, or in nearby inns. Supplies had to be bought to feed the visitors; they had to be stored somewhere, too. Stabling, or at least pasture, must be found for the horses. As the day of the royal visit grew near, the harbingers, whose role it was at the queen's remove to provide lodging for 'all the queen's men, all lords, ladies and chief officers [and] needful men', arrived to check that everyone who merited a bedchamber had one, that the beds were aired and that there was enough fuel for the fires.[16]* They went through sleeping arrangements with the host and produced sleeping charts to show who got what in the way of lodgings, and when everybody arrived they handed out tickets apportioning particular sets of rooms and beds to each individual staying in the house.

The very act of arrival was a spectacle in itself. According to William Harrison's *Description of England* (1577), 'when the queen's majesty doth remove from any one place to another, there are usually 400 cartwares [teams of horses], which amount to the sum of 2,400 horses, appointed out of the countries adjoining, whereby her carriage is conveyed safely unto the appointed place'.[17] The first sight of a vast convoy of wagons and carriages a mile or so long snaking through the countryside, with its armed outriders and banners, coupled with the knowledge that they were all making their way to your door, must have caused more than one host to rue the day he or she accepted the honour of a visit from the Queen.

We can gauge the upheaval involved in a visit by the Queen and her court from the accommodation arrangements made by Lord Burghley when Elizabeth came for a five-day visit to his great mansion of Theobalds in May 1583, as part of a mini-progress into Hertfordshire and Middlesex. Theobalds (pronounced 'Tibbles', like the cat) had been begun by Burghley in 1564 as a fairly modest house for his younger son Robert, on whom his dynastic hopes rested. Thomas, the elder son, was hardly fit to govern a tennis court, according to his father. Elizabeth first came there in that year, and she stayed at Theobalds at least eleven more times between then and Burghley's death in 1598. During that time Burghley transformed Theobalds until it had grown into a vast mansion arranged around half a dozen courtyards, with galleries, elaborate gardens and a set of state rooms made especially for Elizabeth.

In 1583, Theobalds' final apotheosis still lay a few years in the future. Even then it was an enormous mansion – but not enormous enough. A sleeping chart, probably written by one of Burghley's secretaries but with annotations in his own hand, details the accommodation arrangements. Elizabeth was bringing a large retinue, including Leicester and Warwick, the Earl of Lincoln, Lord Howard of Effingham and Lord Hunsdon, her captain of the gentlemen pensioners. They all brought their own servants, and Burghley was hard put to find room for everyone. Secretaries, gentlewomen of the bedchamber and their servants, household officials, grooms and clerks – all needed somewhere to lay their heads. Moreover,

---

* Ninety years later Lady Anne Hobart used to air the beds in preparation for visitors by having her maid lie in them.

Eliza Triumphans: the
famous painting by
Robert Peake the elder
of Elizabeth I being
carried in procession,
surrounded by her court
(c.1601).

that somewhere had to be appropriate for their rank. The Queen herself was given a suite consisting of bedchamber, withdrawing chamber and privy chamber, with her gentlewomen of the bedchamber next door. She used the hall at Theobalds as her great chamber, with a room that usually served for the house carpenters being brought into use as a hall for Burghley's own household. The Queen's cooks, who always prepared her food when she was on progress, were given a chamber over the brewhouse, while Burghley ate in a gallery at the top of the house. The Earl of Leicester had a chamber in a tower at one end of a long gallery which was given over to the Queen's use, with her bedchamber at the other end.

Maintaining any great house was a costly business. 'His officers affirm', said Lord Burghley's first biographer, 'that at his lordship's being at Theobalds, it cost him fourscore pounds in a week.'[18] When the Queen came to call, those costs escalated dramatically. Burghley's biographer again:

> His lordship's extraordinary charge in entertainment of the queen, was greater to him than to any of her subjects; for he entertained her at his house twelve several times, which cost him £2000 or £3000 every time, lying there at his lordship's charge, sometimes three weeks, a month, yea six weeks together . . . Her majesty sometimes had strangers and ambassadors come to her at Theobalds, where she hath been seen in as great royalty, and served as bountifully and magnificently, as at any other time or place; all at his lordship's charge, with rich shows, pleasant devices, and all manner of sports, could be devised, to the great delight of her majesty, and her whole train . . .[19]

Yet a host didn't bear all the costs of a royal visit. 'Every nobleman's house is her palace, where she continueth during pleasure and till she return to some of her own,' wrote William Harrison; and by assuming symbolic ownership of her host's house, the Queen – or rather her household staff – also assumed some of the responsibilities for running that house. As at Theobalds, she always arrived with her own cooks, and some at least of her own food. She seems to have paid for the diet of her court, as she would have done when at Whitehall or Greenwich. And there were other expenses, chiefly to do with transportation: twopence a mile for the owners of all those carts; hundreds of pounds for hay for the horses. The most accurate account of royal outgoings comes from the 76-day progress she made into Essex and Suffolk in 1561, when the cofferer of the household, Thomas Weldon, reckoned the court's expenses at £8,540, or just over £112 a day.[20]

In most years, the costs of Elizabeth's progresses came to less than that. Burghley reckoned that a long progress added between £1,000 and £2,000 to the annual budget for the royal household. Bread cost a penny a loaf more to bake on progress than in the royal bakehouse; there were material and labour costs for putting up temporary kitchens; the carriage of beer and wine added nearly £300 to the bill. (This last was in any case a major item of expenditure, wherever the Queen happened to be: in one year alone *600,000 gallons* of beer and ale were carted to the court.[21]) And the Queen's habit of changing her itinerary at the last moment meant needless expense on the hire of carts and the preparation of houses that would never welcome her. 'The days appointed for removes in time of her majesty's progresses may be as little changed as needed shall be, and the alterations of places avoided as near as may be conveniently', was one suggestion for reducing the expense. 'A good order if it may be kept', was Burghley's weary response.[22] Like sovereigns before and after her, the Queen subscribed to the dictum articulated in the early seventeenth century by Sir Thomas Chaloner, chamberlain to Henry, Prince of Wales: 'In the king's house some prodigality is not so dishonourable as a little saving.'[23]

———

WHEN MARY TUDOR DIED AT ST JAMES'S PALACE on 17 November 1558, her half-sister had inherited not only the throne of England, but well over fifty royal houses. Elizabeth I never managed to visit many of them, in spite of reigning for the next forty-five years. In any case, some were in such a poor state that they were barely habitable. At least five fell down during the Queen's lifetime.

But that still left a formidable group of country houses, castles and palaces. Most were so-called outlying houses, like Grafton Regis and Woodstock Manor, left in the care of a skeleton staff for months or years at a time, and only brought into use when the Queen announced that she planned to visit during one of her annual progresses. Then an army of joiners and painters and builders would descend in a frenzy of activity to repair doors and windows, sweep the chimneys and clear the drains. The Queen and her entourage would arrive and stay for a week, a night, an afternoon, and then move on, leaving the house to resume its slumbers and the workmen to wait for their wages.

That wasn't the case with the group of eight 'standing houses', mostly scattered along the Thames valley and hence accessible by barge, which were in regular use as royal residences: Windsor, Oatlands, Hampton Court, Richmond, Whitehall, St James, Greenwich and, on the old Watling Street to Gravesend and the Cinque Ports, Eltham. All of these were in use during Elizabeth's reign. She liked to hunt at Windsor and spent weeks in the autumn at Hampton Court. The palace of Placentia at Greenwich, where she was born in 1533, was one of her favourite houses. But the royal palace which saw most of Elizabeth I was Whitehall.

The Queen occupied the set of lodgings at Whitehall that her father had used. Her dressing chamber, dining chamber, privy chamber, bedchamber, bathroom and library overlooked the elaborate garden and orchard begun by Henry VIII, an Elysium of walks and topiary filled with thirty-four painted beasts set on columns. The centrepiece was a fountain and a sundial which stood beside it and 'which shows the hours in thirty different ways', according to Lupold von Wedel, a Pomeranian soldier of fortune who was shown round the palace in 1584. Fountain and sundial formed quite a feature. Another visitor, the nineteen-year-old Bohemian nobleman Zdeněk Brtnický, Baron Waldstein, noted that water from the fountain squirted the unwary; a third, Paul Hentzner, explained that while strangers were peering at the sundial, 'a quantity of water, forced by a wheel which the gardener turns at a distance, through a number of little pipes, sprinkles those that are standing round'.[24]

Thanks to tourists like von Wedel, Waldstein and Hentzner, members of a wave of Protestant travellers from Europe who came to explore England as part of a grand tour, we can glimpse something of the opulence of Elizabeth I's privy lodgings, with their gilded ceilings, their rare paintings and jewels. Hentzner remarked on the royal library, stocked with Greek, Latin, Italian and French books, all bound in velvet with clasp of gold and silver. He was also shown the Queen's bed, 'ingeniously composed of woods of different colours, with quilts of silk, velvet, gold, silver and embroidery'.[25] Young Waldstein was impressed. The palace 'is a place which fills one with wonder', he wrote, 'not so much because of its great size as because of the magnificence of its bedchambers and living rooms which are furnished with the most gorgeous splendour'.[26] He commented on the richness of the Queen's couch, woven with gold and silver thread, the rich tapestries in her bedchamber, and her bathroom, which adjoined the bedchamber and was fitted as a kind of grotto: the water poured from oyster shells and different kinds of rock, he wrote.[27]

Henry VIII had installed a number of bathrooms both at Whitehall and in the other main palaces. They were often quite elaborate affairs, with tiled walls, sunken pools, boilers and ceramic stoves. The Queen's bathroom at Hampton Court had a coal-fired stove in it by July 1600, when Waldstein commented on the fact. 'By heating this the room itself is warmed,' he said, although such stoves were used for producing steam as well as for keeping the royal occupant of the bathroom warm.

Bathing was all the Queen did in her bathrooms. Close stools were on hand for other needs – wooden boxes covered in velvet, with padded seats, pewter pans and the royal monogram 'ER' embroidered on them. Elizabeth's father was content to have a groom beside him when he relieved himself. She was more fastidious, retreating beneath a canopy of crimson silk and cloth of gold, with curtains which buttoned up to hide her from view.[28] The lodgings of senior household officers were also provided with close stools, at the crown's expense. Less privileged servants had to use the common house of easement. No example survives from the Tudor royal palaces, but fragments of the house of easement at Hampton Court show an enormous structure with fourteen seats on two levels, built over a culvert. Pots and lead troughs were also stationed here and there about the palace for those who couldn't wait, or couldn't be bothered to use the house of easement.

WITH ELIZABETH'S ACCESSION TO THE THRONE in 1558, England, Wales and Ireland had a single female ruler for only the second time in history: the first was her half-sister Mary, who reigned alone for seventeen months before marrying Philip of Spain. As a queen without a consort, Elizabeth's close household was dominated by women. The gentlemen, grooms and gentlemen ushers of the privy chamber, who during the reigns of her father and her half-brother Edward VI formed the core of the sovereign's personal servants, were mainly involved in fetching food and fuel, regulating access to the privy lodgings and carrying messages. The Queen's body servants were female; so were the gentlewomen and maids of honour who attended her and amused her without actually carrying out any menial tasks.

The number of Elizabeth's female attendants fluctuated during her reign, but there were usually somewhere between twenty-five and thirty: three or four ladies of the bedchamber; around a dozen ladies, gentlewomen and maids of the privy chamber; half a dozen maids of honour under the supervision of the mother of the maids; and three or four chamberers, who were in effect the Queen's chambermaids. Some received fees – the chamberers' wages were £20 a year, and ladies of the bedchamber and gentlewomen of the privy chamber were paid £33 6s. 8d. Maids of honour received nothing, although they were entitled to bouche of court. The more aristocratic members of the household had servants of their own, some of whom lived in and took their meals, not always legitimately, at the crown's expense, while others were lodged nearby in Westminster or the City.

In theory, the Queen's servants and attendants were supposed to be on hand unless they had licence to leave. The organised rotas that would be adopted by later monarchs – one week on and three weeks off, or one month twice a year, or something similar – were not in operation, and in fact no one at court had any regular periods of time off at all. But they weren't prisoners: when things were quiet, they might visit friends and relatives in Westminster or further afield. And they seem to have enjoyed themselves in other ways during their off-duty hours. Sir Francis Knollys, Elizabeth's treasurer of the household, had his sleep disturbed by the Queen's ladies and maids of honour, who used to 'frisk and hey about in the next room, to his extreme disquiet at nights'. After asking them to be quiet, without success, Knollys hit on the idea of embarrassing them into silence: having got a servant to bolt the main door to their chamber so that they couldn't escape, he entered their room through a connecting door dressed only in his shirt and a pair of spectacles, and read aloud from a pornographic work by Pietro Aretino. 'What a sad spectacle and pitiful fright these poor creatures endured', wrote the seventeenth-century teller of this tale, 'for he faced them and often traversed the room in this posture above an hour.'[29]

THE QUEEN'S DAY BEGAN BETWEEN 8 AND 9 A.M. 'You know I am no morning woman,' she once confessed.[30] When she did get up, she tended to swan around in her nightgown while she ate breakfast and perhaps strolled in her privy gallery or sat at her bedchamber window. The famous incident in 1599, when the Earl of Essex rushed back from negotiating an unauthorised peace with Irish rebels and burst into her bedchamber to find her 'newly up, her hair about her face', took place about ten in the morning.[31] She was vain, and male courtiers who happened to see her *en déshabille* were liable to catch the edge of her tongue, or worse. On May Day 1578 Gilbert Talbot was walking in the tiltyard at Greenwich at eight in the morning when he looked up and saw the Queen, who was sitting in her window. Their eyes met and 'she showed to be greatly ashamed thereof', he reported to his father, the Earl of Shrewsbury, 'for that she was unready, and in her nightstuff'.[32] When she saw Talbot later that day, she hit him on the head, 'and told my lord chamberlain, who was the next to her, how I had seen her that morning, and how much ashamed thereof she was'.[33]

When the Queen finally did decide to dress, it was the ladies of the bedchamber and the chamberers who helped her with a task which must have lasted for an hour or more. Her clothes were the responsibility of the Wardrobe of Robes (a department rather than a cupboard) and stored in the palace of Whitehall, although the privy lodgings in all the standing houses had chambers where clothes could be kept for immediate use. Any items transferred between the main store and these other chambers had to be listed and signed for by whichever of the Queen's women happened to be on the scene at the time. Jewels and furs must also be signed for, and the woman signing for them was held responsible for their safe return – not an easy task when one knows how careless Elizabeth was with her possessions. She was always losing things. A 'small fish of gold with a diamond in it' came off her hat one day in September 1574; at Nonsuch Palace in 1582 a gold acorn and oak leaf broke off a cluster and vanished.[34] The next day she lost three buttons and an aglet from the same gown. At Richmond the following year, a great diamond fell out of a clasp of gold given her by the Earl of Leicester.[35] At Whitehall another diamond, 'one of the fairest', fell out of a cluster attached to her dress.[36] As one recent historian has it, she shed jewels wherever she went 'like some perambulating Christmas tree'.[37]

Dressed, bejewelled and bewigged, the perambulating Christmas tree was at last ready to show herself in public. Baron Waldstein, who was presented to Elizabeth in the presence chamber at Greenwich one Sunday morning in 1600 as she was about to enter the Chapel Royal, was overwhelmed. His attention was drawn first to the maids of honour, who were all dressed in white and silver and whose 'beauty and shapeliness had no difficulty in diverting the eyes'. (He was nineteen.) But when Elizabeth herself arrived in procession, he only had eyes for her. 'Glittering with the glory of majesty and adorned with jewellery and precious gems, [she] entered into the view of the whole assembly and stretched her arms wide as if to embrace everybody present.'[38] The moment she arrived, everybody got down on their knees.

Most foreigners were impressed by their first sight of the Queen.

Lupold von Wedel watched her pass on her way to the Accession Day joust, an elaborate tournament held every November to commemorate her coming to the throne. She was alone, wearing a white gown and seated in an open gilt carriage under a canopy of red velvet embroidered with gold and pearls. And she 'looked like goddesses are wont to be painted', said von Wedel.[39] Paul Hentzner, who like Waldstein saw her in the presence chamber at Greenwich as she passed in procession on the way into chapel, was a little more critical:

> Her face oblong, fair, but wrinkled; her eyes small, yet black and pleasant; her nose a little hooked; her lips narrow, and her teeth black (a defect the English seem subject to, from their too great use of sugar); she had in her ears two pearls, with very rich drops; she wore false hair, and that red; upon her head she had a small crown … her hands were small, her fingers long, and her stature neither tall nor low; her air was stately, her manner of speaking mild and obliging. That day she was dressed in white silk, bordered with pearls of the size of beans . . .[40]

Hentzner also commented on the fact that wherever she turned to look as she walked along, everybody fell on their knees. She was accompanied by her maids, 'very handsome and well shaped', and again dressed in white; and she was guarded by two lines of gentleman pensioners wielding gilded halberds.[41]

While the Queen was at her prayers, Hentzner and the other onlookers were allowed to watch her table being set for her dinner. First two men came in, one carrying a rod of office, the other a tablecloth. Both knelt three times 'with the utmost veneration', before the second carefully spread the cloth on the table. They knelt once again and left, and their places were taken by two more men, one with a rod and the other with a salt-cellar, a plate and some bread. This pair also knelt three times. One placed the salt-cellar, plate and bread on the table and then both knelt again and withdrew. Next came two of the Queen's women. One, dressed in white silk, 'when she had prostrated herself three times in the most graceful manner, approached the table, and rubbed the plates with bread and salt, with as much awe, as if the queen had been present'. After a brief pause, the yeomen of the guard paraded into the chamber, bringing with them twenty-four dishes, mostly on gilt plate. One of the women took a sample of each dish and offered it to the man who had brought it to taste, an ancient ritual but also a sensible precaution against both inedible food and poison. The bringing of the food lasted for about half an hour and was accompanied throughout by music from twelve trumpeters and two drummers, who made the hall ring with their music.

Finally, when everything was ready, more of the Queen's women appeared – but not the Queen herself. They picked up the food and carried it into an inner chamber, where Elizabeth was waiting to choose what she wanted. The rest went to the ladies of the court. She ate privately.

The Scottish courtier Sir James Melville, who was sent south in 1564 to discuss Mary, Queen of Scots' claims to be heir to Elizabeth's throne, told a rather touching story of the Queen's vanity and vulnerability. During a stay at Hampton Court he was given an audience in which she mischievously asked him which was the fairest, his mistress or her. Melville countered that 'she was the fairest queen in England, and ours the fairest queen in Scotland'.[42] That wasn't enough. She pressed him, and when he replied (rather desperately, one imagines) that they were both the fairest ladies of their courts, she asked which of them was taller. Mary, he replied, at which she said that in that case Mary was too tall, whereas she was neither too tall nor too short. This slightly awkward interview ended after Melville mentioned that his mistress played the virginals. How well? Reasonably for a queen, he replied.

That afternoon, the Scot was taken aside by Lord Hunsdon, the recently appointed captain of the gentleman pensioners and hence the man in charge of the Queen's personal safety. Hunsdon led Melville to a 'quiet gallery' where, like Polonius, he was directed to stand behind a tapestry and listen while the Queen played the virginals in the chamber beyond. She played 'excellently well' and, intrigued, the Scot pulled aside the tapestry and watched for a moment. But Elizabeth turned and saw him, 'and came forward seeming to strike me with her left hand … alleging that she used not to play before men, but when she was solitary here alone'. Melville claimed he had been passing the chamber when the sound of music drew him in, 'I wist not how'.

They both knew this was a lie. But instead of striking him she beckoned him in and, as he knelt, 'gave me a cushion with her own hand to lay under my knee'. Then, having observed the proprieties by calling in one of her attendants from the next room as chaperone, she asked which queen played the better.

And that was the point. Melville, of course, said that she did: in the circumstances, he could hardly say anything else. The encounter suggests something more than vanity – a need for reassurance, a desire to impress. While Melville knelt on his cushion, Elizabeth talked to him in French, Italian and Dutch; she talked of theology and history. She actually delayed his return to Scotland for two days, so that he could watch her dance at some court entertainment. Then, inevitably, she asked him which queen danced the better.

The incident also shows how carefully Elizabeth and her household officers stage-managed her life. Her appearances in public, her encounters in private, everything was meticulously organised. On the very rare occasions when she was alone, as she was when Melville walked in on her, people were always close at hand: her captain of the gentleman pensioners was stationed outside the door, her women were in the next room. The Elizabethan royal household's role was not merely to make life easy for its mistress: to provide her with food when she called for it, to clothe her and transport her and keep her safe. It also played a crucial part in managing her contact with the outside world.

———————————————•———————————————

T HE BATTLE TO CURB THE EXPENSES of the royal household was one that Elizabeth's advisers never won, but it was one they never stopped fighting. The administrative structure of the household was basically the same as it had been in Henry VIII's time. There were the three principal officers: the lord chamberlain, who supervised operations above stairs; the lord steward, who ran things below stairs; and the master of horse, most of whose work was done by the chief clerk of the stable, the avenor, whose job it was to ensure that the Queen's horses, which ranged in number from 220 to 275, had sufficient oats, hay and litter.

The stables aside, most of the spending was done by the lord steward's department. From 1570 until 1581 there was no lord steward, however, and the business of management was given jointly to the treasurer and the comptroller of the household. Even when there was a lord steward, the treasurer and the comptroller did most of his work. There were five treasurers and five comptrollers in the course of Elizabeth's 45-year reign, but the two men who dominated the posts were Sir Francis Knollys, the Queen's kinsman, who was treasurer from 1570 until his death in 1596; and Sir James Croft, whose family had served in the royal household for generations and who was comptroller from 1570 to 1590.

Neither man was a paragon of virtue. (But then, who in Elizabethan England was?) Both were politically active at court, both were privy counsellors, and neither had much interest in the workings of the household. When Knollys was eventually taken to task over neglecting his job, he wrote a disingenuous letter to his mistress, begging her 'to consider how far mine office doth stretch and that other men's fault may be imputed to me; for never any treasurer could see all men's doings under him'.[43] Never mind that this was his job, for which he received board and lodging, a range of perks and a salary of £130 16s. 8d. a year.

Lord steward, treasurer and comptroller were often referred to as the white-stave officers or whitestaves, from the wands of office they were entitled to carry. By and large they left the work of dealing with the accounts to career officials. Immediately beneath them was the cofferer, effectively the chief cashier, who had the 'receiving and disbursing of all her majesty's money for household affairs'; and beneath him were two groups of clerks. The clerks of the Green Cloth kept the books and prepared the cofferer's accounts. The clerks comptroller patrolled the palace, checking the quality of the foodstuffs and sending back 'all meats and drinks unsavoury or not convenient to be spent'.[44]

The whitestaves and their assistants held sway over more than twenty different household departments, from major purchasing operations like the acatery, which bought all the provisions needed to furnish the larder, and the bakehouse, which bought vast quantities of wheat, down to the laundry, whose officers 'do wash all the table clothes, towels, napkins, and cupboard-cloths, which are used for the chamber and household', according to *The Book of Household of Queen Elizabeth*.[45] (For modesty, the Queen's personal linen was washed by a separate laundress of her own.) They also had charge of twenty-five servants of the hall, whose job it was to serve up food to the counting house staff and to see that the hall was kept free of 'vagabonds, boys and disorderly persons'.[46] Last but not least, they were meant to supervise the cart-takers, another vital household department. The Queen didn't keep a permanent fleet of wagons and carts, so the yeoman cart-taker and his grooms had the task of commandeering all the necessary transport 'to remove her majesty and her whole house, at every time her highness goes from house to house'.[47]

Without a firm hand at the tiller, the expenses of a household this size and this complicated could easily get out of control. And they did. In 1563, Parliament voted to give Elizabeth a fixed allowance from crown revenues to pay for the running of her household. The figure they arrived at was based on three documents: a book of diet, which laid out the food allowed to the Queen and her household; a bouche of court, which set out how much bread, wine, beer, fuel and light went to each individual in the household; and a book of ordinary, which listed everyone who had a right of entry into her house. Taking all these factors into account they

CHAPTER TWO

Behind the Masque

ELIZABETH I'S FINAL PROGRESS BEGAN AND ENDED on 28 April 1603. Her entire household accompanied her: the clerks of the Green Cloth; her master of the horse and master of the household; the comptroller and the treasurer of the household; her gentlewomen and maids of the privy chamber; her doctors and cooks and musicians, her brewers and purveyors and carters. Some 1,600 people formed up in a vast procession which wound its way through the streets of Westminster. And at the heart of this convoy of humanity, surrounded by knights in black hoods and cloaks who held aloft a canopy to protect her and proclaim her status, was Elizabeth herself, Gloriana, with flaming red hair, piercing blue eyes and rouged cheeks.

Except that it wasn't Elizabeth. It was her effigy, a life-size doll made of wood and wax. The real Queen Elizabeth had been dead for five weeks. Now, safely embalmed and hidden from view in a lead-lined coffin, she made her last journey to Westminster Abbey, where she was to be buried in the vault of her grandfather Henry VII.* The knight marshal's men went ahead of the cortège, clearing the way; they were followed by 240 poor women walking four by four, then the Queen's household servants, ambassadors and nobles. Her master of horse, the Earl of Worcester, followed the hearse, leading 'the palfrey of honour'. The chief mourner was Helena Gorges, Marchioness of Northampton, one of Elizabeth I's favourite gentlewomen of the privy chamber. The marchioness was flanked by the Earls of Dorset and Nottingham, lord treasurer and lord high admiral respectively; her train was carried by the vice chamberlain of the household, assisted by fourteen countesses. Finally came the captain of the guard with all the guard following, five by five, their halberds pointed downwards. 'Her hearse (as it was borne) seemed to be an island swimming in water, for round about it there rained showers of tears,' wrote the playwright Thomas Dekker.[1] 'The city of Westminster', claimed the antiquarian John Stow, 'was surcharged

---

* Three years later her body was exhumed and placed in the north aisle of Henry VII's chapel, under a monument erected for her by James I (and on top of the coffin of her half-sister Mary I).

The *Chariott drawne by foure Horses vpon which Chariott stood the Coffin couered wth purple Veluett and vpon that the representation. The Canapy borne by six Knights*

footemen

with multitudes of all sorts of people in their streets, houses, windows, leads, and gutters … There was such a general sighing, groaning, and weeping, as the like hath not been seen or known in the memory of man.'[2]

The funeral procession of Elizabeth I: 'Her hearse seemed to be an island swimming in water, for round about it there rained showers of tears.'

The Queen's funeral was an opportunity for expressions of grief and loyalty (although in truth she was considerably less popular than she had been in the 1570s and 1580s), and for a public acknowledgement of the transfer of power to her successor, at a time of uncertainty. It was also an enormous drain on the Treasury. Estimates of the cost, which included dishing out 12,000 yards of black fabric to the mourners, range from £11,600 to £20,000.

No handover of power on the scale of nations is ever entirely happy. Crown appointments ceased with the death of a sovereign, and inevitably this left some members of Elizabeth's household feeling anxious about their future. Some dashed off to the north to offer their services and their best wishes to her nearest royal relative and nominated successor, James VI of Scotland. Others retired gracefully from the field, reconciled to the fact that they must make way before the Scottish invasion.

When they came, the changes were sweeping. The new queen, Anne of Denmark, replaced Elizabeth's senior women with her own people: the Marchioness of Northampton, for example, having carried out her duty as chief mourner at Elizabeth's funeral, stood down as a gentlewoman of the privy chamber and retired from public life. The King established a male household, drawing on Scottish courtiers who had accompanied him or followed him to London, and on members of that English circle who had seen which way the succession was likely to go some time before and had assiduously smoothed the way for the new king. At Elizabeth's death Sir Robert Carey, an MP and minor courtier, rode non-stop from Richmond Palace, where she died, to Holyrood Palace in Edinburgh, determined to be the first to give James the news. He accompanied the sad tidings with a request to be made a gentleman of the bedchamber, a request that James granted.* 'After this there came daily gentlemen and noblemen from our court,' Carey wrote later.[3]

HOUSEHOLD ECONOMY – economy of any kind, in fact – was not James I's strong point. Lavish with his largesse and keen to make an impact on his new kingdom, in the first year of his reign he created nineteen English peerages along with seven Scottish and Irish titles, and hundreds of new knights. Over the course of his 22-year reign he created 111 peerages in England, seven times as many as Elizabeth had bestowed in a reign that lasted twice as long. Some already had noble titles, but around half were new peers, who expected that a certain proximity to the king would go along with their new status.

At the same time, the new king entertained on a magnificent scale. In July 1603 he held a dinner at Windsor Castle to celebrate the installation of his eldest son, nine-year-old Prince Henry, as a knight of the Most Noble Order of the Garter, the prestigious chivalric order founded 250 years before by Edward III. Lady Anne Clifford, who watched the events in the great hall, commented that 'there was such an infinite company of lords and ladies and so great a court as I think I shall never see the like'.[4] Three weeks later, on 23 July, 393 gentlemen were dubbed knights in the garden at Whitehall. As if that weren't enough, the next day James knighted seven more.

By mid-September 1603, when the King and Queen were on progress through Wiltshire, Berkshire and Oxfordshire, spending on the household looked as though it was reaching a rate of £100,000 a year, twice the amount that Elizabeth had spent. 'Think what the country feels,' wrote secretary of state Robert Cecil.[5] It was Cecil, whom the king called his 'little beagle', who tried to bring in some household economies. The little beagle's father, Lord Burghley, had tried and failed, and Cecil went through the same processes that Burghley had wrestled with during Elizabeth I's reign. He knew who was entitled to eat at the sovereign's expense, and how much they should have. But all too often,

---

* Carey was soon demoted to the less prestigious post of gentleman of the privy chamber. He had to wait until the accession of Charles I in 1625 to be made gentleman of the bedchamber again.

the amount of food and drink to which an officer was entitled was much more than he or she could consume. Some of the surplus went to feed personal servants, but the rest enabled petitioners, hangers-on, friends and relatives to live at the King's expense. Then there were the staff perks. The master-cooks were entitled to all the salmon tails, the heads of porpoises, pigs, lambs and kids, and shares (with the sergeant of the acatery) of the skins and tallow from all the oxen presented to the King and Queen. The sergeant, yeomen, grooms and pages of the chandlery had the leftover candle ends, 'and also the wax that runneth off at the searing of the torches'. The yeomen of the scalding house had the down of the geese and swans, 'and the garbage of poultry'. On top of everything, custom and practice dictated that the officers of the Green Cloth and the acatery were entitled to one-third of the profits on all backdoor sales of hide and tallow.

Obviously, these officers had no interest in economising. The more salmon was served up, the more salmon tails came the way of the master-cooks. More candles and lighted torches meant more wax for the staff in the chandlery. More geese and swans meant more down for the yeomen of the scalding house. More oxen consumed meant more for the clerks of the Green Cloth.

At one point, someone on the Privy Council suggested the radical step of doing away with diets altogether, and giving members of the household money instead. That came to nothing, although it was still being rumoured in the autumn of 1604, when the MP Philip Gawdy reported that 'all tables in the court shall be put down, and all the attendants shall be turned to grass'.[6] In the meantime, new ordinances were issued as from the King, with the object of reducing waste and reforming the running of the household. Some proposals were remarkably specific. Leading the way, the King and Queen agreed to reduce their daily thirty dishes of meat down to twenty-four. One of their physicians had his diet replaced with a quarterly payment; so did the apothecary for the household. Sir Edward Cary, the master of the jewel house, had been quietly taking seven dishes at a meal since the time of Elizabeth, without any authority. That had to stop.

Other proposals were more general. In recent times, everyone had taken to drinking sack (white wine imported from Spain and the Canary Islands), 'contrary to all order, using it rather for wantonness and surfeiting': from now on its appearance on the table was to be strictly regulated, and the sergeant of the cellar was allowed to dole out twelve gallons a day and no more.[7] People were told to stop walking off with silver dishes from the privy chamber and the presence chamber. The master-cooks were reprimanded for their 'evil custom' of removing pieces of raw meat from dishes for their own use. And because all kinds of rogues and masterless men were hanging around the royal palaces, every person who was allowed lodging and diet at court was to send in the names of their servants to the lord chamberlain, who would decide who should and who should not be at court.[8] The Green Cloth would then prepare a register of authorised persons which was to be kept by the porters, and used by them to decide who had the right of entry into the palace.

The Treasury wasn't the only department to express anxiety about the need to control supply at the beginning of the reign. There were also mutterings in the Commons, and indeed in the country at large, that purveyance was getting out of hand. This was the traditional and much-derided system of provisioning the royal household. Purveyors were appointed by the Board of Green Cloth to go out into the country and obtain wheat, beer, meat and poultry, fish and wax and rushes – anything and everything, in fact, that was needed to maintain the royal household, and to requisition wagons and carts to transport their purchases back to wherever the royal household happened to be. They roamed around villages and towns and private estates, accosting farmers taking their cattle to market and poor women with a few chickens. Their commission authorised them to take goods in return for reasonable prices and payments, which in practice meant at a hefty discount on their real value. Anyone who tried to talk up the price was aware that while purveyors were supposed to pay in cash for goods worth less than forty shillings, they only had to give a receipt for goods over that amount, leaving the hapless vendor to retrieve his money as best he or she could. And when the crown did pay up, its clerks had a habit of deducting a further discount of one penny in the shilling.

The numbers of purveyors and their deputies fluctuated – Lord Burghley noted thirty-eight in 1586, and a report made three years later lists fifty-six purveyors and 111 deputies. There was a hierarchy, as there was in every royal department, with page purveyors, groom purveyors, yeomen purveyors (who seem to have done most of the actual sourcing and purchasing) and at the top, sergeants, one for each department. There were plenty of abuses: it was common practice, for example, to take bribes from people who didn't want to sell their goods at a low price, or to buy more at the discounted price than the sovereign required and then sell it on privately at a handsome profit. Contemporaries reckoned that purveyors took between three and twenty times as much as they actually delivered to the royal household.

James's larger and more extravagant household required more provisions, and hundreds of commissions were issued to purveyors to obtain those provisions at prices which were far below market rates. The politician Sir Francis Bacon stood in the withdrawing chamber at Whitehall in April 1604 and told the King to his face that 'there is no grievance in your kingdom so general, so continual, so sensible, and so bitter unto the common subject, as this whereof we now speak'.[9] The purveyors took post-horses for their own use. They even took horses out of ploughs in the fields, and the animals were so badly treated that they sometimes died on being returned to their owners. They offered a quarter of the true value for goods and services; they felled timber without the owner's permission and without a price being agreed, and then sold it on for their own profit. If anyone complained, they were threatened with imprisonment.

Periodic attempts had been made to reform the system. Counties were allowed to compound for particular goods: that is, they could enter into a contract to supply a specified quantity of wheat, or mutton, or poultry each year at a fixed price. But that didn't prevent the purveyors from seeking out other types of provisions in those counties. In 1610, James I's little beagle proposed 'the Great Contract' – in essence, a plan whereby the King would give up certain ancient rights, including purveyance, in return for Parliament agreeing to pay off his debts and provide a fund for emergencies, and to award him an annual grant to cover his expenses. As the Earl of Northampton explained to the Commons, 'as long as there is a monarchy, you must maintain the monarch'.[10] Negotiations continued throughout 1610, but neither side felt happy with the arrangement. On the King's side, it would mean radical household reform, a lessening of royal prestige and royal power. Parliament worried about how to raise the taxes to pay for the Great Contract, and some MPs at least warned their colleagues that if they gave the King so much, he wouldn't need a parliament. The project was quietly shelved.

IN 1610 JAMES AND ANNE HAD THREE CHILDREN LIVING. The youngest, Charles, Duke of York, was a sickly ten-year-old, unnaturally short and bow-legged with a stammer which he attempted unsuccessfully to cure by talking to himself with his mouth full of pebbles. Next came fourteen-year-old Elizabeth, beautiful, high-minded and fiercely Protestant – much to the annoyance of her mother Anne who, after being raised a Lutheran, had rebelled against the hard, austere brand of Protestantism which permeated her husband's Scottish court and converted to Catholicism in the 1590s.

The couple's eldest child, the boy destined to rule over two kingdoms, was the archetype of the prince as hero. The sixteen-year-old Prince Henry was good-looking and always dressed in the latest fashions. He was an athlete, an expert horseman and tennis-player; a discerning patron of the arts who collected paintings and rare manuscripts and Renaissance bronzes and antique coins. And he was pious in his Protestantism, having prayers said twice a day and insisting that his servants attend. (Otherwise they were made to go without their food.) 'His magnetic virtue drew all the eyes and hearts of the Protestant world,' wrote a contemporary, 'his person being as a saint, his court as a temple'.[11] Joseph Hall, one of his twenty-four chaplains, went further: Henry was 'the glory of the nation, ornament of mankind, hope of posterity, a glorious saint, a prince, whose life was able to put life into any beholder'.[12] Everybody loved and admired Prince Henry.

Everybody, that is, except his father. The prince's popularity both at court and in the country at large displeased James I. It was as if Henry were unconsciously holding up a mirror to the monarchy and, simply by being who he was, reminding everyone of the King's many faults – his extravagance, his indolence, his embarrassingly indiscreet behaviour with a succession of young favourites. 'It would seem', reported the Venetian ambassador, 'that the king was growing jealous.'[13]

But a perfect prince had his value. In 1609, the cash-strapped James I resurrected an all-but-forgotten feudal levy, 'anciently due by the common law of England', which could be exacted for Henry's knighting when he reached the age of sixteen.[14] The proceeds from this tax went towards paying James's debts. The following year, as Robert Cecil began negotiations over the Great Contract, he saw an opportunity for a public display which would impress Parliament while at the same time reinforcing the King's claim on the nation's purse. On Thursday 15 February the little beagle brought the themes together, telling a joint committee of the Lords and the Commons that there were only two reasons for convening a new session of Parliament: to agree the King's supply, and 'to make you witnesses … of those great honours and favours which his majesty intendeth to

The best king England
never had: Henry, Prince
of Wales, painted by
Robert Peake the elder
in 1610, when the prince
was sixteen years old.

perform to his royal son in creating him Prince of Wales and Earl of Chester'.[15]

The appearance of this popular and handsome youth before Parliament would stir feelings of loyalty to the crown among peers and MPs, feelings which Cecil hoped might be monetarised to the benefit of the impecunious king. But the move also brought problems. For one thing, there hadn't been an investiture of a Prince of Wales for 106 years, not since February 1504, when the future Henry VIII was installed. No one was entirely sure how to go about the thing. For another, the King and Cecil were uncomfortably aware of the long-term financial implications. The installation of Henry as Prince of Wales wasn't simply a matter of idle ceremony or public spectacle, expensive enough in themselves. It would also involve the transfer of considerable estates from James to his son, and the establishment of a separate royal household with costs which would be outside Cecil's control. And this when the King was massively in debt and Cecil was desperate to curtail royal expenditure.

James was initially uncertain about Henry's 'creation', as contemporaries called it. But he was won round. On the morning of Monday 4 June 1610, father and son went by water from the Privy Stairs at Whitehall to Westminster Bridge. From there, the King went to a chamber set aside for him in the palace of Westminster, where he was dressed in his purple robes and crown. The prince went separately to another chamber in the palace, where he and the eight earls who were attending him were robed.

As the audience watched, trumpets sounded and the prince's train entered the hall. First came the earl marshal and lord chamberlain; then the twenty-five knights of the Bath in purple satin, and Garter King-at-Arms, carrying the letters patent. Next came six earls, carrying various items of regalia: the prince's robes of purple velvet; his train; his sword, ring, and rod of gold; his cap and crown. At last the prince himself appeared, in a coat of purple velvet.

> Presenting himself before the king with very submissive reverence, [Henry] kneeled upon the uppermost step leading to the state, while his patent was read by the Earl of Salisbury, till it came to the putting on of his robes, sword, and the rest, by the Lords who carried them: but the crown, rod, ring, and patent, were delivered to him by the king's own hands.[16]

The ceremony over, everybody went back to Whitehall by water. The King dined in his privy chamber, but the sixteen-year-old Prince of Wales ate in the great hall, where he was served in such state, said one contemporary, 'that greater could not have been done to the king himself'.[17]

THE MAN APPOINTED to run the Prince of Wales's new household was his old governor, Sir Thomas Chaloner. Chaloner was no ordinary career courtier. Born in 1563, as a young man he went up to Magdalen College, Oxford, where he distinguished himself as a poet before fighting with the English army in France and travelling on the Continent, especially in Italy, where he sought out the leading scholars of the day.[18] Back in England he interested himself in chemistry and alchemy, collecting rare and curious alchemical texts and writing his own: in 1584, when he was barely twenty-one, he published *A short discourse of the most rare and excellent vertue of nitre*, in which he urged the medicinal use of saltpetre as a cure for a range of ailments, from sweaty armpits and swollen testicles to jaundice and scurvy. ('Rub the places with powder of nitre, mixed with dog's urine when it may be come by.')[19]

After Henry's creation as Prince of Wales, his newly independent household expanded to meet his new status, becoming in effect a smaller version of those of his mother and his father. And only slightly smaller, at that: by now there were 426 in his household, not counting another thirty-five craftsmen – tailors and builders and plasterers and painters. He even had his own department of works, headed by Inigo Jones as surveyor. (This was the first architectural post for a man who would go on to be one of the seventeenth century's greatest architects, although Jones doesn't seem to have designed any buildings for the prince.) Chaloner was appointed chamberlain. Henry's secretary was Adam Newton, who had been his tutor when he was still in Scotland; his groom of the stool and gentleman of the robes, Sir David Murray, had also served him in Scotland. Other officers were English. Henry's treasurer, Sir Charles Cornwallis, was a Suffolk-born diplomat under the patronage of Robert Cecil. His comptroller, Sir John Holles, was a veteran of the wars in Europe.

Significantly for the prince's intellectual development, these senior figures were all men of culture, poets and scholars as well as men of action. Newton was a distinguished Latin scholar and a collector of paintings. Holles was interested in trends in Continental architecture, possessing a copy of Palladio's *Quattro libri* and borrowing works by Serlio, Alberti and others. Murray was a published poet; Cornwallis had been James I's ambassador to Spain. While Henry also gathered round him young men who, like himself, were athletic, skilled at horsemanship and the martial arts, these senior household officers ensured that he didn't neglect the life of the mind.

The prince immediately laid down some rules for the governance of his house, presumably with guidance from Chaloner. They were not the usual household ordinances – lists of names and wages and duties, details of who was entitled to which dishes for their dinner. Instead, they explored the kind of behaviour that Henry expected from his servants, and that they might expect from him – 'some especial matters', he told them, 'that I would have precisely looked unto, and duly observed as well for the advancement of my service, as for the honour of my court'.[20]

To begin with, the sixteen-year-old's officers were to know that he took his religion seriously. Every one of his servants had to attend divine service in the prince's private chapel when he did, and must take communion there four times a year, including Christmas and Easter. Anybody who absented themselves without having a good excuse should beware: 'for the which kind of people my court shall be no shelter, nor my service any protection'.[21]

Henry's court was a young court and the prince was aware that young men were prone to fighting. Quarrels, he said, should always be referred to his chief officers, and anyone who felt he had been wronged must under no circumstances 'revenge himself by violence, or with the sword'.[22] That wasn't the way things were done in 'a well disciplined court, as neither agreeing with piety nor civility'.[23]

Henry was anxious that wherever his court happened to be resident – Richmond or Greenwich or St James's Palace – his marshals must act to remove 'that scum of vagrant and idle rogues, that follow the train and my stables with their wives and children, committing many disorders and stealths'.[24] In spite of the rigid hierarchies and deference, palaces in the seventeenth century were public places, their courtyards filled with hawkers and whores, beggars and tapsters and curious country cousins come to gaze on royalty. These people were blamed for fights and petty thefts, and by Prince Henry, at least, for bringing 'danger of infectious sickness to my court'.[25]

There was another reason for excluding strangers. In May 1610 the prince's namesake, Henry IV of France, was stabbed to death by a Catholic fanatic while his coach was stopped in traffic on the Rue de la Ferronerie in Paris. The prince was profoundly shocked: he had always looked up to the French king, dreaming of one day fighting under him in a great crusade against the Habsburg Empire. When he heard of the assassination he took to his bed, saying over and over again, 'My second father is dead.'[26] The following year he personally laid Henry IV's standard, sword and helmet before the altar of the Chapel Royal at Windsor, still visibly upset at the death of this French king.

So when Prince Henry's household orders were published five

months after his second father's murder, security was a prominent issue, bound up inextricably with what was due to him as prince and heir to the thrones of England and Scotland. 'Considering the danger and practices of these times', he announced, the distribution of double keys, which gave access to restricted areas, must be strictly regulated. When he was hearing divine service in his public chapel there must always be two guards at the door. Likewise, when he was playing tennis or exercising, two guards must always be on hand. 'Sometimes when I have been at the tennis play there hath scarcely been six persons about the tennis court, and most of them but lackeys or pages, which is neither safe nor fit for the state of a prince.'[27] Arms and ammunition should always be available wherever he happened to be living. And he expected his guards to be fit and active men, able to wrestle, to shoot a musket and wield a sword and a pike and not just to stand holding a halberd. Better still, they should be veterans of the European wars, experienced in arms and fighting.

ON SUNDAY 25 OCTOBER 1612, Prince Henry dressed and went into the chapel at St James's Palace to hear one of his favourite preachers, Robert Wilkinson, speak on Job 14:1, 'Man that is born of a woman is of few days, and full of trouble'. Not content with one sermon, he then went over to Whitehall to hear his father's chaplain preach. But he wasn't feeling very well, and after dinner he began to shiver with a fever. That night he complained he was thirsty, and said the candlelight in his chamber hurt his eyes.

The prince was coming down with typhoid fever. The next day, Monday 26 October, James I's physician, Sir Theodore Mayerne, was called in: he prescribed an enema, which worked well enough for the prince to get up and play cards with his brother Charles. 'Yet his Highness for all this looked ill and pale, spake hollow, and somewhat strangely, with dead sunk eyes', according to his earliest biography, *The Life and Death of our Late Most Incomparable and Heroique Prince, Henry Prince of Wales*, which existed in manuscript form by 1613.[28] Mayerne suggested a diet of cordials and cooling juleps, broths and jellies. When this didn't work, the young man was given a laxative of senna pod and rhubarb, 'infused in cordial and cooling liquors, with syrup of roses'.[29] It had the desired effect, but Henry's condition didn't improve. His servants noticed that his tongue and throat were ulcerated, and although he tried to get up and dress he felt so dizzy when he stood that he had to go back to bed. Other doctors were brought in, but nothing seemed to do him any good. On the Thursday evening his household officers noticed a rare lunar rainbow hovering over St James's Palace, 'a fatal sign'.[30]

On 31 October the fever was worse, and the prince slipped into delirium. 'This night was more cruel and unquiet unto him than any other.'[31] For several days Mayerne had urged bleeding, in the face of opposition from the prince's other doctors, who were of the opinion that cordials and purges would bring out the fever. On Sunday 1 November, one week after he was first taken ill, they relented and he was bled in his right arm. In the afternoon his father, mother, brother and sister came to visit. According to one account, his twelve-year-old brother Charles pressed into his hand a little bronze horse by Giovanni Bologna.

As Henry's condition worsened over the next six days, another doctor was brought in, Henry Atkins, who diagnosed 'a corrupt putrid fever, the seat whereof was under the liver in the first passages'.[32] It was serious, said Atkins, who obviously wasn't afraid to state the obvious; but he had nothing to say about treatment. Mayerne wanted to bleed Henry again, but the others advised against it. Instead, they gave him cordials for his thirst, they shaved his head and gave him an enema and applied cupping glasses.

Nothing did any good. He raved and went into convulsions, singing and calling out for his clothes and his rapier. Desperate, although still reluctant to bleed him again, the doctors resorted to ever more bizarre treatments. They ordered a cockerel to be split in two, and the halves applied to the soles of his feet. More doctors came, but all they did was argue. James had given Mayerne authority to override the rest, but he wouldn't accept the challenge, saying he wasn't going to be held responsible for killing the King's eldest son. The Archbishop of Canterbury, George Abbot, prayed with Henry and gently prepared him for death.

The last days were terrible. The King couldn't bear to see his son's suffering. Looking 'more like a dead, than a living man', he rode off to Theobalds to wait for the bad news that he and everyone else now expected. The prince's two closest household officers, Sir Thomas Chaloner and Sir David Murray, stayed by him. Henry kept calling for Murray, crying out 'David, David, David' over and over again. When Murray asked what he wanted, his only reply was, 'I would say somewhat, but I cannot utter it.'

In the early hours of 6 November, Archbishop Abbot was called in again. Weeping, he knelt by the prince's bed and whispered, then shouted in his ear, 'Sir, hear you me! Hear you me! Hear you me! If you hear me, in certain sign of your faith, and hope of the blessed resurrection, give us for our comfort a sign, by lifting up of your hands.'[33]

With an effort, the prince lifted both his hands. He died shortly before eight o'clock that evening.

The death of Prince Henry was met with an outpouring of sorrow. For months afterwards, James I would burst into tears without warning, crying, 'Henry is dead! Henry is dead!' Foreign diplomats were warned not even to mention the boy's name in front of the Queen, for fear she would be overcome with grief.

Henry's death propelled his short, stammering, bow-legged younger brother into the limelight as heir to the two kingdoms. Reserved, inclined to outbursts of petulance and lacking in personal charm, Prince Charles was a poor substitute for his dead brother – something of which he was made painfully aware throughout his adolescence. When he was created Prince of Wales in November 1616, a few days before his sixteenth birthday, Anne of Denmark refused to attend because she couldn't bear the way the ceremony dredged up memories of her dead son. Some of Charles's feelings of being second best had been resolved by the time he inherited the crown from his father in 1625. But as king, he was too quick to remind others of his God-given status, too anxious to appear the strong leader that he so patently was not. That was to be his downfall.

ONE OF THE MORE OBVIOUS ROYAL EXTRAVAGANCES to cause concern among James I's advisers was an enthusiasm for costly court masques, and the more elaborate the better. At its most basic, the masque involved a dozen masked and costumed courtiers being presented on something like a pageant float – perhaps a pasteboard castle, or a ship – with speeches or songs performed by professionals and accompanied by professional musicians. The twelve masquers, who were either exclusively male or exclusively female, descended to the floor and, after a choreographed formal dance, invited members of the audience to join them in more dancing before being recalled to their float by a final speech or song.

A few days before Christmas 1603, when James had been on the English throne for less than nine months, Sir Thomas Edmonds mentioned to the Earl of Shrewsbury that 'both the King's and Queen's Majesties have an humor to have some masques this Christmas time'.[34] The result was *The Vision of the Twelve Goddesses*, put on at Hampton Court on 8 January 1604 with Queen Anne as Pallas, 'in a blue mantle with a silver embroidery of all weapons and engines of war, with a helmet-dressing on her head'.[35] The action involved Pallas and the other eleven classical deities, played by women of her household, descending from a 'mountain' at the screens end of the great hall and making offerings at the Temple of Peace at the upper end, then executing a series of dances to the sounds of viols and lutes before inviting men in the audience to join them in 'certain measures, galliards and currantos' before returning to Olympus. The author, the poet Samuel Daniel, thought his work 'not inferior to the best that ever was presented in Christendom'.[36] Others, it must be said, disagreed.

The Vision of the Twelve Goddesses wasn't a terribly expensive production. Daniel received £40 for writing it, and £250 went to constructing the pasteboard mountain and temple. No record of the amount spent on creating the costumes has survived, although it was presumably not exorbitant since items from Queen Elizabeth I's wardrobe were recycled for the occasion. One member of the audience commented on the fact that Anne's clothes 'were not so much below the knee but that we might see a woman had both feet and legs, which I never knew before'.[37]

It was Anne who took the lead in promoting the masques, which became a regular feature of Twelfth Night and Shrovetide festivities at court. The masque staged at Whitehall Palace the following Christmas was more ambitious than Daniel's *Vision*, and it was driven by her. With words by the poet Ben Jonson and designs by Inigo Jones (the first of around thirty collaborations between the two men), and music by viol-player and extraordinary groom of the privy chamber Alfonso Ferrabosco, *The Masque of Blackness* took its name from Queen Anne's desire that she and her ladies should appear as blackamoors. It may not be a coincidence that the King's company of players had performed *Othello* at court only two months earlier.

Jonson's plot, such as it was, involved the god Niger and his twelve black daughters (the masquers, played by the Queen and her ladies) arriving at the English court in a large scallop shell, accompanied by the sea god Oceanus and his female torch-bearers. Niger explains that they have come in fulfilment of a prophecy of the moon goddess, Aethiopia, who told them that when they found a land whose name ended in '-tannia' they would also find a cure for their blackness. Oceanus is in the middle of telling the travellers that they are out of luck because this land is called Albion, when all of a sudden Aethiopia appears 'in the upper part of the house, triumphant in a silver throne' and crowned with a sphere of light.[38] The land is no longer called Albion, she (or rather he, since convention dictated that speaking parts be played by males) tells them. 'With that great name Britannia, this blest isle | Hath won her ancient dignity...' Moreover, Britannia is ruled by a sun 'whose beams shine day and night, and are of force | To blanch an Aethiop and revive a cor[p]se'.[39] With that, the twelve black nymphs dance for the audience and then take their pick of men to join them in their dancing. Finally they return to their shell, as Aethiopia tells them that if they bathe in the sea 'thirteen times thrice, on thirteen nights', they will wash away their blackness 'and for your pains perfection have'.[40]

The Masque of Blackness raises so many questions about ethnicity, gender and Jacobean colonialism that it has spawned an academic literature all of its own. Its original audience gave it mixed reviews. The Venetian ambassador, Nicolò Molin, thought it 'was very beautiful and sumptuous'.[41] The English diplomat Sir Dudley Carleton, on the other hand, was shocked that instead of wearing masks, as convention demanded, the Queen and her eleven fellow-masquers relied on blacking up as a disguise. 'Their black faces and hands which were painted and bare up to the elbows was a very loathsome sight,' he reported to his friend John Chamberlain. 'I am sorry that strangers should see our court so strangely disguised.'[42] To a fellow diplomat, Sir Ralph Winwood, he wrote, 'You cannot imagine a more ugly sight than a troop of lean-cheeked Moors.' He was amused or bemused (it is hard to tell which) by the sight of the Spanish ambassador dancing with the Queen and then gallantly kissing her hand, 'though there was danger it would have left a mark on his lips'.[43] And he was unimpressed with Inigo Jones's costumes – 'too light and courtesan-like for such great ones' – and his stage sets, which included moving waves with images of sea-monsters ridden by Moors: 'all fish and no water'.[44]

The King's advisers were less concerned about the artistic merits of *Blackness* than they were about the cost. John Chamberlain was told before Christmas that the Queen 'hath a great masque in hand against Twelfth-tide' and that £3,000 had been supplied to finance it.[45] (The early 21st-century equivalent is somewhere in the region of £8.5 million.) By 17 December the Privy Council was voicing its concerns to James I, and urging him not to lay the expense on his courtiers, who could ill afford to pay for his – or rather Anne's – extravagance. But as always when the subject of cutting back on the royal budget came up, prestige took precedence over household economy. Abandoning the masque at such a late stage, the council conceded, 'would be more pernicious than the expense of ten times that value; for the ambassadors of foreign princes will believe that the masque has been forborne because the king or the queen lack £4,000'. [46] Note that £4,000: *The Masque of Blackness* was well over its enormous budget, and by the time it was staged there were grumblings of discontent at the lavish expenditure involved.

With *Blackness*, the masque was established as the most prominent court entertainment of James I's reign, and his wife commissioned and presided over several more masques in the next five years, before stepping back and allowing her husband's favourite, the Duke of Buckingham, to take on the role of producer. After this, she and her ladies were relegated to the role of dancing partners in the revels. The King, as one recent historian of the masque put it, 'much preferred to watch male dancers'. [47]

Anne's performances included the *Masque of Beauty*, the sequel to *Blackness*, which was performed on 10 January 1608 at her own expense. *Beauty* is as problematic to modern eyes and ears as its predecessor: the black nymphs, now sixteen in number and again led by Anne, have followed the moon's instructions and lost their blackness, only to be kidnapped by Night, who is 'mad to see an Aethiop washed white'. Saved by the Moon, they appear on a floating island, and the 'throne whereon they sat seemed to be a mine of light struck from their jewels and their garments'. [48] The Venetian ambassador was awe-struck by the production. 'The apparatus and the cunning of the stage machinery was a miracle,' he reported, 'the abundance and beauty of the lights immense, the music and the dance most sumptuous. But what beggared all else and possibly exceeded the public expectation was the wealth of pearls and jewels that adorned the queen and her ladies, so abundant and splendid that in everyone's opinion no other court could have displayed such pomp and riches.' [49]

It is hard to imagine the sheer spectacle of a big Jacobean masque, the sights and sounds of a major royal entertainment. Half the household was involved in some way or another. The writer would agree the basic concept with the royal or noble producer and come up with a one-page outline; the designer brought in carpenters and painters from the palace office of works to make the mountains which opened and clouds which sailed across canvas skies and islands which floated on pasteboard oceans. Inigo Jones, who emerged as the chief designer of masques at this period, produced costume designs which were refined and revised, copied in paper and then made up by tailors and haberdashers and shoemakers, who would sometimes try out two or three different patterns or colour combinations before deciding on the one that worked best. Specialist mask-makers produced carefully crafted masks of painted, moulded and perfumed leather.

Professional actors from the King's Company were hired for the speaking roles and for the anti-masque. This was a grotesque or comic prologue to the main event which Jonson first introduced in the 1609 *Masque of Queens* after Anne commanded him 'to think of some dance, or show, that might precede hers, and have the place of a foil or false masque … a spectacle of strangeness'.[50] Different members of the King's Musick composed pieces for their own particular consort: the violins for the dances, the lutenist-singers for the songs, the loud wind band for the processions.[51] Dancing masters in the royal household choreographed the dancers and took the masquers through their steps.

Rehearsals might go on for five or six weeks, with the masquers practising separately and together. In 1622, the Queen's privy chamber at Whitehall was set up for Prince Charles to practise in over a four-day period, and the great hall there was prepared for twenty days of rehearsals. Two weeks before the performance of *The Masque of Queens*, Anne was in the banqueting house holding 'daily rehearsals and trials of the machinery'.[52] Preparing for the 1613 *Somerset Masque* one performer, the courtier Sir Henry Bowyer, overdid things and, 'over-heating himself with practising, fell into the smallpox and died'.[53]

Occasionally, these rehearsals took place in front of a small invited audience. In 1640, for example, Charles I's queen, Henrietta Maria, noted that the French ambassador and his wife were returning to Paris on the day that a new masque was to be performed. 'The queen was pleased he should be honoured with a sight of the practice of the dances and of the motions of the scene, three or four days before the masque was to be acted.'[54] The ambassador and his wife were conducted into a private box from where they could watch the company being put through its paces.

AFTER THE FIRST CHRISTMAS ENTERTAINMENT of James I's reign at Hampton Court, masques usually took place at Whitehall. The early masques were set in a temporary building erected in 1581 for the arrival of French diplomats to discuss Elizabeth I's proposed marriage to the Duke of Alençon. It was made of thirty enormous wooden masts, each forty feet high, covered in canvas painted to resemble stone and fitted with 292 panes of glass. The interior was tiered and painted with ivy and holly and spangled with gold. The ceiling was painted with stars, clouds and sunbeams, and according to a contemporary account, the roof was hung with 'all manner of strange fruits, as pomegranates, oranges, pompions [pumpkins or melons], cucumbers, grapes, carrots, pease with other such like'.[55] It took 375 workmen twenty-four days to put the building up at a cost of nearly £1,745.

Although it was originally intended as a temporary structure, the Elizabethan banqueting house remained in place for almost a quarter of a century. It was here, beneath the spangled gold and the dangling carrots and cucumbers, that *The Masque of Blackness* was staged. But in 1606, as the masque's importance in the royal year grew, James I decided to replace the rather decrepit old building with something more substantial. His new banqueting house was finished in time for the performance on 10 January 1608 of *The Masque of Beauty*. The only description we have of the interior comes from Orazio Busino, chaplain to the Venetian ambassador, who twelve years later described a large hall fitted up like a theatre, with boxes all round and the king's chair of state placed beneath its canopy in front of the stage. The roof was supported on two orders of columns, Doric below and Ionic above, carved and gilded. From the roof hung festoons and angels.

On the night of a performance, the banqueting house was packed. People fought for invitations, complained loudly about being seated behind one of the columns, and complained even more loudly about not being able to find any seat at all. Foreign ambassadors squabbled over who had precedence and stormed out over slights, real or imagined. 'The Spanish ambassador in ordinary makes vigorous efforts to be invited [to *The Masque of Queens*],' reported the Venetian ambassador. 'He puts in motion all his supporters.'[56] Once seated, the heat from the hundreds of naked flames which lit the house was intense; the stench of sweat, almost but not quite masked by heavy perfume, was overpowering. The noise of the wind band that played as the masquers processed echoed round the rafters. The songs, in contrast, were hard to make out, and their lute accompaniment inaudible. It wasn't unknown for the singer to come and stand directly in front of the throne as he sang so that the King, at least, could hear the words. The high point was not Ben Jonson's exquisite poetry, or Inigo Jones's remarkable stage machinery – it was the dance, the newly learned, newly devised steps which the stately, glittering masquers took, the jumps and pirouettes and carefully rehearsed gestures. This was the focus of the Jacobean court masque. This was what entranced the noisy, overheated, overcrowded banqueting house at Whitehall.

Sometimes it wasn't alright on the night. The highlight of Thomas Campion's *Somerset Masque*, staged in the banqueting house on 26 December 1613 to celebrate the marriage of the Earl of Somerset to the Countess of Essex, involved a dozen knights appearing as if by magic when the Queen lifted the spell that enchanted them. Unfortunately, Inigo Jones, who had been Campion's collaborator on his previous two court masques, was in Italy with the Earl of Arundel that year, and his replacement as set designer, a Florentine architect named Constantine de Servi, was not very good. So the cloud which was meant to descend out of the air to reveal the enchanted knights was a lumbering affair: 'one could see the ropes that supported it', reported the Savoyard diplomat Giovanni Battista Gabaleoni, 'and hear the pulleys, or rather wheels, making the same noise as when they raise or lower the mast of a ship'. And by the time the winches and pulleys could be made to work, the song which was supposed to accompany the knights' arrival was over. In the silence which followed, 'the lords came down without any music, with no other sound but the screeching of the wheels'.[57]

Just as bad as the technical hitches on the stage were the organisational failures. Court masques often took place late at night: Campion's *Somerset Masque*, for instance, began at eleven and finished at two in the morning, and the audience might have to wait for several hours before the King arrived and the performance could begin. People were getting restless by then, and the household officers weren't always able to control the crowds when the show was over. After *The Masque of Blackness* finished and the King had left, people poured out, jostling and pushing each other. The tables holding a banquet which had been prepared for James I were overturned with the food hardly touched. Women lost jewels and purses in the melee. And as the diplomat Sir Dudley Carleton noted rather cryptically, one woman 'lost her honesty ... being surprised at her business on the top of the terrace'.[58]

Worst of all was when poor performance and inadequate crowd control combined with royal heckling to produce a nightmare to remember. Although he didn't take part in masques, James I frequently interrupted a performance to joke with the performers or to ask for certain songs to be repeated. And he was equally unrestrained when the action didn't meet with his approval. *Pleasure Reconciled to Virtue*, written by Ben Jonson with sets by Inigo Jones, was a notable example of a perfect royal storm. Put on for Twelfth Night 1618, it was the first time that the seventeen-year-old Charles, Prince of Wales performed as chief masquer, and great things were expected.

Those expectations weren't fulfilled. John Chamberlain said the masque was dull. Inigo Jones's designs were regarded as poor, and Jonson's words didn't impress, either: 'divers think fit he should return to his old trade of bricklaying again'.[59] (As a youth, Jonson was apprenticed to his bricklayer step-father, a fact which unkind critics frequently brought up.)

The action, which involved Hercules, a personification of Mount Atlas which rolled its eyes, a chubby Bacchus, masquers dancing as wine barrels and wicker flasks and a dozen boys dressed as frogs, failed to please the King. The climax came when twelve masked male dancers, led by Prince Charles, each took a lady and, accompanied by twenty-five or thirty violins, 'performed every sort of ballet and dance of every country whatsoever', according to the chaplain to the Venetian ambassador, who was bewildered by the whole thing. 'They sang some trifling things which we did not understand,' he wrote afterwards. Towards the end the dancers began to flag, and that was too much for James I. He began to shout. 'Why don't they dance? What did they make me come here for? Devil take you all, dance!' James's favourite, Buckingham, did his best to placate the King, springing forward and 'cutting a score of lofty and very minute capers', but after kissing his son and patting Buckingham on the face the King rose from his chair and swept out, taking his guests with him. After walking through the palace until he reached a hall laid out with food – mainly seasoned pasties on glass dishes, with painted pasteboard table ornaments – he left. That was the signal for the rest of the court to fall on the food 'like so many harpies'. They upset the table and the dishes smashed on the floor. 'The crash of glass platters', said the Venetian ambassador's chaplain, 'reminded me precisely of a severe hailstorm at midsummer smashing the window glass … disgusted and weary we returned home.'[60] It was 2.30 in the morning.

IN 1619, A YEAR AFTER THE PERFORMANCE of *Pleasure Reconciled to Virtue*, the King's new banqueting house burned down. Two men who were sweeping the room accidently set light with their candles to some oil-cloth sets. They panicked and 'fearing to be known that they did it', they ran away, shutting the doors behind them. By the time the fire was discovered, it was too late to save the building.[61]

James I immediately decided that it must be rebuilt. The responsibility for building and repairing royal palaces lay with the surveyor of the King's Works; and, since the death in 1616 of the previous incumbent,

Simon Basil, that post had been occupied by the set-designer Inigo Jones, who received a salary of about £200 and a house in Scotland Yard, on the edge of the Whitehall complex. As it turned out, Jones was quite good at his new job. The Queen's House at Greenwich, begun for Anne of Denmark and completed for her daughter-in-law Henrietta Maria, the Queen's Chapel at St James's Palace and a host of other work for the crown show him as the champion of Renaissance classicism at a time when England was regarded as an architectural backwater by the rest of Europe. Jones understood proportion, he understood the correct application of the classical orders, he understood that beauty – the beauty of Palladio and Scamozzi – springs from the control of space. The new Banqueting House at Whitehall is his masterpiece: restrained, almost austere in the ebb and flow of its rhythmic geometry, it was remarked upon from the outset as a building which possessed a sophistication that no one expected from the English.

And from the outset it was intended as more than just a performance space. After it was finished in 1622 it became a presence chamber, with a huge blue and gold alcove at the south end to take James I's throne. This was where he received foreign ambassadors and delegations from Parliament. It became the ceremonial heart of Whitehall, the setting for displays which proclaimed kingship at a time when men were beginning to ask exactly what gave a king the right to rule over them. As parliamentary opposition to James I's successor, his son Charles I, grew in the 1630s, the Banqueting House was the setting for Rubens's great ceiling canvas depicting James being raised into heaven to take his place among the gods, an affirmation of the divine right of kings. And after that right was questioned and then rejected so dramatically by Parliament in the civil wars of the 1640s, it was from the Banqueting House that Charles I would step out onto the scaffold on a cold day in winter.

S.ᵗ Iohn Finett
Master of y.ᵉ Ceremonies
to King Iames y.ᵉ I.ˢᵗ

Quoniam superest
at mea 38.

engraving etc.

CHAPTER THREE

Diplomats and Fools

I N ELIZABETH I'S TIME, foreign diplomats were welcomed by one
of her twenty-five gentleman pensioners. Whoever happened to be
available was despatched to meet and greet, to conduct them to their
lodgings and to carry messages or escort them to audiences with the
Queen. That meant a lack of continuity – 'never one being sent twice'
was a complaint by the French ambassador in 1597[1] – and a risk that
ambassadors and envoys, who were notoriously prone to imagined
slights, might feel they weren't being accorded the respect they deserved.

In May 1603, barely two weeks after he entered London as king,
James I sought to address this issue. He appointed Sir Lewis Lewknor to
care for strangers of quality at an annual salary of £200. Lewknor, who
spoke fluent Spanish, was to make sure that visiting foreign dignitaries
were treated with respect. He had to arrange suitable accommodation
for them and their entourage, which might consist of well over a
hundred servants. He had to ensure that this accommodation was
properly equipped with hangings, bedding, sheets, stools and tables, all
provided out of the King's standing wardrobe. He must explain exactly
what the King would pay for – usually food, beer and wine, coal, lights
and torches, but only for a fixed period, after which the ambassador had
to find payment himself. And he had to arrange for coaches to carry
the diplomat to and from his audiences with the King. The position of
master of ceremonies was a new one, although commentators gave it a
spurious air of antiquity by claiming it as 'an ancient office … a long
time void and almost forgotten'.[2] In 1605 Lewknor was confirmed in
the post for life and given three helpers: a marshal of ceremonies and
two assistants.

In 1612 John Finet, a 41-year-old minor courtier with experience
of several European courts and a knowledge of French, Spanish, German
and Italian, was appointed as one of Lewknor's two assistants. Finet was
a conscientious deputy – so conscientious, in fact, that he was often on
bad terms with Lewknor, who felt his efficiency reflected badly on the
master's own relaxed performance in office. Finet's first foray into the
world of international diplomacy tested him to the limit. On Sunday

Sir John Finet (1570/71-
1641), master of
ceremonies to Charles I.

14 February 1613 in the chapel of Whitehall Palace, James I's daughter Elizabeth was married to Frederick V, Count Palatine of the Rhine and elector of the Holy Roman Empire.

The marriage was preceded by spectacular entertainments. On the evening of Friday 12 February, the King and Queen, Princess Elizabeth and the count palatine, 'and the rest of the nobility of England' gathered at the windows of Whitehall Palace to watch a show of fireworks on the Thames. A fight between a fiery dragon and an equally fiery St George was followed by a flaming hart being hunted over the water by a pack of hounds 'made all of fire burning'.³ On the Saturday afternoon there was a sea battle on the river, depicting an assault on Algiers and ending in the capture of the city and the liberation of Christian slaves. It was watched by the King and Queen and others from the Privy Stairs at Whitehall.

On Sunday came the ceremony itself. To a fanfare of trumpets, the young groom processed from the Banqueting House wearing a white suit decorated with gold and pearls. Then came his bride, looking stunning in a gown of white satin and a gold crown, with pearls and diamonds. Her train was carried by fourteen or fifteen women, all in white satin. Afterwards there was a feast in the Banqueting House, and dancing. The celebrations continued on the Monday and Tuesday. There were masques and revels.⁴ Everything went off to perfection.

Almost everything. The day before the wedding the lord chamberlain, the Earl of Suffolk, sent John Finet to Ferdinand de Boiscot, the ambassador of the Spanish Netherlands, with a formal invitation. The Spanish Netherlands were ruled by Archduke Albert VII of Austria and the Archduchess Isabella on behalf of the Spanish crown; any invitation to court had to take account of the fact that the ambassadors of Spain and France, and their respective allies the Spanish Netherlands and Venice, had been locked in a struggle over precedence for years now. James I's answer was never to invite them to anything together, if he could possibly help it.

Finet was shown into Boiscot's presence, where he told him that the King had invited the French and Venetian ambassadors to attend 'the first day's solemnity'. Would he like to attend on the second or third, either dinner or supper or both? There was a pause before Boiscot asked with a frown if the Spanish ambassador was going.⁵ The Spanish ambassador was sick, said Finet. After another pause, Boiscot wanted to know why the Venetian ambassador was present on the first day of the wedding celebrations, and he was only being asked to the second or third. If he weren't the representative of a great prince, he would accept any kind of invitation, even to serve up a dish at the bride's table. But he was. And if precedence was being given to Venice, 'a mean republic, governed by a sort of burghers, who had but a handful of territory in comparison to his master', then he wasn't coming. Working himself up into a rage, he told Finet he didn't know what he had done to deserve such treatment. The Venetian ambassador was always being invited to things, and he wasn't. Eventually he dismissed Finet, following up the interview with a letter to the lord chamberlain in which he repeated that the invitation 'was in a second place to one who was far from all colour of reason to precede him' and that he was therefore unable to be there.[6]

Boiscot was left to cool off while the wedding celebrations went ahead. Finet was despatched to his residence once again with a long letter explaining that no offence had been intended, that no one day was more important than another, but – a masterstroke, this – that if one day were the most important, it was the third day, the Tuesday (which was also Shrove Tuesday):

> To argumentize thereupon, it might be alleged that the last day should be taken for the greatest day, as it is understood in many other cases, and particularly upon the festivals of Christmas wherein the twelfth day or the festival of the three kings which is the last is taken for the greatest day. And in many places Tuesday is taken for the chiefest day of Shrove-tide; wherefore the masque at court composed of noble men and ladies was assigned for that day as being the greatest of the festivals.[7]

Boiscot was unconvinced.

In the meantime, Finet was also having to deal with the French and Venetian ambassadors, who, as he put it, 'were not free from punctillios'.[8] One said that as the representatives of crowned heads they ought to precede Prince Charles at the wedding. The other insisted that they must be provided with chairs at the wedding feast, even though the only people to have chairs were the bride and groom. Even Prince Charles had only a stool to sit on. These claims were sidestepped, and neither man seemed keen to press them, particularly after James I took them aside at the wedding and told them he wasn't minded to pay attention to the absent Boiscot's protests, which meant they had scored over the Spanish Netherlands and thus over Spain. But another disaster loomed when the lord chamberlain tried to place the French ambassador's wife at the dinner table beneath the countesses but above the baronesses, only for Viscountess Effingham, who also occupied this intermediate place at

The true Effigies of ẏᵉ Alkaid, (or Lord) Jaurar Ben Abdella, Embassador from ẏ high and mighty Mully Mahamed Shegue, Emperourr of Morocco, King of Fess and Suss. etc.

G. Glover fe:

The Moroccan ambassador Jaurar ben 'Abd Allah, whose unexpected arrival in England in 1637 threw the court into confusion.

and prominent citizens, all on horseback, who escorted him to the house in Wood Street.

Jaurar was still sick, so his audience with Charles I was delayed until early November, with the allowance of £25 a day steadily mounting up. Finally, on 5 November 1637, he rode out to Whitehall to meet the King. It was quite a sight. The procession was led by a mounted City marshal with half a dozen servants on foot, who cleared the way. Then came seven trumpeters on horseback, and the four Barbary horses which formed part of the sultan's gift to the King, two of them equipped with their gold-plated saddles and bridles, and each led by a black Moroccan in red livery. The four hawks were absent from the parade: they hadn't flourished during the long journey from Morocco, and it had been thought best to present them to the King four or five days earlier in case they died before he saw them. After the horses came sixteen English slaves, freed by Sultan Mohammed and clothed all in white at the ambassador's expense. Then six or seven City captains in plumed hats and ten gentlemen of the privy chamber.

Finet came next, alone, and leading the ambassador, who was flanked by the Earl of Shrewsbury and Robert Blake. Blake was told to keep back slightly, 'to express a difference' in status.[10]

Jaurar ben 'Abd Allah cut a striking figure. As the procession snaked through the City, past the vast bulk of the medieval St Paul's Cathedral and on, through Ludgate and along Fleet Street and the Strand, all eyes were on him. It was usual for diplomats to travel by coach – not him. He told Finet beforehand that he must ride: 'he had an express order from the king his master to pass not otherwise to his public audience than on horseback,' reported Finet.[11] One of his servants carried his gilded scimitar and another his slippers and part of his horse's golden harness. 'At each side of him walked four footmen in blue liveries, and behind him eight of his more eminent followers, Moors in their country habits on horseback.'[12]

The procession attracted a crowd of thousands. When it reached Temple Bar, the Westminster militia, 400 strong and led by one of the grooms of the bedchamber, met Jaurar and led him into Whitehall, where they formed a guard of honour. Eventually he was led through crowds who had come to gape at this exotic curiosity, and into Inigo Jones's Banqueting House. There he met the King and Queen. He spoke first to Charles I, bowing to him three times before delivering his master's letter.

The ambassador turned then to Queen Henrietta Maria and, although he knew Spanish and Italian, spoke briefly to her in Arabic, which was duly translated by Blake. A private conference followed, after which he and the King walked down the flight of stairs opening into the park, where Charles received the present of the horses and inspected the freed captives. By now darkness was falling, and no one could find the ambassador's own horse. Finet had to take him back to his lodging in one of the royal coaches.

The pageantry that enveloped Jaurar ben 'Abd Allah's public

appearance wasn't just meant to honour a new ally. It was an affirmation of the success of Charles I's foreign policy, a vindication of his imposition of the ship-money levy. 'The reason of all is the shipping money,' muttered Viscount Conway.[13] Other commentators were quick to point out that no matter how grand the Moroccan ambassador was, this Moor was awed by the majesty of the English court. As he entered the Banqueting House at Whitehall, wrote one, 'the resplendency of the royal majesties, the lustre of the nobility, and the variety of eye-dazzling beauties made him wonder beyond admiration, and admire past all former wonder'.[14]

Towards the end of March 1638, the Moroccan ambassador decided his business at court was over. Charles I ordered two warships to Portsmouth to take the Moroccan party home, as a precaution against pirates; and Finet began the business of buying suitable presents for both Jaurar and his master, Sultan Mohammed.

Those hawks and horses and gold-plated harnesses called for something equally impressive. Or, as the lord chamberlain whispered in the King's ear, 'how fit it would be, and how to his majesty's honour, to disengage himself of the debt he might seem to remain in to the king of Morocco for the present he had sent him'.[15] A warrant for £2,000 was issued out of the Exchequer. A conservative estimate would put this at about £285,000 at today's values, while a less conservative estimate would put it in the millions. The money was spent by Finet and Blake on a coach gilded and painted with flowers and lined with crimson velvet, four Denmark horses to draw it ('with a fifth spare'), another six or seven horses and mares, a hundred lances, an assortment of cloth, and copies of Van Dyck's portraits of Charles I and Henrietta Maria.

Gilt plate to the value of £800 was the usual parting gift for ambassadors from monarchies, with those who represented republics or other lesser states also getting plate, but only to the value of £420. Blake told Finet that its use was forbidden in Morocco, so instead the master of ceremonies arrived at Wood Street with an array of fine cambric and linens, and a selection of muskets, pistols and other weapons to the value of £800. In return, the ambassador handed Finet 120 pieces of gold as a gratuity for himself and another thirty for his assistant. Blake received a gold chain and medal to the value of £210, which was the normal parting gift for an agent.

The policy on the value of parting gifts was fixed, although of course that didn't mean that it was always accepted. When Juan de Necolalde, who was in England as an agent of Spain (rather than a resident ambassador), was preparing to leave for home in 1637 he was outraged to hear from Finet that he was only getting a chain. 'He rose up from his chair in a passion, such as I had not seen him subject to,' said Finet, who was so taken aback that he immediately sent a report of the incident to secretary of state Sir Francis Windebank, asking for help.[16] Windebank told the King, the King said that Necolalde was only an agent, and Finet had to go back and tell the Spaniard that it was a chain or nothing. Necolalde opted for nothing.

Occasionally a departing diplomat would ask for something other than the normal present of gilt plate. In 1631, for example, the Count of Montanero and Castelletto, an ambassador extraordinary from the Duchy of Savoy who had come to congratulate Charles I on the birth of his first son, asked Finet if he could have a jewel instead, explaining that it was difficult to transport plate all the way home to Savoy, it was rarely used there and – the real reason for his asking, one suspects – the first time there was a great feast his master, the Duke of Savoy, would ask to borrow the plate and he would never get it back.

A problem with varying the type of parting gift was that it led to protests from Sir Henry Mildmay, the master of the Jewel House. The Jewel House was responsible for making, weighing and keeping the king's plate, and for providing plate for departing dignitaries; and as master, Mildmay had the right of presenting the gift, which meant he could usually pocket a gratuity of up to £40 from the recipient. This was perfectly normal practice. But the Jewel House also contrived to make a profit from gilt plate and gold chains in other ways. The gifts were often slow in coming, and when they finally did arrive, they weighed rather less than they should. The crown put a fixed value of eight shillings an ounce on the plate, so in theory a gift worth £800 should weigh 2,000 ounces. When a gold chain proved to be twenty per cent lighter than it should have been, or a gift of plate twenty-five per cent lighter, diplomats complained and Finet was embarrassed. Mildmay, however, always brazened it out and kept the money, which could amount to a considerable sum when crown expenditure on diplomatic gifts averaged more than £3,600 a year.

Sir John Finet's life revolved around formality and form. There was another side, though, to this most punctilious of men. We have a glimpse of it in January 1618, when James I was staying at Theobalds and, according to the great letter-writer John Chamberlain, Finet sang him a song 'of such scurrilous and base stuff, that it put the king out of his good humour, and all the rest that heard it'.[17] The song, in which Finet was accompanied by nine or ten courtiers who joined in with the chorus, is regrettably lost, leaving us to speculate on exactly what it was that caused Chamberlain to marvel that no one had the sense 'to see how unfit it was to bring such beastly gear in public before a prince'.[18]

One of Finet's partners in song on that occasion was George Goring, a gentleman of the privy chamber and a man noted for 'a peculiar jocularity of humour'. And it seems that Finet and Goring were often involved in the kind of idiotic buffoonery which James I enjoyed (as long as it didn't go too far). According to the *Court and Character of James I*, which first appeared in 1650, Finet and Goring, along with the courtier Sir Edward Zouch, were the King's 'chief and master fools': 'Zouch his part it was to sing bawdy songs, and tell bawdy tales; Finet's, to compose these songs; then was a set of fiddlers brought to court on purpose for this fooling, and Goring was master of the game for fooleries.'[19] They organised dances and horseplay for the King's amusement, riding round on each other's backs in imitation jousts 'till they fell together by the ears'.[20] In earlier reigns, these antics might have been the preserve of the court jester, the fool whose role it was to amuse the sovereign and who in return claimed what Erasmus called 'the peculiar privilege of fools to speak the truth' with impunity.[21] And in fact James I had a jester, Archibald Armstrong, and Armstrong did indeed play a part in these games with Finet and the others, riding on the back of the other fools like a knight in the tiltyard.

Although the king's fool was coming to seem a little dated by the seventeenth century, he had been a fixture in the Tudor royal household, where fools came in many forms. Henry VII had several 'naturals' or 'innocents', individuals who were intellectually disabled and who accompanied him on progresses. They were clothed and fed at the King's expense, and placed in the charge of a keeper, 'the fool master'.

Cardinal Wolsey's fool, known as 'Patch', achieved a slight place in history as a reluctant pawn in the game of thrones which the cardinal lost to Henry VIII. Wolsey and his entourage were en route from Putney to Westminster in 1529 when they were met by Sir Henry Norris, the groom of the stool, with a message reassuring the cardinal that he was still in favour with the King. Wolsey was beside himself with relief (a misplaced relief, as it turned out) and, casting round for a gift to send the King, offered his fool. Patch remained with the King until the summer of 1535, when he brought his career at court to an abrupt end by saying nice things about Henry's ex-wife Catherine of Aragon and calling his current wife, Anne Boleyn, a trollop and her daughter Elizabeth a bastard. Henry nearly murdered him there and then, and he was banished from court.

Anne Boleyn also kept a fool, an unnamed woman for whom she bought a new gown and a green satin cap in 1536. So did Henry's eldest daughter, Mary Tudor: her fool, Jane, was taken on by the King's last wife, Catherine Parr, for a while in the 1540s. There was also a succession of dwarfs at court, kept as playthings and curiosities. Elizabeth I showered her dwarf, Thomasina, with gifts, presenting her with gowns and gloves, ivory combs and gilt rings.

The Family of Henry VIII (c.1545). The king is flanked by his third wife, Jane Seymour, and his son, Prince Edward, later Edward VI. Princess Mary, later Mary I, stands on the left, and Princess Elizabeth, later Elizabeth I, on the right. The figures in the archways are thought to be Princess Mary's fool, known only as Jane, and Will Somers, one of Henry VIII's fools.

The Tudors also kept conjurers and jesters, men (and occasionally women) who played the fool for the entertainment of the sovereign. Throughout the 1520s and 1530s 'the King's juggler', as he was called in Henry VIII's household accounts, was Thomas Brandon. Brandon was more of a stage magician than a juggler in the 21st-century sense of the word. One of his tricks was to paint a picture of a dove on a wall and then, pointing to a real pigeon sitting on the roof, prick the picture with his knife: the pigeon would fall from the roof, stone dead. Will Tarleton, actor, dancer and comedian, achieved national fame as Elizabeth I's court fool. 'He told the queen more of her faults, than most of her chaplains,' wrote the seventeenth-century historian Thomas Fuller, 'and cured her melancholy better than all of her physicians.'[22] Elizabeth loved Tarleton's brand of low comedy, his jokes and drunk acts, the way he pretended to do battle with her little dog, waving his sword and longstaff about so effectively that she ordered him out of her presence for making her laugh too much.

James I, famously dubbed the wisest fool in Christendom, kept a fool of his own. One of the many legends and myths surrounding Archibald Armstrong, 'the best fool of state' on his own estimation, tells of how, condemned to death for sheep-stealing, he pleaded with the King for his life.[23] He had recently come across the Bible, he said, and wanted to read it 'for his soul's sake': would James postpone his hanging until he had finished it? The King is said to have agreed, at which Archie replied, 'Then devil take me if I ever read a word of it as long as my eyes are open!' This answer amused the King so much that he took him into his service and brought him down to England in 1603.[24]

Armstrong was soon exercising the royal fool's prerogative of telling the King a few home truths. When James complained that his mount was on the lean side, Armstrong replied that the best way to fatten up the beast would be to make him a bishop. Yet this fool was no fool. Armstrong had a happy knack of making influential friends and acquiring money, although he seems to have been none too scrupulous about how he came by it. His friend the poet John Taylor dedicated his *Praise, Antiquity, and Commodity, of Beggary, Beggars and Begging* (1621) to 'the bright eye-dazzling mirror of mirth … and regent of ridiculous confabulations', wishing Armstrong 'a nimble tongue, to make other men's money run into your purse, and quick heels to outrun the hue and cry'.[25] And he managed to stay on as court jester to the altogether less relaxed Charles I, which suggests a tact and diplomacy which is conspicuously absent from most of the tales told about his royal career.

As tensions rose in the lead-up to civil war, Archibald Armstrong found out the hard way that the court jester's prerogative to mock with impunity no longer held good. At Whitehall in March 1638 he happened to meet the Archbishop of Canterbury, William Laud, who was on his way to a meeting of the King's council. News had just arrived that Laud's attempts to enforce uniformity of worship in Scotland had been met with widespread protests north of the border, and Armstrong mentioned this and asked, 'Who's the fool now?' Laud went straight into the council and complained to the King, with the result that Charles immediately ordered his fool to be sacked and banished from the court. The lord chamberlain of the King's household was ordered to act, 'and immediately the same was put in execution'.[26] Armstrong's career as court jester had come to an abrupt end.

He wasn't quite the last royal fool. That title went to his replacement, a man called 'Muckle John', of whom nothing is known except for his high sartorial standards: there are entries in the household accounts for crimson silk hose, silk and silver garters, gloves of stag's leather fringed with gold and silver, a feathered hat and a pair of perfumed gloves lined with sable, all 'for Muckle John'.[27] Then in 1642 came the war, making fools of every man.

CHAPTER FOUR

A Court without a King

O N 10 JANUARY 1642 KING CHARLES I LEFT LONDON. He wouldn't see the city again until he returned to die in it seven years later. A week before his departure, he had sent a message to Parliament demanding the surrender of five of his most vociferous opponents in the House of Commons and the leader of the Puritan faction in the House of Lords, accusing them all of treason. Parliament refused to give them up, and he withdrew in dismay, first to Hampton Court Palace, then north to York. All through the spring and early summer of 1642 he and his adversaries in Parliament, after sparring for several years over religion, the constitutional role of the sovereign and the rights of his subjects, began to organise arms and armies for the civil war that everyone saw approaching, but that no one seemed able to prevent. On 22 August Charles rode into Nottingham with a group of nobles and watched as a huge royal banner was unfurled from the highest tower of Nottingham Castle. A herald-at-arms read out a proclamation calling his loyal subjects to come to his aid.

It wasn't a wild success. The King had made so many last-minute changes to the proclamation that with all the crossings-out and insertions the herald couldn't read it properly. And that night, the bright red standard, emblazoned with the royal arms and the motto 'Give Caesar his due', blew down in a high wind. But that day marked the beginning of four years of bloody war.

On 29 October 1642 the King arrived in Oxford, 'the only city of England that he could say was entirely at his devotion', according to his trusted adviser Edward Hyde.[1] The following month, after the Earl of Essex's parliamentarian forces had halted the royalist advance on London at the Battle of Turnham Green, Charles withdrew to Oxford, which would remain the royalist headquarters until it surrendered to the parliamentarians in June 1646. As men and women loyal to the crown began to drift into the city, the King's alternative court began to take shape, and his lodgings, at Christ Church, came to mirror the arrangements at the palace of Whitehall, although with more emphasis on his personal security. He kept a presence chamber and a privy chamber:

Charles I, king and martyr, depicted wearing the clothes in which he was executed.

two grooms were stationed at the foot of the stairs leading up to them, and were instructed 'not to permit any unknown or mean person to pass up the stairs toward that room'.[2] As a second line, a gentleman usher guarded the door to the privy chamber, in case anyone got past the grooms. Another was positioned 'at the upper end of our presence and privy chamber' to vet anyone trying to enter the King's withdrawing chamber, while a page of the bedchamber guarded the backstair, preventing access to Charles to all but the nobility, counsellors of state, judges, bishops and members of the King's council of war. When the King went out, guards were to stay close, 'and be vigilant in observing all persons making any address toward us or coming near our person'. And when he walked in the gardens, two or more yeomen of the guard were to keep watch 'and not to permit any mean or unknown person to enter'.[3]

A S IT TURNED OUT, nothing could keep the King safe. The royalists were routed by Parliament's New Model Army at the Battle of Naseby in June 1645, a defeat which signalled the end for Charles I. By the time Oxford surrendered to the New Model Army's commander-in-chief, Thomas Fairfax, one year later, the King had fled north to become a pawn in a bigger game being played out between competing factions in Parliament. On 19 January 1649, with the war over and the royalist high command in exile or in tatters, the defeated Charles I was brought as a prisoner to St James's Palace, where he spent the last eleven nights of his life.

While he had been away, Parliament had clung to the notion that it was making war not on the King, but on his wicked advisers. There was no intention of deposing Charles himself, still less of beheading him. In the meantime, MPs mulled over the problem of what to do with his palaces and possessions until he returned and took up his throne, a sadder and a wiser man. According to one story, the radical politician Henry Marten and the Puritan poet George Wither stormed into Westminster Abbey in the early days of the Civil War and broke open the great iron chest that held the royal regalia. 'With a scorn greater than his lusts and the rest of his vices, [Marten] openly declared that there should be no further use of those toys and trifles,' wrote the chronicler Anthony à Wood.[4] Marten then dressed Wither in the royal robes, and the poet proceeded to prance around with Edward the Confessor's crown on his head and 'with a thousand apish and ridiculous actions exposed those sacred ornaments to contempt and laughter'.*

That smacks of royalist propaganda. But there were certainly some deplorable acts of religiously motivated vandalism. At Easter 1643, for example, soldiers led by Marten broke into the Queen's Chapel at Somerset House, smashing statues and burning vestments. Sir John Clotworthy, a fiercely anti-Catholic MP, climbed onto the altar and, calling for one of the troops to hand him a halberd, ripped apart the altarpiece – a large Crucifixion by Rubens. A parliamentary committee for the 'demolition of monuments of superstition and idolatry', headed by Sir Robert Harley, was formed the following month; and in 1644 and 1645 it commissioned the destruction of images in the chapels at St James's Palace, Whitehall, Greenwich and Hampton Court. Stained glass was replaced with plain glass, communion rails were removed, and altar steps were levelled. Wall paintings were whitewashed, and statues and paintings destroyed. Organs were removed from Greenwich and Hampton Court. In December 1645 John Rutland was paid £9 16s. for dismantling the east window in the chapel at Hampton Court.

The Commons ordered other depredations in the royal palaces which had nothing to do with imposing Protestant values. In November 1644, some 13,000 ounces of plate from the palaces were melted down and converted into coin to finance the parliamentarian war effort. And by 1648, faced with the need to raise money for the army's pay arrears, Parliament realised that godly reformation and enterprise weren't mutually exclusive. Another parliamentary committee was asked to consider the tapestries in the palaces and to pick out 'such of them as have superstitious and idolatrous pictures in them'. These could be sold to provide 'fire, candles, and other necessaries' for the soldiers at Whitehall.[5]

Throughout the Civil War, Parliament was mindful that the responsibility for safeguarding the King's goods in his absence (those that hadn't been smashed, ripped or melted down) lay with them. The Earl of Pembroke, who had been lord chamberlain of the household until he came out against the King and was dismissed, was asked by the House of Lords to ensure that nothing left Whitehall without authority. MPs were to be present when searchers went through any of the palaces

*The antiquary John Aubrey wrote that when Wither was captured by royalists during the war and in danger of being hanged, Sir John Denham interceded with Charles I to save his life, saying that while Wither lived Denham 'should not be the worst poet in England'. Andrew Clark (ed.), 'Brief Lives': Chiefly of Contemporaries, Set Down by John Aubrey, Oxford: Clarendon Press (1898), vol. I, 221.

looking for goods belonging to courtiers who had taken the King's side, to ensure that none of the King's property disappeared during those searches. In January 1649, as the prospect of a dramatic transfer of ownership of property from the King to the state became ever more real, the Commons asked for the names of suitable persons 'for taking an inventory, and for preserving all the goods in the King's several houses'.[6]

That transfer of ownership occurred dramatically in front of Inigo Jones's Banqueting House at Whitehall on 30 January. It was in that place and on that day that sentence was carried out on Charles Stuart, King of England, standing 'convicted, attainted and condemned of high treason and other crimes' and sentenced 'to be put to death by the severing of his head from his body'.[7] Three weeks later, Oliver Cromwell, MP and second-in-command of the army, reported from the Council of State, which had become the executive body responsible for the government of the nation under the direction of the Commons. 'Divers goods belonging to the state are in danger of being embezzled,' said Cromwell. Books, statues and pictures formerly belonging to the King should be committed to the Council of State, and the Council 'be empowered to dispose of such of them as they think fit'.[8]

In June, the Council of State recommended that Parliament should hold on to the dead King's principal residences: Whitehall, the palace of Westminster, St James's, Somerset House, Hampton Court, Theobalds, Windsor and Greenwich. As for the rest of the royal possessions, on 4 July 1649 Parliament passed an act for the sale of the goods and personal estate of the late King, and those of his widow Henrietta Maria and his eldest son, the Prince of Wales, both of whom were then in exile on the Continent. Trustees were appointed to seek out, secure and value paintings, furniture, tapestries – everything from crystal cabinets to chamber pots. England was about to see the greatest sale of art objects in the nation's history.

———— • ————

THE TRUSTEES WHO SUPERVISED THE SALE of the late King's goods were a mixed bunch. George Wither, the poet who was supposed to have pranced around Westminster Abbey with Edward the Confessor's crown on his head, was one; another was Edward Winslow, the erstwhile governor of Plymouth Colony, who had travelled to England in 1646 to represent the interests of Massachusetts and who decided he would rather build the city on a hill in London. One of the

What I WAS, is passed by;
What I AM, away doth flie;
What I SHAL BEE, none do see;
Yet, in that, my Beauties bee.

The poet George Wither, one of the trustees appointed to seek out, secure and value the late King Charles I's personal property, in what became one of the biggest art sales in British history.

most active trustees was Anthony Mildmay, who had served in the King's household as a gentleman of the privy chamber and who waited on him during his imprisonment. Mildmay's inside knowledge must have been particularly useful. His brother Sir Henry was master of the king's jewel house, and active in the parliamentarian cause. (He was the same Sir Henry Mildmay who used to short-change John Finet when it came to providing parting gifts for diplomats.)

The trustees were given Somerset House, a residence of queen consorts Anne of Denmark and Henrietta Maria. It was brought into use now as offices and lodgings, and the great hall was fitted up as a sale room. For the next five years, the trustees brought together the late King's goods, valued them and passed them on to contractors who were authorised to negotiate sales. The trustees themselves were entitled to take sevenpence in the pound, slightly less than three per cent, from those sales. But there were also benefits in kind. Some items, for example, found their way to the trustees' lodgings: George Wither equipped his own apartment with £238 15s. worth of royal furnishings, including a suite of Brussels tapestries, fifteen chairs and stools and a set of damask bed curtains 'with strings to it of silver and gold, laced and fringed', as the valuers noted.[9]

The first £30,000 raised by the sales of royal goods were earmarked for the use of the Commonwealth's navy. After that, priority went to the royal family's creditors and household servants. Some creditors were given straight cash payments out of the proceeds of sales; others accepted goods at the valuation set by trustees, and sold them on. Fourteen syndicates of creditors called 'dividends' were set up to accept goods in lieu or to buy them; collectors and their agents then dealt directly with the leader of a syndicate, who negotiated a resale and distributed the profits among his fellows. The late king's embroiderer, upholsterer and glazier all had some of his pictures and antique sculptures in their homes awaiting sale in 1652. Emanuel de Critz, who later claimed on rather slender evidence to have been Charles I's sergeant-painter, had three rooms full of royal paintings plus the King's bust by Bernini which had been at Greenwich, and which had been valued by the trustees at £800.

The royal upholsterer mentioned above was Ralph Grynder, who had redecorated Henrietta Maria's bedchamber at Somerset House in the 1620s. Grynder was the leader of a particularly active syndicate. On one day, 23 October 1651, he negotiated the purchase of forty lots, valued at a staggering £4,775 10s. They included paintings by Dürer, Titian, Carracci and Mytens; antique statues of Diana and Jupiter from Greenwich Palace; and two barges that had belonged to Charles I and the Prince of Wales. The most expensive single acquisition was 'ten pieces of arras hangings of the old and new law' from Richmond Palace, which were valued at £1,817 10s. A set of tapestry hangings with the same name was listed among the possessions of Catherine of Aragon after her death in 1536.

Acquisitions on this scale suggest that Grynder's syndicate was either owed a great deal of money or had some powerful financial backers who could see a potential for profit. That was certainly true of some private individuals. John Hutchinson, a Nottinghamshire landowner, soldier and

MP who had been one of the signatories to Charles I's death warrant, bought twenty-three paintings for £1,349, as well as carpets, furniture and brass figurines. 'These he brought down into the country,' recalled his wife, 'intending a very neat cabinet for them.'[10] They didn't stay in the cabinet for long. Hutchinson sold the pick of the bunch, Titian's *Venus of the Pardo*, to Cardinal Mazarin, chief minister to the infant Louis XIV of France. He told Mazarin's agent in London, Antoine de Bordeux-Neufville, that he'd paid £6,000 for it, then £7,000. He couldn't possibly take less, he said. 'So as not to lose it,' Bordeux-Neufville reported, 'I was today obliged to finalise the purchase of £7,000 … I have promised £2,000 for Monday and the remainder three weeks later.'[11] Hutchinson had actually paid £600 for the painting.

Bordeux-Neufville also dealt with contractors, syndicates and dealers to acquire royal busts and tapestries. Other European buyers competed for the best pictures: the Spanish ambassador, Don Alonso de Cárdenas, acquired twenty-four chests of pictures, hangings and household stuff and shipped them off to his master, Philip IV, in Madrid, having first negotiated a deal with the Council of State which allowed him to export the goods without paying any duty on them. Nor were sales confined to kings and consortiums. Edward Miller of Drury Lane bought an assortment of bits and pieces, including 'many broken crystals in an open leather case', valued at £1 but sold to him for £2, a flower pot, a 'very old' leather cradle and some hangings from Hampton Court which were also 'very old'.[12] Miller bought a lion for £38, but it turned out to be the wrong lion, and he demanded his money back.

THE COUNCIL OF STATE reserved to public use £20,000 worth of goods and appointed yet another parliamentary committee to choose them. These reserved goods were needed to furnish government buildings. The Armada tapestries which Elizabeth I had demanded during her visit to Lord Howard of Effingham went to decorate the House of Lords. Other hangings and furnishings were used to fit out the Commons, the Courts of Justice and the official lodgings of various foreign ambassadors. The bulk were used for the palace of Whitehall.

When they first assembled in February 1649 the 41-member Council of State, which was effectively the government of England, met at Derby House in Canon Row, Westminster. Within a couple of months, the Council decided that the palace of Whitehall would provide them with more suitable premises. In May, they ordered the army officers who were occupying the palace to move out, and voted themselves £10,000 worth of art and furnishings from the late king's goods. The gallery was repaired, doors were fitted with new locks and keys, chaplains were appointed to preach in the chapel every Sunday, and officers were recruited to look after the privy lodgings.

Initially only a handful of officials were actually granted lodgings there. (They included the poet John Milton, who was the Council's secretary for foreign tongues.) But it was accepted that any Council member who wanted to move into the palace was entitled to do so, and over the summer and autumn many did, voting that 'such hangings, carpets, chairs, stools, and beds as can be had [should] be reserved for furnishing the lodgings of the council of state'.[13] As keeper of the palace, the Earl of Pembroke already had lodgings in the Whitehall Cockpit, which was a labyrinth of rooms overlooking St James's Park that had grown up around the site of Henry VIII's tennis court, tiltyard and cock-fighting arena. It was from his chamber window there that on 30 January 1649 the earl 'looked upon the king, as he went up stairs from the park to the gallery in the way to the place of his death'.[14] Pembroke died in 1650, and his lodgings in the Cockpit were given to Oliver Cromwell, who was appointed captain-general and commander-in-chief of the army that same year.

Was this gradual occupation of Whitehall by the Council of State a case of power corrupting? The royalist propaganda machine certainly presented it that way. A fabulously scurrilous 1649 tragi-comedy, *New-Market-Fayre, or a Parliament Out-Cry of State Commodities Set to Sale*, portrayed Cromwell bidding against Thomas Fairfax, who had been commander-in-chief of the army before him, to buy the crown 'that Colonel Marten took from the Abbey at Westminster some four years since'.[15] Meanwhile, according to the anonymous author, Lady Fairfax cheated on her impotent husband and Mrs Cromwell hopped into bed with the army officer and MP Herbert Morley. When one reads that in the closing scene Thomas Fairfax turns into a zombie, Oliver Cromwell goes off to Ireland possessed by devils, Mrs Cromwell is stabbed to death by Lady Fairfax and the people decide to petition 'royal Charles' to come home, one realises that the play must be treated with a certain amount of caution.

In truth, the adoption of Whitehall Palace by the Council and its various committees had less to do with personal ambition than with a collective move to establish a government which functioned as a replacement for the King. That meant the palace had to be properly staffed and secured. The Council recruited secretaries, a sergeant-at-arms and eight officers, two chaplains, four clerks and twelve messengers. Richard Nutt, who was the master of the Commonwealth barge, had £60 a year, the same salary as his predecessor, the keeper of the King's barge.

The soldiers who guarded Whitehall were urged to make sure that 'no clamorous women nor spies be permitted to come within the walls of this house'.[16] Gates and doors were to be kept locked, and the doors of houses on the edge of St James's Park, which abutted onto Whitehall, were nailed shut to prevent intruders. The council room was only unlocked for members, and twenty armed men were kept in the guard chamber and told to be 'well and fully armed' every afternoon that the Council was in session.[17] The armoury at the Tower was asked to send over forty halberds for the use of these guards.

Meanwhile complaints grew that the King's old household servants, artificers and suppliers were living in poverty while the Council reserved the best items from the sale of the King's goods to themselves, and the trustees dragged their feet over the thing. Critics hit out at the delays, predicting that 'the king's poor creditors and servants may gape long enough for sale of the king's goods to pay their debts: they (poor souls) are left to starve while these Saints triumphant revel in their master's goods and houses'.[18] In July 1654 the old household servants petitioned the Council, saying that many were in a starving condition, and that the trustees had disposed of goods unjustly when those goods or the proceeds from their sale should have been coming to the petitioners.

An exasperated Council of State countered robustly. The three leaders of this petition, they said, were the keeper of the tennis court at St James's Palace, who had already had more than his due; Charles I's clerk of the kitchen, who had gone with the King to Oxford and therefore wasn't owed anything; and a chap called Jackson who had bought many of the creditors' debts at a heavy discount in the hope of making a profit. Council members did acknowledge that there were still some debts outstanding to household servants and suppliers. The problem was, they were short of men who understood the workings of the King's household. 'Unless you employ knowing men', an anonymous adviser warned the Council, 'you will be abused.'[19]

But this was in the summer of 1654, and by then everyone in London knew the real reason for the delay. The previous December Oliver Cromwell had been sworn in as lord protector, with the powers to exercise 'the chief magistracy and the administration of the government

Oliver Lord Prot. *Elizᵗʰ Lady of Oliver.* *Richᵈ Lord Protʳ.*

R. Hancock Sc

Oliver Cromwell, his wife Elizabeth and their son Richard, who briefly succeeded his father as Lord Protector of England. The monkey on Lady Cromwell's shoulder is a deliberate insult, implying that she has ideas above her station.

over the Commonwealth of England, Scotland and Ireland … and the people thereof'.[20] The Council of State was replaced by a much smaller body and the lord protector moved out of the lodgings he occupied in the Cockpit and into extensive apartments in the palace of Whitehall itself, which were to be furnished according to Lady Cromwell's instructions.

Oliver and Elizabeth Cromwell had been married for twenty-four years by 1654. They were both in their mid-fifties with six surviving children, four daughters and two sons. Richard, the eldest boy, was assigned lodgings of his own in the palace, almost certainly those which had belonged to Charles I: however, he divided his time between Whitehall and his father-in-law's estate at Hursley in Hampshire, where his wife was busy producing children at yearly intervals. The Cromwells' other son, Henry, was made commander of the English army in Ireland in 1654, and moved there the following year, staying until 1659.

Bridget, the eldest girl, had been married to Henry Ireton, a senior commander in the New Model Army during the Civil War. After his death on campaign in Ireland in 1651, she married Charles Fleetwood, another senior military figure and a close colleague of her father: Fleetwood was commander of the army in Ireland from 1652 until he was replaced by Henry Cromwell, whereupon he and Bridget came back to England and took up lodgings in Derby House in Westminster.

The other three Cromwell daughters, Elizabeth, Mary and Frances, all lived in their parents' household. Mary and Frances were teenagers and unmarried; Elizabeth, who by all accounts was Oliver's favourite, was the wife of another military man, John Claypole, who was appointed the lord protector's master of horse, which meant that he and Elizabeth had lodgings of their own both at Whitehall and at the second of the lord protector's residences, Hampton Court.

The Cromwells moved into the palace of Whitehall proper and technically took up residence at Hampton Court on 14 April 1654, five months after Parliament had resolved that Whitehall, Hampton Court and various other ex-royal residences 'be vested in the present Lord Protector, and the succeeding Lords Protectors, for the maintenance of his and their state and dignity'.[21] The move hadn't been easy. The republican Edmund Ludlow, who admittedly was a strong opponent of Cromwell's acceptance of the protectorship, claimed that Elizabeth Cromwell 'seemed at first unwilling to remove thither, thou afterwards she became better satisfied with her grandeur', unlike her mother-in-law, 'who by reason of her great age was not so easily flattered with these temptations'.[22]

But the real reason for the delay wasn't Elizabeth's reluctance to move in, so much as the reluctance of others to move out. Various committees and commissioners were still being urged to vacate their lodgings at Whitehall at the end of 1654. There were bigger problems at Hampton Court Palace. It had actually been sold, and the purchasers had sold on or leased out parcels of land and some of the buildings. They demanded a fair profit to give up their title.

In 1655 Parliament granted Cromwell £80,000 a year for his household expenses. This was reduced to £64,000 a year the following February. In the autumn of 1657, he was allowed £100,000 a year expressly for the purpose of 'defraying the expenses of his Highness's household, and for answering the disbursements for repairs to his Highness's houses'.[23] By this time, the lord protector had established a routine of spending Monday to Thursday at Whitehall, and Friday to Sunday at Hampton Court Palace.

He was also assuming the trappings of royalty. In the spring of 1657 a faction in the Commons urged him to assume the title of king, but although he was attracted by the idea, he could not bring himself to believe that it was God's will: 'I would not seem to set up that which Providence hath destroyed and laid in the dust', he declared, 'and I would not build Jericho again.'[24] He did, however, accept a second investiture as lord protector in June 1657, at which he sat in Edward I's coronation chair in Westminster Hall (he had it carried from the abbey for the purpose). He wore a purple velvet robe lined with ermine, and took his oath clutching a Bible, a sword and a golden sceptre. As one recent historian observed, 'only a crown was missing'.[25]

Cromwell's court included a lord chamberlain, the moderate parliamentarian grandee Sir Gilbert Pickering, and a board of Green Cloth with its own comptroller and cofferer. There were two stewards, who worked in tandem for much of the protector's 'reign'. Like his royal predecessors, he kept two kitchens – the household kitchen and 'his Highness's kitchen' – and more than sixty staff to service them, which suggests that the business of feeding the court went on much as it had in the past.[26] A report in the *Weekly Intelligencer* in March 1654, when preparations were in hand for the Cromwells to move from the Cockpit at Whitehall into the Privy Lodgings, listed the expected 'tables for diet'. They included one for the protector, another for his wife, and separate tables for 'chaplains and strangers', 'the steward and gentlemen', 'the gentlemen', 'coachmen, grooms and other domestic servants' and, lastly, 'inferiors, or sub-servants' – seven tables in all.[27]

The Cromwells' establishment also included rather a lot of relatives.[28] Not only did the lord protector appoint his son-in-law master of horse, but a string of cousins and kinsfolk found themselves with posts in the protectoral household. John Barrington and Edward Rolt, two of Cromwell's new gentlemen of the bedchamber, were distant cousins; so was the joint steward and later master of the household, Nathaniel Waterhouse. Richard Beke became captain of the lifeguards shortly after marrying Cromwell's niece. Oliver Fleming, the master of ceremonies, was a first cousin. (To be fair, Beke was already lieutenant-captain of the lifeguards, and Fleming had been master of ceremonies since the early 1640s – just because you were a relation didn't mean you weren't the best person for the job.)

The evidence for exactly how the protector's household functioned is fragmentary, and has to contend with two things: the flood of vitriolic royalist propaganda which portrayed Cromwell and his circle as amoral country bumpkins who wallowed in their quasi-royal status; and the fact that most of the relevant documents disappeared when Charles II was restored to the English throne in 1660, when those who had played key roles as either courtiers or servants to Cromwell were understandably reluctant to broadcast the fact to the new regime.

But we do know that Cromwell's court was a lively place, far removed from the dour gloom which is supposed to permeate the puritanical Commonwealth period. The protector kept a master of music, the organist and composer John Hingston, who supervised 'his Highness's Musique', a band of eight musicians and two boys.[29] Hingston gave organ lessons to the youngest Cromwell daughters on an instrument installed at Hampton Court, which their father had removed from the chapel at Magdalen College, Oxford. After a day of public thanksgiving in February 1658, following an unsuccessful attempt on the protector's life, MPs were invited to Whitehall for dinner in the Banqueting House. According to the newssheet *Mercurius Politicus*, when dinner was over 'his Highness withdrew to the Cockpit and there entertained them with rare music, both of instruments and voices, till the evening'.[30] And at the Whitehall wedding of Frances Cromwell, the protector's youngest daughter, there were three or four days of music, dancing and feasting, according to one contemporary.[31] Another reported that 'they had 48 violins and 50 trumpets and much mirth with frolics, besides mixt dancing (a thing heretofore accounted profane) till 5 of the clock yesterday morning'.[32]

Cromwell was roundly criticised by royalists and republicans alike for taking on the trappings of kingship. But those criticisms failed to acknowledge that he was head of state. And as a head of state, there were certain expectations about the magnificence of his residences, the size of his court, the way he should conduct himself.

On the day in April 1654 that England concluded a peace with the States General of the Dutch Republic, ending the first Anglo-Dutch War, Allart Pieter van Jongestall, who had represented the States General during the talks at Westminster, was invited with his wife and daughter and the other Dutch negotiators to have dinner with Cromwell. In his role as master of ceremonies Sir Oliver Fleming arrived at their lodgings at 1.30, accompanied by Walter Strickland, one of the leading English negotiators, and two coaches which carried the party to Whitehall. On their arrival, the Dutch diplomats were greeted with a fanfare from twelve waiting trumpeters. Their wives were presented to the lord protector, and then taken to a separate room where they dined with Elizabeth Cromwell and one of her daughters, while the men ate with Oliver Cromwell, who sat alone on one side of the table while Jongestall and the others sat opposite. Music played throughout the meal. Afterwards

the lord protector had us into another room, where the lady protectrice and others came to us, where we had also music, and voices, and a psalm sung, which his highness gave us, and told us, that it was yet the best paper, that had been exchanged between us; and from thence we were had into a gallery next the river, where we walked with his highness about half an hour, and then took our leaves, and were conducted back again to our houses, after the same manner as we were brought.[33]

The episode suggests a mixture of informality – the joke about the psalm, for one thing – and traditional ritual.

We can get another glimpse of the lord protector in residence from the correspondence of Peter Julius Coyet and Christer Bonde, two Swedish diplomats who came to England in the 1650s to negotiate trade agreements on behalf of the Swedish king, Charles X. Coyet arrived in London ('this inordinately expensive place'[34]) in March 1655 and, after a series of delays caused first by illness and then by Cromwell being too busy to see him, he was given an audience at Whitehall on 11 April.

The lord protector's coach arrived for him at his lodging, drawn by six Oldenburgs, stately carriage horses bred in Lower Saxony. It would have been driven by Cromwell's coachman and postilion and accompanied by ten footmen who ran alongside dressed in the protector's livery, a coat of grey cloth trimmed with velvet, silver and black silk lace. Once he arrived at the palace of Whitehall, Coyet acquired an entourage of German and Austrian nobles who happened to be in London and who were anxious for a glimpse of the protector.

The meeting was brief. Cromwell was flanked by members of the Council of State, secretary of state John Thurloe and Sir Oliver Fleming. Coyet addressed Cromwell in Latin. Cromwell answered in English. Fleming translated the protector's speech into High German. And that was that.

In July 1655 Coyet's countryman, Christer Bonde, arrived in London to take up his post as ambassador extraordinary. His reception was much more formal than that of Coyet: Fleming came to Gravesend to greet him, taking him aboard the lord protector's yacht and sailing him up the Thames to the Tower, from where he was driven in state to lodgings in Westminster. He was granted two audiences with Cromwell a few days later: the first a formal affair, followed by a private meeting later in the day, when Fleming took him by barge from his lodgings to the palace, where he spent nearly two hours with the protector:

At our conference, he ordered all who were present to withdraw – Secretary Thurloe with the others; which has never happened before, for the secretary is his intimus. I must admit that my English comes in extremely handy, and the Protector is very glad of it: when I excused myself in case I should not be able to express myself as I ought, he answered that it was a matter of grief to him that he had been so ill educated that he scarcely ventured to speak any other language than English, and that he was therefore the happier that he could speak to me in confidence without an interpreter or other assistance.[35]

Bonde was one of only a few foreign dignitaries who were invited down to Hampton Court. Not much was done in the way of business, but the two men spent a Saturday afternoon relaxing. They listened to music, walked in the park, killed a stag and played a game of bowls. Bonde was introduced to Elizabeth Cromwell, 'Protectress Joan', whose hand he kissed, and three of the couple's daughters, Bridget, Mary and Frances, of whom he later wrote unchivalrously that 'ugly they were'.[36]

O LIVER CROMWELL DIED OF PNEUMONIA at Whitehall on 3 September 1658. His wax effigy lay for weeks at Somerset House in a room hung entirely with black velvet, while mourners filed in to pay homage, as a contemporary account described:

> The bed of state whereon he lay, was covered with a large pall of black velvet, under which was a Holland sheet, borne up by six stools covered with cloth of gold. About the bed was placed a complete suit of arms; and at the feet of the effigy stood his crest. This bed had fixed about it an ascent of two steps. A little from thence stood eight silver candlesticks, about five foot high, with white wax tapers standing in them, of three foot long. All these things were environed with rails and balusters, four square, covered with velvet; at each corner whereof, there was erected an upright pillar; which bore on their tops, lions and dragons, who held in their paws streamers crowned. On both sides of the bed were set up in sockets, four great standards of the Protector's arms … About the bed stood men in mourning, holding in their hands black wands, and also standing bare-headed.[37]

Oliver Cromwell's lying-in-state: 'About the bed stood men in mourning, holding in their hands black wands, and also standing bare-headed'.

The state funeral didn't take place for nearly three months, to allow time to organise what was a royal pageant in all but name. (The actual burial had already taken place in a private ceremony some weeks previously, 'by reason of the great stench thereof'.[38]) The funeral was a ticket-only affair. Invitations began:

> You are desired to attend the funeral of the most serene and most renowned Oliver, late Lord Protector, from Somerset House, on Tuesday the 23d of November instant, at eight of the clock in the morning at the furthest, and to bring with you this ticket; and that, by Friday night next, you send to the Heralds' Office, near Paul's, the names of your servants that are to attend in mourning, without which they are not to be admitted.[39]

It was a funeral fit for a king. The streets were lined with soldiers, all dressed in new red coats with black buttons. Along with senior figures from the army, the navy, the judiciary, the clergy, the government and the City of London, as well as drummers and trumpeters and an unknown number of 'poor men of Westminster', the procession included 'all the servants of his Highness, as well inferior and superior'.[40] There were staff from his board of Green Cloth, his steward and lord chamberlain, grooms of the chamber, carvers and sewers and ushers and waiters, the master of the music and the master of the barge, his gunsmith, his shoemaker, hatter, tailor and upholsterer, his master-carpenter and master-joiner and master-mason, the staff who worked in his kitchens.

According to one eye-witness the effigy, which was mounted on a chariot, was 'vested with royal robes, a sceptre in one hand, a globe in the other, and a crown on the head'.[41]

CHAPTER FIVE

We Have Called You Gods

KING CHARLES II WAS DETERMINED that if he ever regained the throne he lost to Parliament, he would keep a household which was much leaner than the one which had drained his father's resources and kept him cushioned against reality. He was going to put an end to 'those excesses which were known to be in great offices'. He was going to 'reform all extravagant expenses'.[1]

That was his plan, formulated while he was poor and in exile during the 1650s, in France and the Netherlands. He was restored to the throne of England in 1660, after the brief and disastrous 'reign' of Oliver Cromwell's son Richard had been brought to an end by a military coup, and the leaders of that coup had themselves been ousted by forces who were sympathetic to the royalist cause. But now Charles found there were debts to repay, for service to his father's cause in the Civil War, for loyalty when friends were few. There were promises that he had made when promises were all he had to offer. And there was the politics of realism and reward.

The first person to embrace Charles II when he landed at Dover on 25 May 1660 was General George Monck, the man who had effectively brought about the end of the republican experiment by suppressing radical elements in the army, occupying London and brokering Charles II's restoration. Charles showered Monck with honours and gifts. He was confirmed as captain-general of the army, created Duke of Albemarle and given grants of land, an annual pension of £700 and apartments in the Cockpit at the palace of Whitehall. Charles also appointed him a gentleman of the bedchamber in the newly restored royal household and, while the lawyers were preparing his titles and grants, he asked Monck what office he would most like at court. Monck chose to be master of horse.

The diarist Samuel Pepys couldn't understand it: 'That blockhead Albemarle hath strange luck to be beloved,' he wrote later.[2] Charles II's lord chancellor, the Earl of Clarendon, accused Monck of being 'an immoderate lover of money' and claimed that through the malign influence of his even more avaricious wife Anne, he sold offices in his gift to whoever offered the most cash.[3]

Charles II's choice for the office of lord chamberlain was Edward Montagu, 2nd Earl of Manchester. He had been a senior parliamentarian commander who had lost his taste for war when he witnessed the terrible slaughter at the Battle of Marston Moor in 1644 and had retired from military service soon afterwards; and he had fallen out of favour during the Commonwealth after speaking out against the trial of Charles I. But the fact remained that his relationship with the crown was complicated. With so many veteran royalists clamouring for preferment, Charles II's decision to appoint Manchester as lord chamberlain (thus, incidentally, handing him a major role in the coronation, at which he carried the sword of state) was an indication of the restored King's determination to build bridges. It was also a lucrative and influential post: the lord chamberlain had at his disposal well over 400 offices, including tradesmen, artists, chamber attendants and several more senior posts, such as the master of ceremonies.

The third great household office, the lord stewardship, went to a more predictable choice. James Butler, Marquess of Ormonde had ruined himself and his family in the royalist cause, trailing around France and the Netherlands after the court in exile and occasionally indulging in rather theatrical bouts of clandestine activity. In January 1658, for example, he dyed his hair and travelled to London to meet with royalist conspirators who were plotting a rising against Cromwell. Now, as lord steward, Ormonde had in his gift the appointment of around 250 household officers, from yeomen and grooms down to children in the kitchens. In theory, promotion from within – the so-called 'Ancient Order of Succession' – should have acted as a brake on new appointments, and there were hundreds of petitions from men who claimed to have been ejected by Parliament from posts they had held in the old king's time, or promised the reversion of this post or that. But such things were hard to check.

Other court posts went to men who had stayed with Charles II during the dark years of exile, regardless of their fitness for a particular office. The poet Sir John Denham, who had served with Queen Henrietta Maria's court in Paris and acted as both a fundraiser for the cause and a mediator between Charles and Parliament, was made surveyor of the King's Works, the most senior architectural role in the country, even though he had no knowledge of building. Sir Henry Bennet, later 1st

Lord Arlington and one of the two 'A's in the King's CABAL, was made keeper of the privy purse, a reward for thirteen years in royal service all over Europe. The groom of the stool, effectively head of the royal bedchamber and a job that brought with it not only intimate access to the king, but also remuneration of £5,000 a year, went first to the Duke of Somerset, who had been one of the pallbearers at Charles I's funeral at Windsor in 1649; and then, after his death in October 1660, to Sir John Grenville, a royalist soldier who had been a gentleman of the bedchamber to Charles II when he was Prince of Wales and who acted as a go-between in Charles's clandestine negotiations with Monck in the months leading up to the restoration.

In spite of his good resolutions, neither the King nor his courtiers were in much of a mood for thrift in those first years. The size of the royal household ballooned, as Charles worked hard to enjoy the trappings of kingship after more than a decade in which he had depended on the charity of others. It is hard to find precise figures, but more than 1,200 officers and servants were sworn in by October 1660: about 800 in Manchester's department, 290 in Ormonde's and 130 in Monck's. What one modern author describes as a 'sense of untrammelled profligacy'[4] can be seen in a royal warrant of that month, which granted diet to just about every officer who had held it in the old king's time. By the following spring the principal household officers were keeping open table at the King's expense, and the household was living far beyond his means. 'All those excesses, which the irregular precedents of former times had introduced, and which the king had so solemnly resolved to reform,' reappeared, wrote Charles's adviser Edward Hyde, who was created Earl of Clarendon at the King's coronation. 'He directed his own table to be more magnificently furnished than it had ever been in any time of his predecessors; which example was easily followed in all offices.'[5]

Within a couple of years the new king's household owed so much money that its officers could no longer get credit. Yet costs continued to mount, exacerbated in May 1662 by the arrival of Charles's bride and queen, Catherine of Braganza, whose attendants swelled the court and whose presence meant the expensive refurbishing of the queen's lodgings at Whitehall. Courtiers were forced to borrow almost £60,000 from City goldsmiths, simply to keep the household afloat.

The situation couldn't continue. At the end of 1662 the practice of providing diet was halted for almost everyone. There were redundancies, too, particularly in the royal kitchens, which now had far fewer people to cater for. But it wasn't enough. In August 1663 a warrant was issued

Celebrations in Lisbon for the marriage of Catherine of Braganza and Charles II.

suspending 'all diets — chamber messes, bouche of court, pensions, board wages and allowances of any kind whatsoever, except wages to the household servants above and below stairs'.[6] Only the King and Queen, the King's cousin Prince Rupert and the maids of honour were exempted, along with the stables, which were left untouched through the influence of the Duke of Albemarle. Old servants were cashiered, there were protests, and the old argument that a sovereign must live like a sovereign was rehearsed once more, very loudly. "Tis the most unadvisable thing that was ever attempted,' wrote the Earl of Anglesey. 'Surely this is no time to level the court, but rather to cure that humour in the people, and if it be fit the stable be well provided for, much more the king and queen and family.'[7]

The situation was so serious, however, that at one point the King considered dissolving his household altogether and living privately. Although some of the cuts of 1663 didn't last, most of the diets that disappeared would never be reinstated: now, when senior household officers provided hospitality to visitors, they did so at their own expense, while junior officers had to rely on board wages, which were often slow in coming. Things would never be the same again.

FROM THE BEGINNING OF HIS RESTORED REIGN, Charles II made himself accessible to his subjects. Less than a month after his return, for example, the word went out that he was going to reinstate the practice of touching for the king's evil. Dating back to the eleventh century, the belief that a touch from royalty could cure scrofula, a swelling of lymph nodes in the neck, was still widely held in England. Charles I, for whom the practice was intricately bound up in notions of sacred majesty and the divine right of monarchs, had last touched in January 1649, eleven days before his execution. On that occasion he miraculously restored the sight of a blind woman who reached out to grasp his coat as he was being escorted out of Windsor on his way to London, like the woman who touched the hem of Christ's robe as He made His way to the house of Jairus in Luke 8. There were also reports of upwards of twenty instances of afflicted persons being cured of their scrofula by the touch of scraps of a handkerchief dipped in the King's blood immediately after his beheading.

In exile, Charles II had kept up the ceremony. According to one account he touched 260 people during the last thirty-six days of his stay in Breda in the Netherlands before he set sail to reclaim his throne. And as with his father, the miraculous healing could take place in his absence. When he was on the run after being defeated by Cromwell at the Battle of Worcester in 1651 and suffered a bad nosebleed, the handkerchief with which he wiped his nose was whisked away by Father John Huddleston, a Catholic priest who was helping him to escape. It passed to a Mr Brithwayte, who kept it as a royal relic and a remedy for the king's evil.

The official reason for resuming the ceremony of touching so promptly was that the kingdom had, as members of Parliament noted, been plagued with scrofula because of the absence of a king. At the same time it was an obvious and very public expression of kingship restored, a fact which was emphasised by the choice of venue for this first magical act of the restoration – Inigo Jones's Banqueting House, the scene of Charles I's execution eleven years earlier. On Saturday 23 June a huge and scrofulous crowd gathered in the pouring rain in the gardens at Whitehall, waiting for their new king to provide them with a miracle.

Supplicants first had to present themselves to the King's surgeon, who after assuring himself that they did indeed have scrofula would issue them with an admission ticket. At the start of the ceremony the King sat in a great chair, with one of his chaplains on his left and a clerk of the closet on the right, who held a quantity of coins tied to ribbons of white silk.[8] The coin used was traditionally a gold angel, then worth ten shillings. The surgeon took one of the diseased supplicants by the hand and after both surgeon and patient had made three low bows to the King, he brought him or her forward. The sufferer knelt close to the King's chair and, while the chaplain intoned a line from Mark 16:18 – 'They shall lay hands on the sick, and they shall recover' – Charles laid his hands on their two cheeks.

Once everyone had been touched, they were all brought before the King for a second time. The chaplain recited John 1:9, 'That was the true Light, which lighteth every man that cometh into the world', and Charles hung one of the coins around each sufferer's neck. After further prayers, the gentleman usher brought up a basin, ewer and towel and handed them to the Duke of Buckingham and the Earl of Pembroke, who knelt before the King while he washed and dried his hands. A wise move, one feels.

King and court were unprepared for the popularity of the reinstated touching ceremony. Charles touched around 600 people in the Banqueting House that first Saturday. 'It took a very long time,' noted

The Royal Gift of Healing

R.White sculp.

Charles II touches for the king's evil, while one of his chaplains intones a line from Mark 16:18, 'They shall lay their hands on the sick, and they shall recover'.

a contemporary newssheet.[9] Ten days later 250 more diseased subjects turned up, although not everyone was as scrofulous as they claimed to be. 'When his Majesty was delivering the gold', reported another newssheet, 'one shuffled himself in out of an hope of profit, which had not been stroked; but his Majesty presently discovered him, saying, "This man hath not yet been touched."'[10] In an attempt to regulate things, touchings were fixed for Fridays, with a maximum of 200 at each sitting; and rather than overwhelming the sergeant-surgeon, a Mr Knight, with demands for tickets on the day, petitioners were informed that he would be at his house in Covent Garden every Wednesday and Thursday from 2 p.m. until 6 p.m. 'And if any person of quality shall send to him, he will wait upon them at their lodgings, upon notice given to him.'[11]

People still tended to clutter up the precincts of Whitehall, and new ordinances emphasised that none of the sick were to be allowed into the palace until the day of the healing. The King also often touched after Sunday service in the chapel at Whitehall, while the diarist John Evelyn noted in March 1684 that 'there was so great a concourse of people with their children to be touched for the Evil' that six or seven were crushed to death as they struggled to get in to see the surgeon.[12]

The question of how much a monarch should engage with his or her subjects has puzzled kings, queens and courtiers since before the days of Elizabeth I. Remain too remote, and the sovereign risks being seen as uncaring or out of touch. Become too accessible, and he or she may find that familiarity breeds contempt. Queen Elizabeth I achieved a balance, showing herself both on her regular progresses and in a relatively open court, yet still retaining the mystery. The young Bohemian nobleman Baron Waldstein found it easy enough to arrange an audience with the Queen while staying in London in 1600; but when he spoke to her and of her as 'some goddess come down from the skies', he was participating in a cult which managed to keep her simultaneously close and distant.[13] Subjects of the crown require their sovereign to be 'just like us' and yet at the same time keep him or her shrouded in a mystique which allows them to maintain that he or she is somehow special. It is a difficult balancing act. As James I put it in his advice to his son, Prince Henry, 'for augmenting your Majesty ye shall not be so facile of access giving at all times as I have been: and yet not altogether retired or locked up like the kings of Persia'.[14]

The need to maintain a certain distance from one's subjects was set out clearly in the late 1650s by William Cavendish, Marquess of

AVDIENCE QVE DONNE LE ROI D'ANGLETERRE
A SON ALTESSE MONSEIGNEVR
LE PRINCE DE LIGNE
EN QUALITÉ D'AMBASSADEVR EXTRAORDINAIRE

Charles II receiving the Spanish ambassador, the Prince de Ligne, at Whitehall in 1660: a rare depiction of the Banqueting House in use.

Newcastle. Cavendish had been governor to Charles twenty years before, and now wrote him a letter of advice, in which he warned:

> [Do] not make yourself too cheap, by too much familiarity, which as the proverb says, breeds contempt. But when you appear … show yourself gloriously, to your people; like a god, for as the holy writ says, we have called you gods. And when the people see you thus, they will down on their knees, which is worship and pray for you with trembling fear, and love, as they did to queen Elizabeth.[15]

Charles didn't take Newcastle's advice. Almost every action of his was carried out in public, and more private acts were nevertheless the topic of conversation both at court and beyond. Bumping into Samuel Pepys at Whitehall one day in January 1664, one of the King's surgeons gossiped freely that Queen Catherine, who had been feeling poorly, was much better, and that 'the king lay with her on Saturday night last'.[16]

At Whitehall, Charles II dished out keys to all and sundry. In 1661 alone the royal locksmith cut more than 150 double keys, which gave access to the state rooms and opened ordinary doors, and at least ten treble keys, which opened state rooms, ordinary doors – and the King's bedchamber.

The first step towards controlling access to Charles was to establish just who had a right to be within the precincts of the palace – and who didn't. It is tempting to think of the royal palaces as glorified country houses, regulated and segregated and run by armies of discreet and efficient staff, like some regal version of Downton Abbey. Nothing could be further from the truth. Whitehall was more like a vast apartment complex with service restaurants, shops and an irritable but ineffectual residents' association. No one knew how many people lived there, although there were potentially around 1,500 lodgings for servants, household officials and courtiers, government officials, tradesmen and hangers-on. There were at least eighteen separate kitchens, a barber's shop, a milliner's, a herb-seller and a professional scrivener. Menials slept in closets and corners. There were squatters.

Part of the problem was the old story that while some of the occupants of Whitehall were there by right of their office, others were given lodgings almost on a whim by the king or his senior officers, while others still simply camped out there and hoped no one would notice. George Vaux, who was under-housekeeper at Whitehall in the early 1660s, received a rather desperate instruction from the lord chamberlain in January 1661: 'I am informed that diverse persons have possessed themselves of lodgings in his majesty's palace of Whitehall without my order having right to no lodgings there. These [instructions] are therefore to will and require you forthwith to take an express of all the lodgings in Whitehall and who are in them and by what right they are so possessed.'[17]

Plans for a new, more modern Whitehall to replace what the Frenchman Samuel Sorbière dismissed as 'nothing but a heap of houses erected at diverse times' were being aired almost as soon as Charles II returned to the throne. John Webb drew up plans for a massive new palace in 1661, and although nothing came of them, in 1664 the Venetian ambassador reported that the King had decided to rebuild the palace 'in the style of the Banqueting Hall'. Events, in the shape of plague and fire, intervened to postpone Charles II's plans, but in March 1669 an ambitious young Oxford professor of astronomy named Christopher Wren was appointed surveyor of the King's Works, and everyone believed that one of his first tasks would be to transform the muddle of old buildings

The Palace of Whitehall, by Hendrick Danckerts, 1676-1680. Inigo Jones' Banqueting House, all that survives of the palace today, is on the left.

and courts and alleys into a palace fit for a modern king. Within weeks of Wren's arrival at the Office of Works, the occupants of lodgings at Whitehall were given notice that they must 'permit Dr Wren … and such persons as he shall appoint to come into your lodgings and yards' to take a measured survey.[18] Daniel Fabureau de la Fabvolière, a military engineer, was given the task; but while he was trying to survey Prince Rupert's lodgings he got into a fight with some of the prince's servants, who hit him over the head with his own sword and kicked him down the stairs. Since the servants belonged to the King's cousin, it was de la Fabvolière who ended up in prison, charged with drawing his sword in the precincts of the royal palace.

The commission then went to Ralph Greatorex, an instrument-maker with premises at the sign of Adam and Eve in the Strand. Greatorex had made mathematical instruments in the past for Wren and others in his circle; he had also recently completed a survey of the Royal Arsenal at Woolwich. Between February and October 1670, he and his assistants surveyed the entire palace.

Charles II never did rebuild Whitehall. He remodelled his own apartments in the early 1680s, but his dreams of a new Whitehall were overtaken first by a grand design for an English Versailles, which Wren began to build for him at Winchester, and then in 1685 by death. But the Greatorex survey (or to be more accurate, since the survey itself has not survived, the plans which were made from it) provide a remarkable snapshot of the primary royal residence at a moment in time. It shows the position of not only the lodgings assigned to the King, the Queen and members of the royal family – Prince Rupert, the Duke of York and the King's bastard son, the 21-year-old Duke of Monmouth – but also many of the service areas: the fish and flesh larders, the Queen's laundry, the King's music house and his mistresses' kitchens. It shows Wren's house in Scotland Yard, on the edge of the palace precincts; the location of the King's herb house; his locksmith's workshop.

Above all, the Whitehall plan of 1670 confirms the sheer complexity of a palace which had evolved organically, without shape or strategy, for nearly a century and a half. There were all kinds of anomalies, and they continued throughout the reign. Sir Stephen Fox, who was clerk comptroller of the Green Cloth in 1660–1, was assigned three unimpressive rooms when he took up his post. An exceptionally wealthy man – largely as a result of the profits he made from another of his other roles, that of paymaster-general to the army – he obtained permission to extend his lodgings at his own expense. Before long he had an enormous house with balconies overlooking the Thames and a coach house and stables of his own, all within the palace. The Duke of York's treasurer, Thomas Povey, built himself a set of grand lodgings with their own front door, leading off the Stone Gallery. All kinds of building work went on, both authorised and unauthorised, with courtiers and other officials swapping lodgings, sub-letting and extending. The Treasury issued orders to Wren saying that 'no new or additional building be for the future made or erected or any great or considerable alterations made' without permission, which was all very well, but when the surveyor was faced with an influential courtier demanding improvements to his lodgings, it was hard for him to refuse. There were occasions when Charles II, having permanently assigned lodgings in the palace to one officer or another, was forced to rent them back for his own use.

By the 1670s, the King had grown rather fed up with the way that minor officials, and even members of the public, were free to wander around Whitehall. Technically, responsibility for maintaining order fell to the knight marshal and his six deputies; their role was to control members of the King's household, who, because they were members of that household, had special privileges which could place them beyond the reach of the common law. The knight marshal's jurisdiction had once radiated outward for twelve miles from the monarch's person, the 'verge' within which members of the royal household were exempt from prosecution by the normal courts; offenders could be brought before the Court of the Marshalsea, which sat every Friday to hear grievances by or about the king's men. By the seventeenth century the verge had been redefined as an area within a twelve-mile radius of Westminster, rather than of the sovereign's person, but the marshal's men, effectively the king's bailiffs, were still active in the palace precincts, besides having a ceremonial role 'in all publick cavalcades, at declaring of war, proclaiming peace, publick entries and processions made by the sovereign'.[19]

But what was annoying Charles II wasn't anything criminal. It was simply that the palace was cluttered with people. Courtiers tended to gather in the privy galleries rather than where they were meant to gather, in the state rooms of the palace. Pages and footmen congregated all over the place. And they smelled. Smoking in the guard chamber was banned, and the lord chamberlain instructed officers that there must be 'no ill savour of beer or anything else' in the passages. In the morning doors and windows should be left open and perfume burned in the rooms 'to take away the scent of the watch of the night'.[20]

A new set of household ordinances, probably issued early in 1679, complained that a great throng of people tended to walk about the King's chapel talking loudly to each other while the service was taking place. 'We command that none presume to walk or talk there in time of divine service and sermon, upon pain of our displeasure.'[21] The ordinances also attempted to set out – yet again – exactly who was allowed where in the palace. 'No mean, idle, or unknown persons shall be permitted to pass into the privy chamber upon any pretence whatsoever.' The only people allowed there were noble and privy counsellors, servants whose duties dictated their presence, and anyone who might attend on the Queen, the Duke and Duchess of York or Prince Rupert, when they came to visit the King. Liveried servants could only enter when the Queen or the duchess required to be carried out in their chairs. However, 'all ladies of the nobility, and ladies and gentlewomen that belong to the queen's majesty, and gentlewomen of good rank and fashion, have liberty to pass through the privy chamber on their way into the queen's presence chamber'.[22]

And some had liberty to remain. Until the early twentieth century, most British kings kept mistresses. Even Charles I, long held up as a paragon of conjugal fidelity, is now thought by some to have had a hesitant sexual relationship with Jane Whorwood, the step-daughter of a groom of the bedchamber. But Charles II was in a different league, acquiring and discarding lovers with bewildering speed both while in exile (when he fathered at least three bastards, including the future Duke of Monmouth) and on his return to England. During his honeymoon at Hampton Court Palace in 1662, there was an embarrassing scene in the presence chamber when he presented one of his long-term mistresses, the Countess of Castlemaine, to his new wife. His aim was to bully Catherine of Braganza into appointing Castlemaine as one of her ladies of the bedchamber, something she was understandably reluctant to do. Initially the Queen didn't realise who Castlemaine was; when it dawned on her she promptly burst into tears in front of the court, had a nosebleed and dropped down in a dead faint. But Charles was determined, telling the Earl of Clarendon that

> I wish I may be unhappy in this world, and in the world to come, if I fail in the least degree of what I resolved, which is of making my Lady Castlemaine of my wife's bed-chamber, and whosoever I find endeavouring to hinder this resolution of mine, except it be only to myself, I will be his enemy to the last moment of my life.[23]

He got his way, but only by publicly flaunting his relationship with Barbara Castlemaine and ignoring his wife, and encouraging the rest of the court to do the same. The Queen finally gave in and agreed that Castlemaine could be appointed as her lady of the bedchamber in June 1663, on condition that she never lived at court. Charles responded by giving her her own set of lodgings at the palace of Whitehall. When the court moved to Oxford to escape the plague in September 1665 he stayed at Christ Church, and deposited both his wife and his heavily pregnant mistress at Merton, with a breathtaking lack of tact. A paper was pinned to the door of Castlemaine's lodgings there. It read: 'The reason why she is not ducked | 'Cause by Caesar she is fucked.'[24]

There was nothing clandestine about the King's extramarital relationships. He didn't attempt to keep them secret, and nor did his

'My dearest, dearest
Fubs': Louise de
Kérouaille, Duchess of
Portsmouth and Aubigny,
by Simon Peeterz Verelst,
c.1670-72.

lovers. After he took up with the actress Mary Davis at the end of 1667 and bought her an expensive ring, she showed it off to everyone, 'and owns that the king did give it her', wrote Samuel Pepys, whose wife called her 'the most impertinent slut … in the world'.[25] The Catholic Louise de Kérouaille, Duchess of Portsmouth, who was the King's chief mistress (but far from the only one) from the early 1670s onwards, had a vast set of lodgings at Whitehall which consisted of some twenty-four rooms. John Evelyn, who saw them in 1675, reckoned they were furnished 'with ten times the richness and glory beyond the queen's'. Eight years later they were even more opulent, filled with French tapestries, silver sconces and candelabra, and some of the King's best paintings. 'Lord what contentment can there be in the riches and splendour of this world, purchased with vice and dishonour?' asked Evelyn, with touching naivety.[26] It was common knowledge that 'my dearest, dearest Fubs', as the king called de Kérouaille, was in a relationship with him. It was her to whom yet another royal mistress, Nell Gwyn, was referring in the famous anecdote when, surrounded by an angry anti-Catholic mob, she put her head out of her carriage window and said, 'Pray good people be silent, I am the *Protestant* whore.'[27]

The fact that courtiers and commoners all knew with whom Charles II was sleeping meant that while they were in favour, his mistresses were able to wield considerable political influence. Courtiers, government ministers and foreign diplomats all beat a path to the opulent apartments of the Countess of Castlemaine, the Duchess of Portsmouth and the others, where they could bump into the King as if by accident, perhaps play a game of cards with him, and, if the moment was right, begin an entirely informal, spontaneous and carefully rehearsed conversation about policy or business. A mistress could provide personal access to the King. At the very least she could whisper in his ear while he was in her bed, asking for favours for her friends or torments for her friends' enemies.

CHARLES II SPENT THE NIGHT of Sunday 1 February 1685 in bed with the Duchess of Portsmouth. The next morning his speech was confused, and the worried duchess called for Dr Edmund King, one of the royal physicians. While King was with him, Charles had a fit: 'he looked black, and his eyes turned in his head,' wrote the contemporary chronicler Gilbert Burnet.'[28] Dr King bled him and he regained consciousness. Over the coming days, however, a succession of senior Anglican clerics arrived to bid him reflect on eternity. He ignored them. All the while, said Burnet, 'Lady Portsmouth sat in the bed taking care of him as a wife of a husband.'[29]

On the Thursday, the King had a second fit, and everyone expected the worst. His brother James, himself a Roman Catholic, sent for Father John Huddleston, the Catholic priest who had helped Charles to escape after the disastrous Battle of Worcester in 1651. Huddleston and the Duke of York were with the king for thirty minutes, accompanied only by the Earl of Bath, the King's groom of the stool, and the Earl of Peterborough, the duke's groom of the stool. Behind a double-locked door the priest administered the last rites.* After everyone was admitted again, Charles refused to receive the sacrament from the Anglican bishop Thomas Ken, or to declare that he would die in the communion of the Church of England. His last words were to his brother, begging him to look after Louise de Kérouaille and his various bastards, and ending with the famous plea for the welfare of Nell Gwyn: 'Let not poor Nelly starve'. He said nothing of his wife, or his subjects, or his servants, or his religion. He died about eleven o'clock on the morning of Friday 6 February, aged fifty-four.

---

* According to Burnet, Huddleston didn't have the host with him, and had to borrow it from a fellow-priest. When he explained what he needed it for, the priest was so panic-stricken that he ran out of the palace and straight into a post. 'He seemed to be in a fit of madness with fear,' said Burnet (History, 2:282).

CHAPTER SIX

The Catholic King

C HARLES II'S DEATH LEFT HIS BROTHER JAMES, Duke of York as king. It also posed a problem for the English establishment. Like Charles, James was raised as a Protestant, but unlike Charles, he converted to Catholicism in the mid-1670s. He had never officially declared for Rome, allowing something of a don't-ask, don't-tell policy towards the practice of his religion during the last decade of Charles II's reign. In theory, that policy didn't hold for officers in the royal households. Although Charles argued that who he or his wife or the Duke and Duchess of York decided to appoint was entirely their own affair, the waves of anti-Catholic hysteria which swept over the nation in the 1670s and early 1680s led to the passing of various pieces of legislation which barred Catholics from public office, and this should have precluded them from serving in any of the royal households. Otherwise, reasoned the Commons, a wicked Jesuitical papist would seize the opportunity to kill the king. There was, for example, an outcry when the Duchess of Portsmouth persuaded Charles II to appoint one of her own servants, a French Catholic named Peter de Rains, as yeoman of the confectionery. Clearly, said one pamphleteer, 'the aforesaid French papist … has such opportunity to poison his sacred Majesty, by mixing poison in the sweetmeats'.[1]

The Test Acts of 1673 and 1678 required all office-holders to take the oaths of supremacy and allegiance (thus acknowledging the king of England as supreme head of the church) and to declare against transubstantiation, the invocation of saints and the sacrament of the mass. In November 1673, the lord steward and lord chamberlain were ordered to prevent Catholics from frequenting Whitehall, St James's Palace and St James's Park, and this injunction was extended in 1678 to cover anywhere within a ten-mile radius of London. The royal palaces were searched for Catholics, and anyone whose religion seemed suspicious was hauled before the knight marshal and made to take the Tests.

So the upheaval that always occurred in the royal household when a new sovereign came to the throne was much worse this time. James sought to bring in his own servants and to reward those who had stood by him when he converted to Roman Catholicism in the mid-1670s. He made no secret of the fact that he wanted the repeal of the Test Acts. In any case, as happened so often with draconian legislation in the seventeenth century, the Acts seem to have been quietly ignored, and both James and his wife Mary of Modena had numbers of Catholics in their households already.

Charles II was scarcely cold before rumours began to circulate that 'Dismal Jimmy', as the pathologically earnest new king was known, planned some dramatic domestic reforms. The entire household was to be dismissed; he was to live as privately as when he was Duke of York; the Queen Dowager, Catherine of Braganza, was laying off her staff, and there was sure to be 'great frugality in fashion'.[2] On 11 February, John Evelyn noted with approval that 'the face of the whole Court was exceedingly changed to a more solemn and moral behaviour; the new King affecting neither profaneness nor buffoonery'.[3] The King broke off relations with his mistress, Catherine Sedley, as an example to the rest of the court. The example was short lived: he resumed their affair three months later.*

Very soon after his accession, the lord chamberlain and the first lord of the Treasury wrote to Dismal Jimmy suggesting sweeping reforms to the household. In the letter accompanying their proposal they said that they 'have humbly offered here to your Majesty some retrenchment of the number of servants retaining the old number only in offices, where the service cannot be performed with less; and some officers we have totally suppressed as useless. And the payments and wages we have reduced of most of them.'[4]

Their main proposal was to reduce diets dramatically, and to stop paying both wages and board wages to most of the household, amalgamating them into a single payment. That meant there was less work for the staff who prepared and served the food: the household kitchen was merged with the King's privy kitchen with the loss of thirteen jobs; the Queen's privy kitchen was reduced by nearly fifty per cent. Another eighty jobs were lost in the bakehouse, the cellar, the larder, the pastry and other food preparation areas. Daily waiters, who had served in the Hall, were made redundant, and other posts weren't filled when they fell vacant. The royal chiropodists went. Twenty-two messengers and fourteen musicians were dismissed.[5] All in all, the establishment below

* Sedley was at a loss to understand James's devotion to her: 'It cannot be my beauty, for I have none; and it cannot be my wit, for he has not enough to know that I have any.' Quoted in Maurice Ashley, *James II* (London: J. M. Dent, 1977), 94.

stairs was cut from 208 to around 100; eighty-five posts disappeared from above stairs; and the 152 places in the stables were cut to eighty-eight. At a stroke, the size of the King's household was reduced from over a thousand to around 600, and the administration of that household took a significant step away from the outmoded medieval model which had held it back for so long.

A S THE FIRST CATHOLIC to come to the throne since Mary Tudor 132 years earlier, James II's accession sent shivers through the court and the fiercely anti-Catholic nation at large. Within weeks 'the Romanists [were] swarming at Court with greater confidence than had ever been seen in England since the Reformation,' muttered Evelyn.[6] Fears were alleviated, temporarily at least, when James took steps to reassure the nation that he was not about to impose popery, announcing at his first appearance at the Privy Council, the day after his brother's death, that he intended 'to preserve the government in church and state as it is by law established', and confirming his intention before Parliament on 22 May 1685. Nevertheless, he had only been king for ten days when he attended mass with his wife in her closet chapel at St James's Palace, ordering that the doors of the chapel should be kept open – his first public avowal of Catholicism.

As far as the practice of religion within the household was concerned, there was an established precedent for Catholic worship within the royal palaces. Not only were James II's sister-in-law Catherine of Braganza and his wife Mary of Modena Catholics, but the two queens of England that preceded them, Anne of Denmark and Henrietta Maria, had been Catholic, too. Inigo Jones had designed Henrietta Maria's Catholic chapel at Somerset House, which opened in December 1635 with a sung mass. Charles II had rebuilt the Catholic chapel at St James's Palace for Catherine of Braganza's use, and she maintained an entourage of Catholic priests and servants throughout her married life.

King James began by preaching religious toleration. His own chapel, he said, 'should be continued in its splendour and order for their use and conveniences, but as for himself he would content himself with his wife's little chapel'.[7] The situation wasn't perfect: the public attendance of the monarch at divine service every Sunday was a celebration of his role as head of the Church of England. Now an empty chair had to stand in for the king.

Mary of Modena,
by William Wissing,
1685.

In January 1687 the staunchly Anglican John Evelyn reported that there was talk around town that the senior household officers and others were going to be dismissed for sticking to their religion: 'The Lord Jesus defend His little flock, and preserve this threatened church and nation!'[8] The King does seem to have made attempts to persuade senior courtiers to his religion, although in fact few converted. The most prominent was the Earl of Peterborough, whose offices under James included the post of groom of the stool. In March 1687 Peterborough declared himself a Roman Catholic, although according to Thomas Bruce, Earl of Ailesbury, he told the churchwarden at St Margaret's, Westminster, that he was keeping his pew because he might need it again in the future. The Earl of

Rochester lost his post as lord high treasurer after failing to be convinced by the arguments of the King's priests, and in spite of being the King's brother-in-law. (His sister was Anne Hyde, James's first wife and another convert to Catholicism.) James's lord chamberlain of the household, the Earl of Mulgrave, was 'indifferent to all religions', according to Gilbert Burnet, and this flexibility enabled him to accompany the King to mass, although he resisted attempts to make him convert. Percy Kirke, an extraordinary groom of the bedchamber, responded to suggestions that he might like to change his religion by joking that 'he was already pre-engaged, for he had promised the King of Morocco [whom he had met on a diplomatic mission to Meknes in 1681] that if ever he changed his religion, he would turn Mahometan'.[9]

Henry Howard, 7th Duke of Norfolk, was more forthright. Howard was hereditary earl marshal and, as a member of one of the great Catholic families of England, he might have been expected to embrace the new regime with enthusiasm. However, Howard had converted to Protestantism in the 1670s, and he held to his new religion. Burnet recalled a day when James II gave Howard the sword of state to carry before him into chapel. The duke remained at the door, 'upon which the king said to him, My Lord, your father would have gone further: To which the Duke answered, Your Majesty's father was the better man, and he would not have gone so far'.[10]

The accession of a Catholic king left the Chapel Royal – an institution rather than a place, and one of the larger household departments – in something of a quandary. Its head was the dean of the Chapel Royal, a position which in Tudor times had been a recognised staging post on the road to a bishopric. By the time of the Restoration, however, the dean of the Chapel Royal was usually already a bishop, and in his frequent absences the management of the department was the responsibility of the sub-dean, who between 1674 and 1689 was William Holder, brother-in-law to Sir Christopher Wren.

The sub-dean had the management of a small army of clerics and lay officers. There were around thirty-two gentlemen of the Chapel Royal, twelve of whom were clergy and the rest laymen; and a dozen boy choristers, who were taught, fed and boarded by the master of the children, who had the right to pressgang any promising young singers into the royal service. In Edward IV's time, the *Liber niger* had stipulated that the gentlemen must meet certain requirements: 'of their music showing in descant clean voiced, well realised and pronouncing, [and] eloquent in reading'; and there seems no reason to doubt that such requirements remained in place in the later seventeenth century. There were also forty-eight chaplains in ordinary, managed by the sub-dean. They were appointed to wait, four assigned to each month of the year, with duties that included preaching in the chapel on Sundays and other holy days, and in the morning to the household; reading divine service to the sovereign; and saying grace when the sovereign had dinner.

James wasn't about to do away with the clergy and lay staff of the Chapel Royal, although he did cause some anxiety when the court decamped to Windsor for the summer of 1686 and he decided to take over the chapel there for his own use, displacing the Anglican clergy. In principle, however, he wanted a Catholic Chapel Royal to function in parallel with the existing Anglican department, and by degrees he got it. The Roman Catholic Chapel Royal came to include a music master, a master of the nine Gregorians, a dozen instrumentalists, six preachers, five chaplains, eight children and a Latin master to teach them, two sacristans, a man to pump the organ and a necessary woman called Tilsley whose job it was to make the wafers.

This new religious establishment needed a suitable setting for its worship, and within three months of his accession James had commissioned Sir Christopher Wren, who remained as surveyor of the King's Works, to build one. It was part of a major remodelling at Whitehall, involving new lodgings for the Queen and new lodgings and offices for the lord chamberlain and other senior courtiers. James wanted his new Catholic chapel at the west end of the old privy lodgings.

Wren's estimate of £14,325 went in on 15 May 1685, and demolition work on the old range began three days later. The King and Queen moved out. Furniture was stored in the Banqueting House; timbers and tiles were stacked in the privy garden for reuse; Portland stone window surrounds and other carved work on the old buildings were carefully dismantled and lowered down on tackles. By the following February the chapel was roofed and carpenters were at work in the new council chamber and the Queen's lodgings. The first service was held in the chapel on Christmas Day 1686.

Some of the new Whitehall interiors were lavishly decorated. The ceilings of the Queen's bedchamber and closet were painted by the great Italian muralist Antonio Verrio, and new furniture for her apartment included a suite of blue and gold velvet chairs and stools for her withdrawing room, musk velvet hangings for her closet, and flowered velvet chairs for her eating room. Her bedchamber was particularly grand, with a marble chimneypiece carved by Grinling Gibbons and gilded with burnished gold. (John Evelyn, when he saw it in January 1687, declared it to be 'incomparable'.)

But the high point of all this new work was the chapel, a straightforward rectangular box, with a vestry to the south, and a first-floor gallery to the north which allowed the King and Queen to arrive in their pew via the privy garden range without having to enter the body of the chapel. Over 10,000 leaves of gold were used on the ceilings; the doors were cedar-grained and the detailing picked out in gold. The pulpit, which was also gilded, was carved by Gibbons; and there were Persian carpets on the floor and crimson damask curtains edged with gold and silver for the organ loft. James and Mary sat beneath a canopy of crimson velvet embroidered with gold and silver and festooned with wooden putti, again carved by Gibbons. Even the strings to draw the curtains were of silver.

But in the midst of all this sybaritic and wonderfully unspiritual splendour, one feature dominated the chapel. Designed by Wren and carved by Gibbons and his partner, Arnold Quellin, the massive altarpiece – nearly forty feet high and twenty-five feet wide – filled the entire east end. There were life-size statues of St Peter and St Paul, flanked by Faith and Charity, with angels on the upper storey and a huge framed painting of the Annunciation, perhaps by Verrio, who also painted the Assumption of the Virgin in the vault of the ceiling. John Evelyn, who witnessed the celebration of mass in the new chapel when it was opened to the public on 29 December 1686, was awed by its grandeur and appalled by its purpose. After sneering at the waving of censers and what he regarded as the superstitious antics of the Jesuits, and grumbling about their 'divers cringes' and the 'world of mysterious ceremony', he wrote that 'I could not have believed I should ever have seen such things in the King of England's palace, after it had pleased God to enlighten this nation'. But he still had to admit that 'nothing can be finer' than the Gibbons altarpiece.[11]

SUNDAY 10 JUNE 1688 WAS TRINITY SUNDAY. At eight o'clock Anne, Countess of Sunderland was in the Anglican chapel of St James's Palace, waiting for the communion service to begin, when a messenger came in and asked her to attend on her mistress, the Queen. When she had finished her prayers, she said; but moments later, while she was actually at the altar, another messenger burst into the chapel and told her it wouldn't wait. She had to come now. The Queen had gone into labour.

Mary screamed at the midwife, 'Oh, I die! You kill me, you kill me!' The Earl of Middleton, one of the King's secretaries of state, was appalled: he said later that Mary shrieked so long and loud that he wondered how anybody could hold their breath so long. The Earl of Peterborough put his fingers in his ears to block out the sound of her screams.

Wilks simply said, 'This one pain, madam, and it will be over.' Moments later she emerged from under the bedclothes cradling a baby. Mary had asked particularly not to be told the sex until she was better able to cope, although of course this was exactly what everyone else in the room was desperate to discover. It was the reason most of them were there. Now she whispered, 'Pray do not tell me what it is yet!'

An elaborate pantomime followed. The nurse, Mary Anne de Labadie, who was handing cloths to Wilks, whispered in her ear, 'Is it a girl?' 'No,' was the reply. At the same time, the midwife caught the Countess of Sunderland's coat and gave it a little tug, a pre-arranged sign that the child was a boy. Everyone was momentarily distracted by the Queen, who suddenly screamed, 'The child is dead! I do not hear it cry!' Reassured by Wilks that the baby was alive and kicking, the Queen then began to demand that the umbilical cord mustn't be cut until she had delivered the placenta, having been told by someone that this was the safest way. Calm as ever, Wilks said it would be best to cut it now. 'Do it then,' said Mary. Then she cried, 'Where is the King gone?' When he told her he was beside her (having just been taking a look at his new son), she asked plaintively, 'Why do you leave me now?' So he knelt on the bed, until Wilks announced that the afterbirth had come away safely, when he stood up and said to the assembly, 'Pray, my lords, come and see the child.' Labadie took the child into a room next door and sat down by the fire with it on her lap. The King followed her, with half the Privy Council on his heels. She answered the question before anyone had a chance to ask. 'It is a boy.' 'Let me see it!' demanded the King. The nurse unfolded the cloth and showed the prince. 'This is what you wish to see,' she said.

There remained one small, almost magical ritual to be performed. Two of Queen Mary's previous children had died of convulsions, and someone among her women said that a charm against convulsions was to give a new-born infant some of its own blood to drink. After conferring with the doctors, who were sceptical but agreed it couldn't do any harm, Wilks took a small knife and slit the umbilical cord. Putting three or four drops of blood into a tiny spoon, she mixed it with a little black cherry water and fed the concoction to the baby.

THE MUCH-WITNESSED ARRIVAL OF THIS LITTLE PRINCE, James Francis Edward Stuart, the heir to the three kingdoms, changed the course of British history. However loudly the conspiracy theorists howled that the baby was illegitimate, or that it was someone else's child who had been smuggled into the Queen's bedchamber in the warming pan or some other contrivance, the fact was that as long as he lived, the Catholic succession was assured. Three weeks after his birth, seven dissident nobles, the so-called Immortal Seven, issued an invitation to James II's son-in-law, the Protestant Prince William of Orange, to deliver them from the evils of popery. Not one in a thousand believed the little prince to be the Queen's child, the letter claimed.

The Glorious Revolution, as the last military overthrow in British history of a reigning monarch has become known, began when William of Orange landed at Torbay on the south coast of England with 14,000 troops on 5 November 1688. James II's attempts at resistance collapsed in weeks; and at 2 a.m. on 10 December 1688, Mary Anne de Labadie and Mary of Modena, who was disguised as a washerwoman, carried the baby prince out into the privy garden at Whitehall and through a little gate to where a coach was waiting. The party went down to Gravesend, where they boarded a yacht for France.

Prince James Francis Edward Stuart never saw England again.

A contemporary print showing a rather dramatic version of Mary of Modena's escape from Whitehall with the baby Prince James Francis Edward Stuart in December 1688.

CHAPTER SEVEN

Mrs Morley and Mrs Freeman

'A FRIEND WAS WHAT SHE MOST COVETED.' That sentence, from the beginning of Sarah, Duchess of Marlborough's self-justificatory *Account of the Conduct of the Dowager Duchess of Marlborough from Her First Coming to Court* (1742), goes a long way towards explaining the extraordinarily close relationship that existed between a sovereign, Queen Anne, and one of her household officers. The duchess went on to describe that closeness, and the way that she and the daughter of James II deliberately adopted personae which would allow them to be more familiar with each other than protocol allowed:

> For the sake of friendship (a relation which she did not disdain to have with me) she was fond even of that *equality* which she thought belonged to it. She grew uneasy to be treated by me with the form and ceremony due to her rank; nor could she bear from me the sound of words which implied in them distance and superiority. It was this turn of mind, which made her one day propose to me, that whenever I should happen to be absent from her, we might in all our letters write ourselves by feigned names, such as would import nothing of distinction of rank between us . . . and from this time Mrs Morley and Mrs Freeman began to converse as equals.[1]

There were other examples of relationships between monarchs and their courtiers. Queen Elizabeth I was on intimate terms with her master of the horse, Robert Dudley, Earl of Leicester. She may even have slept with him, although that is unlikely. James I almost certainly did sleep with *his* master of the horse, George Villiers. The King christened him 'Steenie', an allusion to St Stephen, who is described in the New Testament (Acts 6:15) as having 'the face of an angel'.

But intimacy need not involve a sexual relationship. Queen Anne's friendship with the Duchess of Marlborough began in 1673, when she was eight years old. Her mother, Anne Hyde, had died two years previously of breast cancer (her last words to her husband, the future James II, were 'Death is terrible! Death is very terrible!'). Her only surviving brother Edgar died a few months later at the age of four. In

1673 her father had married the fifteen-year-old Mary of Modena; and one of Mary of Modena's new maids of honour was the thirteen-year-old Sarah Jenyns, youngest daughter of an impoverished Hertfordshire MP. The two girls used to play together, recalled Sarah, 'and she even then expressed a particular fondness for me'.[2]

Move forward ten years. Sarah was now the wife of an ambitious young soldier named John Churchill, and Princess Anne was married to Prince George, the amiable thirty-year-old son of Frederick III of Denmark, with a household of her own and lodgings in the Cockpit at the palace of Whitehall. Sarah was everything that Anne was not: beautiful, confident, charming and outspoken. And instead of resenting this inequality, Anne came to idolise her friend. She asked her to be her second lady of the bedchamber – her first lady was her aunt the Countess of Clarendon, who had been foisted on her without her consent[*] – and when it seemed her father might veto the appointment, she grew frantic, weeping and promising Sarah she would persevere with her father, reassuring her that 'you have not a faithfuller friend on earth nor that loves you better than I do'.[3]

The young princess succeeded in changing the Duke of York's mind, and when the Earl of Clarendon was made lord lieutenant of Ireland in 1685 and his countess went with him, she promoted Sarah to first lady of the bedchamber. It was Sarah who smuggled Anne down the backstairs and out of Whitehall on the night of 25–26 November 1688, after she had decided to support her brother-in-law William of Orange and the Glorious Revolution against her own father. Anne had never seen her backstairs before: as she fled down them her comment was that they needed painting, and as soon as she reached safety she issued an order to have them decorated.

Sarah didn't like Mary II, Anne's sister and the wife of William of Orange. The new queen 'wanted bowels', she said, by which she meant she lacked gravitas; she talked too much, and she was flighty. Sarah was present at Whitehall to welcome Mary when she arrived in England from the Netherlands to take up her crown in February 1689. She was shocked when Mary ran around her apartments like an excited girl, poking into closets and turning up the quilts on the bed. Having deposed her own father, 'she should at least have looked grave, or even pensively sad, at so melancholy a reverse of his fortune'.[4] Neither Sarah nor Anne liked William, either. Anne had agreed to put aside her claim to the throne

---

[*] 'She looked like a mad-woman, and talked like a scholar', was Sarah's memorably damning verdict on the Countess (*Conduct*, 10).

Sarah Churchill,
Duchess of Marlborough,
by Charles Jervas.

in William's favour, and she and Sarah both thought she should have a degree of financial independence as a reward, something which her sister resisted.

There were also resentments over more trivial matters – trivial to posterity, at any rate, but not to the siblings. For example, Anne and Prince George wanted to move from their Whitehall lodgings in the Cockpit, to be nearer to the King and Queen – not because of any filial affection, but to bring them closer to the heart of the court. The Duchess of Portsmouth had gone back to France after Charles II's death, and her lodgings, which lay on the east side of the palace complex between the privy garden and the Thames, were vacant. Anne asked her brother-in-law if she could have them, and he said 'Yes'. But that wasn't quite enough: Anne and George had quite a considerable household of their own, and Anne also asked for the lodgings next door, for the use of her servants.

That was where the trouble started. William Cavendish, Earl of Devonshire was one of the 'Immortal Seven' who had put their names to the letter inviting William to come over and save England from popery. One of his many rewards was the post of lord steward of the household, which came with lodgings at Whitehall; and he decided that he also wanted Lady Portsmouth's old apartments. 'There was a fine room for balls,' said the palace gossips, and 'it would give him a very magnificent air.'[5] Forced to choose between upsetting Anne and disobliging one of the men who had put them on the English throne, the King and Queen suggested a compromise, whereby Anne could have the Portsmouth lodgings, but she couldn't move her servants into *their* new lodgings next door until the earl had decided whether he wanted them, or whether he would take part of the Cockpit. This infuriated Anne, who told her sister she would stay where she was, 'for she would not have my Lord Devonshire's leavings'.[6] In fact she still took the Duchess of Portsmouth's apartments and used them for her children while she stayed in the Cockpit. Come what may, she wasn't going to let Devonshire get his hands on them.

In 1691 John Churchill, who had deserted James II when William of Orange landed at Torbay (a step which had earned him a peerage as Earl of Marlborough), was found to have been in contact with the exiled James, and this, coupled with Mary's growing suspicion that Sarah Churchill was encouraging Anne in her feud with her sister, led her to tell Anne that her first lady of the bedchamber must go.

The princess refused point blank. Sarah offered to resign her post, but Anne 'fell into the greatest passion of tenderness and weeping that is possible to imagine'.[7] She was prepared to put up with any indignity rather than submit to William and Mary's demands. Otherwise, she told Sarah, 'how would that Dutch abortive [her pet name for King William] laugh at me and please himself with having got the better?'[8] When Mary sent the lord chamberlain round to tell Anne that Sarah was forbidden to appear at Whitehall, Anne left the palace, borrowing the Duke of Somerset's Syon House, ten miles to the west of London, so that she could stay in contact with her friend.

The death from smallpox of Queen Mary at the end of 1694 led to a rapprochement of sorts between Mrs Morley and the Dutch abortive. William and Mary had no children, so Anne was now the next in line to the throne, and she was welcomed back at court. Sarah, who was always ready to see the worst in people she disliked, put the King's relaxation of his policy of isolating his sister-in-law down to self-interest. Now that she was his heir, the nobility wouldn't be dissuaded from paying her court. 'And he was well aware that everybody, who had a mind to show they did not care for him, would certainly do it by making their court to her.'[9]

William's death in 1702, following a fall from his horse, brought no lessening of Anne's devotion to her Mrs Freeman. She immediately appointed her as groom of the stool, mistress of the robes and keeper of the privy purse, combining these crucial household offices in a way that had never been seen before. Not surprisingly, Sarah began, as she put it herself, 'to be looked upon as a person of consequence, without whose approbation, at least, neither places, nor pensions, nor honours were bestowed by the crown'.[10] As keeper of the privy purse, she held the Queen's private funds when Anne's annual allowance was between £20,000 and £26,000. As mistress of the robes she not only took charge of the Queen's clothes and jewellery, but was also able to contract with individual tradesmen and purveyors on the Queen's behalf. As groom of the stool, she was in charge of the royal bedchamber, with the right to regulate access to the bedchamber and closet; even when she wasn't there, she could determine who was and who wasn't welcome. These posts brought in around £5,600 a year, and gave her her own lodgings at St James's Palace, Kensington Palace, Hampton Court Palace and Windsor Castle. As if that weren't enough, the Queen also appointed Sarah as ranger of Windsor Great Park, which brought with it the use of the lodge there – 'a very agreeable place to live in,' said Sarah.[11] And at the end of 1702 Anne made Sarah's husband John a duke.

Sarah was a tremendously effective gatekeeper, dealing with importunate petitioners and shielding Anne from difficult conversations. She was also very supportive, in her forthright way. This of itself nurtured the Queen's emotional dependency on her friend, and fostered the kind of relationship in which one side sought to control the other and the controlled went to great lengths to keep the other happy.

The rock on which this strange and unequal friendship would founder was politics. Sarah, the new Duchess of Marlborough, supported the Whigs, whose policies included continued war with Louis XIV of France, toleration for religious dissenters and the supremacy of Parliament over the crown. Her royal mistress supported the Tories and believed that the Whigs were the implacable enemies of the crown and the Church of England. As far as Sarah was concerned, Anne's views were stupid; they arose from a simple misunderstanding of the world that she took it upon herself to correct. 'I undertook to moderate her Majesty's partiality to the tories,' she recalled, 'and to engage her to a better opinion of their opposites.'[12] Anne proved reluctant to see the error of her ways, but Sarah returned again and again to the subject, explaining Anne's mistakes to her and supremely confident that she was bound to come round in the end.

———————————

WHEN WILLIAM OF ORANGE'S HORSE, Sorrel, stumbled over a molehill in the park at Hampton Court on 20 February 1702, catapulting him into eternity and his half-sister onto the throne, Queen Anne inherited a clutch of royal residences rather different in character from those which her father had left behind when he fled to France fourteen years before.

For a start, the palace of Whitehall was no longer the primary royal residence. In fact, to all intents and purposes, the palace of Whitehall was no longer there. On the afternoon of 4 January 1698, a servant lit a charcoal brazier in an upper room and left some wet linen hanging round it to dry. In her absence the linen caught, and the fire soon spread to 'the hangings, wainscots, beds, and what not, and flamed and smoked in such a violent manner, that it put all the inhabitants thereabouts into consternation, as well as confusion'.[13] Sir Christopher Wren was in his office in Scotland Yard, on the edge of the Whitehall complex, when a bricklayer named Henry Evans burst in to say that fire had broken out in the royal lodgings. Wren told the bricklayer to gather up the books and papers from his closet for him, while he went across to see what was happening. Within seconds he was back, yelling, 'We are undone!' The fire was moving westwards through the old privy lodgings, and threatened Inigo Jones's Banqueting House. 'For God's sake let all things alone here,' the surveyor told Evans, 'and try to save that fabric.' Evans organised a team of bricklayers to block one of the windows on the south side of the building, thus saving the scene of Charles I's execution and one of the most hallowed shrines in Stuart hagiography. (He was awarded £5 for his efforts.) In spite of attempts to prevent the flames spreading further by blowing up around twenty buildings in its path to create a firebreak, the rest of the palace was destroyed.

King William wasn't terribly upset. What the Duke of Saint-Simon described as 'the largest and ugliest palace in Europe' had never been a favourite of his.[14] It was too public, and William recoiled from public

Leonard Knyff's bird's-
eye view of Whitehall
from the east, a year or
two before the palace
was destroyed in the fire
of 1698.

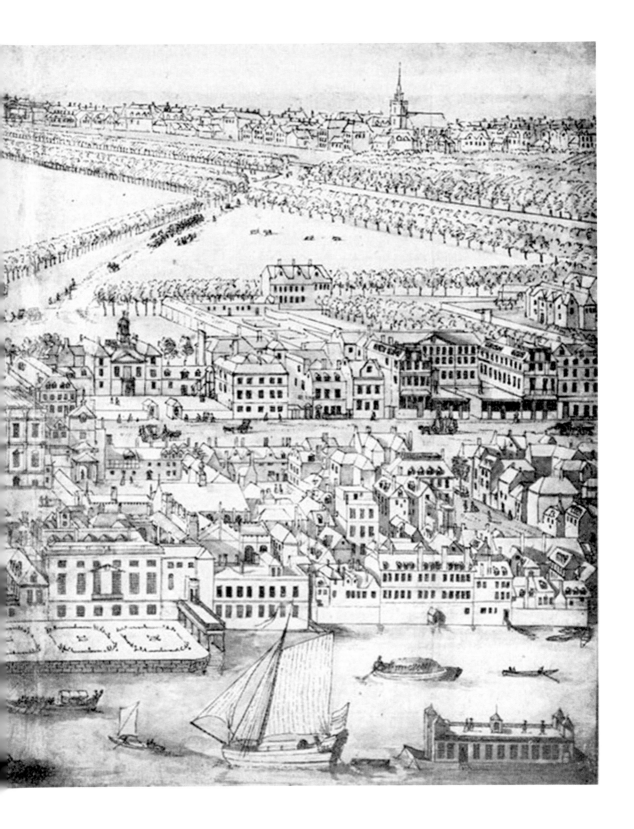

St James's was never big, and never properly planned; but under Anne it made the transition from St James's House to St James's Palace, the official residence of the sovereign – a role it retains to this day, in theory if not in practice.

Out of town, Queen Anne favoured Windsor, rarely spending much time at Hampton Court, although she did sometimes go there from Windsor on Sundays to meet members of her cabinet who travelled down from London. The cabinet was a relatively new political entity, consisting of the lord chancellor (or lord keeper), the treasurer, the president of the council, the lord privy seal, the lord-lieutenant of Ireland, the commander-in-chief, and the two secretaries of state, along with one or two other nobles whose power and influence earned them a place at the table. The practice of holding Sunday evening cabinet meetings, begun by William of Orange and continued by Queen Anne, led to Alexander Pope's lines on Hampton Court in *The Rape of the Lock*:

> Here thou, great Anna! whom three realms obey
> Does sometimes counsel take – and sometimes tea.[17]

She was rarely at Hampton Court for more than a night or two, however, and never for more than a couple of weeks, preferring to hold court and to entertain at Windsor or St James's Palace – although 'entertaining' isn't the word her guests would have used to describe her receptions. Jonathan Swift recalled being present at a reception at Windsor in 1711 where the food was excellent – he ate at the board of Green Cloth, calling it 'much the best table in England' – but the company was not. 'We made our bows, and stood, about twenty of us, round the room, while the queen looked at us with her fan in her mouth, and once in a minute said about three words to some that were nearest to her; and then she was told dinner was ready, and went out.'[18]

Neither Queen Anne nor her devoted and frequently drunk husband George was particularly good at socialising. 'Nobody can maintain that she was … entertaining in conversation,' wrote Sarah, Duchess of Marlborough, and while the duchess's opinions were rarely kind, in this case she was right (as she often was). 'Neither good nor bad, but he is a bit fat,' said the French ambassador of Anne's consort,[19] while Charles II is supposed to have exclaimed that he had tried George drunk and tried him sober, 'but God's fish! There was nothing in him.' Both Anne and George would be accused of having same-sex relationships by the Duchess of Marlborough, but there was no evidence for the accusations. The couple were extraordinarily close, while the fact that Anne had seventeen pregnancies in the first seventeen years of their marriage is convincing evidence that the mutual attraction had its physical side. The fact that not one of those seventeen children survived infancy (all were dead by the time Anne came to the throne in 1702, in fact) united them in grief.

Anne's close household was predominantly female. She kept six maids of honour, decorative young women who passed their time in 'dressing, dancing, seeing and acting of plays, hunting, music, all sorts of diversions', as one maid put it.[20] They were given an allowance of £300 a year and special one-off payments to buy themselves suitable clothes for formal entertainments. 'There was dancing,' another maid told her father in 1704, 'but it was not called a set ball, which distinction is very fatal to us maids having no allowance for clothes, which was never known before.'[21] Parents had to subsidise their daughters heavily, but it was worth it: the prizes on offer included an advantageous match with an eligible courtier, and a dowry of £3,000 which the Queen presented to her maids of honour when they married with royal approval. Inevitably the fact that the girls were marriageable meant a high turnover: in the course of her twelve-year reign Anne had eighteen maids of honour.

She also kept between eight and eleven ladies of the bedchamber, all noblewomen and managed by the Duchess of Marlborough as groom of the stool. They received £1,000 a year and lodgings when they were in waiting. They kept the Queen amused, accompanied her when she went out and helped her women of the bedchamber to dress and undress her.

The women of the bedchamber were Anne's body servants. In 1728 Henrietta Howard, a bedchamber woman to Queen Caroline who was battling with one of Caroline's ladies of the bedchamber as to who was supposed to do what, asked a friend to find out exactly what were the duties of a bedchamber woman in Queen Anne's day. The friend asked someone who had worked as one of Anne's women, and this was the reply:

> The bedchamber-woman came in to waiting before the queen's prayers, which was before her majesty was dressed. The queen often shifted [dressed] in a morning: if her majesty shifted at noon, the bedchamber-lady being by, the bedchamber-woman gave the shift to the lady without any ceremony, and the lady put it on. Sometimes, likewise, the bedchamber-woman gave the fan to the lady in the same manner; and this was all that the bedchamber-lady did about the queen at her dressing.

When the queen washed her hands, the page of the back-stairs brought and set down upon a side-table the basin and ewer; then the bedchamber-woman set it before the queen, and knelt on the other side of the table over against the queen, the bedchamber-lady only looking on. The bedchamber-woman poured the water out of the ewer upon the queen's hands.

The bedchamber-woman pulled on the queen's gloves, when she could not do it herself.

The page of the back-stairs was called in to put on the queen's shoes.

When the queen dined in public, the page reached the glass to the bedchamber-woman, and she to the lady in waiting.

The bedchamber-woman brought the chocolate, and gave it without kneeling.[22]

This, one of the most detailed accounts we have of a body servant's role in the royal household, is interesting not only because of the glimpse it offers into the rituals of daily life, but also because of who is saying it: Abigail Hill, a cousin to Sarah, Duchess of Marlborough. When Hill's father, a Smyrna merchant, went bankrupt and then died leaving the family in desperate financial straits, Sarah stepped in to help, bringing the young woman into her own household and asking Anne, who was not yet queen, to find her a place as one of her women of the bedchamber when there was a vacancy. By 1700 Hill was Princess Anne's mother of the maids, a chaperone to the maids of honour; and when Anne came to the throne in 1702 she was confirmed as one of her women of the bedchamber with a salary of £500 a year.

In 1707 Hill, now in her late thirties, married a man nine years younger: Samuel Masham, groom of the bedchamber to Prince George and another protégé of the Duchess of Marlborough. The marriage took place without Sarah's knowledge, which was unusual in that as she was Hill's patron, it would have been good manners to ask for her approval beforehand. When she found out about the match the duchess was cross, but in her own words, 'I was willing to impute it to bashfulness and want of breeding, rather than to any thing worse.'[23] But when she then discovered that the Queen had attended the wedding without telling her, she began to suspect that Abigail Masham was exerting an undue influence in the bedchamber.

Sarah's fears were influenced by the political scene at the time. She supported the Whig faction at court and in government, and she was relentless in her pursuit of the Whig interest, doing her best to bully and cajole Anne into supporting Whig policies. She lost no opportunity to influence the Queen in favour of the lord high treasurer, Sidney Godolphin (whose son was married to Sarah's daughter); the secretary of state, the Earl of Sunderland (who was married to another Marlborough daughter); and the captain-general of the army and master-general of the ordnance (who was Sarah's husband, the Duke of Marlborough). A younger brother of the duke, George Churchill, was a senior figure at the

An imaginative Victorian portrayal of the Duchess of Marlborough (left) berating Queen Anne. Abigail Masham cowers behind the queen.

Admiralty and another groom of the bedchamber to Prince George of Denmark; but he didn't toe the Whig line, leading Sarah to inform Anne on no evidence at all that he was having an affair with her husband.

Sarah was a difficult friend, but a terrifying enemy. Accusations of homosexuality as a way of attacking court favourites were common at the turn of the seventeenth century. Gossips claimed that Thomas Wentworth, groom of the bedchamber to William III, owed his advancement to his sexual relationship with the King; and when another of William's favourites, Hans Willem Bentinck, was replaced by Arnold van Keppel, Bentinck told the King that there were some very nasty stories circulating about the two men, 'things I am ashamed to hear'.[24] Sarah hurled charges of sexual deviancy without the slightest evidence. Abigail Masham was related to the Tory politician Robert Harley, who was suspected – quite rightly, as it turned out – of using his cousin to gain access to the Queen and to undermine the Whig government. And as Sarah's unease grew, she began to hint, both behind Anne's back and to her face, that there must be a sexual element to the Queen's relationship with her bedchamber woman. When the truth came out, she wrote to the Queen, it 'will make her character so very different from that which has always been given by her faithful Freeman'.[25] And as their relationship deteriorated, Sarah's secretary, Arthur Maynwaring, composed a nasty ballad about Masham, calling her a 'slut' and 'a dirty chambermaid', and claiming that her role was 'the conduct and the care | Of some dark deeds at night'.[26]

Sarah helpfully showed this ballad to the Queen, with several more in the same vein. When Anne expressed anxieties about her reputation, her friend responded by saying her reputation was already lost. 'Nor can I think the having no inclination for any but of one's own sex is enough to maintain such a character as I wish may still be yours.'[27]

This was an astonishing way to behave towards the queen of England. There was worse to come. For all the duchess's snide remarks about Anne's sexuality, it was Sarah who began to behave like a spurned lover – suspicious, prone to fits of jealous rage and given to recrimination and public quarrels. In August 1708, the Queen attended a service of thanksgiving at St Paul's Cathedral for the allies' victory over the French at the Battle of Oudenaarde, a key moment in the War of Spanish Succession and a landmark in the career of the Duke of Marlborough, who was in command. Sarah accompanied Anne to the cathedral in her capacity as mistress of the robes, but while they were riding in the coach she noticed that the jewels the Queen was wearing weren't the ones she had laid out for her. She leapt to the conclusion that this was Masham's work – and that, because they were less spectacular than those which she had intended, it was a deliberate slight on her husband, calculated to tell the world that the Queen didn't think so much of his achievement at Oudenaarde. This was bizarre, but what was worse was that she started berating the Queen, and continued to berate her while they climbed out of their carriage and walked into St Paul's. When Anne tried to defend herself, Sarah told her to shut up or people would notice.

A month later there was another quarrel, this time at Windsor and behind closed doors. After the duchess left, the Queen's eyes were red with weeping.

Sarah's jealousy was frightening, and verging on paranoia. At the end of October 1708 Prince George died at Kensington Palace. He had been in poor health for some time, but Anne was distraught with grief. The duchess immediately took charge, insisting that the Queen must leave Kensington for St James's Palace that afternoon rather than remain 'within a room or two of that dismal body', although the real reason was that she was afraid that Anne would look to Masham for solace if she was left at Kensington. When the Queen later shut herself up in her husband's closet with her sorrow, Sarah was sure she knew the real reason for that, too: 'The true reason of her majesty's choosing this closet to sit in, was, that the back-stairs belonging to it came from Mrs Masham's lodgings, who by that means could secretly bring to her whom she pleased.'[28]

Through all these troubles, Abigail Masham sailed serenely on. The Duchess of Marlborough was quite right – the bedchamber woman *was* facilitating her cousin Robert Harley's private visits to Queen Anne, and she was using her influence to persuade her mistress to Harley's Tory point of view. But if the duchess thought that haranguing and bullying the Queen would make her act to get rid of Masham, she was wrong. 'I desire nothing but that she would leave off teasing and tormenting me,' Anne wrote to the Duke of Marlborough in 1709, 'and behave herself with that decency she ought both to her friend and queen.'[29]

The duchess's behaviour grew ever more erratic. She absented herself from court without the Queen's permission. She threatened to resign all her posts, but was held back – and outraged still further – by the fact that Anne was reluctant to honour an undertaking given years earlier to grant those posts to Sarah's three daughters. In March 1708, she had borrowed £12,000 from the privy purse without telling the Queen; she replaced it, but when her accounts were presented there was no record of the transaction, and she borrowed a further £21,800 between August 1708 and January 1710, again without the Queen's authorisation. She sent the Queen a list of her (Anne's) failings, telling Lord Godolphin that she wanted to 'convince even her stupid understanding that she has used me ill'.[30] And she talked openly of having a 'hatred' for Anne.

By the end of March 1710 Queen Anne had had enough. She was happy for Sarah to keep her posts, as long as she didn't have to see her ex-friend more often than was absolutely necessary. But the objects of Sarah's paranoia now included not only Abigail Masham, but also Elisabeth, Duchess of Somerset, one of the ladies of the bedchamber. Sarah was convinced that the duchess and her husband, who was master of the horse, were spreading lies about her, and just before Easter she decided she must have things out with Queen Anne. On 3 April, she wrote to ask for an audience. Anne refused, saying it would be better if they communicated by letter. Three days later, on Good Friday, 6 April, Sarah sent Anne another letter, saying that she was coming to see her at Kensington Palace. Before the Queen had a chance to refuse, Sarah tore round to the palace and stationed herself outside Anne's lodgings. Then she grabbed a page of the backstairs and ordered him to tell the Queen she was waiting to see her. After a long delay, during which the Queen was evidently trying to make up her mind about how to handle the situation, Sarah was shown in. Immediately the Queen announced she was intending to write, and advised her also to put anything she had to say in a letter.

'I think there is nothing you can have to say, but you can write it,' said Anne.

'Won't Your Majesty give me leave to tell it you?'

'Whatever you have to say you may write it.'

'Indeed, I can't tell how to put such sort of things into writing.'

'You may put it into writing.'

'Won't Your Majesty allow me to tell it you now I am here?'

'You may put it into writing.'

'I believe Your Majesty never did so hard a thing to anybody, as to refuse to hear them speak, even the meanest person that ever desired it.'

The exchange went on like this for some minutes. The Queen turned her back on Sarah, who after trying to say she hadn't come about Masham, launched into a diatribe about the 'thousand lies' that her enemies were telling about her. Eventually the Queen said she was leaving, only for Sarah to block her way and burst into tears, saying, 'I only beg to know what you have heard, that I might be able to clear myself in anything in which I was wronged'. The Queen refused to answer her.[31]

This was the last time that Mrs Morley spoke to Mrs Freeman. The Queen held off from dismissing Sarah, partly for political reasons and partly because the duchess threatened blackmail. When Anne asked for the return of her letters, Sarah refused, saying she had drawers full of them and that 'I cannot yet find it in my heart to part with them'. The prospect horrified Anne, who thought back to the times when the two women were so much closer than they were now. 'When people are fond of one another they say many things ... they would not desire the world to know.'[32]

At the beginning of 1711, with a new Tory-dominated administration under Harley in power, Anne decided to remove Sarah from all her

Queen Anne and the Knights of the Garter, by Peter Angelis, c.1727. The painting is thought to show the institution of new Knights of the Garter at a ceremony held at Kensington Palace on 4 August 1713, the year before the queen's death.

places. Nor would she give those places to Sarah's daughters, whom she neither liked nor trusted. The duchess threatened blackmail again. She sent letters of apology for her behaviour. She sent her husband to plead her case. None of it did any good. Having told the duke several times that she wanted Sarah's gold key of office, at an audience with him on the evening of 18 January to discuss army matters Queen Anne announced that she wasn't going to discuss anything until she had that gold key. He went home, got into bed with his wife and told her what had happened. She made him get up again and take the key to the Queen at once.

Mrs Freeman wasn't quite done with Mrs Morley. Before Sarah handed over her privy purse accounts she helped herself to £18,000, which she claimed was owed to her. And when she finally left her lodgings in St James's Palace in May, having been ordered out by the Queen, she took the brass locks with her. She didn't publish Anne's correspondence with her during the Queen's lifetime (perhaps as part of a tacit agreement whereby Anne signed off Sarah's privy purse accounts, knowing them to be open to question). But in 1742 she did publish a justification of her behaviour, the *Account of the Conduct of the Dowager Duchess of Marlborough* mentioned at the beginning of this chapter. There she quoted at some length from letters written when Anne was princess and when she was queen. They suggest an ardent friendship: 'If you should ever leave me, be assured it would break your faithful Mrs Morley's heart.'[33] 'As long as I live, I must be endeavouring to show, that never any body had a sincerer passion for another, than I have for Mrs Freeman.'[34] 'Whilst I have life, I will endeavour to show my dear Mrs Freeman, I have a grateful heart that is most passionately and faithfully at her command.'[35] Whether they suggest anything more than friendship is unlikely.

But the more interesting feature is what those letters tell of Anne's vulnerability, her emotional dependence on a senior member of her household. The balance of power within the relationship was wrong. Sarah was prepared to exploit this one-sided friendship to her own ends (as was Abigail Masham). Her manipulation of the Queen amounted to controlling behaviour, and her rudeness towards her sovereign would have landed her in the Tower only a generation or two earlier. Perhaps the most surprising thing about this, the most famous friendship between a sovereign and a courtier, is that no one stepped in to end it earlier.

Aɴɴᴇ's ᴛʀᴀɢɪᴄ ᴏʙsᴛᴇᴛʀɪᴄ ʜɪsᴛᴏʀʏ — those seventeen deaths and stillbirths and miscarriages — meant there was no British successor to the throne. Anne's ousted father, James II, had died in 1701, and her closest royal relative was her half-brother James Francis Edward Stuart, Mary of Modena's 'warming-pan baby', who was still living in exile in France. But James Stuart had laid claim to the throne on his father's death (and had been recognised as James III by various Catholic states in Europe), which led to him being attainted for treason in 1702. In early 1714, when it was clear Anne hadn't long to live, there were clandestine attempts by British ministers to persuade James to convert to Protestantism as a means of smoothing his path to the throne. He refused, saying with typical Stuart arrogance that he had chosen his religion, and it was for others to change their attitude towards him. That effectively put a stop to moves to offer him the crown on Anne's death, and in June 1714 Parliament offered a colossal reward of £100,000 to anyone who brought him to justice should he land or attempt to land in Great Britain or Ireland.

In any case, the Act of Settlement of 1701 had already determined Anne's successor. It was to be Sophia, Electress of Hanover, a good Protestant, a granddaughter of James I and a daughter of Elizabeth of Bohemia, sister of Charles I and wife of Frederick V, Count Palatine of the Rhine and elector of the Holy Roman Empire.

Queen Anne died at Kensington Palace on the morning of Sunday, 1 August 1714. She had managed to outlive Sophia of Hanover (whom she never liked) by just seven weeks. And so it was that Britain never had a Queen Sophia. Instead, it was her son and heir, the 54-year-old George Ludwig, Elector of Hanover, who ascended the throne as George I.

CHAPTER EIGHT

Happy Families

GEORGE I WAS A SHY MAN. He didn't like to eat in public, or to appear at receptions or balls. In fact he didn't really like people very much. On a typical day the King of Great Britain, France and Ireland, Duke of Brunswick-Lüneburg, defender of the faith, archtreasurer and prince-elector of the Holy Roman Empire, didn't leave his bedroom until around noon. And then it was only to step into his closet next door, where he conducted necessary business with his ministers. He dined alone at two, went for a walk in the gardens at St James's Palace and spent the evening shut up in his mistress's apartment, where his supper was served.[1] Although he had the usual complement of British gentlemen and grooms of the bedchamber, they had very little to do, since he kept a parallel household of German attendants and body servants.[2]

He had no wife. In 1682, when he was twenty-two, he had married the sixteen-year-old Sophia Dorothea, the eldest child of the Duke of Brunswick-Lüneburg. To begin with, the couple got on as well as might be expected for the partners in any arranged marriage, but after having two children, a boy and a girl, they grew apart. By the early 1690s George had begun a relationship with Melusine von der Schulenburg, one of his mother's maids of honour, while Sophia Dorothea was seeing a dashing Swedish soldier, Philip Christoph, Count von Königsmarck, who was in service with George's father at the Hanoverian court.

Sophia Dorothea's affair wasn't a problem, but her lack of discretion was. She and Königsmarck were warned to take more care, but they paid no attention, and when Sophia Dorothea asked for a degree of financial independence from her husband and the Swede took another post with Frederick Augustus I of Saxony, it was obvious that they were preparing to elope. In the summer of 1694, Königsmarck set off for the Leineschloss, the residence of the rulers of Hanover, to meet Sophia Dorothea. He was never seen again. The likelihood is that Sophia's father-in-law, Ernest Augustus, had the Swede killed.

George and Sophia Dorothea were divorced six months later. She was forbidden to remarry, and confined to Schloss Ahlden in Lower Saxony for the rest of her life. When George Lewis came to the throne of Great Britain as George I, he never referred to her; nor would he allow his children to mention her name. Instead, he installed Melusine von der Schulenburg and her daughters in apartments at St James's Palace. According to Lady Mary Wortley Montagu, 'she was duller than himself, and consequently did not find out that he was so'.[3] He created her Duchess of Kendal, dined most evenings with her, and on those occasions when he did appear in public, she was by his side. When news of his ex-wife's death at Ahlden came in 1726, he refused to allow mourning. That same night he appeared in public at the theatre with Madame Schulenburg.

George I also brought over his half-sister, Sophia von Kielmansegg, whom everyone at court assumed to be another of his mistresses, and who competed fiercely with Schulenburg for influence and attention. (After the latter was made Duchess of Kendal in 1719, Kielmansegg campaigned for a title of her own, becoming Countess of Leinster in the Irish peerage in 1721 and Countess of Darlington in the British peerage the following year.) The great gossip and social commentator Horace Walpole, who saw both women as a child, remembered years later that they made a striking pair. Schulenburg was 'long and emaciated', while Kielmansegg terrified him: 'two acres of cheeks spread with crimson; an ocean of neck that overflowed, and was not distinguished from the lower part of her body; and no part restrained by stays'.[4] They were known behind their backs as the Maypole and the Elephant.

The King wasn't popular with his courtiers or with his people. His domestic situation was complicated by his strained relationship with his son. The Prince of Wales, George Augustus, was more outgoing than his father: Lord Hervey, who would later serve as his vice chamberlain, reckoned that 'the pageantry and splendour, the badges and trappings of royalty, were as pleasing to the son as they were irksome to the father'.[5] The prince spoke English (George I had only a few words, preferring French and his native German). And he had a socially adept princess and wife in Caroline, daughter of the Margrave of Brandenburg-Ansbach.

The prince and princess stepped willingly into the social vacuum at court left by the King's reluctance to engage with his subjects. During their first winter in England, Caroline held an evening drawing room twice a week, and gave balls at Somerset House on the Strand and St James's.[6] When George returned to Hanover for an extended stay in the summer of 1716, the prince and princess moved to Hampton Court, where they began to entertain on a lavish scale which hadn't been seen since the days of Charles II.

John, Lord Hervey, who served as vice-chamberlain in George II's household from 1730 until 1740, when he was made Keeper of the Privy Seal. He is shown holding his purse of office in this 1741 painting by Jean-Baptiste van Loo.

There was a reason for all this socialising, a reason which had nothing to do with fulfilling social obligations or being dutiful. Father and son had always had a rocky relationship, and it was made worse when, although George I made George Augustus regent in his absence, he refused to give the 31-year-old all the powers of a regent. He didn't trust him.

So while the King was away, the prince moved to head a political faction in opposition to him. He surprised ministers with his diligent attention to the business of government, asking to see despatches and enquiring about finances. 'By some things that daily drop from him,' said the politician and statesman Sir Robert Walpole, 'he seems to be preparing to keep up an interest of his in parliament independent of the king's.'[7] When George I returned to England early in 1717 he initially behaved as he had before he left, keeping away from his courtiers and spending all his time with Madame Schulenburg and his Hanoverian body servants. But as it became clear that his son was courting popular acclaim and gathering the King's political opponents around him, men who were out of government and thought they should be in, men who thought the King wasn't giving enough of his time to his new country, George I – prompted by Schulenburg and Kielmansegg – decided it was time to fight fire with fire. He moved to Hampton Court for the summer and began to entertain as he never had since the beginning of his reign. He dined in public every day, held morning levees and mixed with his courtiers each evening. Drawing rooms were held six nights a week.

These entertainments proved so popular that polite society flocked to Hampton Court. The lord chamberlain's office had to send down card tables from St James's Palace, and 'four dozen cane chairs' for extra seating.[8] The audience chamber couldn't accommodate everyone who wanted to be part of the fun, in spite of it being the biggest state room at the palace, and the assemblies moved first into the tennis court and then, when that proved expensive to heat and light, to the cartoon gallery. The King arrived at around ten each night, and stayed for a couple of hours, 'with a constant serenity in his countenance and universal affability to all about him', according to one witness.[9]

Ministers and nobility were impressed by this change of tone. 'The king obliges the nobility and others very much at Hampton Court by inviting them to sit down with him at table', commented the essayist Joseph Addison, who was sure the King had 'gained many hearts by his affable and condescending way of life'.[10] When George I returned to London in November, he launched thrice-weekly evening drawing rooms at St James's, and established a public table there to entertain his friends and supporters, at a cost of more than £700 a month.

The prince kept away from the King for several weeks after his return to London. When he did pay his respects, it was tense and formal: he turned up at one of the St James's drawing rooms when the King was playing cards, bowed to him and left. That was all. In turn, the gossip was that the King hadn't bothered to visit the princess, even though she had presented him with a new grandchild that month.

It was at the christening of this child, Prince George William, that the antagonism between the King and his son spilled over into rage.

The quarrel began, as such things do in families, over a relatively trivial matter – who was going to stand godparents to the baby. The prince and princess wanted the King's brother, the Duke of York, and the prince's sister (who was now queen of Prussia), and had written to ask them. The King, knowing nothing of the arrangement, overruled them and said that he and his lord chamberlain, the Duke of Newcastle, would stand, together with the Duchess of St Albans. This infuriated the prince, and when the ceremony was over he stalked over to Newcastle, whom he held to blame, and whispered in his ear, calling him a rascal and a villain and saying, 'I will find you.' Unfortunately, the duke heard this as 'I will fight you', and thinking he had been challenged to a duel for obeying a royal command, he complained directly to his master the King.

The next day, a furious George I sent no fewer than three dukes round to see his son with a message demanding to know exactly what had been said. The prince admitted the name-calling but explained that there had been a misunderstanding about the duel. He was told, in effect, to go to his room and stay there; and although over the weekend he wrote two letters of apology to his father, the vice chamberlain arrived with a handwritten note from the King ordering him out of the palace. Princess Caroline could go with him or not as she pleased. Their four children were to stay where they were.

At nine o'clock that night the prince and princess left St James's Palace. They had been lent a house in Dover Street, off Piccadilly. When they got there the prince cried for two hours. His wife fainted.

If courtiers thought this was a temporary spat, they soon found out they were mistaken. The King sent an account of the quarrel to foreign diplomats, telling them that if they visited the prince, they wouldn't be welcome at St James's. Every courtier and servant who had posts with the King and the prince was told to give up one or the other. Ladies in waiting whose husbands were in the King's service were told they had to leave the princess's household. Although several of the prince's supporters visited him during the first days of his exile, not many went after this. Meanwhile, the rumours flew. According to one newsletter:

> It is said this day [19 December 1717] that the king has acquainted their highnesses with the conditions and terms which he expects from them, in order to their returning to his palace, and they say that he demands a surrender of their patent for £100,000 [granted to the prince by Parliament for the upkeep of his household], and that he shall not pretend to the regency, when the king goes abroad,

and that he shall go with him to Hanover, and that he shall have none about him but what are approved by his Majesty.[11]

The King continued to hold his drawing rooms three times a week, as though nothing had happened. And he continued to put pressure on his son, telling all peers and peeresses, and all politicians and their wives, that if they went to see Their Royal Highnesses they would not be allowed into his presence. He took legal advice over retaining custody of his grandchildren. The prince and princess acquired Leicester House, a seventeenth-century mansion on the north side of Leicester Fields (now Leicester Square), from where they maintained an alternative shadow court, attracting those who were discontented with George I and his ministries, those who calculated that it was to their advantage to trade royal favour in this reign for royal favour in the next, and those who had nothing to lose. The baby at the heart of the quarrel died in February 1718, aged three months. There was a reconciliation of sorts between the King and his son two years later, but the breach was never really repaired.

I T WAS WEDNESDAY 14 JUNE 1727, and the Prince of Wales was in the middle of an afternoon nap with his wife. Suddenly a lady in waiting appeared and woke him to announce that Sir Robert Walpole was at the door. He had urgent news and it wouldn't wait.

Walpole was ushered into the bedchamber. All he said was, 'I am here to acquaint Your Majesty with the death of your father.' After complaining of stomach pains whilst on the road to Hanover, something he attributed to a surfeit of strawberries, George I had suffered a stroke on the morning of 9 June.[12] He died at Osnabrück two days later. The prince was now a king.*

George II and Caroline of Ansbach were crowned king and queen of Great Britain and Ireland on 11 October 1727 in Westminster Abbey, walking along a route carpeted in blue cloth. Young women in white scattered flowers along the way. Handel composed four anthems for the occasion, including 'Zadok the priest', which has been sung at the coronation of every British sovereign since. The people cried out, 'God

---

* According to Thackeray, George's reaction was to roar, 'Dat is one big lie!' W. M. Thackeray, *Thackeray's Lectures: The English Humorists and The Four Georges* (New York: Harper & Brothers, 1867), 340.

save King George the Second! Long live King George! May the King live forever!'[13] Odes and panegyrics poured from the pens of the nation's poets:

> Lo, the majestic form appears,
> Sparkling in life and manly years:
> The kingdom's pride, the nation's choice;
> And Heaven approves Britannia's voice.[14]

It was left to the social commentator Lady Mary Wortley Montagu to give an edge to the proceedings, in a snide critique which shows how savage the age of elegance could be when it chose to bare its teeth:

Some languished and others strutted; but a visible satisfaction was diffused over every countenance as soon as the coronet was clapped on the head. But she that drew the greater number of eyes was indisputably Lady Orkney [the septuagenarian former lady in waiting to Mary II, and mistress to her husband William III]. She exposed, behind, a mixture of fat and wrinkles, and before a very considerable protuberance, which preceded her ... 'tis impossible to imagine a more delightful spectacle. She had embellished all this with considerable magnificence, which made her one of the largest things of God's making, if my Lady St John had not displayed all her charms in honour of the day. The poor Duchess of Montrose crept along with a dozen black snakes playing round her face, and my Lady Portland (who is fallen away since her dismissal from Court) represented very finely an Egyptian mummy, embroidered over with hieroglyphics ... I, who dread growing wise more than anything else in the world, was overjoyed to find that one can never outlive one's vanity.[15]

George II proved to be no more popular than his father, either during his lifetime or after it. He cared for nobody, and nobody cared for him, according to Lord Hervey, his vice chamberlain: 'He gives without obliging, is served without being respected, and obeyed without being loved.'[16] In the nineteenth century, William Makepeace Thackeray's verdict was even more damning: 'Here was one who had neither dignity, learning, morals, nor wit – who tainted a great society by a bad example – who in youth, manhood, old age, was gross, low, and sensual.'[17]

Another thing the King had in common with his father was a difficult relationship with his eldest son. George and Caroline's first child, Frederick Lewis, was born at the Leineschloss in Hanover in 1707, and

The Music Party, by Philip Mercier, 1733. The artist shows Frederick, Prince of Wales and his sisters Amelia, Anne and Caroline. The Dutch House at Kew is in the background. Mercier was principal painter to the prince and drawing master to the princesses.

left behind to act as ceremonial head of the family when his parents and grandparents decamped to England in 1714, taking his three sisters, Anne, Amelia and Caroline, with them. He remained in Hanover for the next fourteen years, while his father Prince George established himself in St James's Palace and fought with Frederick's grandfather, and while his mother Caroline produced four more children, including William, born in 1721 and destined to be his parents' favourite.

In 1728, a year after his accession to the British throne, George II was persuaded to send for Frederick. By now they were strangers, and Frederick, who at twenty-one was used to having his own way at the Hanoverian court, found it difficult to settle into life at St James's Palace. The King is supposed to have said with contempt, after interviewing Frederick on his arrival, 'This is not a son I need be much afraid of.'[18] He was wrong: Frederick was at ease with people while the King was boorish. He was cultured while the King was not. And he was ambitious for power and money.

In 1697, Parliament had established the principle that the costs of government should be separate from the costs of supporting the sovereign, assigning an annual amount of £700,000 for the king or queen and his or her household. When George I came to the throne, Parliament voted him £700,000 on the civil list, as this parliamentary grant was known, and £100,000 more for the Prince of Wales – a situation which subsequently infuriated the King, since it prevented him from bringing his son to heel by withdrawing his allowance.

George II learned from this. With the help of Sir Robert Walpole, he secured a parliamentary guarantee of £800,000 a year, and for the first time Parliament allowed the king to keep any surplus. Everyone assumed that he would settle £100,000 a year out of this on his eldest son. But he didn't. Instead he gave him £24,000 a year. (Frederick also had around £9,000 a year from the Duchy of Cornwall estates.) It was enough for the prince to maintain a small household of his own, but not quite enough for him to live a princely life.

In April 1736 Frederick married Augusta of Saxe-Gotha in the chapel royal at St James's Palace, and a few weeks later King George left for Hanover, pointedly leaving the Queen as regent rather than his eldest son. Queen Caroline did her best to make friends with Augusta, inviting the newly-weds to dine with her, even though she thought her new daughter-in-law was both stupid and boring. Relations with the prince were still fraught: Caroline told Lord Hervey that she couldn't be offended at anything her daughter-in-law did because she knew the girl never did anything unless the prince ordered it. 'Poor creature, if she were to spit in my face, I should only pity her for being under such a fool's direction, and wipe it off.'[19] There were petty squabbles, and the Queen was right to think that Frederick would cheerfully use his wife to annoy his mother. For example, the prince started to make a point of bringing his wife into chapel at Kensington after the service had begun, so that Augusta always had to squeeze past the Queen or, if Caroline was on her knees, hover awkwardly beside her until she could get by. After this had gone on for two or three Sundays the Queen told the princess's chamberlain to bring the girl in by the door which the ladies of the bedchamber used, at which Frederick told his wife that if she wasn't ready to go into chapel with the Queen she shouldn't go in at all.

George II stayed in Hanover rather longer than anyone expected, leading his disgruntled subjects to complain about his neglect. Someone stuck up a bitter notice on the door of the Royal Exchange: 'It is reported that his Hanoverian Majesty designs to visit his British dominions for three months in the spring.' Another, on the gate at St James's, read: 'Lost or strayed out of this house, a man who has left a wife and six children on the parish.'[20] And Frederick made the most of his father's absence — and his father's unpopularity. When a fire broke out in the nearby legal district, he went down in the middle of the night to direct the firefighting operations, an act which impressed the crowd so much that they shouted 'Crown him! Crown him!'

George II finally returned to his kingdom in January 1737, and promptly came down with a bad case of haemorrhoids. While he languished at St James's Palace, Frederick decided to press home his advantage and lobby Parliament for an independent allowance of £100,000. His strategy was to tell anyone who would listen that he was sorry not to be able to reward his supporters for the time being, but he promised to make it up to them when he came to the throne, 'with strong insinuations at the same time how near the King's health seemed to bring that happy day'.[21] George II offered his son £50,000, but Frederick rejected it. Caroline's advisers urged her to speak privately with her son and persuade him to give up his scheme to appeal directly to Parliament for his money, something which would be hugely embarrassing to the King if it went through. But the Queen refused point blank, saying her son was such a liar that he was capable of claiming that anything had been agreed. In the past, when she had had private conversations with him she deliberately left her dressing room door half open and posted one of her daughters behind it as a witness to what passed between them. Now she was beside herself with hate and anger. One day shortly before the parliamentary debate on the £100,000, she was standing at the window of her dressing room when she saw Frederick strolling across the courtyard below. She went red with rage and hissed, 'Look, there he goes! That wretch! That villain! I wish the ground would open up this moment and sink the monster to the lowest hole of hell.'[22] Both she and her husband have been credited, if that is the right word, with saying of Frederick that 'my dear first-born is the greatest ass, and the greatest liar, and the greatest *canaille* [vulgar person], and the greatest beast in the whole world; and I most heartily wish he was out of it'.[23]

Frederick's friends lost the debate over his £100,000, and George II and Queen Caroline both wanted to turn their son out of St James's, as George's father had turned him out twenty years before. The prime minister, Sir Robert Walpole, persuaded them against it, arguing that if he left and set up a court of his own they would have even less control over him than they did now, while the nation would feel sorry for him. Walpole also persuaded the King (with a great deal of difficulty) to honour his offer of a £50,000 allowance; and relations between king, queen and prince returned to a semblance of normality. Frederick remained at St James's, coming to drawing rooms and levees, dining in public with his parents. 'But the king never seemed to see or know he was in the room', recalled Lord Hervey, 'and the queen, though she gave him her hand on all these public occasions, never gave him one single word in public or private.'[24]

To cap it all, Princess Augusta was expecting her first child. Her husband had been dropping hints that she might be pregnant since soon after their marriage, while she ostentatiously took to playing with a large jointed doll, dressing and undressing it at the window of her apartment – until her sister-in-law told her to stop it because, according to Hervey, 'the sentinels and footmen used to stand and stare and laugh during this performance'.[25] By the early spring of 1737 it was obvious that she really was pregnant – a cause for joy and reconciliation, one might think, as the dynastic ambitions of the House of Hanover stood a fifty-fifty chance of being secured for another generation.

Queen Caroline didn't see it that way at all. As far as she was concerned, this was another example of Frederick's treachery, a deliberate attempt to prevent his brother William, her favourite, from inheriting the throne. Worse, the Queen managed to convince herself both that her daughter-in-law wasn't really expecting a child ('I do not see that she is big'), and that Frederick wasn't capable of getting Augusta pregnant. That wouldn't stop the villain from ruining William, though: he would get another man to lie with Augusta, or smuggle a baby into her lying-in as James II was supposed to have done.

The most vivid account of the extraordinary events that took place over the summer of 1737 comes from the pen of Lord Hervey, who was present during most of them. But we should remember that Hervey was not an impartial observer. In fact he hated Frederick as passionately as did Frederick's mother. The two men had once been friends. They had shared a mistress – Anne Vane, of whom it was uncharitably remarked that although she was one of the Queen's maids of honour, she was 'willing to cease to be one on the first opportunity'.[26] But the bisexual Hervey loved Frederick, and the prince did not love him back; and after he was replaced as favourite by George Bubb Dodinton in the early 1730s, Hervey turned into one of the prince's most implacable enemies, a silver-tongued courtier who fed the King's anger and the Queen's hatred at every opportunity. Nevertheless, his eye for detail and his ear for gossip are hard to resist.

After the chaos and suspicion surrounding the birth of James II's son nearly fifty years earlier, there were certain rituals which were meant to surround the birth of a royal baby. Most importantly, there must be reliable witnesses to the birth. Once it was known that Princess Augusta was expecting a baby, the King ordered that she should have it at Hampton Court, where the court was living over the summer. The Prince of Wales wanted his first child to be born at St James's Palace, if for no other reason than because his father didn't. Still, the couple moved to Hampton Court with the King and Queen that summer.

On the evening of Sunday 31 July, the princess was taken ill in her apartment. As soon as the prince realised she was going into labour, he called for a coach, and, helped by her dancing master and one of his equerries, he hustled the unfortunate Augusta through passages and stairways until they got outside. As they walked, her waters broke, and her contractions were coming so violently that she couldn't put one foot in front of another. For God's sake, she begged, wouldn't the prince just leave her where she was? His reply was to say it would soon all be over, and to bundle her into the waiting coach, along with two of her dressers and her lady in waiting. Frederick's valet, who happened to be a surgeon and midwife, was perched on the coach box, while the equerry and two others hung on behind.

St James's Palace is about fifteen miles from Hampton Court. The coach set off at a gallop; by the time it reached London the princess was in a pitiable state, 'notwithstanding all the handkerchiefs that had been thrust one after another up Her Royal Highness's petticoats'.[27] According to Hervey there was nothing ready when they reached the palace. There weren't even any sheets, and she was put to bed between two tablecloths while the midwife sent out to the neighbours for napkins, a warming pan, 'and all other necessary implements for this operation'.[28] Mindful of the need for witnesses to the birth, the prince had sent a messenger ahead when he was leaving Hampton Court to summon Spencer Compton, lord president of the Council. He also roused Lord Godolphin, lord privy seal, who lived by St James's. (He summoned the lord chancellor and the Archbishop of Canterbury as well, but the first was out of town and the second didn't arrive until it was too late.)

Augusta gave birth to 'a little rat of a girl, about the bigness of a good large toothpick case', just before eleven that night. In the meantime, and when he was sure it was too late for them to be there, Frederick sent word to the King and Queen that they were about to become grandparents. The Queen's woman of the bedchamber, Mrs Titchburne, woke them at 1.30 in the morning.

'What is the matter? Is there a fire?' asked Caroline.

No, the princess had gone into labour.

'My God, my nightgown!' said the Queen. 'I'll go to her at once.'

'Your nightgown, Madam, and your coaches too; the princess is at St James's.'[29]

The King started shouting at his wife, saying that 'a false child' had been put upon them. 'This has been fine care and fine management for your son William.' But rather than listening to his recriminations, Caroline dressed as fast as she could, ordered coaches, and at 2.30 set off in pursuit of her new grandchild, accompanied by her two eldest daughters, their servants, and a gaggle of noblemen, including Lord Hervey.

They arrived at St James's at four in the morning, to be greeted by the prince in his nightgown and nightcap. He gave them the news that he was the father of a girl, and proceeded to tell his mother all about it at some length, first in English and then in German. What with holding his wife in the coach and keeping her pillows in place, he added, 'he had got such pains in his back he could hardly stir'.[30] The poor chap.

The Queen was polite. She spoke with her daughter-in-law, and was shown the new baby. Then she went downstairs and said to Hervey, in front of her daughters, 'Upon my honour, I no more doubt this poor little bit of a thing is the princess's child, than I doubt of either of these two being mine.' All the way from Hampton Court to St James's she had suspected 'some juggle', she said. But the sight of the baby reassured her. 'If, instead of this poor, little, ugly she-mouse, there had been a brave, large, fat, jolly boy, I should not have been cured of my suspicions.'[31]

In the days that followed, the prince's courtiers explained his bizarre behaviour by claiming that the princess had agreed to the late-night coach-ride, and that the reason behind it was that there was no midwife, or linen, or nurse at Hampton Court; in the circumstances it made more sense to go to them, rather than send a messenger to bring them to his wife. 'For before they could have come she would have been brought to bed without help, which might have been of dangerous consequence to her and the child'.[32]

The King was having none of it. After the Queen and the princesses had paid another couple of visits to Augusta and the baby and had been snubbed by the prince, he flew at his wife, telling her with his customary elegance and wit that 'she was well enough served for thrusting her nose where it had been shit upon already'.[33] That is Hervey's version, anyway: the Earl of Egmont, a less biased observer, had it from the prince's page that it was the Queen who snubbed her son, and that the prince had twice begged his father's permission to 'throw himself at his feet and ask his pardon for coming away so suddenly from Hampton Court', but had had no answer.[34]

At the beginning of September 1737, when the baby was scarcely two months old, the storm broke. Egmont arrived at his London home to find a note had been delivered by one of the King's messengers:

> Notice is hereby given to all Peers, Peeresses, Privy Councillors and their Ladies, and other persons in any station under the King and Queen, that whoever goes to pay their Court to their Royal Highnesses the Prince and Princess of Wales will not be admitted into His Majesty's presence.[35]

History was repeating itself. Less than twenty years after George II had been thrown out of St James's Palace by his father, he was doing the same thing to his own son. Ordering him to leave the palace with his wife and child and their servants as soon as the princess was able, he condemned his son's behaviour and forbade him even to reply:

> This extravagant and undutiful behaviour in so essential a point as the birth of an heir to my crown is such an evidence of your premeditated defiance of me, and such a contempt of my authority and of the natural right belonging to your parents, as cannot be excused by the pretended innocence of your intentions, nor palliated or disguised by specious words.[36]

In a coda to the letter, the King ominously announced that he was leaving the care of his granddaughter to her mother the princess 'until a proper time calls upon me to consider of her education'.[37]

The move backfired, as it was bound to do. Sympathy went with the prince and princess, forced out of their home with their little baby. Elements in the opposition clustered round. The Duke of Norfolk rented the couple his house in St James's Square, while the nobility and gentry beat a path to their door. The old Duchess of Marlborough, who knew more about feuds than most, offered Frederick her house near St James's. The Duke of Bedford offered his. The Earl of Egmont's son offered his house in Pall Mall for the use of the prince's household, if he should need it.

The prince and princess left St James's Palace on Monday 19 September 1737. There were cheering crowds to see them off. Voices shouted 'God bless you!' to which Frederick replied, 'God bless the King and God bless the poor.' People wept openly. In a petty gesture, the King ordered the guards on duty not to salute his son as he left. One soldier admitted afterwards that 'the tears trickled down my cheeks'.[38]

THE WARRANT WAS DATED 13 AUGUST 1762. In neat copperplate, it read:

> This is to certify that I have sworn and admitted the Right Honourable Lady Charlotte Finch His Majesty's servant in the place and quality of Governess in Ordinary to His Royal Highness the Prince; to have, hold, exercise and enjoy the said place together with all rights, profits, privileges and advantages thereunto belonging.[39]

It was signed by the Duke of Devonshire, lord chamberlain of the household.

Lady Charlotte Finch was thirty-seven years old, and immersed in the life of the Georgian court. Her father had been master of horse to Queen Caroline, her mother a lady of the bedchamber. Her husband, who was nearly twice her age, had been vice chamberlain of the household for the past twenty years, and her brother George was made a gentleman of the bedchamber eleven days before her own appointment.

Finch's employer, George III, had been on the throne for less than two years. Born eleven months after his ugly she-mouse of a sister, and in rather less dramatic circumstances, he had become heir presumptive to his grandfather's kingdom when his father Frederick died unexpectedly in 1751. He succeeded George II nine years later and in September 1761 at the chapel royal, St James's Palace, he married the sensible, cheerful and genteel Princess Charlotte of Mecklenburg-Strelitz.

The marriage was a happy one. George and Charlotte produced the biggest royal family in British history, so that by the time she retired in January 1793, Lady Charlotte Finch had looked after fifteen royal charges, and her nursery and its various offshoots had grown into an enormous department employing fifty-eight people. The eldest child, the Prince of Wales, was thirty with his own establishment; the youngest, Princess Amelia, was nine. As each new baby arrived there were wet nurses and dry nurses, rockers and dressers and nursemaids and necessary women.

Lady Charlotte Finch,
governess to the children
of George III, by John
Robinson, c. 1740-45.

As they grew, teachers and tutors were employed; for the princes there
was a fencing master, a dancing master, writing and drawing masters, and
a riding master, James St Amour, who had been an equerry of the crown
stables. The boys (there were nine of them) were given their own separate
households when they were seven or eight, and their own governors
who came and went. But Finch remained, for more than thirty years.

Her role was no sinecure.* She and her sub-governess, Henrietta
Cotesworth, worked hard. Decades later the Princess Royal, another

---

* Something that can't be said of everyone in her staff. In 1783 a Mrs Margaret Scott
was receiving a salary of £200 a year for acting as wet nurse to the Prince of Wales. He
was twenty-one.

Charlotte, recalled that to begin with there was no English teacher, and Finch and Cotesworth taught her and her brothers and sisters to read. By this time there were seven or eight little princes and princesses, and Cotesworth was suffering from ill-health. It was said that she had turned to drink. 'Lady Charlotte could not teach us all, and begged mamma to take some clergyman's daughter to assist her.'[40] Even then the governess would read with the two older girls for an hour or two every day.

Finch's position brought her into frequent contact with the Queen, who relied heavily on her judgement. The two women got on well together: there was only one occasion when they had a serious difference. In 1774 the drunken Cotesworth (if indeed she was drunk) left royal service and the question arose of appointing a successor. Finch believed that it was up to her to choose the new sub-governess. The King and Queen did not, and Queen Charlotte wrote and told her so. 'This place is not to be disposed of by either governor or governess but by us alone,' she said. 'Their recommendations are taken as well and in preference to others, but the choice and determination lies solely in us.'[41] Her tone was polite, genial even. But it didn't invite contradiction.

Lady Charlotte Finch fought back. She hadn't meant to suggest that it was her right to appoint the new sub-governess, she said.

> [However], the Person with whom I must be so connected from my Place, should be One, whose Principles and Sentiments were known to *Me* to be such as I could recommend as correspondant [*sic*] to my own, nothing being so detrimental in Education as a Contrariety of Opinions in those that are to act together in so important an Undertaking. Therefore I assure your Majesty I did not mention it as a claim on any other Foundation but the Reason of the thing, having really nobody I wish particularly to recommend.[42]

What really annoyed her in this exchange was that she had asked that when the new person was appointed, she might be allowed to take two days off a week. The Queen agreed, but said Finch should increase her attendance in the nursery on the other days. Increase it? As it was, she replied, she was in attendance for between four and six hours every morning, and again from seven in the evening until the Queen dismissed her, 'besides numberless occasional additional attendances'.[43] How could she be expected to do more? She was growing old, she said (she was not quite fifty); and she was finding the work hard. 'Your Majesty must know what an uncommon stock of Spirits and Cheerfulness is necessary

George III and Queen Charlotte listening to music at Buckingham House. 'The king generally directs them what pieces to play, chiefly Handel.'

to go through the growing attendance of so many and such very young People in their Amusements, as well as Behaviour and Instruction, besides ordering all the Affairs of a Nursery.'[44] The implied threat of resignation hovered, unsaid. But it didn't come: Lady Charlotte Finch stayed with the royal family for another two decades, supporting the Queen through the deaths of two of her sons, 'my dear little angel Alfred', who died in 1782 after a smallpox inoculation when he was a year old; and four-year-old Octavius, who also died after being inoculated, just six months later.[*]

M USIC-MAKING PLAYED AN IMPORTANT PART in Georgian court life. George III kept an orchestra of twenty-two musicians, led in the 1780s by the blind organist and composer John Stanley, who was paid £200 for his services as master. (There was also a conductor who received £100 a year, but Stanley appropriated that post for himself, along with the salary that went with it.) The previous master of the King's band, William Boyce, was deaf. At Windsor, the band played every evening from 8.00 to 10.00, with George himself choosing the programme. 'The king generally directs them what pieces to play, chiefly

[*] The royal archives still contain an envelope with a little lock of Alfred's hair 'cut off during his Illness' and sent by the Queen to Finch with a request that she wear it in remembrance of him.

Handel,' wrote the octogenarian bluestocking Mary Delany in 1785.[45]

Queen Charlotte kept her own ten-person Band of Musick, consisting of four violins and a cello, two oboes, an organ, and two singers, a tenor and a bass. She also had a separate four-piece Chamber Band, which was led by the viola da gamba player Carl Friedrich Abel, famous in Georgian London for collaborating on a series of fashionable public concerts with Johann Christian Bach, youngest son of Johann Sebastian Bach. At one stage J. C. Bach was teaching music to the princesses and giving lessons to Queen Charlotte, and occasionally accompanying King George's flute-playing on the pianoforte. 'These two players, Bach and Abel,' recalled a contemporary, 'introduced modern music into this country.'[46]

The rest of the royal family was just as fond of music. The King's brothers, the dukes of Gloucester and Cumberland, both employed the Italian violinist Felice de Giardini as their director of music; so too, when he was old enough to have a household of his own, did the young Prince of Wales, who had a fine singing voice and played the cello 'with taste and precision'.[47] The prince joined in the regular musical quartet evenings, presided over by Giardini, which became a feature of life at Windsor. All seven of the King's surviving sons belonged at one time or another to the Noblemen and Gentlemen's Catch Club, a weekly dining club founded in 1761 to encourage the composition of catches, canons and glees.

The nightly performances at Windsor were more in the way of background music than formal concerts. The King would sometimes come in and play a game of backgammon with one of his equerries. The Queen often sat next door in the drawing room the whole time, and the musicians didn't see a sign of her. Household officers were expected to make up the audience. Equerry Philip Goldsworthy, the brother of sub-governess Martha Goldsworthy, complained that each night he had to go and stand there – no seats – and 'hear over and over again all that fine squeaking' while he tried not to fall asleep on his feet:

> Sometimes, when my poor eye-peepers are not quite closed, I look to the music books to see what's coming; and there I read 'Chorus of Virgins': so then, when they begin, I look about me. A chorus of virgins, indeed! Why, there's nothing but ten or a dozen fiddlers! … Then, when we've stood supporting the chimney-piece about two hours, why then, if I'm not called upon, I shuffle back out of the room, make a profound bow to the harpsichord, and I'm off.[48]

A less jaundiced view of these evenings came from Mary Delany, who was occasionally present at the Queen's Lodge while the band played Handel next door. The whole family would sit around a big table covered in books, pencils and paper:

> The Queen has the goodness to make me sit down next to her; and delights me with her conversation, which is informing, elegant, and pleasing, beyond description, whilst the younger part of the family are drawing and working, &c. &c., the beautiful babe, Princess Amelia [then about two years old], bearing her part in the entertainment; sometimes in one of her sisters' laps; sometimes playing with the King on the carpet.[49]

Delany's sensations as she watched this domestic scene were, she said, 'respect, admiration, and affection'.[50]

The picture of domestic harmony painted in such loving detail by Delany — the King crawling around the carpet with his youngest child while the others sat drawing at the table and their mother looking on fondly — was too good to last. As the years passed, the King and Queen's fondness for their daughters turned into possessiveness. Three of the girls, Augusta, Amelia and Sophia, had affairs with three of the King's equerries, Major-General Sir Brent Spencer, Colonel Charles Fitzroy and Major-General Thomas Garth. Sophia had a child by Garth.

There was pressure on the seven surviving boys to make their way, to do the right thing, but be a credit to their parents. For the Prince of Wales's eighth birthday, his mother gave him a pocket book and a long letter of advice, so as 'not to have anything to reproach myself with hereafter', she told Lady Charlotte Finch. The advice was conventional enough: fear God, abhor all vice, respect your parents, love the King. 'Be charitable to everybody, not forgetting your meaner servants … Look upon yourself as obliged to set good examples.'[51] They were good rules to live by. As he grew to manhood the prince managed to flout every one.

CHAPTER NINE

An Agitation of Spirits

AT THE END OF OCTOBER 1788, the people around the fifty-year-old George III noticed he was more irritable than usual, and given to talking at length on anything that came into his head. His personal physician, Sir George Baker, gently hinted that it was 'essential to his health to be less frequent and earnest in his conversations'.[1] The King thanked him for the advice. But he kept on talking.

He had been ill over the summer, with what Baker diagnosed as gallstones. This time was different, though. 'An agitation of spirits bordering on delirium', noted the doctor.'Frequent and sudden transitions from one subject to another.'[2] A few days later, George III's behaviour was so erratic that the equerries who weren't already in waiting hurried to the Queen's Lodge at Windsor, where the King and Queen were in residence, to see what they could do to help.

There were five equerries altogether, and they were all military men. They included the King's chief equerry, Colonel Philip Goldsworthy, whose sister Martha was sub-governess to the princesses and one of Queen Charlotte's closest confidantes; and Robert Fulke Greville, a lieutenant-colonel in the Grenadier Guards and a loyal, good-hearted servant of the King. The equerries found that their master, who had now been advised by Baker to sleep in a separate room from his wife, was hardly sleeping at all, and had taken to wandering in the night in search of her. Her servants sat up to guard her; pages patrolled the corridors and waited in ante-rooms. One night at dinner with the rest of the royal family the King had 'broken forth into positive delirium', and then had leaped up and thrown the 26-year-old George, Prince of Wales against the wall. The prince burst into tears, the Queen had hysterics and the princesses 'were in misery', recorded the diarist Fanny Burney, who was a member of the Queen's household at the time.[3]

Over the next few weeks the King remained in an excitable state. He took against Philip Goldsworthy, and ordered him back to London. He insisted he wanted Fulke Greville to be in attendance; no one else would do. On 22 November, he told General Budé, private secretary to his son the Duke of York and a regular companion at

chess, that he had seen Hanover through a telescope. Then he began to talk obscenely, 'the most beastly indecency both of word and actions'; and had an obvious erection which lasted for some hours, 'a bodily complaint which I cannot describe', the MP James Bland Burges told a friend, 'but [which] you will find in the folio dictionary under the article Priapism'.[4]

The King's doctors – and there were now quite a lot of them – were at a loss as to what to do next. Sir George Baker had only been appointed as physician in ordinary to the King in July 1787, having already been physician to the Queen's household and then physician in ordinary to the Queen. He was immensely distinguished: the president of the Royal College of Physicians, a fellow of the Royal Society and the author of influential books on colic, dysentery and inoculation for smallpox. But he was only one member of an extensive royal medical establishment

George III, Queen Charlotte and their six eldest children, by Johan Zoffany, 1770. The royal family all wear 'Vandyke dress', fashionable at the time for costume balls.

which included Richard Warren, Sir Lucas Pepys and Henry Revell Reynolds, all eminent society doctors. At the time of the King's illness there were four physicians in ordinary to the King, one physician in ordinary to his household, four physicians to the person extraordinary, two apothecaries to the person, one apothecary to the King's household, two sergeant surgeons to the person and one to the household, and a surgeon oculist. This was replicated on a smaller scale, and with variations, in the households of Queen Charlotte and the Prince of Wales; and as if this weren't enough, additional physicians were brought in as and when they were needed.

They were needed now. While the physicians in ordinary converged on Windsor Castle, the Queen brought in William Heberden, a local man who lived in Windsor town. Then Dr Anthony Addington arrived on 27 November: 'old and indeed nearly superannuated,' reckoned Fulke Greville,[5] although in contrast to the other doctors, Addington actually had experience of treating mental illness, having kept a private asylum in Reading for some years.

But Addington's first intervention was disastrous. He told the King there would be no harm in his seeing Queen Charlotte, and the result was that George III ran naked into her room and tried to throw her on the bed, telling her women that they should stand by 'to see whether he did well'.[6] Two days later he tried to assault his daughter Charlotte, the Princess Royal. 'She was rescued from him with great difficulty and he was in such a rage at his disappointment as to strike the queen.'[7] When he was told that his doctors ordered him detained in his bedchamber by his attendants every night, he reacted by slapping one of his pages across the face.

The King's disinhibited sexual behaviour was upsetting for everybody. He spoke obsessively and freely about his sexual feelings towards Elizabeth Herbert, Countess of Pembroke, the fifty-one-year-old lady of the bedchamber to Queen Charlotte. But his delusions were sometimes more poignant. On Christmas Day, Fulke Greville recorded that he had taken a pillow into his bed which he named as his dead son Octavius, 'who he said was to be new born this day'.[8]

The Queen was overwhelmed at her husband's actions. In the early days of his madness her servants would find her 'with her hands and arms stretched across a table before her, with her head resting upon them'.[9] 'She looked like death, colourless and wan,' wrote Fanny Burney, who as second keeper of the robes under Juliane von Schwellenberg was in waiting on the Queen at the time. Charlotte wept uncontrollably, couldn't eat or drink, and it was all Madame Schwellenberg could do to persuade her to her bed. Even then, she insisted on Martha Goldsworthy sitting up and reading to her throughout the night.

The doctors decided it would be best if the King was moved to the little group of royal residences at Kew, between Windsor and Westminster. There would be more privacy there, but the King had never liked the place, and Queen Charlotte was anxious about how the move from Windsor was going to affect him. For several weeks, the staff at the White House at Kew, where he was to be kept, were in a frenzy of preparation to receive the household. The forty-foot-long dining room was converted into a living room for the king: one of the six west-facing windows opened to the ground, so he could step out to take some exercise in the garden without being overlooked. (One of the objections to his staying at Windsor was that the private garden there could be seen from the terrace, which was open to the public.) The King's bedchamber was next to the converted dining room. Soldiers who usually occupied an adjoining guardroom were moved out, and the guardroom was converted into an ante-room which contained accommodation for the King's footmen and pages. Two more rooms close to the King's bedroom were prepared for his doctors.

Saturday 29 November 1788 was the day appointed for the move. When it came, everyone entered into an elaborate conspiracy to lure the King out of his bed at Windsor and into a carriage for the fifteen-mile drive. 'Princes, equerries, physicians, pages – all conferring, whispering, plotting, and caballing, how to induce the king to set off!' wrote Fanny Burney.[10] The Queen went at ten in the morning with Lady Charlotte Finch and the three older princesses. The three younger girls were to stay behind and wait on events. The doctors ordered that none of them could be allowed to see their father, something which was too much for Finch, who broke down and wept.

When Burney arrived at Kew with some of the Queen's things an hour or so later, she wasn't allowed to unpack, so convinced was the Queen that the King wouldn't come. Burney also found that the Prince of Wales had turned up earlier that morning and taken charge of arranging the various apartments in a high-handed fashion, choosing who should have which room and personally scrawling the intended occupant's name on the door with a piece of chalk.

Back at Windsor, Prime Minister William Pitt was chosen as the first to go in to George III, who was still in his bed and showing no signs of wanting to get up and dress. The youthful Pitt (he was only twenty-

Devoted equerry
Robert Fulke Greville.
'Heavens!' he wrote,
'What a spectacle to
see the dear afflicted
king standing in a strait
waistcoat.'

eight) walked into the royal presence and said breezily what a fine day it was. Wouldn't the King like to set out for Kew, since the Queen had just gone there? George responded by saying that she had left without permission, and that she had better get back to Windsor right away to ask his pardon.

Then it was the turn of Robert Fulke Greville. He went in with William Harcourt, one of the grooms of the bedchamber, and said the King's carriage was ready. Wasn't it time he dressed? 'He became very angry and hastily closed the bed curtains,' recalled Fulke Greville, 'and hid himself from us.'[11]

Now four of his doctors walked into the room in a body. Catching sight of Dr Richard Warren, to whom he had taken a dislike, the King ordered him to leave and when he didn't go, leapt out of bed and lunged at him. Fulke Greville and a couple of pages restrained him – and he went back to bed.

Everyone was losing patience. By now it was early afternoon, and the winter light would soon be fading. The doctors told George that if he didn't dress and get into the waiting carriage of his own accord, he would be taken to Kew. By force, he asked? Yes, they said, by force. He tried one more trick: he would dress, but only if the doctors left the room. As soon as they were gone he lay back down on his bed. But it was no good. The equerries reminded their king that he had promised to get ready, and told him that if he didn't, the doctors would come back and make him. A little before four o'clock he finally climbed into his carriage, with Fulke Greville and Harcourt beside him and an escort of cavalry.

The tragi-comedy continued when the party reached the White House. As the carriage drew up at the door, the King got out and walked nonchalantly into the central hall. Then without warning he made a sudden dash for the suite of apartments which the Queen usually occupied, only to find the door locked. Fulke Greville and the others gave him no time to reflect on this: they threw open the doors to his own apartments, which were lighted and ready to receive him. He went in, but was unsettled by the unfamiliarity of the rooms. There was a new water closet and a new bed, which he didn't like. He announced he wasn't going to sleep in it. Instead he would sit up all night and tire out his attendants. Fulke Greville later wrote:

> He remarked to us that he was very strong and active, and in proof
> of this he danced and hopped with more agility than I could have
> suspected had been in him. But the sight of such an exhibition
> in our dear king and so much unlike himself affected me most
> painfully.[12]

The King was as good as his word. He kept his pages up until four in the morning, and when they tried to put him to bed he pulled the hair of one and kicked out at another. Over the next couple of days, he plotted escape, swore at his servants and continued to use language which was so sexually explicit that it shocked his household officers.

———————— • ————————

THE EXACT NATURE OF GEORGE III'S ILLNESS has exercised historians and medical men for the last two centuries. His family's attitude was straightforward and clear – they thought the King was a lunatic. The British newspapers were discreetly non-committal, talking of 'His Majesty's indisposition' and suggesting that 'some indifferent act or acts in others may have overcharged his mind'.[13] Correspondents to *The Times* diagnosed gout in the head or blamed the drinking of mineral waters, which were well known (claimed one) to be 'pernicious to the head and bowels in particular, by violently affecting the one and greatly disordering the other'.[14] More recently, in 1941 the American psychiatrist Manfred S. Guttmacher diagnosed manic depressive psychosis. Sixteen years later J. H. Plumb, an otherwise distinguished British historian, proposed that the King's flight from reality was caused by 'the sexual strain of his marriage to so unattractive a woman as the queen'.[15]

Then in the late 1960s, two British psychiatrists, Ida Macalpine and Richard Hunter, suggested that the causes of the King's indisposition were physical; that he was not in fact insane, but a victim of porphyria. This is a rare group of metabolic disorders, usually inherited, in which abnormally high levels of organic compounds called porphyrins accumulate in the body.[16] In an attack of acute intermittent porphyria, symptoms might range from pains in the arms and confusion to psychosis, hallucinations and seizures. Macalpine and Hunter's theory gained some acceptance in the 1970s and 1980s, to be challenged in 2010 by Timothy J. Peters and Allan Beveridge, who argued convincingly from a study of George III's medical records that Guttmacher was right, and that the king suffered from recurring bouts of manic-depressive psychosis.[17]

George III's own doctors were less precise. As far as they were concerned, the King's wits were disordered. They were all eminent men in their fields. But with the disastrous exception of the co-opted Dr Addington, those fields didn't include mental disorders. Up to now, their treatment had involved bleeding, purging, applying blisters to the patient's legs, encouraging him to sleep and hoping he would get better. That wasn't working.

On Friday 5 December Dr Warren arrived at Kew with a new physician, Francis Willis. The seventy-year-old Willis ran a successful private asylum at Greatford in Lincolnshire, 'a madhouse … for the reception of any number of lunatics not exceeding ten'.[18] According to one account, he had been sent for on the urging of his son Thomas, who was a chaplain to the King and confessor to Queen Charlotte. However, in the royal archive at Windsor there is an unsigned testimonial from someone with personal knowledge of Francis Willis's expertise as a mad-doctor, stating that Willis was experienced in dealing with 'the sad disease that every British heart is now lamenting … [having] received

The king's mad-doctor:
Francis Willis, painted
by John Russell in
1789, when Willis had
achieved celebrity by
'curing' George III's
madness.

into his house as boarders a variety of ladies and gentlemen, most of
which have been restored to their families as perfectly well in every
respect as before they were under the sad necessity of being separated
from them'. The anonymous writer noted that one of Willis's successes
was 'a near connection of my own', and after admitting that the doctor
and his son John, who acted as his assistant, used 'coercive' measures, the
writer concluded by suggesting that 'if by any means the father and son,
one or both, could be procured', they might 'be found very useful on the
present lamented occasion'.[19]

The mad-doctor's initial meeting with George III passed off uneventfully. The King knew who Willis was, and asked him how many patients he had under his care. He complained about his treatment, and noticing that Willis was wearing clerical dress (he was an ordained clergyman as well as a mad-doctor), asked him if he belonged to the Church.

'I did formerly, but lately I have attended chiefly to physics [medicine],' Willis replied.

'I am sorry for it,' answered the King. 'You have quitted a profession I have always loved, and you have embraced one I most heartily detest.'[20] Then he offered to make Willis Bishop of Worcester, if only he would give up medicine.

That evening Willis had a second, more confrontational interview with the King, who was disturbed and railing against his physicians. Willis told him to his face that 'his ideas were now deranged, and that he required attention and management'.[21] That made the King even more agitated. He started to shout, and tried to push Willis out of the room with both hands. The doctor held his ground and said that unless the King controlled himself he would put him in a straitjacket. To show he was as good as his word, he went out of the room and came back, carrying one under his arm. 'The king eyed it attentively,' recalled Robert Fulke Greville, 'and alarmed at the doctor's firmness of voice and procedure, began to submit.'[22] He promised to go to bed, at which Willis wished him good night and left. The King burst into tears.

FRANCIS WILLIS'S APPEARANCE MARKED THE START of a new regime for George III. It was brutal, coercive and horribly effective. Robert Fulke Greville, whose official three months as equerry in waiting were about to begin, went up to London for a few weeks to arrange his affairs. He returned to Kew on 16 December to find that all the other equerries had been dismissed for the time being. The King's pages were still there, but Willis had brought in men of his own to manage the patient. And while the royal physicians still came and went, Willis remained. 'And he only, in constant attendance, now regulated principally in every direction.'[23]

Under his direction, the King was forcibly held down in his chair if he became agitated; he was tied to his bed if he tried to leave it; and between mid-December and the end of January 1789 Willis used a straitjacket on him at least twenty-two times. He also used it as a threat when the King was excited or disturbed. He should be calmer, the doctor would say, 'or he would certainly talk himself into a strait waistcoat'.[24] Sometimes the sight of one of Willis's men ostentatiously hanging the straitjacket on a dressing screen was enough of itself to calm him.

At the end of December, Willis announced that Queen Charlotte could visit her husband for the first time since before the move to Kew – but only in his presence and for no longer than fifteen minutes. Fulke Greville, five pages and two of Willis's men watched in an ante-chamber as she walked into the King's chamber and closed the door behind her. They could hear the King's voice, although they couldn't make out what was being said, since the conversation was mostly in German. 'At times, he appeared to us as if he was crying.'[25]

Queen Charlotte stayed much longer than her allotted fifteen minutes. She was with her husband and the doctor for nearly an hour. Willis later reported that the King sat beside her and kissed her hand and frequently burst into tears. But after she left – and she had difficulty extricating herself, and needed the help of two of Willis's attendants – George III burst into a torrent of abuse, saying she was mad and that he wasn't going to let her into his bed for the next five years. Greville later confided to his diary that he wished he had not heard some of the things the King said about the Queen.

The visit unsettled George, who by now was being routinely put under restraint. Willis pinned a paper over the chimneypiece in the ante-room to the king's bedchamber: 'No one but the pages are at any time to go into the King's Apartment, without being introduced by, or having leave from, Doctor Willis.'[26] He persuaded his patient to wear his straitjacket unfastened underneath his own waistcoat, so that it would be easier for the attendants to strap him in when he became violent or agitated.

One evening at the beginning of January, George summoned Fulke Greville to play cards with him. Willis was there too; but when the mad-doctor left the room for a moment, the King opened his coat to show his equerry the straitjacket underneath.

> After this melancholy display, it was necessary to pull off his coat to set it to rights again. He stripped and never shall I forget the painful, and unpleasant sight. Heavens! What a spectacle to see the dear afflicted king standing in a strait waistcoat, and tucking up himself, the sleeves and strings, until they might be wanted!![27]

Buckingham House was bought by George III for Queen Charlotte in 1762 and renamed 'the Queen's Palace'. Their son, George IV, decided to make it his principal residence in the 1820s and Buckingham Palace, as it became, has been the seat of the monarchy ever since.

Queen Charlotte was keen that the world outside Kew shouldn't be given too pessimistic a view of the King's condition. To begin with, the royal family had done everything in their power to keep news of his illness from reaching the public, 'but it is now no more possible,' the Duke of York told his brother Prince Augustus on 3 December. 'He is a complete lunatic.'[28] Daily bulletins issued by the King's doctors were vague without being deliberately misleading. 'His Majesty was more unquiet than usual in the evening of yesterday. His Majesty slept four hours in the night at intervals, but is not better this morning.'[29] 'His Majesty has slept for four hours last night, and continues the same as yesterday.'[30] After one of the daily bulletins was too forthright about George III's being restrained, the Queen insisted on seeing every bulletin before it went up to London, and she made a point of amending the gloomier reports. For example, she altered the Boxing Day bulletin, which originally read 'His Majesty was yesterday in the afternoon disturbed, had an indifferent night, and is calm this morning', to 'His Majesty was yesterday in the evening less calm, had an indifferent night, and is calm this morning'.[31]

Francis Willis was sure the King was on the mend, and engaged in shouting matches with the other doctors over improvements which he claimed to be able to see, but they couldn't. After one particularly heated exchange with Richard Warren, the latter refused point blank to issue a bulletin stating that 'the king continued mending'. 'You will not allow him to be mended until he is well,' stormed Willis, to which Warren calmly replied, 'Yes, whenever I see him one hour under the direction of his reason and judgement, I will say he is well.'[32]

At the beginning of the new year, the professional rivalry between these two men spilled over into the public arena. On 7 January 1789, they were ordered to appear before a parliamentary committee that had been appointed to discover the state of His Majesty's health. Four more of the King's doctors – Sir Lucas Pepys, Sir George Baker, Henry Revell Reynolds and Thomas Gisborne – were also commanded to attend. The hearings went on for a week, and it was clear from the line of questioning that the committee was after something more than the current state of the King's health. MPs were eager to know exactly who signed off on the bulletins which went up to St James's Palace each day. They asked Baker about disagreements over the wording of these bulletins, and he described to the committee an occasion when Willis had insisted that the daily report should say that 'His Majesty has had a very good night'. Baker and Pepys had disagreed. The King had slept for four or five hours: they should say it was 'a good night' and leave it at that. No, said Willis. It should say 'a very good night' or he would refuse to put his name to it. The other two gave way to him.

Warren said that Willis had 'written letters to the Prince of Wales, expressing his Majesty to be much better than I apprehended his Majesty to be ... declaring progress in cure that I could not discover'.[33] He also told the committee that he had heard Willis had sent a similar letter to Prime Minister Pitt, saying 'that his Majesty was greatly better, and was likely to be speedily well'; and this at a time when in Warren's opinion the King was 'remarkably bad, and under coercion'.[34] Neither Warren nor Baker held out much hope for the King's recovery, although Warren was currently carrying out research among similar cases at Bethlehem Hospital to see how many regained their senses. The other royal physicians were more guarded, and none of them was prepared to say more than that the King was quieter than he had been.

Only Willis was convinced that the patient was mending. The King did everything in a more rational way than before, he told MPs. His

George III, by Peter
Edward Stroehling,
1807. The king stands
on a terrace at Windsor
Castle wearing the
distinctive Windsor
uniform which he
designed himself.

powers of concentration were improving, so that he was able to read
several pages of a book at a time, where before he hadn't been able
to manage more than a line or two. And he could comment sensibly
on what he was reading. (Slightly unfortunate, this, since one of the
complaints made against Willis was that he had been insensitive enough,
or careless enough, to give George a copy of *King Lear*.) Warren directly
contradicted Willis in front of the committee, saying he had never seen
the King read more than a line and a half at a time.

Accusation and counter-accusation followed fast on each other's
heels. Willis said he had been intimidated by Warren into agreeing to

overly pessimistic reports on the King's health. Warren claimed that although all the royal doctors agreed that anything the King could use to harm himself should be kept away from him, 'the very next day [Willis] put a razor into his Majesty's hand, and a penknife'.[35] Warren also brought up the Lear episode.

To be sure, this squabbling had a lot to do with professional rivalry. Warren kept reminding the committee that he was 'first physician' to the King, and there is no doubt that he disliked playing second fiddle to a Lincolnshire mad-doctor. Willis in his turn testified that he had been told personally by the lord chancellor that although he should consult with the other doctors, 'I was to follow my own line, and do as I had been used to do with patients at home'.[36]

But beyond professional courtesies and the lack of them lay the fact that Willis and Warren were soldiers in a proxy war. The backdrop to their appearance before the parliamentary committee was a struggle for power between the Tory government, led by William Pitt, and the Whig opposition, led by Charles James Fox and supported by George, Prince of Wales, who was on bad terms with his father and who, like his grandfather and great-grandfather before him, had established himself as patron of the opposition.

When the King first fell ill, Parliament stood prorogued. According to constitutional custom and practice, it was the monarch who must appoint the time of the next meeting and the monarch who would open Parliament again with a speech from the throne, or at least appoint commissioners to do so. Until that was done, neither Lords nor Commons could conduct business.[37] And when they did conduct that business, bills passed by both Houses needed the royal assent for them to become law: this was, and still is, signified by letters patent signed by the sovereign and bearing the Great Seal.

The Privy Council had already met with the King's doctors at Whitehall at the beginning of December 1788, before Francis Willis arrived on the scene. Then, they testified that George III was incapable of coming in person to Parliament or of attending to any kind of public business. At that point, the doctors all thought he might eventually recover, although none offered any evidence beyond the rather vague assertion that most people with his affliction did recover. But until he did, Parliament couldn't meet, unless a regent was appointed to act on his behalf. That required legislation; and in a thoroughly British catch-22, the legislation couldn't be passed without the King's assent, which he was incapable of giving.

Pitt put together an entirely unconstitutional scheme under which the lord chancellor, Edward Thurlow, was authorised by both houses to affix the Great Seal to a royal commission for the opening of Parliament, and to a Regency Bill once it had been approved by both houses. Needs must. But the problem for Pitt and the Tories was that the obvious choice of regent was the heir apparent, the Prince of Wales; and once the prince came to power, Pitt knew the Tories were likely to be dismissed, and Charles James Fox would be invited to form a Whig ministry. In the meantime, Fox was arguing that since the King was incapable of acting as king he was legally dead, and the Prince of Wales should simply inherit the throne. The King's madness had precipitated a desperate struggle for power, with Pitt stalling for time in the hope that George III would regain his senses, and Fox and the prince pressing Parliament to move quickly on the question of the regency before that happened.

On 30 December 1788, Pitt wrote to the Prince of Wales from Downing Street to inform him of the plans for the Regency Bill. He proposed that Queen Charlotte was to be responsible for the care of the King, for the management of his household and for the appointment of household officers and servants. The prince would be 'empowered to exercise the royal authority in the name and on behalf of his Majesty' – with one or two restrictions.[38] He wouldn't be able to dispose of the King's personal property; he wouldn't be able to make grants or appoint to offices for life; and he wouldn't be able to create peerages.

Pitt's intention was to limit the prince's power to put crown resources behind a new Whig administration, and the prince knew it and was furious. After consulting with Edmund Burke, a leading Whig who helped him to draft his reply, he responded with an angry denunciation of Pitt's plan:

> It is with deep regret the Prince makes the observation that there seems to be in the contents of that paper a project for producing weakness, disorder and insecurity in every branch of the administration of affairs, a project for dividing the Royal Family from each other, for separating the Court from the State and thereby disjoining Government from its natural and accustomed support; a scheme for disconnecting the authority to command service, from the power of animating it by reward, and for allotting to the Prince all the invidious duties of Government without the means of softening them to the people by any one act of grace, favour or benignity.[39]

Nevertheless, the prince grudgingly accepted Pitt's terms.

This was how matters stood when Willis, Warren and the other royal physicians were summoned to appear before the committee of enquiry at the beginning of January 1789. Willis had made no secret of the fact that he supported the Tories and loathed Charles James Fox. Robert Fulke Greville, ever the discreet royal equerry, was shocked at how free Willis was with his political views: 'I begin to think Dr Willis is rather too incautious a man for his present conspicuous and responsible situation,' he wrote in his diary. 'At the least he is certainly unguarded and imprudent, and too much so for a man who strongly leans to a political party.'[40] The Whigs on the committee naturally suspected him. Warren, on the other hand, spent rather a lot of time reporting on the King's health directly to the Prince of Wales. That was perfectly natural, of course; but when the Tories on the committee heard how Warren had insisted on going in to see the King against Willis's wishes, and that he had said 'he must go in, for he was a spy upon them all', they were surprised, and pressed the mad-doctor on the point:

> Are you positively sure that those were the very words which Dr Warren made use of, or do you only mean to state the effect and substance of Dr Warren's words on that occasion?
>
> The very words.[41]

The committee hearings finished on 13 January 1789, with both sides convinced of the rightness of their own position. The Tories believed Willis was right, the King was on the mend, and if they played for time there would be no need for a regent. The Whigs agreed with Warren that George was unlikely to recover, and with the prospect of an indefinite regency before them they fought hard against the proposals to limit the Prince of Wales's powers.

If the Whigs had accepted Pitt's proposals, rather than fighting them every step of the way, the Prince of Wales would have been regent by the middle of January and they would have been on their way to government. But their tactics created delays. Pitt kept the Queen informed of developments in Parliament through Lady Charlotte Finch, to whom he wrote from Downing Street with details of the bill's committee stage. And at Kew, Francis Willis continued to put out optimistic reports of the King's recovery.

T HE POLITICS ASIDE, ONE OF THE PROBLEMS was that the King's behaviour changed dramatically from hour to hour. One moment he was quite coherent and happily playing piquet with the Queen (who was now being allowed to visit her husband); the next he was hurling a chair at an attendant, or lying down in the middle of a walk through Kew Gardens and refusing to move. On one occasion Robert Fulke Greville met Spicer, one of Dr Willis's men, coming out of the King's apartment covered in blood. 'He then informed me that the king had been turbulent, and would do only what he chose – that upon being checked he struck Spicer in the face and cut his cheek, and which attack had put him under coercion.'[42]

Nevertheless, there *were* of signs of improvement. The King's insomnia subsided during the first weeks of February so that he was sleeping for seven hours a night. And while he was still excitable, his understanding was returning. Hearing mention of Parliament, he asked if it was really sitting. It couldn't be, he went on. He had adjourned it, and 'therefore if it was now assembled, it was illegal'.[43] Even Dr Warren had to admit that Willis's optimism finally had some substance. The mad-doctor allowed the King to spend his evenings in the Queen's apartment, to walk regularly in the gardens and to use the library. The lord chancellor came for an interview; then Pitt, the Prince of Wales, the Duke of York and various members of the cabinet. George spoke quite coherently and intelligently, and without any of the inappropriate language which had marked his conversation during his illness.

The bulletins announced that 'his Majesty appears to have an entire cessation from illness'.[44] The doctors decided that they could see the King every other day rather than daily. Talk of the Regency Bill faded away at the beginning of March and instead, the papers spoke of a grateful nation granting Francis Willis a pension of £3,000 a year. The Prince of Wales, who had already written his speech to Parliament as regent assuring both Houses 'how difficult and painful … it may be for me to bear the weight which has fallen upon me by my being called to the Government of the Kingdom under such peculiar circumstances', found that weight unexpectedly lifted from him.[45] He tried not to show his disappointment.

On 10 March 1789 houses, public halls and government offices in London and Westminster were illuminated to celebrate George III's recovery. Queen Charlotte ordered that Kew should be lit up as a surprise for the King, with figures of Providence, Health and Britannia. When everything was ready, the five-year-old Princess Amelia led her father by the hand to the window and handed him a paper containing a poem from the Queen, beginning:

> Amid a rapt'rous nation's praise
> That sees Thee to their prayers restor'd,
> Turn gently from the gen'ral blaze,–
> Thy Charlotte woos her bosom's lord.

There was a postscript:

> The little bearer begs a kiss
> From dear papa for bringing this.[46]

CHAPTER TEN

Regent

GEORGE III'S MENTAL HEALTH REMAINED FRAGILE for the rest of his long life. Between the psychotic episode in 1788–9 and a final, protracted bout of insanity which began in 1810 there were at least two recurrences. The first was in February 1801, and the King's symptoms included weeping, insomnia and feverish agitation. They were exacerbated by his fears that he was losing his mind again. Francis Willis, the mad-doctor whose brutal regime had 'cured' the King in 1789, was then in his eighties, but his sons John and Robert had followed him into the family practice and they were called in. The episode, 'a severe trial' in the words of Queen Charlotte, passed in four or five months.[1] There was another in 1804, which was serious enough for the King to be once more restrained in a straitjacket.

The King's mental problems were compounded by the fact that between 1804 and about 1808 he developed cataracts in both eyes, which became so severe that he was virtually blind. But it was his anxiety over the health of Amelia, his favourite child, which proved the catalyst for another bout of madness. On 25 October 1810, when a small gathering was held at Windsor to mark the fiftieth anniversary of his accession to the throne, it was obvious that all was not well. Cornelia Knight, a companion to Queen Charlotte, described 'the dreadful excitement in his countenance' as the Queen led him round the room. When he came to Cornelia he said, 'You are not uneasy, I am sure, about Amelia. You are not to be deceived, but you know that she is in no danger.' At the same time, he squeezed her hand so hard that she would have cried out if the Queen hadn't dragged him away. She was so shocked that when tea was served she could hardly take her cup, her hand was shaking so much.[2]

The King's concern for Amelia was well founded. At one o'clock on the afternoon of Friday 2 November, his physician extraordinary, Sir Henry Halford, put a lighted candle close to the lips of the twenty-seven-year-old princess and announced that it was over. Her sister Mary kissed her and then left to scribble a hurried note to the man Amelia had loved, royal equerry Charles Fitzroy: 'Our beloved Amelia is no

A VOLUPTUARY under the horrors of Digestion.

The Prince Regent was
not an attractive figure.

more but her last words to me were, "Tell Charles I die blessing him."'[3]

A consumptive, George III's favourite daughter had been in fragile
health for years. The day after her death her brothers and executors, the
Prince of Wales and the Duke of Cambridge, opened her will to find that
apart from a few small bequests, she had left her entire estate to Colonel
Fitzroy. The next day, they summoned the equerry to Windsor, where
the prince gave him a fraternal hug, said he looked upon him as Amelia's
husband, and then suggested that Fitzroy might assign all rights in her
will over to him and his brother. This would mean that his name needn't
appear when the will was proved, and a scandal would be averted. Of
course, it would only be a nominal resignation of his rights as residuary

legatee, said the prince, since the executors would make sure everything was done in accordance with Amelia's wishes.

An honourable man, Fitzroy wrote out a paper formally requesting the prince and the duke 'to accept the office of residuary legatee, to the Princess Amelia's will instead of me Charles Fitzroy'. The wording was checked with the princess's solicitor, Charles Bicknell, who happened to be waiting in the next room; and the equerry was urged to go and spend a few days at Cranbourne Lodge on the edge of Windsor Great Park, the home of Sir George Villiers, a groom of the bedchamber and a friend of Fitzroy's. The prince would send to him very soon, 'as he should wish constantly to confer with him'.[4]

But far from conferring with Fitzroy, the prince and his brother proceeded to dispose of their sister's worldly goods as they saw fit, and without any reference to him. His anguished letters were ignored, or referred to Bicknell, and when he sought legal advice of his own, he was told that short of creating an enormous scandal and going through the courts, there was no chance of him resuming 'the power he has thus imprudently abandoned'.[5]

A month or two after Amelia's death, a cartload of goods arrived without notice at Fitzroy's country house, Sholebrook Lodge in Northamptonshire. They included some empty bookshelves and a small quantity of plate from which the princess's cypher and coronet had been clumsily removed. There was a mahogany box which was open, empty and keyless, and a red box, also keyless, which Fitzroy couldn't open because it was locked. That was all Amelia's lover ever received. He resigned as royal equerry in 1811.

THE TEA PARTY AT WINDSOR ON 25 OCTOBER 1810, where the King squeezed Cornelia Knight's hand so tightly, turned out to be George III's last public appearance. Four days later the prime minister, Spencer Perceval, found the King's language inappropriate, his speech hurried. The politician George Canning was more direct. 'Poor old Knobbs is as mad as ever he was in his life,' he told his wife.[6]

By the end of the month Windsor was once again issuing daily bulletins on 'the melancholy state of his majesty's health'.[7] Amelia's death on 2 November made things worse: Robert Willis was called in, and he judged that the King needed forcible restraint. The Archbishop of Canterbury was ordered to prepare a form of prayer 'to Almighty God for the restoration of his Majesty's health', which was read out in churches across the country: 'Raise, we implore thee, our beloved Sovereign from the bed of sickness and of affliction; soothe his parental cares; restore him to his family, and to his people.'[8]

The doctors' reports over the next month describe George as 'very disordered and irascible, exceedingly talkative and impatient, turbulent and incoherent'.[9] He couldn't sleep, and his condition deteriorated to such an extent that he was kept away from any interactions with the court or even with his family. He suffered from hallucinations, sometimes believing he could raise the dead or even that he was himself dead; he made embarrassingly explicit sexual remarks, and returned to his old fantasy that he was married to 'Queen Esther', the Countess of Pembroke. Thomas Garth, Princess Sophia's old lover and still an equerry, was shocked at the King's language, which he said was 'very incorrect indeed'.[10]

To begin with, everyone hoped – or pretended to hope – that the King's madness was temporary. Addressing the House of Lords on 16 November, Lord Chancellor Eldon reported that 'it was the opinion of the physicians who attended the royal person, that his Majesty's lamented indisposition was brought on entirely by the heavy pressure of domestic affliction, in the illness of a beloved daughter; and that there was no reason for not entertaining confident expectations of his Majesty's recovery'.[11] In the meantime, however, the business of government had to go on. And although he had periods of remission, when he enjoyed playing his harpsichord and his flute, George's unpredictable behaviour meant he was unable to carry out any of his duties as king, and hopes for a swift recovery faded. He showed a degree of irritability, reported the Willis brothers in September 1811, 'which could only be met by coercion, and which was only varied by occasional exclamations and noises without meaning'.[12] On 3 November 1811, they reported that although he was in high spirits during dinner that day, singing and laughing, he refused to make use of a pot and instead wet himself, so that 'a quantity of water was seen running through the chair'.[13]

Long before this, Parliament had resurrected the measures for a regency which had come so close to being put in place in 1788–9. (And there were pointed questions in the House of Commons as to why they hadn't been implemented in 1801 or 1804, when the King, although plainly out of his mind, had continued to give his assent to various bills.) In the third week of December 1810 Spencer Perceval's government prepared a bill 'providing for the exercise of the royal authority, should the king's indisposition unhappily be protracted'.[14] As before, the proposal was to hand limited authority to the Prince of Wales, and as before, the prince objected to any limits being placed on him. This time Perceval overcame them by suggesting that if George III hadn't recovered his wits within a year, the Prince Regent would have full authority to act in the King's place.

So on 5 February 1811 the 'Act to provide for the administration of the royal authority, and for the care of his majesty's royal person, during the continuance of his majesty's illness' passed into law.[15] The Prince of Wales was declared prince regent. His signature, 'George P. R.', was 'deemed and taken to be to all intents and purposes his majesty's royal sign manual'. For the time being, he wasn't allowed to meddle with the composition of the government or to dole out offices, something he rather wanted to do; but if he were still regent in twelve months' time, the full powers of the sovereign were to be his. The care of the King and the management of the royal household were given to Queen Charlotte, who was aided by a council consisting of the lord chancellor, the archbishops of Canterbury and York and a handful of privy counsellors. This Queen's Council had the power to examine the King's physicians under oath at any time, and was tasked with making quarterly reports on the King's health to the Privy Council.

It's fair to say that the forty-eight-year-old Prince of Wales, now *de facto* head of state, had not led a blameless life. 'His professed admiration of the fair sex in general', wrote one of his more discreet biographers, 'was a bar to his entering into an indissoluble engagement with an individual'.[16] He had enjoyed a string of mistresses, in other words, beginning as a teenager when he was said to have had sexual relationships with a groom's wife and one of his mother's maids of honour. His professed admiration of the fair sex in general continued, as he added actresses, friends' wives, prostitutes and statuesque peeresses to his list of conquests.

There was nothing particularly unusual in that. But the fact that he had married one of his mistresses was unusual. So was the fact that Maria Fitzherbert was a Roman Catholic: the 1701 Act of Settlement disqualified anyone who was a Catholic, or who married a Catholic, from inheriting the throne.

The prince had begun his pursuit of Maria Fitzherbert in March 1784. He was twenty-two. She was six years older and already twice widowed. Her initial rejection of him provoked a frenzy of desire: he offered to marry her, and when he heard she was planning to avoid his advances by fleeing to France he stabbed himself, then sent a deputation including his surgeon and his groom of the stool to tell her that he would tear open his bandages unless she came to see him. He wept, he rolled about on the floor, he banged his forehead hysterically. The Whig politician Lord Holland reported that he swore 'he would abandon the country, forego the crown, sell his jewels and plate, and scrape together a competence to fly with the object of his affections to America'.[17] He wrote Maria long, passionate letters, calling her 'my beloved wife' and swearing there was no sacrifice 'that I have not and will not make for thee; thou art a treasure to me I never can part with'.[18]

Eventually she agreed to marry, a reluctant Cinderella with an insistent but unappealing Prince Charming. The couple were secretly wed in December 1785, by one of the prince's chaplains who had been jailed for debt and who agreed to perform the service in Maria's Mayfair drawing room in return for having his debts paid. The union was invalid – the 1772 Royal Marriages Act made any marriage contracted by a member of the royal family without the consent of the sovereign null and void – and the couple couldn't live together in public. Nor did the relationship last for long. By the end of the 1780s there was gossip that 'he is quite tired of her, and in love elsewhere'.[19] Nevertheless, and through a number of separations and reconciliations, the couple remained close right up until the regency, in spite of the prince's numerous affairs and his legal marriage in 1795, to Princess Caroline of Brunswick-Wolfenbüttel. During this second wedding ceremony, the prince was so drunk that he had to be held upright. He spent his wedding night unconscious on the floor before climbing into bed with his new wife the next morning. Their only child, Charlotte, was born nine months later, by which time the royal couple were living apart.

The prince's second marriage was forced on him by his father in return for an agreement to extricate him from one of his periodic financial crises. Almost as a reaction against George III's staid, down-to-earth domestic values, his eldest son had been determined to live beyond his means ever since he had means to live beyond. In 1784, for example, he asked his father for help with debts that already amounted to more than £100,000. That help was not forthcoming, and when he asked again in the spring of 1786, he calculated that he needed £270,000. Again, his plea met with an angry response: 'The Prince of Wales has nothing to expect from me', his father told him, 'till I see reason to expect that the attempt to relieve him may be effectual, instead of probably serving only to involve him still deeper.'[20] The prince responded with a show of petulance, announcing, 'I am compelled to dismiss ... all the gentlemen belonging to my family who have served me with zeal, attachment and fidelity ever since I appointed them.'[21] His grooms of the bedchamber, his gentlemen ushers, his equerries – all were fired. This infuriated the King even more.

One of the main bones of contention between father and son was the prince's town residence, Carlton House. When the prince came of age in 1783, the King had agreed he should have his own household, and gave him Carlton House on Pall Mall, which was a short walk from St James's Palace and boasted a garden front opening onto St James's Park. The prince immediately set about modernising his new home. He commissioned a massive refurbishment from Henry Holland, who had recently designed Brooks's club around the corner, of which the prince was a member. Holland's estimate for the works at Carlton House was £18,000. By 1784 this had risen to £30,250. In 1786, the prince informed his father that £79,700 was needed 'for completing, finishing and furnishing the works and designs now in hand at Carlton House'.[22] The fact that he had slipped this sum into the statement of outstanding debts that he sent to his father (along with a further £30,000 'for incidental charges') sent the King into a rage. 'A moment's reflection', he fumed, 'ought to have made the Prince of Wales sensible of the impropriety of offering such a paper to my consideration.'[23]

Father and son came to an accommodation in 1787, with George III agreeing to pay £161,000 towards the prince's debts and granting him an extra £10,000 a year. The prince re-engaged his household officers, and Parliament voted £20,000 towards the completion of Carlton House, although Holland now reckoned the works 'necessary to be done in order to complete the palace for habitation' amounted to £81,200. And note the use of the word 'palace'.

The prince's financial crises continued into the 1790s, and work on Carlton House was periodically suspended as he failed conspicuously to live within his income. (He was also paying for work on the Marine Pavilion at Brighton, a staid neo-Classical villa designed by Henry Holland, which was soon destined to disappear beneath the weight of John Nash's spectacular blend of Moorish, Gothic and Indo-Chinese.) After Holland's death in 1806 a string of designers, craftsmen and advisers, including the art dealer Walsh Porter, the clockmaker Benjamin Lewis Vulliamy and the architect Thomas Hopper, furnished and decorated Carlton House. James Wyatt and John Nash would later be involved in further remodelling, only for Carlton House to be

GUDGEON FISHING a la Conservatory.

A cartoon satirises the fête held at the Prince Regent's Carlton House on 19 June 1811. Contemporaries made much of the table decorations which included a stream, complete with fish, running down the middle of the prince's dining table.

demolished in 1826 when the Prince Regent, now George IV, decided it was in too public a position and opted instead to move to Buckingham House.

Having yearned for real power for so long – at forty-eight he was the oldest Prince of Wales since Richard of York died at the Battle of Wakefield in 1460 – the prince was shocked to find out that as regent, power, even limited power, brought with it responsibilities. 'Playing at king is no sinecure,' he exclaimed when he saw how many papers he was required to wade through.[24] 'The Prince is very nervous,' wrote one MP that summer, 'as well he may be at the prospect before him, and frequent in the course of the day in his applications to the liquor chest.'[25] Nevertheless, the trappings of power appealed to him, as did the extravagant public display of those trappings. It had been the custom, when George III was well enough, for polite society to gather every June at St James's Palace for a grand ball to celebrate his birthday. Oblivious to advice that with his mad father kept under restraint at Windsor, now wasn't quite the time for a party, the Prince Regent decided that in place of the usual birthday ball he would hold a grand entertainment of his own at Carlton House to mark his elevation to the regency.

Invitations to the fête at Carlton House went out to 2,000 of the nobility and gentry, government ministers, ambassadors and other distinguished foreigners. Doors opened at nine o'clock on the night of

19 June 1811, with one entrance for those who came by coach and another for those who preferred to arrive by sedan chair. The long sequence of state rooms facing The Mall, which included an astonishing cast-iron Gothick conservatory, was filled with supper tables for VIPs – the Prince Regent, the royal dukes, the most distinguished members of the aristocracy and the most illustrious foreign diplomats. The rest were catered for at tables set up under 45,000 square feet of canvas awnings and in marquees in the garden, which was lit by thousands of lights and festooned with artificial flowers. 'There will be 2,000 yards at least of the latter used,' predicted the press.[26]

The *pièce de résistance* was the conservatory, where the prince presided over the festivities:

> The upper end [went the official account of the evening] was a kind of circular boufet, surmounted by a medallion, with the initials G.P.R. lined by festoons and antique draperies of pink and silver, and partly filled by mirrors, before which, on ornamented shelves, stood a variety of vases, candlesticks, &c. of the most gorgeous gold plate … In front of the regent's seat, there was a circular basin of water, with an enriched temple in the centre of it, from whence there was a meandering stream to the bottom of the table, bordered with green banks. Three or four fantastic bridges were thrown over it, one of them with a small tower upon it, which gave the little stream a picturesque appearance. It contained also a number of gold and silver fish.[27]*

Two bands of the Guards in state uniform played to entertain the guests throughout the night. Supper was announced at 2.15 a.m. and everyone lined up to process from the state rooms down to the garden range, a sight which moved commentators to paroxysms of wonder and admiration at the sight of hundreds of women 'in white satin, silks, or muslins, embroidered or spangled with silver, having each a plume of ostrich feathers, from eight to fourteen in number, and they waving on their heads, and reflected in the serpentine brook before them; it was really a silver flood, and these were its tributary streams'.[28] Even the

---

* The stream provoked some laboured wit. 'It was observed by Mr Jekyll [the lawyer Joseph Jekyll] … that the Lords Rivers and Brooke should be Stewards, and Admiral Fish master of the ceremonies. Mr Manners Sutton [brother of the Archbishop of Canterbury] added, "Yes, and the Bishop of Bath and Wells Chaplain." Somebody near said, "The Banks family, I perceive, are on both sides."' *Lancashire Gazette and General Advertiser*, 29 June 1811.

old court at Versailles, declared the *Annual Register*, 'could never have more attractively set forth the elegant fascinations of fashionable life and exalted rank'.[29] Armed soldiers kept guard on all the approaches to the building.

The Carlton House fête was the talk of London. (It was also the occasion of the prince's final break with Maria Fitzherbert, who, when told that she wasn't going to be allowed to sit at the prince's table, went off to Brighton, where local society treated her like a queen for the rest of her life.) The event aroused so much interest that the prince agreed to keep all the decorations for the fête in place and open Carlton House to the public on the following Saturday, Monday, Tuesday and Wednesday. Admission was by ticket and was supposed to be limited to people known to the Prince Regent's household and their connections. Notices were put up at the gate telling visitors not to touch; sticks, parasols and umbrellas were banned; and people were urged to pass through the rooms as quickly as possible out of consideration for those who were still waiting to get in. 'The yeomen of the guard, the livery servants in their state liveries, and the pages in their state uniforms [will] attend to give it the same effect as at the time of the fête,' announced a notice in the *Morning Post*.[30]

The crowds that turned up on the Saturday and Monday were manageable, but on the Tuesday there were between 20,000 and 30,000

The actor Charles Mathews giving a private performance for George IV at Carlton House, 1825. While Mathews (left) was giving his impression of fellow-actor John Kemble, the king interrupted him and gave his own impression, 'with the most powerful similitude to the actor's voice and manners,' according to a contemporary.

people at the door, 'all of them highly respectable', according to the press.[31] The cards of admission (and one wonders exactly how many had been distributed over the preceding week) were generally for parties of seven or eight people, but the size of the crowds gathered at the gate led household officials to begin admitting a few hundred at a time into the

entrance courtyard, and then phasing entrance into the house itself as and when there was room. Those who had toured the state rooms couldn't get out for the crush, and in the end the St James's Park entrance was opened up as an exit point. The prince's men, led by his close friend the Earl of Yarmouth, did their best to control the crowds, but it was a hot day and people lost scarfs and cloaks as they jostled for position. 'Some lost their shoes', reported the *Morning Post*, 'and a variety of ornaments were torn off and trod upon.'[32] Several people fainted. The Earl of Yarmouth was seen hauling victims in at a window of the great hall. Eventually Life Guards were called to control the milling traffic in Pall Mall and to police the entrance gates.

Wednesday was the last day. An announcement had come from Carlton House the previous evening, emphasising that no more cards of admission would be issued or honoured after the gates closed that evening. From six in the morning, carriages began to converge on Pall Mall. By seven, there were several thousand people waiting at the gates, desperate for a glimpse of the wonders within; and when those gates were opened at eleven, soldiers were needed to keep order. People kept arriving, and by mid-afternoon it was obvious that the admission system of allowing no more than 200 at a time into the entrance courtyard, at roughly thirty-minute intervals, meant that most were going to be disappointed. Lord Yarmouth came out to say His Royal Highness asked everyone to be patient, and that he had directed the doors to be kept

The Gothic Dining Room at Carlton House, designed for the Prince Regent in 1814 by John Nash. Eclectic and exuberant, the room exemplified the Prince Regent's extravagant tastes.

open until seven that evening so that as many people as possible could be admitted. Then the gate was opened to admit another 200, and there was a stampede.

Two young women went down and were trampled in the rush. First reports said that one had broken her thigh in two places and was unlikely to live, but it turned out she was only bruised. An elderly woman and a man were knocked over. The Prince Regent's doctor was called out to treat the injured. Female servants ran out into the courtyard with jugs of cold water and 'restorative viands' to revive those who had fainted or collapsed.[33] Horse Guards trying to keep the crowd back were pushed along in the surge, so that their mounts reared up and came down on the people closest to them. The shoes lost in the Carlton House courtyard filled a large tub, and attendants invited those who had lost them in the melee to rummage through and find their property.

> Many ladies, however, and also gentlemen, might be seen walking away in their stocking feet [declared the *Hampshire Telegraph*]. About a dozen females were so completely disrobed in the squeeze, they were obliged to send home for clothes, before they could venture out in the streets; and one lady was so completely disencumbered of all dress, that a female domestic, in kind compassion, wrapped her up in an apron.[34]

Eventually the Prince Regent's brother, the Duke of Clarence, appeared and clambered up a ladder to stand on top of the wall overlooking the courtyard, from where he addressed the crowd. He said that although his brother was happy to gratify the public's curiosity, he had been advised to shut the gates of Carlton House and keep them shut for the rest of the day. As the crowd limped away, notices went up on the walls announcing that the mansion would not be open to visitors again.

⸺•⸺

TOWARDS THE END OF 1811 IT WAS OBVIOUS THAT GEORGE III was still not fit to resume his duties, and Prime Minister Perceval and Lord Liverpool for the government started discussions with the Prince Regent and his advisers on the shape and the financing of the royal household in the longer term. They agreed to continue most of the provisions set out in the Regency Act. George III would be allowed a small household at Windsor, managed by Queen Charlotte. The main household was transferred to the Prince Regent, and resources were split between the court at St James's Palace, which was increasingly becoming a home for ceremonial sinecures, and Carlton House, where the 'real' royal household lived.

Several times during the nine years of the regency Parliament attempted to establish how the Regent was spending the money he received from the civil list. The Commons demanded lists of plate and jewels; they wanted an account of furniture supplied 'for the use of illustrious visitors and their suite'; and they wanted to know what happened to it when those visitors departed. They wanted to know salaries, wages, kitchen expenses, how many horses were kept, how much coal was delivered to Windsor in any one year.

The balance of power between sovereign and Parliament was shifting – had been shifting since the seventeenth century, when Parliament got rid of two kings who thought their right to rule outweighed everything. Now the sovereign ruled, in so far as he or she ruled at all, by consent of Parliament. And Parliament held the purse strings, as the civil list came to be viewed as a straightforward grant of money to the sovereign. The Treasury, rather than the monarch or the regent, had a right to make decisions on how it was spent. If the Prince Regent's expenditure exceeded his income, and it usually did, then the Treasury wanted to know why, and what was being done about it.

If the prince thought things would be different when he was king, he was to be disappointed. George III died on 29 January 1820, leaving his fifty-seven-year-old son to ascend the throne at long last as George IV. The new king was voted £850,000 a year on the civil list: but when he announced that from now on, he would give orders directly to the lord chamberlain, the lord steward and the master of horse, and that departmental finances were to be 'entirely subject to His Majesty's control and government', the Treasury said that wasn't how things were done any more.[35] George IV had to back down.

The King had domestic problems of another kind. Although he and Caroline of Brunswick had separated in 1796, less than a year after their wedding, they were still married. In the first years of the new century rumours began to circulate about her indiscreet behaviour. It was claimed that she had had a child, and in 1806 the Prince of Wales, as he then was, persuaded ministers to appoint a commission of inquiry. The commissioners heard Caroline accused of adultery, or as near as, with a string of people, including Admiral Sir Sidney Smith, a Captain Manby, and the painter Sir Thomas Lawrence, who stayed late when she was sitting for her portrait. 'One night I saw him with the Princess in the

Blue Room [at Montague House, her London residence],' deposed one of her servants. 'When I supposed that he had gone to his room, I went to see that all was safe, and I found the Blue Room door locked, and heard a whispering in it, and I went away.'[36] The proceedings were rather unsavoury. Maids and laundresses were examined about the state of the princess's bedsheets, and forged notes purporting to be from her were produced. However, the commission found no evidence of adultery, although it did censure Caroline for impropriety.

George III had always been quite fond of his daughter-in-law, championing her right of access to her daughter, Princess Charlotte. After the Prince of Wales became regent in 1811 her position was weakened. Her husband's supporters resurrected the old charges, and she eventually found it easier to leave the country, going home to Brunswick and then buying an estate on Lake Como. Princess Charlotte, who by now was married to Prince Leopold of Saxe-Coburg, died in childbirth in 1818, distancing Caroline further from the English court, and she seems to have led a happy if eccentric life in the company of a handsome young Italian named Bartolomeo Bergami.

Then came George III's death, and with it her husband's accession to the throne and the thought that she was queen of Great Britain. Even now she might not have acted on the thought; but George IV demanded that she shouldn't have a part in the coronation, and that she should be excluded from the Anglican liturgy's prayers for the royal family. This, coupled with the fact that foreign courts were failing to recognise her new status, seems to have convinced her to return to England and fight her case.

In a bid to keep her away, the government tried to buy her off, proposing an annuity of £50,000 if she didn't cross the Channel. 'She will not come, unless she is insane,' said Lord Chancellor Eldon.[37] But she did come, landing at Dover on 5 June 1820 and making a triumphal progress into London, where public sympathy towards her as a wronged woman, combined with antipathy towards the dissolute and ungallant king, made her a popular heroine. Women waved handkerchiefs and hung flags from windows; men waved their hats and cried, 'Long live Queen Caroline!' Her coach, accompanied by a horde of riders and carriages, drove past Carlton House, to the embarrassment of the guards on duty, who reluctantly presented arms. After vanishing into the house where she was staying, in South Audley Street, Mayfair, she appeared on the balcony and bowed, to the delight of the crowd. 'The most splendid pageant, the most imposing theatrical exhibition,' declared *The Times*, 'never imparted a more genuine delight than seemed to pervade all ranks of spectators at this instance of condescending kindness.'[38] There were demonstrations of support all over the country. The King's political opponents rallied to Caroline's side. So did the poets:

> The meanest subjects in your royal heart
> Justice and mercy, grace, and honour find.
> May I not claim at least a subject's part
> In all your noble qualities of mind?[39]

The King was determined that Caroline would never be his queen, and just as determined that she wouldn't remain his wife. Never a man to care too much about public opinion, his response to the adulation was to lodge with Parliament a dossier of evidence of his wife's infidelities. This had been compiled in Italy by a three-man commission sent there in 1818 for just this purpose. The government decided it was so serious that an official inquiry was needed, and on 17 August the House of Lords gathered for what became known as the 'Trial of Queen Caroline'.

It wasn't a conventional divorce trial. The King's advisers wouldn't allow that, for fear that Caroline would introduce counter-evidence of her husband's adultery, of which there was plenty. There was also the legal point that in common law, a husband couldn't be said to have suffered any injury if his wife committed adultery while they were separated. The government toyed briefly with a charge of high treason, arguing that the Treason Act of 1351 included an offence of sexual activity by the wife of the king's eldest son and heir. But the relevant clause in the Act was aimed at the *man* who engaged in such activity; and since in this case the act had taken place abroad and the man was an Italian who owed no allegiance to the British king, Bartolomeo Bergami couldn't be said to have committed treason, and therefore Caroline couldn't have abetted him.

In the end Parliament's law officers advised the hearing of a bill of pains and penalties, a rather exotic strategy by which the Queen's marriage could still be dissolved if she were found guilty. Adultery by a queen might not be treason, argued the prime minister, Lord Liverpool, but it was still a crime against the state. ('A bill of pains and penalties is an awkward name,' declared Lady Cowper; 'it sounds to the ignorant as if she was going to be fried or tortured.'[40])

The 'trial', which was actually the second reading of a bill 'to deprive Her Majesty Caroline Amelia Elizabeth of the Title, Prerogatives, Rights, Privileges, and Pretensions of Queen Consort of this Realm, and to dissolve the Marriage between His Majesty and the said Queen', accused the Queen of carrying on 'a licentious, disgraceful, and adulterous intercourse' with Bartolomeo Bergami, 'a foreigner of low station', thereby bringing 'great scandal and dishonour … upon your majesty's family and this kingdom'.[41] It began on 17 August. The Queen was there in person to watch the start of the proceedings: dressed in black and wearing a white lace veil, she was driven from Brandenburg House in Hammersmith, where she had set up her small court, and past Carlton House again on her way to the palace of Westminster, accompanied by cheering crowds crying, 'God bless her!' 'The shouts of the immense multitude which accompanied her, and which, from the appearance of those who composed it, might be said to be a fair representation of the different classes that constitute the frame of society in this country, were the loudest we ever heard,' declared a contemporary.[42]

As the hearing went on – and it went on for nearly three months – the Queen watched as servant after servant was called to give intimate details of her private life. It was a difficult experience. When one of her footmen, Theodore Majocchi, was ushered in and placed before the bar of the Lords, she cried out, 'Theodore! Oh, Theodore! Oh, no, no.' Or perhaps, as the press was swift to speculate, '*Tradidore, Tradidore!*' (Traitor, Traitor!)

The King's Milan commission had done its work thoroughly. A man who had been a mate on a ship which took Caroline and Bergami around the Mediterranean in 1816 was called to testify that they had adjoining cabins, and that he had sometimes seen Bergami 'sitting on the bench near to the main-mast, and the princess sitting on his lap or thigh, with an arm round his neck over his shoulder'.[43] Her cook testified that during the voyage the couple sometimes slept in the same tent on deck. Her maid said that sometimes her mistress's bed had not been slept in. An innkeeper saw them alone in a gondola at Venice. A painter glimpsed them with their arms round each other: 'Were their faces near each other, or how?' he was asked. 'Their faces were at a distance, for she is short and he is tall,' was the common-sense reply.[44]

And so it went on. But the evidence, while compelling, remained resolutely circumstantial. It was given largely by foreigners, and everyone in the chamber and the country knew that foreigners weren't to be trusted. And it took on the nature of a witch hunt, which more and more peers found distasteful. The bill of pains and penalties passed its second reading, but by a much smaller majority than Lord Liverpool had expected. When the third reading passed in the Lords by a majority of just nine, Liverpool realised there was no chance of getting it through the Commons. On 10 November 1820 he rose to tell the Lords that 'he could not be ignorant of the state of public feeling', and that his government 'had come to the determination not to proceed further' with the bill.[45]

The country went wild. A performance at Covent Garden Theatre that night was brought to a standstill by cries of 'The Queen! The Queen!' Eventually, after 'Rule Britannia' failed to satisfy the audience, the orchestra played 'God Save the King', but every stanza concluded with 'God save the Queen!' Private houses were illuminated all over London in celebration, while the homes of politicians who had led the assault on the Queen had to be protected by soldiers. One house in the City was adorned 'with a splendid crown of variegated lamps, supported by C.R., under which was a star', with the initials of all of Caroline's defending counsel, reported *The Times*.[46]

The Queen's supporters organised a public service of thanksgiving for her deliverance. She processed in triumph from Brandenburg House to St Paul's Cathedral in a state carriage drawn by six chestnut horses, with an escort of 150 outriders. Cheering crowds lined every step of her way. Trumpets sounded a grand salute as she entered Piccadilly, 'but the shrill noise of the martial instrument was quickly drowned in the enthusiastic and deafening shouts of the people,' wrote *The Observer*.[47] Elegantly dressed women occupied every window as she passed; they wore white favours, as did the horsemen, many hundreds of them by now, who rode with her up Fleet Street. Their horses sported white rosettes. The lord mayor was there to greet her as she entered the City, along with other dignitaries, who, along with their municipal robes, wore white rosettes and carried white wands decorated with wreaths of artificial flowers and topped with more white silk rosettes.

As Caroline arrived at St Paul's the crowd broke into roars of 'God save the Queen!' and waved a sea of white handkerchiefs, 'in token of their conviction of her innocence', said *The Observer*'s reporter.[48] The choice of psalms at the service wasn't lost on the congregation: Psalm 140, 'Deliver me, O Lord, from the evil man'; and Psalm 141, 'Lord, I call upon thee; haste thee unto me, and consider my voice when I cry unto thee'. The king decamped to Brighton, announcing he was going to stay there for the winter.

But the mob was fickle, and the Queen's reputation had been tarnished by the lurid accounts of her antics with Bergami. She had her annuity of £50,000 settled on her in February 1821, but her popularity waned over the following months, and George IV was adamant that she

'I present to you your
queen, surely it is not
necessary for her to have
a ticket?'

would never be crowned as his consort. The Privy Council supported
him, saying that she couldn't be crowned against the King's wishes.

That wasn't going to stop her from showing herself at the ceremony.
On Coronation Day, 19 July 1821, she arrived at Westminster Abbey at
6.30 in the morning, in a state carriage and accompanied by Viscount
Hood, her lord chamberlain. The doorkeepers were prepared. They asked
to see tickets.

'I present to you your queen, surely it is not necessary for her to have
a ticket?' asked Lord Hood.

'Our orders are to admit no person without a peer's ticket.'

'This is your queen. She is entitled to admission without such a form.'

'Yes,' said a smiling Caroline. 'I am your queen. Will you admit me?'

'My orders are specific, and I feel myself bound to obey them,' said the doorkeeper.

The Queen laughed – a rather strained laugh, one imagines – and Hood produced a ticket to admit one. He suggested that the Queen might go in alone, and she declined. Some of the crowd gathered in the abbey porch burst out laughing, infuriating Hood. 'We expected to have met at least with the conduct of gentlemen,' he said. 'Such conduct is neither manly nor mannerly.'[49]

Caroline's conduct wasn't considered mannerly, either. She lost credit by it, and there were boos from the crowd as she made her way back to her house. She felt unwell that night and took laudanum; three weeks later she was dead of an intestinal obstruction. There were rumours that her husband had had her poisoned. On her deathbed, she asked that her body should be taken back to Brunswick, and that the inscription on her coffin should read: 'Here lies Caroline of Brunswick, the injured queen of England.'

CHAPTER ELEVEN

The Respectable Household

SIXTEEN YEARS AFTER CAROLINE'S DEATH, and seven years after the death of her unlovely husband George IV, an open carriage accompanied by outriders in royal livery drew up at the grand entrance to the Duchess of Kent's apartments at Kensington Palace. Almost immediately a small, slight figure of a girl was seen being helped into the landau, followed by two older women – the girl's mother and her German governess. A line of mounted lancers on Palace Green held back the cheering crowds as the small procession made its way through Hyde Park and along Constitution Hill before passing under the Marble Arch into the great courtyard of Buckingham Palace.

The eighteen-year-old Queen Victoria was moving house.

IT WAS THURSDAY 13 JULY 1837, and Victoria had been on the throne for twenty-three days. She was leaving Kensington Palace, the place where she had been born and brought up, for a new home with an unhappy history. An early eighteenth-century mansion bought by George III for Queen Charlotte back in 1762, Buckingham House, as it then was, was massively remodelled by John Nash for George IV. The remodelling was unfinished at George's death in 1830, largely because his tastes vastly exceeded his purse in this, as in so many things. Incomplete, hundreds of thousands of pounds over budget and universally loathed – *The Times* described it as 'that accumulation of hunchbacks, that mass of architectural warts and bunions'[1] – it had ruined Nash's reputation and finished his career as a public architect. George IV's successor, his brother William IV, heartily disliked the place, which epitomised all the extravagant flamboyance that he deplored in his brother; and after failing to persuade the government that it should be turned into an army barracks, he offered it as a replacement when the Houses of Parliament burned down in October 1834. Parliament politely declined the gift, and William reluctantly decided there was nothing else but to complete it. Thomas Creevey, who was shown round in 1835, was not impressed:

'Never was there such a specimen of wicked, vulgar profusion,' he thought. 'The costly ornaments of the state rooms exceed all belief in their bad taste.'[2] Work on installing the fixtures, fittings and furnishings was continuing in a desultory fashion at the time of William IV's death.

All that changed with Victoria's accession to the throne in 1837. Within forty-eight hours of becoming queen she gave orders to prepare the apartments at the palace for her inspection; and by the beginning of July the newspapers were declaring that the Queen had signified her intention of moving into the palace 'in about a fortnight'.[3]

A week later there were upwards of 300 men working on fitting up the palace. Plate and kitchen equipment were transferred from St James's Palace on 11 July, and two days later Victoria moved in. 'I am much pleased with my rooms,' she wrote in her journal. 'They are high, pleasant and cheerful.'[4] She took Dashy, her pet spaniel, for a walk in the gardens that afternoon before presiding over dinner for eighteen. Afterwards she sang a little for the company and chatted on the sofa with her lord chamberlain of the household, the Marquess of Conyngham, while her mother played cards.

Not only did the new queen now have an extra palace to maintain,

Buckingham Palace as remodelled by John Nash, 1825-1830. The Marble Arch, designed by Nash to stand in front of the palace, was moved to Cumberland Gate in 1851.

but she had rather less money with which to maintain it. William and his queen consort, Adelaide, had received £510,000 a year from the civil list, including a sum of £110,000 for personal expenses, the privy purse; and £301,800 for salaries and wages, tradesmen's bills and other household expenses. Without precedent for a British monarch, they had almost lived within their means. In 1836, the last full year of William IV's reign, spending on household expenses came to £174,048, against an allowance of £172,500. The largest item in the accounts was £11,381 for upholstery and cabinet-making – a consequence of William's reluctant decision to fit and furnish Buckingham Palace. Household laundry that year cost the king and his consort £3,014, plus £3,130 for washing the table linen. They spent £4,979 on butter, bacon, cheese and eggs, a whopping £9,472 on butcher's meat, and an even more whopping £10,569 on keeping up the royal gardens.

Following the precedent set when William came to the throne in 1830, a parliamentary select committee met to review the civil list at the start of the new reign. Arguing, quite reasonably, that a teenage queen reigning alone had less in the way of personal expenses than a married couple, the committee immediately docked £50,000 from Victoria's privy purse, leaving her with £60,000. They slashed the salaries of the lord chamberlain, lord steward and master of the horse, and proposed reducing the number of lords in waiting from twelve to eight, and the grooms in waiting from thirteen to eight. The allowances for household expenses were raised very slightly to £303,760; but when other cuts had been taken into account, Queen Victoria was left with £385,000 – still a considerable sum, of course, but only three-quarters of her uncle William's civil list.

V ICTORIA'S HOUSEHOLD WAS SUBJECT TO PUBLIC SCRUTINY from the moment she came to the throne. First there was the affair of the 'Boy Jones'. At five o'clock on the morning of 14 December 1838, George Cox, one of the gentlemen porters who guarded Buckingham Palace together with two police inspectors and a contingent of sentries, found a soot-covered youth loitering in the Marble Hall at Buckingham Palace.[5] After a chase through the building, around the gardens and out into the street, the youth was finally brought down by a passing policeman. He was found to be carrying a regimental sword which he had taken from the bedroom of the master of the household. Worse, he had some of the Queen's letters – and what the press demurely called 'a quantity of linen', which turned out to be items of royal underwear.⁶

Brought before the magistrate, the youth said his name was Edward Cotton and that he came from a respectable Hertfordshire family. He claimed to have been living clandestinely at the palace for the past eleven months, stealing food from the kitchens and listening in from behind the furniture when the Queen met with her ministers. None of this was true. He was really a builder's boy named Edward Jones, and he had slipped into the palace through a tradesmen's entrance a couple of days earlier, driven by curiosity. He was indicted for theft, but at the Westminster Sessions his counsel presented the whole business as a childish prank, and the Boy Jones, as the papers came to call him, was acquitted.

The prank didn't seem so funny two years later, when Jones was found in the palace again, this time hiding under the sofa in the Queen's sitting room. At the time of the first incident she had been at Windsor Castle. On this occasion, which took place at the beginning of December 1840, she was not only staying at the palace, but was actually in the bedchamber next door to where the Boy Jones was found, having given birth to her first child only eleven days earlier. (Victoria had married Prince Albert of Saxe-Coburg and Gotha in the chapel royal of St James's Palace on 10 February 1840; she became pregnant almost immediately.) It was her nurse who heard the door of the Queen's apartment creaking open. She called out to know who was there and it closed abruptly; so she bolted it and called Victoria's old governess and confidante, Baroness Lehzen, and one of the pages. After they had searched several rooms, Lehzen pushed aside one of the sitting room sofas, 'and there on the ground', wrote the Queen in her journal, 'lay a lad'. He was taken downstairs, protesting that he meant no harm; he just wanted to see the Queen. 'But supposing he had come into the bedroom – how frightened I should have been.'⁷ Jones got three months in the house of correction.

Two weeks after he was released, a policeman on patrol in the grand hall of the palace saw a face pressed against the glass door. It was Jones. He got another three months, this time with hard labour, before being packed off to join the navy.

Victoria believed Jones was half-witted, but Jones, who was polite and self-possessed at his various public appearances, became something of a popular hero, and the subject of some laboured wit. The wags declared that he was so good at finding his way into the palace that he must be descended from 'In-I-Go' Jones.

There was a more serious side. If a builder's errand boy could gain access to Buckingham Palace at will, then so could someone with less innocent intentions. Two extra police sergeants were brought in after Jones's second visit, charged with patrolling the interiors at night – it was one of these who caught him the third time. But he still managed to gain entrance, and when asked how, would only say he came in by the door, or the window. There were calls for an inquiry into security at the palace, and three additional sentries were posted to guard entry points.

THE EXPLOITS OF THE BOY JONES UNFOLDED against a backdrop of more serious concerns about the operation of Victoria's household. On 10 January 1839 the 32-year-old Lady Flora Hastings, lady in waiting to the Queen's mother, the Duchess of Kent, returned to court complaining that she had been feeling unwell over Christmas. That day she consulted Sir James Clark, physician in ordinary to both the Queen and the duchess, who noted that her stomach was distended. He suspected she was pregnant. For some reason, though, he didn't share his opinion with his patient.

Hastings seemed quite well, and continued to perform her duties, walking daily in Hyde Park with her mistress and attending her to church and to the theatre. But people began to talk. One of Victoria's ladies of the bedchamber, the Marchioness of Tavistock, euphemistically suggested Hastings might be 'privately married'. Another, Lady Portman, asked Clark about her condition, and the physician, whose examination of Hastings had been confined to feeling her abdomen through her dress and stays, was shamefully indiscreet, saying she showed all the signs of expecting a child. The Queen and Baroness Lehzen were convinced the woman was pregnant, and that the father was the courtier Sir John Conroy, who was already rumoured to be the lover of Victoria's mother, the Duchess of Kent. The Queen, who loathed Conroy, confided to her journal that 'the horrid cause of all this is the Monster and demon Incarnate, whose name I forbear to mention', before declaring that the whole business 'makes one loathe one's own sex; when they are bad, how disgracefully and disgustingly servile and *low* women are!'[8]

By the middle of February, the gossip was so widespread that Clark told Hastings only a proper examination by himself and another doctor would clear her character 'and satisfy the ladies of the court'. The Queen dispatched Lady Portman to tell the woman that she shouldn't appear at court until that had happened.[9] The distinguished obstetrician Sir

Lady Flora Hastings,
lady-in-waiting to
Queen Victoria's
mother, the Duchess of
Kent. The unmarried
Lady Flora was falsely
accused by members of
Victoria's household of
being pregnant: in fact
she was suffering from
abdominal cancer.

Charles Clarke was brought in, and on 17 February, after an examination which the patient described as having been conducted 'with more than ordinary disregard to delicacy', Clark and Clarke issued a certificate from Buckingham Palace stating that 'there are no grounds for suspicion that pregnancy does exist, or ever did exist'.[10]

Both men failed to diagnose the real cause of Hastings's condition: she was suffering from abdominal cancer. She would be dead in five months.

Meanwhile, Hastings's family was outraged at what her mother, the Marchioness of Hastings, described in a letter to Queen Victoria as 'the atrocious calumnies and unblushing falsehoods against my daughter's reputation'.[11] They demanded the removal of Sir James Clark from his post as the Queen's physician, and a public apology. Neither was forthcoming: Victoria did apologise privately to Lady Flora, and she and Lord Melbourne, her prime minister, mentor and friend, both reckoned that would be enough.

The Times declared that Melbourne's supporters at court were 'generally persons the most unfit in the world to place in attendance upon the person of a pure and modest woman', and repeated a rumour that the Dean of Chester's daughter, Mary Anne Davys, had resigned her post as extra woman of the bedchamber because the prospect of having to mix with the evil-minded women of the household was too much 'for a person of Miss Davys' purity'.[12]

And the Hastings family went public. On 24 March *The Examiner* published a 'statement in vindication of Lady Flora Hastings' from her uncle, Captain Hamilton Fitzgerald. It set out the narrative of what Fitzgerald called 'the deplorable insult which has been lately offered to my niece'. Fitzgerald also named Lady Tavistock and Lady Portman as the two women who were most active against her, and called for the dismissal of the indiscreet Sir James Clark.[13]

When that produced no response, the marchioness sent her correspondence with Queen Victoria and Lord Melbourne to *The Observer*, which duly reprinted it in full. The Queen was roundly condemned for not leaping to Lady Flora Hastings's defence: she was hissed in public, and when she went to the theatre or rode in the park there were cries of 'Dismiss Lady Portman!' Portman was unconvinced by the medical certificate, and her husband only made matters worse by saying publicly that his wife's conduct required no vindication, 'as a few months would testify'.[14]

Hastings herself reckoned that the whole nasty business had been an indirect attack on the Duchess of Kent, whose bad relationship with her daughter tended to be reflected in relations between the two royal households. The conspiracy, Hastings told her sister and brother-in-law, had been got up by Lehzen, who found willing tools in Clark, Tavistock and Portman. It was 'ultimately directed against the duchess,' she said.[15]

Whatever the truth of the matter, the affair exposed to public gaze the flawed nature of Victoria's household. The diarist Charles Greville went to the heart of things when he declared that

> the Court is plunged in shame and mortification at the exposure
> that the palace is full of bickerings and heart-burnings, while the

whole proceeding is looked upon by society at large as to the last degree disgusting and disgraceful … Though such things happen in the servants' hall, and housekeepers charge still-room and kitchen-maids with frailty, they are unprecedented and unheard of in good society.[16]

———————— · ————————

WEEKS LATER, THIS PUBLIC DISSECTION of the royal household was given new momentum by a political crisis that centred again on the ladies of the Queen's bedchamber. Lord Melbourne's Whig government collapsed on 6 May 1839 and, wretched over the loss of her beloved prime minister, Victoria summoned the Duke of Wellington to the palace and asked him to form a minority Tory ministry. The seventy-year-old Wellington declared he was too old and too deaf, and suggested she ask Sir Robert Peel, who was nearly twenty years his junior. Peel was duly summoned to Buckingham Palace. But both he and the Queen were in for something of a shock.

By the nineteenth century, the political nature of the senior posts in the royal household was an accepted feature of life at court. The lord chamberlain, the lord steward and the master of the horse no longer had much to do with the running of the household, and their names were usually put forward to the sovereign by the current prime minister, as were a cluster of others, including the vice chamberlain, the treasurer and the comptroller of the household. When the government was replaced, so were these courtiers. That was expected. What was not expected was that in his interview with Victoria over the formation of a minority government, Peel told the Queen he wanted to replace her ladies in waiting, too.

Victoria was attended by a mistress of the robes and eight ladies of the bedchamber. The mistress of the robes was a largely ceremonial post: its holder, the Duchess of Sutherland, accompanied the Queen to her coronation in Westminster Abbey, for example, and sat with her and the master of the horse in the state coach on the way to the prorogation of Parliament. In theory the duties of the ladies of the bedchamber were only slightly more onerous. Each one waited on the Queen for two weeks in rotation, so that each individual's average attendance was a little over six weeks a year. When they were in attendance they dined at Her Majesty's table, and took their breakfast and lunch with the lords in waiting and the maids of honour in a room of their own at Buckingham

Palace and Windsor Castle. For this they received an annual salary of £500, the same as the mistress of the robes.

In practice, however, the ladies of the bedchamber – some of them, at least – were close to the Queen. They were her companions, her confidantes. Moreover, they were all closely connected to the Whigs. The Marchioness of Tavistock's brother-in-law, for instance, was the home secretary, Lord John Russell; Lady Portman's husband was active in the Whig cause in the Lords. Another of the ladies of the bedchamber, the Marchioness of Normanby, was married to a lord lieutenant of Ireland who would shortly succeed Russell as home secretary. Yet another, the Duchess of Sutherland, was herself politically active, keeping an influential salon at her vast London mansion, Stafford House. (Coming from Buckingham Palace to visit the duchess, Victoria is supposed to have said, 'I have come to your palace from my house.'[17])

The political connectedness of the Queen's ladies, or more accurately their links to senior Whig politicians, was a problem for the Tory Peel. After discussing matters with the men he proposed to bring into his new cabinet, he resolved to tell the Queen that some of her ladies of the bedchamber had to go. 'It would impair the efficiency and stability of the Government in public opinion, if they did not relinquish their situations,' said Peel.[18]

The idea did not go down well. As soon as he had left the palace, Victoria wrote a note to Lord Melbourne, saying that 'Sir Robert Peel has behaved very ill, he insisted on my giving up my ladies, to which I replied that I never would consent … the Queen of England will not submit to *such* trickery'.[19] Peel was back again that evening, confirming that unless she showed her confidence in the new ministry by bringing in Tories to replace at least some of the Whig ladies, he didn't see how he would be able to form a government.

The following morning Victoria sent a letter to Peel, dictated to her by Melbourne:

> 'The Queen having considered the proposal made to her yesterday by Sir Robert Peel to remove the ladies of her bedchamber cannot consent to adopt a course which she conceives to be contrary to usage and repugnant to her feelings.'[20]

Peel replied within the hour. He resigned.

Victorian's 'excellent Lord Melbourne' promptly stepped into the breach and offered to form another government. 'I grasped his hand in both mine with real feelings of the greatest gratitude,' she wrote.[21] And the bedchamber crisis, as it became known, presented the press on both sides of the political divide with a field day. The Whig newspapers were full of righteous indignation at the impertinence of Peel, who dared to tell his queen whom she could and couldn't have about her. The Tory papers, on the other hand, bemoaned the fact that the opportunity had been lost for 'a clearance of the female household because of their profligate character', and reprinted Captain Hamilton Fitzgerald's statement in vindication of his niece, Lady Flora Hastings.[22]

Coming hard on the heels of the Hastings scandal, and involving some of the same people, the bedchamber crisis encouraged yet more gossip about the moral health and efficiency of the royal household. Peel had deliberately alluded to the recent gossip in a memo to his cabinet in waiting:

> I am to provide the attendants and companions of this young girl, on whose moral and religious character depends the welfare of millions of human beings … I wish to have around her those who will be, to the country and to myself, a guarantee that the tone and temper of their character and conversation will lead to her moral improvement.[23]

After Flora Hastings died at Buckingham Palace that July, the Queen decided her own carriage should follow the dead woman's cortège as a mark of respect. But public opinion was running so high against her over her mishandling of the business with Lady Flora that a massive police presence was judged necessary, to prevent the carriage from being attacked by the angry crowds that gathered. One respectable-looking man pointed with his stick at the royal carriage and shouted, 'What is the use of her gilded trumpery after she has killed her?'[24] At the opera one night someone asked the box-keeper if the queen would be there. 'Oh no,' came the reply. 'She dare not come.'[25]

IN JUNE 1844 ELIZABETH LINDSAY AND HER SISTER ELLEN appeared at the Old Bailey, charged with the theft of a monogrammed counterpane marked 'V.R. 1840' and a quantity of towels, blankets, linen sheets and dusters to the value of £21 2s. 2d., 'the goods of our lady the queen, their mistress'.[26]

The sisters had been employed at Buckingham Palace for fourteen or fifteen years: Elizabeth was a servant in the linen department, and

Ellen was a housemaid. The gist of the charges was that they had stolen the items from the palace and delivered them to their brother James, a surgeon who lodged in Pimlico and who was accused of 'feloniously receiving the said goods, well knowing them to have been stolen'.[27] James's landlord had become suspicious at the arrival of several large chests and, when James was out, he peeked inside, found the linen and reported the matter to the police. All three Lindsays were arrested and examined by a magistrate at Bow Street police station. The matter was serious enough for the lord chamberlain of the household to be present throughout the interviews, which lasted four hours; and for the prosecution, when what the press dubbed as 'the Buckingham Palace case' was heard at the Central Criminal Court, to be led by the solicitor-general himself, Sir Frederick Thesiger.

When the case came to court, all three got off, in spite of being caught red handed with their loot. Some of it was still marked 'V.R.' or 'W.R.' in blue thread, and some clearly showed the royal monogram in blue where the thread had been cut out. Nor were their explanations convincing. James Lindsay, who had the items in his possession, flatly denied knowing anything about them. 'He had charge of them for his sisters, whose perquisites they were, [and] he had nothing more to do with them.' Elizabeth claimed to have been using her own linen for the royal household whenever there was a shortage, and said she took new sheeting to replace it when it wore out. Ellen said she must have mixed up the monogrammed counterpane with one of her own. Both sisters denied all knowledge of what they called 'the duster' and claimed it must have been accidentally put away with the linen, which rather overlooked the fact that there were actually fifty-four brand-new dusters, and that one corner of each — the corner which usually showed the royal mark — had been carefully washed.

Their acquittal was due partly to their previous good character: even Sir Frederick Thesiger had to admit 'there was not the slightest stain upon their characters prior and up to the present transaction,' reported the press.[28] But the jury gave more weight to the testimony of a string of witnesses called by the defence to describe the disorder that prevailed at Buckingham Palace. Four housemaids and three charwomen, all employed there, came forward one after the other to say that it was normal practice to find unmarked towels, dusters, sheets and pillowcases issued to them along with those bearing the royal mark, giving weight to Elizabeth Lindsay's claim that she issued them with her own linen when the need arose. The Queen's laundress, Sophia Harding, testified that over the previous ten years she had frequently received unmarked linen from Elizabeth Lindsay, especially when Victoria (and before her, William IV) was in residence and the palace was busy. 'Some of them had not any mark,' she said under cross-examination by the solicitor-general. 'Others had marks which were not Her Majesty's marks. There were various letters, M and L, and a variety of letters. I have seen towels, dusters, sheets and pillowcases so marked.'

'Do you mean', intervened the incredulous judge, 'that there have been for this length of time things coming which you knew not to be the Queen's property?' The thought that Victoria and her prince consort might have been drying themselves on someone else's towels and sleeping in someone else's sheets appalled him. Not the laundress. 'I cannot say to whom they belonged,' snapped Harding. 'I never made any inquiry how they came there. They were sent with the others, and I of course thought it was right.' When the foreman of the jury pronounced the Lindsays not guilty on all counts, there was cheering and applause in the gallery, and Elizabeth and Ellen both fainted in the dock.

The Buckingham Palace case highlighted the chaotic nature of the royal household, much of which was due to the political nature of the appointments of the three heads of department, which meant frequent changes of personnel as ministries rose and fell. In the fourteen years since William IV had come to the throne in 1830 there had been four masters of the horse, five lord stewards and six lord chamberlains. And since none of them lived at Buckingham Palace, they were often forced to delegate their authority on an ad hoc basis to junior servants who were not up to the job.

Worst of all, there was no coordination between the three departments. Christian Friedrich, Baron Stockmar, a German physician who had been advising Victoria since her accession to the throne and who after her marriage in 1840 continued to act as a sort of unofficial counsellor to her and Prince Albert, set out the weaknesses in the household as he saw them in a memorandum of 1844. His 'Observations on the present state of the royal household, written with a view to amend the present scheme, and to unite the greater security and comfort of the Sovereign with the greater regularity and better discipline of the royal household'[29] pointed out that all the important court appointments were ministerial arrangements, without a proper system of delegation. But Stockmar reserved most of his exasperation for the ridiculous lack of cooperation between departments. The housekeepers, pages and housemaids were under the authority of the lord chamberlain, while all the footmen and

Baron Stockmar, whose investigations into the running of Victoria's household found 'ludicrous divisions' of labour.

under-butlers were under the master of the horse. The rest, including the kitchen staff and the porters, were the responsibility of the lord steward.

> These ludicrous divisions [said Stockmar] not only extend to persons, but they extend likewise to things and actions. The lord steward, for example, finds the fuel and lays the fire, and the lord chamberlain lights it ... The writer of this paper, having been sent one day by her present Majesty to Sir Frederick Watson, then the master of the household [and a member of the lord steward's department],

to complain that the dining room was always cold, was gravely answered, 'You see, properly speaking, it is not our fault; for the lord steward lays the fire only, and the lord chamberlain lights it.'[30]

For the same reason, the lord chamberlain's staff provided all the lamps at the palace, but the lord steward's servants had to clean, trim and light them. The lord chamberlain's people might decide to clean the inside of the windows in the Queen's boudoir; but it was for the master of the horse, who had authority over the woods and forests and hence the exterior of the palace, to decide when to clean the outside of the windows.

> If a pane of glass, or the door of a cupboard in the scullery, requires mending, it cannot now be done without the following process: a requisition is prepared and signed by the chief cook, it is then counter-signed by the clerk of the kitchen, then it is taken to the lord chamberlain's office, where it is authorized, and then laid before the clerk of the works, under the office of woods and forests; and consequently, many a window and cupboard have remained broken for months.[31]

In fact, the main reason for the failings over the Boy Jones affair, argued Stockmar, was that no one person had been on hand to take responsibility for the security of the palace.

The most significant of the baron's proposals for reform involved a fresh look at the job description of the master of the household, who operated rather vaguely as a subordinate officer in the lord steward's department. If all three heads of department would agree to delegate their authority to a single resident master of the household, most of the inefficiencies listed by Stockmar would vanish. This master would be responsible to all three heads, 'but at the same time be able to secure unity of action in the use of the power delegated to him'.[32]

Prince Albert, who took on the responsibility for reforming the royal household, agreed with Stockmar's ideas. At the end of 1844 the existing master of the household, Charles Murray, was edged out and left to pursue a diplomatic career which was notable for two things: as consul-general to Egypt he acquired the first hippopotamus ever brought to England; and as minister-plenipotentiary to the Persian court, he slept with the married sister of the Shah's principal wife and provoked the Anglo-Persian War of 1856–7. His successor as master of the household was Colonel George Bowles, a veteran of the Peninsular and Napoleonic wars, who had seen service at Salamanca, Quatre Bras and Waterloo and who was personally recommended to the Queen by the Duke of Wellington. In line with Stockmar's plan, he was to live at court and take over day-to-day management of the entire domestic establishment. The master of the household's salary was raised from £500 a year to £1,158 in recognition of his new responsibilities.

Bowles was as English as they come, and as reputable – the son of Wiltshire landed gentry, the brother of one admiral and the grandson of another. But the fact that the process of court reform was being driven by two Germans, Stockmar and Prince Albert, didn't go unnoticed. One newspaper helpfully reminded everyone that in the fourteenth century Richard II's chamberlain had been impeached for introducing aliens into the royal household. Even before the Queen's marriage in 1840 to Albert, a move which had provoked a wave of anti-German feeling, suspicions were regularly being voiced over foreign members of the young Victoria's household, especially Louise Lehzen, her governess and confidante, who was held by some to be the person responsible for the Lady Flora Hastings scandal.

This mistrust of foreign influence at court manifested itself in curious ways. When a German palace servant had trouble with his evidence at one of the Boy Jones trials, the gallery laughed at his broken English and the magistrate poked fun at him quite openly. British servants in the household, both high and low, resented interference in their work by Prince Albert, Stockmar and the Germans in Albert's entourage. After Albert appointed a fellow-countryman named Heller to be page of the chambers, one of the English pages over whom he had been placed threatened in front of the prince to throw the man down the stairs, telling Albert to his face that he 'would not be insulted by a foreigner'.[33]

Colonel Bowles served six years as master of the household, overseeing a far-reaching scheme of domestic economies drawn up by Albert at the end of 1844 in an attempt to demonstrate, in the words of one of the prince's earliest biographers, that 'the royal establishment, as it was first in dignity, should also be first in purity, in efficiency, and not least in well-regulated economy'.[34] Bowles and Albert were ably assisted by a Mr Norton, the deputy comptroller of the household and a man of combative disposition: in 1841 Norton had got into an argument at the palace in front of forty-odd members of staff with Charles Francatelli, the chief cook of the royal kitchen. It turned into a fracas which ended in a policeman being sent for to take Francatelli into custody.

Staff who died or left weren't replaced. In recognition of the fact that they only worked for half the year, the royal housemaids – around forty at Windsor and forty at Buckingham Palace – had their wages slashed from £45 a year down to between £12 and £18, depending on length of service. The twenty-five members of the Queen's private band had their wages cut by a third; their traditional allowance of supper with a pint of wine at the end of evening performances at court was abolished. So was the 'red room wine', an allowance of thirty-five shillings a week for officers who sat in the red room at Windsor to supervise the Queen's guard. The guard had been removed years before, but Prince Albert found that the under-butler still took the thirty-five shillings. The practice of replacing all the candles in the palace every day, whether they had been used or not, was stopped, and Albert insisted that candles should stay in place until they had burned for a reasonable time.

The Queen praised Bowles for the way he had 'set many things in the house to rights, placed all on its present admirable footing, kept everything so strait and brought economy into all the departments'.[35]. But by 1851, although he was only sixty-four, his health and his memory were failing. Fortunately, as Albert reported to Stockmar that July, 'the Lieutenant of the Tower, with £700 a year, has been so good as to die, and Bowles is in rapture at being nominated his successor'.[36] Stockmar, who was just about to leave for Europe, sourced Bowles's replacement, a forty-one-year-old army major named Thomas Myddleton Biddulph.

This careful household management led to some startling savings. Between 1843 and 1852 the civil list savings on salaries, household expenses and 'unappropriated monies' – a contingency fund of £8,040 a year – amounted to nearly £55,000. This figure halved over the next ten-year period, perhaps because the royal family now had nine children and were living in Osborne House on the Isle of Wight and Balmoral Castle in the Scottish Highlands as well as at Buckingham Palace and Windsor. But over Victoria's entire reign more than £800,000 in savings were made.[37]

That money didn't go back to the government. Instead, it was transferred to the Queen's privy purse, a case of 'waste not, want not' and a powerful incentive to continue the economies. According to George Anson, keeper of the privy purse from 1847 to 1849, the Queen's affairs were so well managed by the time he took up his post that he thought she would be able to pay for the building and furnishing of Osborne House, at a cost of £200,000, out of her income.

Outside the royal circle there were frequent calls for the civil list to be reduced, and cutting the cost of the royal household was the obvious solution. In 1848 a book called *Sketches of Her Majesty's Household* appeared. It purported to be 'A Guide to Situations in the Sovereign's Domestic Establishment', helping prospective candidates for a place by pointing out whose patronage mattered and where. In fact, by giving its readers details of salaries, duties and pensions in the royal household, it built up into a devastating critique. Why, for example, did the queen need a hereditary grand falconer at a salary of £1,200 a year, when she didn't possess a single hawk? Why were salaries paid to so many ladies and gentlemen of the court for doing absolutely nothing? Did Prince Albert (who had been granted a personal annuity of £30,000 on his marriage) really need the £500 a year he received as ranger of Windsor Home Park? Was the master of the tennis court really worth his salary of £132 a year, since 'there is no tennis court attached to the royal household'? And did the Queen really need a medical team of thirty-three men, including two apothecaries to the person, three apothecaries to the household,

two apothecaries extraordinary and two apothecaries resident on the Isle of Wight? 'In the present lamentably distressed state of the country,' concluded the author of *Sketches*, 'with the alleged necessity for increased taxation staring us fearfully in the face, it may be worthwhile to endeavor to ascertain if some reduction of Her Majesty's civil list could not be effected.'[38] He proposed a saving of £29,104 on salaries paid out of the civil list, which could be achieved by cutting or abolishing sinecures. He also urged the Queen to pay income tax.*

Citing the information in *Sketches of Her Majesty's Household*, the Liverpool Financial Reform Association, a radical free trade group, launched a series of tracts attacking the royal household's finances. 'These remnants of a decayed feudalism appear sufficiently absurd,' declared

Victoria and Albert with their children on the terrace at Osborne House. 'It might be made an excellent home,' declared the queen when she first set eyes on the house in 1844.

* Sir Robert Peel reintroduced income tax in 1842, and suggested to the Queen that she should set an example to her subjects, even though she was not obliged to do so. She paid tax on the privy purse and on her allowance for household expenses, and deducted tax from the salaries of the household. But this was not made public for some time and as a result she was frequently criticised for not paying up.

the association in 1848, 'and would, probably, have gone out with other kindred mummeries which the good sense of this nineteenth century has extinguished, had it not been that, under cover of an antiquated and unmeaning pageantry, many branches of the aristocracy and their needy dependants have been enabled to quarter themselves on the public purse.'[39] The association, whose president was Robertson Gladstone, brother of Liberal statesman William Ewart Gladstone, had a simple solution: immediately cut the civil list from £385,000 to £200,000, and fix it at £150,000 for the Queen's successors. The association didn't presume to suggest from where these cuts might come, beyond arguing that senior officials 'who delight to bask in the sunshine of Court favour, should find in the privilege of so doing their sole reward'.[40]

In 1856 the association returned to the attack. Working through the different departments and offices in devastating detail – *thirteen* porters to bring in the coal? *eleven* members of staff to support the master of the household? – the anonymous author of Tract 14, 'The Royal Household: A Model to Parliament and the Nation', poured scorn on almost all of them. The ladies of the bedchamber should be ashamed of themselves for accepting £500 a year for the honour of keeping the Queen company for six weeks. Viscount Drumlanrig, the current comptroller of the household, was paid £904 for checking the accounts of the lord steward's department, even though that duty 'is, of course, purely imaginary, so far as any vulgar dabbling with figures by the heir to the Marquisate of Queensberry is concerned'.[41] It was a disgrace that the eight lords in waiting took a salary: 'the honour of dining with the queen ought to be sufficient compensation to noblemen who, if they had any chivalrous feeling, would scorn to descend to the class of menials, by taking wages for waiting'.[42] As for the falconless hereditary grand falconer, his role was 'as gross an absurdity as would be that of Hereditary Grand Dragon and Griffin Keeper'.[43]

I
N SPITE OF THE PUBLIC CRITICISM, Victoria and Albert resisted any further attempts to rationalise the household. 'Everything else changes, but the life here never does, and is always exactly the same from day to day, and year to year,' wrote Georgiana Osborne, one of the Queen's maids of honour.[44] That was in 1844, when the wave of household reforms was at its height. She wouldn't have noticed much difference ten or even fifteen years later.

With two exceptions. The first was that in the intervening years the royal couple acquired an army of children, beginning at two o'clock on the afternoon of 21 November 1840, when Victoria gave birth in her bedroom at Buckingham Palace. 'Alas! A girl and not a boy,' she wrote in her journal. 'We were, I am afraid, sadly disappointed.'[45]

Albert was there for the birth. In the next room, the Archbishop of Canterbury, the Bishop of London, the prime minister, the foreign secretary, the lord steward and the master of the horse sat and listened to the labour, heirs to that tradition which held that the birth of a royal baby must be in the presence of the great and the good, there to prevent a clandestine swap.

The baby, Victoria Adelaide Mary Louise, was immediately provided with a wet nurse, Mrs Ratsey, the wife of an Isle of Wight sail-maker. After spending her first week of life in the dressing room next door to Victoria and Albert's bedroom, the little princess was moved to a nursery in the attics. 'Pussy', as she quickly became known, was brought down to her besotted mother twice a day, and the Queen occasionally ventured up to the nursery. 'The baby was looking in great beauty when she was brought down to me' was a typical comment in her journal. And, more colloquially, 'looked such a duck'.[46]

Three hundred and fifty-four days after Pussy's arrival, Victoria gave birth to a boy, the future Edward VII. 'Oh! how happy, how grateful did I feel to that Almighty Providence Who has so greatly blessed me,' wrote the Queen.[47] In February 1841 she had appointed Mrs Southey, sister-in-law of the poet Robert Southey, as superintendent of the nursery; but with the arrival of an heir to the throne, both Victoria and Albert felt a noblewoman would be more appropriate – not a political appointee who was governess in name only, as had happened when the Queen was a child, but someone who lived with the children, with a sub-governess under her.

Their choice was Sarah Spencer, Lady Lyttelton, a widow in her fifties with five grown-up children of her own and a woman who already knew the household well, having been a lady of the bedchamber since 1837. They weren't sure she would accept the role: she had already been left in charge of the children at Windsor for four days during a state visit by the king of Prussia, and she had been anxious then about the responsibility. It was brought home to her each night as she went to check on the access to the children's apartments with General Wemyss, the Queen's aide-de-camp. 'The intricate turns and locks and guardrooms, and the various intense precautions, suggesting the most hideous dangers, which

In *The Royal Family in 1846* Franz Xaver Winterhalter sought to combine regality and domesticity. Although Victoria and Albert were delighted with the painting, it was criticised in the British press: the *Athenaeum* wrote that it displayed 'such a want of taste as to make us frankly rejoice that it is not from the hand of an Englishman'.

I fear are not altogether imaginary, made one shudder!' she confessed to her daughter. 'Threatening letters of the most horrid kind (probably written by mad people), aimed directly at *the children*, are frequently received.'[48]

Victoria and Albert launched a two-pronged assault. First, the Queen took Lady Lyttelton out driving in the park and began to talk, in a roundabout way, of the need for a lady superintendent of the royal children. From there, '[I] gradually felt my way, until I mentioned what was in my mind'.[49] Lyttelton was flattered, but diffident. She said she must talk it over with her brother, Earl Spencer. The next day Albert urged her to think hard about the offer.

Privately, both Victoria and Albert were convinced she would accept: and they were right. A week later they had her in to see them again and talked through the arrangements for the children. 'She is so reasonable and sensible about everything', said Victoria, 'that I am sure it will be an immense advantage to have her at the head of the nursery.'[50]

Lady Lyttelton remained as lady superintendent of the royal children for the next eight years, until in 1850 the death of one of her own daughters in childbirth persuaded her she should leave the household to look after her motherless grandchildren. By then she had a flock of seven princes and princesses in her charge. The latest was Arthur, 'a fine fat prince of blood royal' according to Lyttelton, who arrived on 1 May 1850.[51] Two more arrived in the 1850s, so that by 1857 there were nine children under the age of seventeen in the royal household. So many meant that the nurseries and schoolrooms at Buckingham Palace formed a department of their own, with tutors, governesses and sub-governesses, nursemaids and under-nursemaids. Pussy had a French tutor by the time she was eighteen months old, and a German tutor was appointed for her when she was three and a half.

Lady Lyttelton would show off her charges to other members of the household. At Windsor Castle on Boxing Day 1842, for example, she led two maids of honour and a lady of the bedchamber to the nurseries for a sight of the Princess Royal and the Prince of Wales. Bertie, who was only a year old, had a cold; Pussy ran about and showed off two new frocks given to her by her grandmother, the Duchess of Kent. 'She is very fat,' noted one of the visitors.[52]

As heir to the throne, Bertie's upbringing and education were considered particularly important.* Baron Stockmar argued that the prince's education should make him responsive to change in a rapidly changing world: 'Above all attainments, the Prince should be trained to freedom of thought, and a firm reliance on the inherent power of sound principles, political, moral, and religious, to sustain themselves and produce practical good.'[53]

The regime which Prince Albert and a succession of tutors developed to achieve these high ideals was arduous. Henry Birch, a former Eton master who was brought in as tutor in 1849, taught arithmetic, English and geography, with specialists giving lessons in German, French, handwriting, drawing and music. Drill sergeants coached the young prince in gymnastics, and there were riding masters.

Bertie didn't get on well with the regime or with Birch. The tutor's daily reports to the Queen made it clear that the royal pupil was a problem. 'A very bad day. The Prince behaved as if he were mad, made faces and spat. Poor Dr Becker [Albert's librarian, and Bertie's German

---

* It was left to one of Bertie's tutors to explain the succession to him when he was ten years old. Up until then he had assumed Pussy would inherit the throne.

tutor] complained of having heard a naughty word.'[54] Things were not much better with Birch's successor. Frederick Waymouth Gibbs, a young barrister, took over the education of Bertie and his brother Alfred in 1852, assisted by Becker, the queen's domestic chaplain Gerald Wellesley, and their French master, Dr Voisin. Gibbs increased their hours of study, so that Bertie and his brother Alfred had six or seven one-hour lessons every day except Sunday, beginning at 8.00 a.m. and finishing at 6.00 p.m. Gibbs's fellow-tutors thought this too much: Albert did not, and the regime continued until Gibbs's retirement in 1858 when Bertie reached the age of eighteen. It didn't earn him the affection of the Prince of Wales, who declared how much he missed Birch, and who as a young teenager continued his spitting, swearing and stone-throwing in class.

Parental expectations were high and discipline was strict. Albert authorised the use of corporal punishment on Bertie, who frequently had his ears boxed and his knuckles rapped with a stick. Pussy sometimes flew into shrieking rages and tried to bite Lady Lyttelton. When she was found out for lying that she had permission to put on a favourite pink bonnet, she was shut up in her room with her hands tied together as a punishment. 'As a rule, children are a bitter disappointment,' wrote the Queen, 'their greatest object being to do precisely what their parents do not wish and have consciously tried to prevent.'[55]

·

T HE SECOND GREAT CHANGE in Victoria and Albert's domestic arrangements was the acquisition of two extra homes. In March 1844, they bought the Osborne House estate near Cowes on the Isle of Wight, as a holiday place by the sea. 'I am delighted with the house,' wrote Victoria when they visited that October. 'With some few alterations and additions for the children, it might be made an excellent home.'[56] Under Albert's supervision those few alterations turned into a major remodelling, so that by 1848 an unassuming Georgian block had been transformed into a vast Italianate palazzo with towers and terraces and a self-contained pavilion for the royal family.

The statesman Lord Rosebery said he thought the drawing room at Osborne was the ugliest room in the world – until he saw the drawing room at Balmoral. Victoria and Albert leased their second acquisition, 'a pretty little castle in the old Scotch style', in 1848.[57] Staying on their Aberdeenshire estate each September, they lived quite simply. 'Not merely like private gentlefolk', wrote Charles Greville after a visit in

1849, 'but like very small gentlefolk, small house, small rooms, small establishment.'[58] Greville found them attended by only six people: a lady of the bedchamber, a maid of honour, a young page of honour, the keeper of the privy purse, a new governess and Henry Birch, who was presumably there to ensure the young princes kept up their studies during their holidays. No doubt there was also a small army of domestic servants, but it wouldn't have occurred to Greville to mention them. The royal family's only security was a single policeman who patrolled the grounds alone 'to keep out impertinent intruders and improper characters'.[59]

For a while, they were happy. But history repeated itself: the pretty little Scotch castle was too small, and in 1852 they bought the Balmoral estate outright and built a larger, less pretty castle in the Scotch Baronial style. Prince Albert deliberately chose a less accomplished exponent of the style, William Smith of Aberdeen, so that he could retain control of the project (as he had at Osborne, where his partner was the builder and developer Thomas Cubitt). The result, a huge granite complex peppered with turrets and crow-stepped gables and dominated by a 100-foot-high tower which was itself capped with corner turrets and battlements, was everything the couple wished for.

There was a determined Scottishness about life at Balmoral, from the

The Ballroom, Balmoral Castle, by William Simpson, 1882. Queen Victoria looks on from the alcove as guests and members of the household dance a traditional Scottish reel.

traditional Scotch reels which Victoria and Albert danced after dinner to the kilted gillies and the tartan linoleum in the servants' quarters. There were wailing pipers to wake them in the mornings, and sword dances and tartan ribbons. Every September the couple would take their children to see the Highland games at the Braemar Gathering, Albert in his kilt of Royal Stuart tartan, and Victoria and the young princesses decked out in tartan frocks. The Queen even put on a Scottish accent. Set against this, the cold, the gloom, the discomfort of what a later queen, Queen Mary, would call 'sitting on a mountain' didn't seem to matter. Balmoral was a place where they could act out their fantasies of Highland life and domesticity. It was a place where they were happy.

CHAPTER TWELVE

After Albert

NOVEMBER 1861 BEGAN COLD AND DREARY. For Queen Victoria and Prince Albert, settling back in at Windsor Castle after an idyllic two months at Balmoral, the gloom was lifted a little by some intensive entertaining. The Queen's widowed half-sister Feodora, Princess of Hohenlohe-Langenburg, came to stay for a few days, followed by Grand Duke Konstantin Nikolayevich, the second son of Nicholas I of Russia. The grand duke brought with him his duchess, Alexandra of Saxe-Coburg, and their ten-year-old daughter Olga, 'a darling, clever, amusing little thing, with such a pretty face,' thought Victoria.[1] Albert and eighteen-year-old Princess Alice took them to St George's Chapel, and Victoria showed them the state rooms. The day they left was Bertie's twentieth birthday, and there was something of a family dinner, with the younger children coming in afterwards to entertain the party.

As November wore on, the Queen and her family fell into a gentle routine. Albert went out shooting, or up to London on business. Occasionally he would go over to Flemish Farm, a model farm on the Windsor estate where he kept a herd of Hereford cattle. On 25 November, however, he went to Madingley, a country house outside Cambridge that had been rented for the Prince of Wales while he spent a year at Trinity College. The reason for the trip was Albert's recent discovery that his twenty-year-old son had been seeing a well-known London prostitute, Nelly Clifden. Albert had already written an angry if unfortunately worded letter of condemnation to Bertie, complaining that the boy had 'thrust [himself] into the hands of one of the most abject of the human species, to be by her initiated in the sacred mysteries of creation, which ought to remain shrouded in holy awe until touched by pure and undefiled hands'.[2] He followed this up with a stern lecture on morals to his embarrassed but unrepentant son.

Victoria passed her time walking out, choosing Christmas presents, arranging her drawings and playing the piano. One day she sat for a portrait by the Welsh photographer Charles Clifford, wearing her diadem and jewels. Another day, she received the homage of the new Bishop of Durham in the morning, read from Sir Walter Scott's *Heart of*

Mid-Lothian in the afternoon and, after dinner, from the same author's heroic *Marmion*, with its famous ballad of the young Lochinvar. ('So faithful in love, and so dauntless in war, | There never was knight like the young Lochinvar.') When that was finished, she and Albert began the recently published *Silas Marner* by George Eliot, and played piano duets together. The Queen exercised by riding, walking or playing at battledore and shuttlecock. Four-year-old Princess Beatrice, the couple's youngest daughter, 'had her little ears bored today and was good and brave, hardly crying at all'.[3]

It was not an arduous life. Once in a while the prime minister, Lord Palmerston, would turn up to brief Victoria on foreign affairs, and occasionally the business of government intruded in other ways. 'On coming home [after a walk] held a Council for the Prohibition of Exportation of Saltpetre,' ran one entry in her journal. And again, a few days later, 'rather vexed at hearing that I must again hold a Council for the Prohibition of the Exportation of Arms'.[4] But there was really very little in the way of affairs of state to distract the Queen from her poetry and her walks.

Albert was sleeping badly, though. He complained of neuralgia, and kept getting pains in his back and legs. The difficult talk with the Prince of Wales had taken place during a long private walk in the rain, and he had apparently caught a chill as a result. Victoria was quite anxious for him, but after a hot bath and a rest he seemed better.

The respite was temporary. On 1 December, a Sunday, the couple went to chapel, but the Queen thought her husband looked very ill, 'and not fit to go through all the kneeling, as he did'.[5] He couldn't eat any lunch, and she called in Sir James Clark, her recently retired physician in ordinary (who had so spectacularly misdiagnosed Lady Flora Hastings's stomach cancer), and his distinguished colleague Sir William Jenner, a specialist in the treatment of fevers. Both men said they hoped the prince would soon be better, which was not what you would call a proactive response.

That night Victoria joined Albert in bed, and found him shivering with cold and unable to sleep. In the morning, she sent for Jenner again. 'I was terribly nervous and distressed,' she wrote in her journal.[6] But Jenner assured her there was no reason to be alarmed. Clark confirmed this. It looked as if it might turn into a low fever, he told the Queen, but he was sure Albert would soon be better.

Albert continued to be restless and fretful. He was unable to eat anything but a little orange jelly. Victoria sat with him, but her fright was growing. 'My anxiety is great and I feel utterly lost', she wrote, 'when he to whom I am wont to confide all, is in such a listless state and hardly can smile!'[7] In the early hours of 5 December he was so wretched that the Queen sent for Clark, who administered ether.

Albert's condition continued to deteriorate, and Jenner finally came up with a diagnosis. The Prince Consort was suffering from bowel fever, he told the Queen. There was no cause for alarm, but the fever must be allowed to run its course. 'I seem to be living in a dreadful dream,' wrote Victoria that night.[8] The following day Albert said he wanted to hear music, and she had a piano brought into the room next door for their eighteen-year-old daughter Alice to play some of his favourite hymns and chorales. A member of the household recalled later that unlike her mother, the princess never lost her self-control in Albert's presence:

> She sat by him, listened to all he said, repeated hymns, and then, when she could bear it no longer, would walk calmly to the door, and then rush away to her room, returning soon with the same calm and pale face without any appearance of the agitation she had gone through.[9]

The prince's mind was clearly wandering, although his doctors – there were now at least four or five attending him – continued to tell Victoria they were pleased with his progress. On the morning of 11 December, she went into Albert's room and found him trying to sit up and take some breakfast. He was so weak that she had to support him against her shoulder. 'He said, "It is very comfortable like that, dear child," which made me so happy, though it almost moved me to tears!'[10]

In spite of all their reassurances, Albert's doctors were very worried indeed. Sir Charles Phipps, keeper of the queen's privy purse and a long-time confidant of the prince, cabled Palmerston on 12 December to say that the prince's life was in danger. The news, replied Palmerston, struck him 'like a thunderbolt … One can only hope that Providence may yet spare us so overwhelming a calamity.'[11]

On Friday 13 December Albert's breathing started to give cause for concern. His pulse was racing. That morning Victoria went out for a short drive with her lady of the bedchamber, the Duchess of Atholl. When she got back she went straight to Albert's room and helped him on to a sofa, which was rolled into another room so that he could look out of the window. The doctors prescribed brandy every half-hour, to prevent his getting too agitated, and continued to reassure the Queen

THE LAST MOMENTS OF H.R.H. THE PRINCE CONSORT.

Prince Albert dies, surrounded by his family and an assortment of courtiers, clergymen and physicians. The Prince of Wales leans over to bid farewell to his father on the left of the bed, while the queen sits to the right. A group of disgraced doctors stands apart to the left of the scene, having conspicuously failed to save Albert's life.

that all would be well. She stayed with her husband all of Friday evening, and then lay down on the sofa next door. Doctors came in to keep her informed at frequent intervals, telling her that the brandy was improving Albert's breathing, that his pulse was improving, that 'we have decidedly gained ground within the last three hours'.[12]

The Prince of Wales, summoned from Cambridge that night, arrived at Windsor in the early hours of Saturday morning and went in to see his father after breakfast. Victoria had already been in with Albert: she went to his room first thing. 'Never can I forget how beautiful my darling looked, lying there with his face lit up by the rising sun, his eyes unusually bright, gazing as it were on unseen objects.'[13] It was clear to everyone now that Albert was dying. When Victoria asked if she might go out for a breath of air, Clark and Jenner warned her not to go far, or be too long. She walked out on the terrace with Alice where, incongruously, they listened to the music of a military band. The Queen broke down in tears and hurried back inside.

That evening, as Albert drifted in and out of consciousness, the Victorian way of death played itself out in all its comfort and sentimentality. The prince's bed was moved out into the centre of the room to make access easier, and the children were brought in to kiss their father goodbye, as were some of the senior courtiers.

At about 10.45 there was a change for the worse. The Queen had just left the sickroom to rest, but Clark told Alice to fetch her back. She found Albert barely breathing, and when she took his hand it was cold. She knelt down at one side of the bed, and Alice did the same at the other. Bertie and Princess Helena knelt at the foot, while the doctors hovered close by, along with the Dean of Windsor, the prince's German valet Rudolph Löhlein and an assortment of courtiers. 'It must have cheered the last moments of the illustrious patient to see his wife and nearly all his children round his bed,' commented *The Observer*, rather optimistically.[14] Altogether some fifteen people gathered to watch Albert die; which he did, quietly, shortly before 11.00.

HISTORIANS STILL SPECULATE over the cause of Albert's death. The newspapers of the day put it down to his visit to his son at Cambridge (without of course knowing the reason for that visit). While he was there, noted *The Observer* reprovingly, 'he went out shooting, got wet through, and, it is said, was imprudent enough to sit in his wet clothes'.[15] Victoria agreed, and never forgave Bertie. Others blamed the doctors: 'They are not fit to attend a sick cat.'[16] *The Lancet* diagnosed typhoid fever and blamed the drains at Windsor. Renal failure, cancer and, most recently, Crohn's disease have been suggested. The Queen refused to allow a post-mortem, and that means any definitive diagnosis is ruled out.

After Albert's death, his widow retreated from public life. She spent increasingly long periods at Balmoral, staying for months at a time. A 35-foot-high pyramidal cairn to her husband's memory was 'raised by his brokenhearted widow Victoria R.', as the inscription said. Balmoral held happy memories for her, and she loved the place.

Everyone else hated it. Ministers and government officials complained that they had to travel more than 500 miles to speak with the Queen. Visitors complained of the cold, and of the Queen's habit of keeping fires to a bare minimum. Courtiers complained of the boredom. One household officer recalled a typically excruciating dinner, where the prolonged silences were broken only by coughs, and the sound of the servants 'dropping plates and making a clatteration of noises'.[17] When

Lady Dalhousie, wife of one of the Queen's lords in waiting, came to visit and was asked if she thought the house pretty, she said that 'a frank question requires a frank answer; and I will tell you I never saw anything more uncomfortable or that I coveted less'.[18]

Those members of the household who made the two-day trek from London were faced with weeks, months even, of isolation and strict discipline. No one was allowed out until the Queen herself had left the castle, not even to go to church. The equerry wasn't allowed to give orders to any of the Highlanders who waited about the place getting drunk and being rude. The maid of honour couldn't walk out with any of the gentlemen of the household unless a chaperone accompanied her.

The Queen sometimes retreated to her rooms for days on end, communicating with the rest of the household through notes passed on by her woman of the bedchamber. When she did appear, the household dreaded being invited to dine with her. (There were four dinners – for the Queen, the household, the upper servants and the lower servants.) Conversation was a minefield. On one occasion her private secretary, who happened to be sitting next to Princess Beatrice, mentioned that a mutual acquaintance was engaged to be married. An awkward silence fell over the dinner table and afterwards the Queen, who was determined that her youngest daughter should remain by her side for ever, sent the secretary a message that on no account must marriage ever be mentioned in young Beatrice's hearing. When one of the ladies of the bedchamber commented, apropos some item in the newspapers, that even temporary unhappiness might lead someone to kill themselves, the secretary muttered (out of the Queen's hearing) that if that were the case, suicide would be common at Balmoral.

———— • ————

THE LAST YEARS OF THE CENTURY and the reign were beset by political seesawing and short-lived governments. Between the fall of William Gladstone's second ministry in 1885 and Queen Victoria's death in 1901 there were six administrations, alternating between Conservatives and Liberals.

Whenever the ministry changed, so did the political appointees to the royal household. The Conservative Duchess of Buccleuch came and went as mistress of the robes three times, while the Liberal ministries were so short lived that they didn't get round to appointing a mistress of the robes of their own before they were gone again. General Sir Henry

Sir Henry Ponsonby,
Victoria's private
secretary from 1870 until
1895.

Ponsonby, the Queen's private secretary, was driven to distraction in his
efforts to fill some of the places. 'Blow the lords in waiting,' he confided
to his cousin, the comptroller of the lord chamberlain's department.
'Every one I suggest is objectionable. One has corns, another is dull,
another is a bore.'[19]

The role of private secretary to the sovereign, an increasingly pivotal
position in the royal household, had been created at the beginning of
the nineteenth century. For most of his reign George III had written

his own letters, and kept his own copies of them. But in 1805 the King's failing sight led him to appoint an army officer, Sir Herbert Taylor, as his secretary, in the teeth of strong opposition to the idea that anyone who was not a privy counsellor should be privy to cabinet secrets. Taylor held the post under both George IV and William IV; and although in the early years of her reign Victoria preferred to rely on Baroness Lehzen and Baron Stockmar, after Albert's death in 1861 she took over her husband's own private secretary, General Sir Charles Grey, even though Grey didn't agree with the Queen's retreat from public life, calling her a royal malingerer and criticising the way she pleaded ill-health to avoid carrying out public duties.

Nor did he like the way the Queen used him to convey very personal corrections to members of her household. For instance, when a lady in waiting appeared at court wearing too much make-up, Victoria declared, 'Dear General Grey will tell her.' When he received the message he was heard to mutter, 'Dear General Grey will do nothing of the kind.'[20] But she relied on him heavily, and was grief-stricken at his death in 1870, albeit in the self-absorbed way she had in her widowhood: after paying her condolences to Lady Grey, she wrote, 'How I feel for her, having gone through the same terrible misfortune myself.'[21]

There was a tendency in recruiting to Victoria's household to keep things in the family wherever possible. Henry Ponsonby, who had seen action in the trenches with the Grenadier Guards in the Crimea, was married to General Grey's niece Mary, who was also a maid of honour. He had been an equerry to Prince Albert and during the 1860s he was nominally an extra equerry to the queen, although he spent a lot of his time with his regiment. On Grey's death, the Queen appointed him her private secretary, something Grey himself had wanted. Ponsonby remained with her for the next quarter of a century.

The post was no sinecure, no hereditary grand falconer. Ponsonby's son Arthur, himself a page of honour as a boy, gave some indication of the breadth and complexities of the job a private secretary to Victoria had to perform:

> While his work involved much correspondence, the drafting of reports and abstracts, the mastery of parliamentary Bills, the framing of submissions, the reading of Foreign Office dispatches, conveying messages, conducting interviews and, later, when he became keeper of the privy purse as well [which he did in 1878], a certain amount of administration, organization, accounts and purchases, there was a factor governing much of his work which required something

more than diligence and punctuality … The personality of Queen Victoria must never be left out of account. That required vigilance, discretion and special perception. There could be no official regulations laid down for it. She had established a routine to which he had to fit in. She laid down certain instructions which had to be obeyed. Her technique and the often bewildering consequences of her injunctions had to be mastered. Her predilections and her character had to be studied.[22]

The Queen's habit of communicating in writing with members of the household, even when they were there with her at Buckingham Palace or Windsor or Osborne or Balmoral, meant that Henry Ponsonby's daily duties involved an awful lot of writing, much of it in the form of notes to his mistress, on almost every conceivable topic. When an artist wanted permission to engrave one of the pictures he had painted for the Queen, it was Ponsonby's job to ask. 'Certainly not,' came back the reply. 'They are not good and he is very pushing.'[23] When Oscar Wilde asked permission to reproduce some of the Queen's juvenile verses, Ponsonby sent a note, and had to rephrase her uncompromising response, which was, 'Really what will people not say & invent. Never cd the Queen in her whole life write *one line of poetry* serious or comic or make a Rhyme even. This is therefore all *invention & a myth*.'[24] When a list of preachers for Osborne was put forward by the Dean of Windsor, Ponsonby had to translate Victoria's undiplomatic marginal notes on that list: 'The Dean of Westminster: *too long*. The Dean of Christchurch: sermons are like lectures.'[25] And when Lord Carmarthen wrote on a matter of business, it was up to Ponsonby to convey to him his mistress's candid opinion of his handwriting: 'The Queen cannot help drawing Sir Henry's attention to this atrocious & disgraceful writing for a young nobleman … It is too dreadful.'*[26]

For eight years Ponsonby worked alone. He wrote the memos and sent the letters and submitted the travel arrangements and kept ministers and courtiers at bay. It was only after he was appointed keeper of the privy purse, in addition to his duties as private secretary, that he was given two assistants, both young soldiers: Fleetwood Edwards, a captain in the Royal Engineers, and Arthur Bigge, a lieutenant in the Royal Artillery.

Ponsonby had lodgings in the Norman tower at Windsor Castle, and

---

*Victoria almost always used the third person, even in notes to her private secretary. The only time she dropped the practice was when his mother died: 'I cannot write formally in the 3rd person to you at this moment of overwhelming grief.' *Henry Ponsonby*, 150.

it was there that his wife Mary raised their five children, often in their father's absence. Apart from the domestic staff, most members of the household served for relatively short periods; but the private secretary was constantly in attendance, and Ponsonby was away from his family for up to four months a year. 'To be separated is the unhappiness of my life', he told her, 'and makes me often long to give up everything.'[27] Still he kept on, only giving up his post in January 1895 after being paralysed by a stroke while at Osborne Cottage, a cottage orné in the grounds of Osborne where the family stayed during the summer and at Christmas. He died there ten months later.

As Victoria's private secretary, Henry Ponsonby was well placed to comment on the two most awkward household crises of the Queen's long widowhood.

The first was what the secretary's son and biographer called 'the queen's marked and sustained infatuation' for John Brown.[28] Brown had been a stable boy at Balmoral before Victoria and Albert took the estate, and he stayed on as a gillie, attending on shooting and fishing expeditions. After Albert's death, the Queen grew to rely more and more on him and by the mid-1860s he was accompanying her everywhere 'as my personal servant for out of doors', not only on the Balmoral estate but at Windsor, Osborne and Buckingham Palace. When Victoria visited Coburg or Lucerne, Brown was there; when a young man aimed a pistol at her as her carriage stood at the garden entrance to Buckingham Palace, it was Brown who leapt on the youth and wrestled him to the ground.

He was frequently drunk, and his manners were rough. 'What a coarse animal that Brown is,' said Lord Cairns, lord chancellor for much of the 1870s.[29] The Queen's family loathed him. The rest of the household, fiercely hierarchical and uncomfortable with the familiar way he behaved towards their sovereign, resented his influence and his legendary rudeness. On one occasion one of the Queen's equerries, General Sir Lynedoch Gardiner, came into waiting and on seeing Brown, asked how the Queen was. 'The Queen's very well,' was the reply. 'It was only the other day that she said to me, "There's that damned old fool General Gardiner coming into waiting and I know he'll be putting his bloody nose into everything that doesn't concern him."'[30]

A lot of nonsense was talked about Brown's relationship with the Queen, both during their lifetimes and later. At the height of Victoria's

Victoria with John
Brown, 'the only person
who could fight and
make the queen do what
she did not wish'.

retreat from public life, there were stories that she had had Brown's child, that they were secretly married, that the Highlander was a medium who was helping her to contact her dead husband. A privately printed pamphlet titled *Mrs John Brown* did the rounds, fuelling the speculation. Later commentators did more than hint at impropriety, but signally failed to come up with any evidence for an intimate relationship between Victoria and her 'beloved friend'. In truth, Brown occupied the role of the fool – privileged, certainly, but more of a pet than a paramour. After visiting Brown's grave at Balmoral (he died at Windsor of a fever in 1883) Ponsonby gave the fairest estimate of his character. He was, said the secretary, 'the only person who could fight and make the queen do what she did not wish'. He may not always have given the best advice, but 'he was honest, and with all his want of education, his roughness, his prejudice and other faults he was undoubtedly a most excellent servant to her'.[31]

Sir Henry Ponsonby was less charitable about the second of his mistress's domestic infatuations. In 1887 two Indians were brought over to Britain as *khitmagars* or servants to enhance the spectacle of Victoria's golden jubilee and to wait on visiting Indian dignitaries. On 23 June she noted their arrival in her journal: 'The one, Mohamed Buxsh, very dark, with a very smiling expression, has been a servant before … the other, much younger, called Abdul Karim, is much lighter, tall, & with a fine serious countenance. His father is a native doctor at Agra. They both kissed my feet.'[32]

At first the Queen treated them like pets, an attitude she never entirely lost: when she sent some of her sketches for inclusion in the 1893 World's Fair in Chicago, they included one of her terrier, Spot; another of Prince Henry of Battenberg's pug; and a third of Abdul Karim. But she grew fond of them both, and particularly of Karim, who was enlisted to help her learn Urdu. When he threatened to go home, she raised his salary and appointed him as her *munshi* or teacher. It was a mistake to bring him over as a servant to wait at table, she declared, since this was something he had never done, 'having been a clerk or munshi in his own country and being of rather a different class to the others'.[33] His father, he told her, was a surgeon-general in the India Army.

Karim was relieved of domestic service, and his name began to appear on court circulars, attending a state ball or accompanying the Queen as a member of her household suite, along with Ponsonby and the assistant secretaries. When the great Italian actress Eleonora Duse performed for her in the white drawing room at Windsor Castle, people noticed that the arm the elderly sovereign leaned on to make her entrance belonged to Abdul Karim.

As far as the public was concerned the munshi was a curiosity. While the court was at Balmoral in 1891 he and a colleague were given a tour of Aberdeen in an open carriage, 'the picturesque costume of the Easterns attracting considerable attention', as the press reports noted. Two years later, his return from a visit to India was national news. 'The *munshi* was accompanied by his wife and daughter,' said *The Times*, 'both of whom were closely veiled, the lady being shrouded in a cloak of yellow stuff and the girl in a darker garment, the Oriental coverings completely concealing the features and figures of the wearers.'[34] (*The Times* got it wrong. Karim had no children, and the two women were his wife and his mother-in-law.) Victoria personally went to meet them at a cottage she had arranged for them on the royal estate at Frogmore, next door to Windsor, and was charmed by the *munshi*'s wife, who wore a beautiful sari of crimson gauze. 'She is nice looking,' wrote the Queen, 'but would not raise her eyes, she was so shy.'[35]

Victoria appointed Karim her Indian secretary, and made him a companion of the Order of the Indian Empire. He ate with the rest of the royal household and had his own houses on the Frogmore estate and at Osborne, and a specially built house in the grounds of Balmoral, which the Queen named Karim Cottage.[*]

The rest of the household was unhappy with his rise. Arthur Bigge asked Sir Henry Ponsonby if it wouldn't be a good idea 'to resist these moves upwards'.[36] Prince Arthur, the Queen's seventh child, was furious at Karim's presumption in standing with the gentry at the Highland games one year. He demanded that Ponsonby do something about it. Knowing that Karim stood where he did by the Queen's express order, the private secretary innocently suggested that Prince Arthur might take it up with her. 'This entirely shut him up,' he wrote.[37]

Disapproval of the *munshi* came to a head in 1894, when it emerged that Victoria was in the habit of showing him sensitive letters and despatches and asking his advice on Indian affairs. As a Moslem, that advice tended to favour the Moslem

Queen Victoria and her *munshi*, Abdul Karim.

interest above that of Hindus. Worse than his obvious partiality, though, was the suspicion that confidential information was being leaked to interested parties in India. Members of the Queen's household, from assistant secretaries to her resident physician and her groom in waiting, complained to her, with the result that she stopped speaking to them. Lord George Hamilton, the secretary of state for India, wrote to say he would find it impossible to send confidential papers to the Queen unless he received assurances that she wouldn't show them to Karim. Courtiers gently tried to explain to her that Indian princes would find

[*] Karim Cottage is available to rent as a self-catering holiday cottage.

Family photograph:
Victoria surrounded by
three generations of her
family in the gardens at
Osborne House, 1898.

it incomprehensible that a mere *munshi* should hold such an important position among the Empress of India's advisers.

There were persistent rumours that Karim had not been entirely frank about his antecedents. When accusations appeared in the press that his origins were very humble indeed, the Queen was furious. Firing off a note to Henry Ponsonby (in the third person, as usual), she said that 'to make out that he is so low is really outrageous … She has known 2 archbishops who were the sons respectively of a butcher and a grocer, a Chancellor whose father was a poor sort of Scotch minister, Sir D. Stewart [presumably Sir David Stewart, lord provost of Aberdeen], and Ld. Mount Stephen [a prominent Canadian philanthropist] both who ran about barefoot as children.' Karim's father, she claimed, had seen good and honourable service as a doctor. The *munshi* 'feels cut to the heart at being thus spoken of'.[38]

The Queen next determined to prove her critics wrong about Karim's background. Ponsonby's second son Frederick, a lieutenant in the Grenadier Guards, was serving in India as aide de camp to the viceroy, the Marquess of Lansdowne. Victoria decided to appoint him as

one of her equerries as a surprise for his father, and she telegraphed him to offer him the post, without consulting her private secretary. According to Frederick, or Fritz, as he was generally known, she also ordered him to go to Agra and seek out Karim's surgeon-general father and so quash the nasty rumours.

Fritz Ponsonby did as he was told, and discovered that, far from being a surgeon-general in the army, or even a physician of any sort, Karim senior worked as an apothecary at the local jail. Fritz duly came back to England, where he was gazetted equerry in ordinary to Her Majesty and took up his duties at Osborne. He was disarmingly frank about what those duties entailed:

Everyone came down to breakfast and then we all went to our work. This was not easy in my case as I had nothing to do, but I went to the equerry's room where I had a writing-table, and having read the newspapers, wrote private letters ... There was little or nothing to be done till dinner, when we all dressed up in knee-breeches and stockings.[39]

His relations with the Queen, however, were rather strained. Not realising he had been dropped into the middle of a major household dispute, he cheerfully told her that he had spoken with Karim's father and that the man was only the apothecary at Agra jail. She responded by saying Fritz must have interviewed the wrong man. No, he said. It was the right man.

Victoria didn't ask him to dinner for a year. When he accompanied her to the south of France for a month in 1895, she didn't speak to him at all until the last day of her stay. Then, as he stood sweltering by her carriage in a tall hat and frock coat, she turned to him and said, 'What a pity it is to leave Nice in such beautiful weather.'[40]

Karim's close relationship with the Queen continued to worry her family and her household. In 1897, when Fritz was again in attendance on her in the south of France, Victoria insisted once more that she had a right to show the *munshi* confidential papers relating to India, and countered every suggestion that he was not to be trusted with the charge that it was 'race prejudice'. The way Fritz described Karim suggests she had a point: 'He happens to be a thoroughly stupid and uneducated man, and his one idea in life seems to be to do nothing and to eat as much as he can. If he had been kept in his proper place, there would have been no harm done.'[41] Fritz hinted that the police had been consulted, 'and have furnished some rather interesting details' about Karim.[42] None of it deterred Victoria, who remained fiercely loyal to her *munshi*.

After his mother's death in 1901, Edward VII had Abdul Karim and his family sent back to India and ordered that all the correspondence between the *munshi* and the Queen should be burned. Concerns that some of it might find its way into the public domain proved totally unfounded. Karim gave it all up, although even then he was given no credit for doing the right thing. Charlotte Knollys, a lady of the bedchamber to Princess (now Queen) Alexandra, declared:

> The Munshi bogie which had frightened all the household at Windsor for many years had provided a ridiculous farce, as the poor man had not only given up all his letters but even the photos signed by [the] queen and had returned to India like a whipped hound. All the Indian servants have gone back so now there is no Oriental picture and queerness at Court.[43]

VICTORIA'S REIGN ENDED AS IT BEGAN – with demands for the royal household to economise. During the 1890s her household expenditure began to expand beyond the limits set at the beginning of her reign, and in 1897 and again after her death in 1901, the Treasury investigated the causes. 'The great increase in the number of the Royal Family in the second and third generation, who pay frequent visits to Her Majesty' was no surprise: she sat at the apex of a vast network of forty-two grandchildren with connections to most of the crowned heads of Europe, and scarcely a month went by without a visit from one royal relation or another. The fact that the Queen's household preferred champagne to cheaper wines was less expected, as was 'an increased expenditure on hot-house flowers, palms, fruits, etc, for entertainments'.[44] The cost of posting letters and sending telegrams had grown until it constituted a serious item of expense to the crown, reckoned at between £2,000 and £3,000 a year.

Golden Jubilee: Victoria leaves Buckingham Palace for a service of thanksgiving at Westminster Abbey, 21 June 1887.

The dining room at Osborne House decorated for Christmas, c. 1873.

The royal kitchen at Windsor, photographed in 1898.

In her old age, the apparently reclusive Victoria had acquired expensive habits. She owned double the number of carriages that she had in 1837 – 187 as against ninety-four, and the cost of maintaining them had gone up, too. There were garden parties, at a cost of about £5,000 apiece, and concerts: 'Though the Queen did not keep open Court, yet of late years there were costly entertainments, like the Opera Company commanded to Windsor, or a theatrical company ordered to appear at Balmoral.'[45] There were professional performances of Charles Gounod's *Romeo and Juliet* and *Faust* in the Waterloo Gallery at Windsor in July 1898 and another performance of *Faust* in July 1900. ('Quite beautiful, and a great treat to hear, though perhaps a little long,' was her verdict.[46]) And her habit of holding all her investitures at Windsor or Osborne rather than at Buckingham Palace entailed special trains, luncheons and extra servants, while the upkeep of Osborne was reckoned at about £17,000 a year, and Balmoral another £20,000.

When Victoria's ministers broke the news to her about the rising expenses, the waste and extravagance in her household, she was genuinely appalled. Her bed broke, and she refused to let her servants have it mended because it would cost too much. She ordered fewer kinds of bread at breakfast. And in a move which surprised her staff, she commanded that toilet paper should give way to newspaper squares in the castle lavatories at Windsor.

CHAPTER THIRTEEN

Court Circular

QUEEN VICTORIA DIED AT OSBORNE, her eldest son by her side, on 22 January 1901. Her last word was 'Bertie'. She had been on the throne for more than sixty-three years, making her the longest-reigning monarch in British history until Elizabeth II. She left detailed instructions about her funeral, which took place at St George's Chapel, Windsor, and her interment alongside Prince Albert in the mausoleum she had built for him at Frogmore.

At Osborne she was photographed on her deathbed wearing white, with her face covered by her wedding veil; in her coffin she lay on Albert's dressing gown, and a plaster cast of his hand was placed in the coffin beside her, along with a large collection of mementoes from friends, family and servants, even a sprig of heather from Balmoral. Once the family had left the room her physician, Sir James Reid, presumably acting under the Queen's instructions, placed a photograph of John Brown and a lock of his hair in the Queen's left hand.

AT LAST ALLOWED THE STATUS OF SOVEREIGN AFTER a lifetime of waiting in the wings, Bertie thrust himself into the glittering rituals of monarchy on his mother's death with the same enthusiasm he had shown in thrusting himself into the hands of the prostitute Nelly Clifden forty years earlier. As Prince and Princess of Wales, he and his wife Alexandra of Denmark had engaged with those royal rituals for nearly forty years, acting as proxies for the mourning Victoria on the frequent occasions when she felt like abdicating her responsibilities but not her throne. But this was different. Now there was no one to disapprove. No one to tell Alexandra how to bring up her children, or how much to spend on new clothes. No one to accuse Bertie of being stupid and irresponsible.

The first levee of the new reign took place on 11 February 1902, and it sparkled like Alexandra's jewels. Levees had been one of the public faces of royalty and nobility since the seventeenth century, when

Charles II adopted the French practice of receiving visitors while he was being dressed. The *London Post* of 19 October 1699 reported William of Orange's return to town by saying that 'this morning there was a very numerous Court at Kensington, all the Nobility and Gentry about Town repairing thither to attend His Majesty at his Levee, and to Complement [*sic*] him upon his Safe and Happy Arrival'.[1] By the eighteenth century they had evolved into morning assemblies and by the nineteenth they were often taking place around two in the afternoon. 'I had my hand kissed nearly 3,000 times!' wrote the young Victoria after one of her early experiences of presiding over a levee.[2]

Bertie had often taken his mother's place as Prince of Wales. Now Edward VII, he decided his levees would take place at noon, and on that bright, cold morning the crowds gathered all along the short route that the King would take from Marlborough House to St James's Palace. From 10.30 onwards contingents of police began to regulate both the traffic and the spectators, some of whom tried to slip through cordons for a closer look. In The Mall, the carriages of those who were due to meet the King were drawn up in four lines stretching down towards Whitehall. There were broughams and landaus, hansom cabs, even a few motor cars 'which, with what seemed like a mixture of shyness and audacity,' reported *The Times*, 'mingled with the carriages of a more sedate and venerable type'.[3]

At 11.30 one hundred men of the Household Cavalry rode out from Horse Guards towards St James's Palace. 'With their white plumes waving over their shining helmets, their cuirasses glittering in the sunshine, their drawn swords and scarlet tunics, they were an ideal bodyguard for a great and powerful sovereign', said *The Times*' correspondent.[4] And, he might have added, they were an ideal advertisement for that sovereign's grandeur and power. The thirty-six-year-old Prince of Wales, the future George V, was glimpsed wearing the uniform of a rear admiral and surrounded by his retinue, making his way on foot from his lodgings in the north-eastern wing of St James's Palace. Diplomats, cabinet ministers, soldiers and sailors in full dress uniform, bishops attended by their chaplains and judges in full-bottomed wigs and flowing robes, all streamed in while the bands of the Household Cavalry and the Coldstream Guards played a selection of music in the garden. 'The whole spectacle … seemed to transport one to the olden times, when costume was more magnificent and when there was more of ostentation than the taste of our somewhat drab days sees fit to approve except upon occasions of state ceremonial.'[5]

At 11.45 the music stopped. Then the Coldstream Guards struck up the National Anthem and the men in the crowd all removed their hats, as three gold and scarlet dress carriages, driven by coachmen in gold lace and escorted by contingents of Life Guards, emerged from the grounds of Marlborough House, where Bertie and Alex had made their home since their marriage in 1863. The procession crossed to the garden entrance to St James's Palace, a distance of no more than a couple of hundred yards, then disappeared inside. Two hours later, the King's return to Marlborough House was accompanied by the same degree of ceremony. The Coldstream Guards played the National Anthem, the Life Guards rode alongside the golden procession, the people cheered and removed their hats.

In the intervening 120 minutes, thirty foreign ambassadors and ministers were introduced to Edward VII. They in turn presented various first, second and third secretaries and military and naval attachés from their embassies and legations – another thirty in all. And then over 500 more men were presented to the King, who was attended by all his senior household officials, including the lord steward, the lord chamberlain, the master of horse, the master, treasurer and comptroller of the household, the keeper of the privy purse. The state rooms were packed and people were kept waiting on the staircase for an hour or more as the king, standing on a carpet of estate in front of the throne, with the Prince of Wales at his shoulder, shook hands with all the ambassadors and received the bows of the rest. It had been the tradition to kiss the king's hand, but this was dispensed with by Edward VII, perhaps because of the need to hurry things along. Each presentee's big moment lasted a little over ten seconds.

But they dressed for the occasion, all the same. Officers from Scottish kilted corps wore their kilts. Bishops wore full canonicals, including black breeches, silk stockings and buckled shoes. Civilians had a choice. The elderly gentleman who yearned for a bygone age might wear old court dress, complete with silk waistcoat, lace ruffles and a wig with a black taffeta bag attached. Those opting for a slightly less antiquated look could choose velvet court dress, which consisted of a black velvet dress coat with steel buttons, knee breeches and silk stockings, a cocked hat and a sword. The modernist might wear cloth court dress: trousers of claret or dark blue, with a gold stripe down the side; a dress coat in dark claret, dark blue or dark brown; and a white waistcoat and white tie. Plus the cocked hat and the sword. There was no getting away without the cocked hat and the sword.

The Ruritanian splendour of the Edwardian royal levee was an exclusively male affair. Throughout Victoria's reign its female equivalent had been the drawing room, at which young women of the right sort were presented to the sovereign when they came out into society, again when they were married, and yet again if their husband was raised to the peerage. Both levees and drawing rooms already had a long pedigree. George III and Queen Charlotte frequently held both. 'The drawing-room at St James's tomorrow will be nearly equal in splendor to a birthday gala,' commented a breathless press in November 1791; 'and several ladies have prepared new dresses for the occasion.'[6]

George IV was less enthusiastic, partly because his severe attacks of gout made it difficult for him to stand for long periods at a time. But he still managed to hold a couple of drawing rooms each year, earning himself praise for the stimulus they were reckoned to give to trades and manufacturing industries through the purchase of new frocks. 'Levees, however frequently held, have no such good effect, because the same sort of Court dress will last a careful man all his life.'[7]

By the time Edward VII came to the throne, the question of who was, and who was not, a suitable person to attend a court drawing room was a matter of debate. 'Formerly', wrote the author of *Manners and Rules of Good Society* in 1898, with icy calm, 'only persons of recognised position considered themselves justified in being presented, but of late years, persons whose social status scarcely comes under this head consider themselves eligible for the honour of a presentation.'[8] Besides the wives and daughters of the aristocracy and gentry, and women whose fathers and husbands were in the professions, those who came from commerce were now included. And 'the daughters of wealthy manufacturers are not debarred from attending drawing rooms if their associations warrant them in so doing'.[9]

It was noticeable that the numbers of women presented had increased substantially during Victoria's reign, from two or three hundred a year in the early 1840s to between eight and nine hundred a year by the turn of the century. It became almost *de rigueur* among the traditional titled classes to sneer quietly at the vulgarity and flamboyance of the Edwardian court and to mutter that money was now the passport to Society. 'Almost anyone who had enough of it', complained the Dowager Countess of Airlie, 'could procure, sooner or later, an invitation to the splendid Court Balls at Windsor and the evening receptions at Buckingham Palace.'[10]

Victoria presided over drawing rooms to the end. Her last was on Friday 11 May 1900, eight months before her death: as usual, she stayed for an hour before handing over to her daughter-in-law Alexandra. She

THE KING'S FIRST COURT AT BUCKINGHAM PALACE: A PRESENTATION

DRAWN FROM LIFE BY SYDNEY P. HALL, R.V.O.

didn't find these occasions particularly appealing. 'Very few people came by whom we knew, and there was not much beauty,' was her verdict on a drawing room she gave in February 1898, when 199 women curtseyed and kissed her hand in quick succession.[11] The actress Lillie Langtry was disappointed to find that Victoria gazed straight ahead the whole time and extended her hand to be kissed in a rather perfunctory manner: 'There was not even the flicker of a smile on her face'.[12] Then again, Lillie was, or had been, sleeping with the Prince of Wales: the experience of having your son's lover presented to you while that son and his wife looked on must have been socially awkward.

Occasionally something happened to enliven the proceedings. In May 1898, while receiving 'a good many uninteresting people', Victoria found that the curtsey proved too much for the octogenarian Lady Esher, who was being presented after her husband was made a viscount. Lady Esher fell flat on her back, grabbing at Queen Victoria's hand as she went over and nearly dragging her sovereign down on top of her. She was 'with difficulty raised up', remarked the Queen.[13]

'Why must a drawing-room be always held in the daytime,'

Presentations at court were formal and lengthy: Edward VII and Queen Alexandra stood while two hundred or more women lined up to curtsey to each of them and kiss the queen's hand.

one newspaper had demanded in 1875, 'in the garish sunlight, when everything looks cold and tawdry which would be warm, brilliant and magnificent at night?'[14] For years there had been complaints about the unsuitability of demanding that women wear full evening dress, with bare shoulders, low bodice and short sleeves, for an event which ran from two o'clock until around four. Edward agreed, and replaced his mother's afternoon drawing rooms with more glamorous evening courts which began at 10 p.m., at Buckingham Palace.

They remained fiendishly ritualised, nonetheless. Edward and Alexandra held two courts before Easter and two after. Strictly speaking, they were attended by those ladies who had been presented to Their Majesties (and by their husbands, although 'gentlemen who come in attendance on their families are not expected to pass the Presence'.[15]) Everyone wore full court dress. Married women were required to wear a court plume consisting of three white feathers; unmarried women wore two white feathers. The feathers had to be prominent enough for the sovereign to separate wives and spinsters at a glance. Those in deep mourning were allowed to wear black feathers. Women were also expected to wear a full train, not less than ten feet six inches long.

Any married woman who had already been presented had the right to present a daughter, or daughter-in-law, or even a friend. (Unmarried women did not have the privilege of making a presentation.) Unmarried women wore white. The author of *Manners and Rules of Good Society* declared that 'it is also the fashion for married ladies to wear white on their presentation, unless their age renders their doing so unsuitable'.[16]

Numbers were limited, and women who wanted to attend one of the evening courts had to send in their name, the name of their husband and the name of any lady whom they wished to present to the King and Queen, to the lord chamberlain's office at St James's Palace. If they met with the lord chamberlain's approval, the presenter would then receive an official summons from him, and the day before the court she had to obtain two cards from his office, each of which she filled out with her name and the name of the woman whom she was presenting. She had to bring these with her, and must hand one to the page in the ante-room and the other to an equerry at the entrance to the throne room. The equerry handed it to the palace comptroller and the comptroller quietly announced the name to Their Majesties.

Frederick Gorst, who served as a royal footman during Edward VII's reign, left a servant's-eye view of an evening court in action. He described how, while nervous debutantes waited with their sponsors in one of five second-floor drawing rooms, the King and Queen entered the ballroom with a roll of drums and the playing of the National Anthem, preceded by the lord chamberlain and the lord steward, who carried their staves of office and walked backwards. 'They turned away simultaneously,' recalled the footman, 'as though they were executing a well-rehearsed dance, in order to allow the royal procession to pass, because no one was permitted to turn his back on their majesties.'[17] The ability to back up in a straight line took years of practice, noted an impressed Gorst.

At last the women to be presented were led in – young debutantes, brides, widows who had married again, peeresses whose husbands were newly ennobled. Before she entered, a lady's train, which until now she had carried over her arm, was taken from her by two officials and spread out behind her with their wands of office. She removed her right glove, resisted the temptation to look behind her to check that the train was properly displayed (a sign of rustic gaucherie) and set off.

As she grew older, Queen Victoria had taken to receiving while sitting down. Edward and Alexandra stood the whole time, while each woman – and there could be 200 or more – curtseyed first to the King, and then to the Queen, kissing the latter's hand. She then backed away from the throne and was escorted back to her seat in the ballroom.

After everyone had been presented, they were shown through to the household dining room, where a buffet was laid out, with tables at waist height. The fathers and brothers and other men joined them, and everyone stood and ate at that level, because it was impossible for the women to sit in their gowns. Champagne was served, along with bouillon, cold entrées of birds, ham and sandwiches, followed by ices and cakes. The King and Queen ate separately in the royal dining room, with just a few friends in attendance.

'I loved to look at the young ladies whose youthful complexions were glowing and heightened by the supreme moment which they were experiencing,' said Gorst. 'Even the plainest of them seemed to become beautiful, illuminated by some inner radiance and expectation.'[18] Around two or three in the morning, when supper was over and the guests were getting ready to leave, the sergeant footman signalled the footmen who were to go on the carriages to go down to the palace entrance and prepare for departure.

And the point of it all? Well, if it wasn't quite Gorst's 'supreme moment', presentation at court was still glamorous, an excuse to dress up. For young debutantes, it was a rite of passage: unless they participated in that rite they were denied access to the dinners and balls which made up the marriage market that was the London Season. It confirmed membership of an elite: an evening court was the closest many of those debutantes would ever get to the King and Queen. And it conferred power. The presentee was placed under an obligation to the presenter, and once she had been presented she magically metamorphosed into a presenter herself, able to pass on the gift to others, in some curious apostolic succession.

ONE THURSDAY IN THE SUMMER OF 1905 an elderly man in a frock coat walked into the showroom of the Lacre Motor Car Company in Soho. 'Good-looking and urbanely contemptuous', he asked to see the service manager, Charles Stamper.[19]

Stamper had met his visitor before. It was Major-General Sir Henry Ewart, knight grand cross of the Royal Victorian Order, knight grand cross of the Most Honourable Order of the Bath, a war hero whose legendary moonlight cavalry charge against an Egyptian army at Kassassin in 1882 was still being talked about in the London clubs. Now retired from the army, Ewart was crown equerry to Edward VII and, according to one contemporary, 'the best mixture of decoration and usefulness among the court's human movables'.[20] As crown equerry he was responsible for coordinating the royal transport arrangements; and his connection with the service manager at Lacre's had begun a few months earlier with a move to formalise driving arrangements at the palace. A rota of specially selected police constables took on the job of royal chauffeurs, and they needed to be trained in basic car maintenance and driving skills. Ewart had arranged for Charles Stamper to come to Buckingham Palace two or three times a week to give them lessons.

Edward VII was an enthusiastic motorist. 'The motor has become as much a part of a courtier's baggage as is the cigarette case,' wrote the anonymous author of *Society in the New Reign* in 1904. 'The king … expects his fashionable subjects to be able to discuss its internal arrangements with the same knowledge that they once possessed or affected of the pedigree of the royal thoroughbreds.'[21] In 1900, while he was still Prince of Wales, Edward had acquired a Daimler tonneau, the first motor car to be bought by a member of the royal family. Within a few years he had a small fleet. There were two big Mercedes and a Daimler, all painted a rich claret colour and trimmed with soft blue morocco leather, and all carrying the royal arms on their door panels and their rear. The King also owned a smaller Renault with a folding canopy over the passenger seats in the rear – a convertible, in effect. Because the Renault was used exclusively for taking the King shopping or paying a call in town, it sported a more discreet royal crown. In spite of the fact that the Motor Car Act of 1903 stipulated that all cars on public roads should display vehicle registration plates, none of the King's did so, a practice which frequently led to them being flagged down by irate police officers whose determination to tear a strip off the driver evaporated when they recognised (or worse, didn't recognise and had to be told) the identity of the passenger within. Queen Alexandra had a Wolseley of her own with distinctive white bodywork. However, it attracted so much attention that she often preferred to be driven in her sister-in-law Princess Victoria's more discreet claret-coloured car.

The larger cars were fitted with four passenger seats, two of which folded down like those in a London cab. They were equipped with interior electric lights, hat cords on which to hang the royal top hat (Edward had a bad habit of denting his hats while climbing in and out of

Edward VII arriving at Goodwood. 'The motor has become as much a part of a courtier's baggage as is the cigarette case', wrote the author of *Society in the New Reign* in 1904.

his cars), and trays to hold a bespoke travelling case, which was transferred from car to car and contained brushes, a mirror and smelling salts.

When Major-General Ewart arrived in the Lacre Motor Car Company's showroom on this particular Thursday in 1905, he had more than driving lessons for royal chauffeurs on his mind. The crown equerry asked Stamper to take him out for a spin with one of the new chauffeurs, and in the course of the drive he suddenly announced that he wanted Stamper to come and work full time in the royal household, 'as His Majesty's motor expert and engineer'.[22]

Stamper accepted the offer without hesitation, and for the next five years he accompanied Edward VII every single time the King went out in one of his motor cars. When the King and Queen went up to Chatsworth (by rail) to spend New Year with the Duke of Devonshire, Stamper was waiting for him with two of the royal cars, ready to take him on afternoon runs around the Peak District. When the King took the waters at Marienbad or stayed in Biarritz or drove in procession across the Clifton Suspension Bridge, Stamper was there in the front seat. He was there when the huge doors of the great hall at Raby Castle in County Durham were thrown open and the King was driven right into the house – the only person to be granted that privilege, 'for fear lest oil should drop on to the flags'.[23]

Yet Stamper never drove the King himself. His role was to keep the royal cars in good running order, supervising the maintenance staff, arranging for the purchase of new vehicles and contracting with suppliers for petrol and tyres. He was directly answerable to Ewart in this. But he always accompanied Edward VII, because his job also involved carrying out the kind of running repairs that any car in the early years of motoring might need during a journey. He changed tyres and adjusted brakes and fixed leaking radiators. The King, who was obsessive about punctuality (in contrast to his wife, who was late for everything), hated delays of any kind; and Stamper often took the decision to investigate potential mechanical problems without asking the chauffeur to stop first. 'I have stood on the foot-board, with the door open, talking to His Majesty, while we were travelling at forty miles an hour,' he recalled, 'and I have been lying stretched along the near front wing with the bonnet open, examining the carburettor, while we were going at the same pace.'[24]

Having started out as a mechanic and service manager, over the five years Stamper served in the royal household he became something more. It was part of his job to act as navigator and tour guide, poring over maps before any royal outing, marking out any points of historical interest along the route, and bearing the brunt of the King's notoriously short temper if he took a wrong turn or lost the way. He had to keep an eye on Edward's delinquent terrier Caesar, who regularly wriggled free of his master and leapt from the car the moment it stopped, ignoring the King's bellowed commands as he disappeared into the nearest park or meadow in search of rabbits. (The dog wore a brown leather collar with a brass name plate engraved with five words: 'I belong to the King.')

Stamper even blew the King's horn. During a visit to Germany, Edward noticed that his cousin Kaiser Wilhelm II had a motor-horn in the form of a bugle, and he wanted one too. Stamper found something similar and, having been taught to play some tunes by Herr Gottlieb, master of one of the King's orchestras, he took to carrying it on his knees as he sat beside the chauffeur. Staff at the various royal residences came to recognise its distinctive tone and threw open the gates to Buckingham Palace or Balmoral when they heard its sound. Motorists – if they were wise – pulled over when they heard it blown behind them.

> Many a time I have heard His Majesty cry, 'Blow your horn,
> Stamper'; and once, when … the window behind me was shut,
> I remember he tapped on the window and I looked round to see
> the King, his cheeks distended and fingers in a line with his mouth,
> winding an imaginary call upon a phantom bugle.[25]

The King's cars were garaged in the Royal Mews behind Buckingham Palace, and brought round to one or other of the palace entrances as required. The procedure was straightforward enough; but when the King *returned* from a drive, there was an element of uncertainty about the business because he refused to decide until the last minute where he wanted to get out. Police telephoned ahead if they caught sight of the royal car coming down Constitution Hill or along The Mall, and there was always the sound of Stamper's bugle; but that left very little time for servants and courtiers to assemble in the right spot. Sometimes they would be waiting at the front of the palace only to see the King sweep past them and into the gardens. 'Then there began a race between the servants and the car,' recalled Stamper. 'The more sprightly would reach the garden entrance as we did, but the rest would come harking after them and arrive just in time to see His Majesty alight.'[26]

ROYAL SECURITY WAS A WORRY FOR EDWARD VII. There had been seven attempts on Victoria's life during her reign, the last at Windsor in 1882, when a lunatic named Roderick Maclean took a pot-shot at her carriage. In April 1900 Edward himself had a miraculous escape at Brussels Nord station, when a fifteen-year-old anarchist jumped onto the royal train as it was pulling out and fired two shots at his head. In 1906 in Madrid another anarchist threw a bomb at the carriage containing Alfonso XIII of Spain and his bride, King Edward's niece Victoria Eugenie, killing or maiming dozens of bystanders. From then on, whenever the British king drove abroad he was always escorted by plain-clothes detectives in a second car.

At home, local police were detailed to keep the roads cleared whenever the King was out in one of his cars, a task they often attacked with enthusiasm, when they weren't flagging down the royal car to point out its lack of registration plates. Imaginary traffic and non-existent crowds were marshalled ruthlessly into side roads; sleeping bootless tramps were shoved into hedgerows in case they interfered with the royal progress; pedestrians who had no intention of stepping off a pavement were sternly commanded not to do so.

When it came to more challenging royal duties, both the elderly Victoria and her son and heir had the benefit of Scotland Yard. Members of the Metropolitan Police Special Branch, formed in 1883 as the Special Irish Branch in response to a Fenian bombing campaign in London, were regularly seconded to protective surveillance duties when senior members of the royal family travelled or appeared in public. They had access to a collection of rather ancient pistols held at Scotland Yard, although they rarely carried them except when travelling abroad. Superintendent Patrick Quin, head of the Special Branch, always accompanied Edward when he travelled in Europe, liaising with detectives from the host nation. Wherever the King slept, a Special Branch officer was on duty all night.

Royal detectives rarely had to worry about anarchists or Bolshevists in Britain. Serious attempts on the lives of the king and queen were mercifully rare, in contrast to continental Europe, where between 1894 and 1914 five heads of state, three prime ministers and one president were assassinated. This was partly because British intelligence networks were effective, and partly because Britain's policy of providing asylum to half the political extremists in Europe made those extremists reluctant to upset the apple cart by blowing up their sanctuary. But as the head of London's Criminal Investigation Department, Sir Melville Macnaghten, wrote in 1914, 'what neither the King's horsemen nor all the Metropolitan Police can guard against is the individual initiative of some crank who, with a very elementary knowledge of chemistry, could fashion a dangerous bomb out of an empty sardine box and some nitro-glycerine'.[27] Royal protection officers were constantly on the watch for the lone lunatic – and they seem to have found plenty. There was the elderly man discovered by a patrolling Special Branch officer banging on the gates of Buckingham Palace: when asked what he was doing, he declared that he had been sent a proposal of marriage from a member of the royal family and he had to get in to see her. Or the chap who broke through the crowds in Whitehall at the state opening of Parliament and hurled himself at one of the royal carriages, waving a piece of paper. When the officers brought him down, they found he was brandishing a petition asking for Hyde Park to be converted into a market garden.

Harold Brust, who joined the Special Branch in 1909, recalled a day at Paddington station when he was on surveillance duty with the King. He was momentarily distracted by a conversation with one of the equerries about transport arrangements, and he turned around to find that an old woman had thrown herself on her knees in front of Edward VII and wrapped herself round his legs. She refused to let go until he listened to her plea for her son, who had been sent to prison a few days earlier. Brust rushed forward to separate sovereign and subject, only for the King to motion him away. Edward helped the old lady to her feet, listened to her story and referred her to his secretary. Then he boarded his train while Brust made sure she was sent home in a cab with money to pay her fare.

Day-to-day security at the royal residences had come a long way since the early years of Victoria's reign, when the Boy Jones outwitted a handful of gentleman porters and night watchmen. Now there was a detachment of officers, all specially selected from 'A' Division of the Metropolitan Police and based at Buckingham Palace. Windsor had an inspector and a handful of men; Sandringham, the King's Norfolk country house, was looked after by a sergeant and one or two constables from the Metropolitan Police. Only Balmoral was left in charge of the local force, and then only when the King was absent. When he was in residence, security duties were handed over to a travelling staff of half a dozen officers who were based at Buckingham Palace but accompanied the King wherever he went in the United Kingdom.

Throughout Edward VII's reign, their boss, and the man in charge of all police duties at the royal palaces, was Chief Inspector Percival Spencer, who had been Edward's chief of police at Marlborough House when he was Prince of Wales. Spencer had lodgings in the Norman Gate at Windsor, and an office just inside the tradesmen's entrance on Buckingham Palace Road. His duties ranged from consulting with Charles Stamper over the safest route for the King's car to take, to returning any speeding tickets which might have been issued to the royal fleet of cars. (The King didn't pay them, on principle.)

Spencer was present at Sandringham in November 1907, when Edward's sixty-sixth birthday was marked by a gift from the Transvaal Colony in southern Africa – the Cullinan Diamond. At 3,106 carats, this gem was twice the size of any diamond previously discovered, and it was insured for £1.5 million. There were rumours that an attempt was going to be made to steal it. So the train carrying the two officials and two Scotland Yard detectives who had charge of the diamond was met at Wolferton station by Spencer and a small army of detectives who were waiting on the platform, supported by a considerable body of county policemen in plain clothes who guarded the outside of the station. Spencer ushered the four men into a closed carriage which was escorted to Sandringham by policemen mounted on bicycles, followed by a convoy of carriages led by Spencer and a gaggle of plain-clothes detectives. The route to Sandringham was lined by uniformed constables. Once the presentation was over the officials clambered into one of the King's motor cars and retraced their steps, 'practically the same precautions being taken as upon their arrival [noted *The Times*] as they were carrying the diamond back to London to be deposited with the other Crown jewels in the Tower'.[28]

No one expected Edward VII's reign to be a long one. Fifty-nine when he came to the throne in 1901, overweight (his friends called him 'Tum Tum' behind his back) and not blessed with the best of health, he failed to make it to his own coronation, coming down days before it with an abdominal abscess which nearly killed him: the coronation had to be postponed. When he died in 1910, from emphysema and heart failure following a series of severe attacks of bronchitis, over 400,000 people filed through Westminster Hall to pay their respects as he lay in state, in an outpouring of grief which surprised everyone, even the mourners. With his love of ceremony and ritual, he had restored glamour to the monarchy. And in the words of his biographer Jane Ridley, 'the dissipated, self-indulgent Prince of Wales had somehow transformed himself into the father of the nation'.[29] It was for his son and successor, George V, to maintain that role in the modern world.

CHAPTER FOURTEEN

That Dear Little Man

Browse through old editions of *Who's Who*, and you might be forgiven for thinking that the twentieth-century royal family was awash with equerries. Entry after entry boasts of crown equerries and extra equerries and chief equerries and honorary equerries, equerries in waiting and equerries in ordinary and acting equerries and temporary equerries. There were equerries to kings and queens, equerries to their consorts and their offspring, equerries to their siblings and occasionally equerries to their rather distant cousins.

The word derives from the French *écurie*, meaning 'stable', although somewhere along the way it became confused with 'esquire' and erroneously associated with the Latin for 'horse', *equus*. Equerries were originally answerable to the master of horse: their chief duties were 'to attend the king on horseback, and on all public occasions'; and to manage the stables and 'instruct the pages of honour in horsemanship'.[1]

Their numbers fluctuated from reign to reign. Charles II had a dozen; his brother James II kept six. William III designated one as equerry of the crown stable, the ancestor of men like the urbanely contemptuous Sir Henry Ewart. When Robert Fulke Greville was watching in horror the antics of his poor mad master George III, there were four equerries who came into waiting for a month at a time, with two months off, and by then the role had evolved into a blend of attendant, escort and companion, a sort of aide-de-camp who fetched and carried and generally made sure the sovereign's life ran smoothly. All the members of the royal family who maintained their own households appointed equerries of their own. By the end of the eighteenth century they were invariably military men, going back to their regiments when they were not required. Sovereigns also appointed extra equerries from time to time, although their duties were largely ceremonial.

When Edward VII's son came to the throne as George V in 1910, he maintained a semblance of continuity in the royal household by retaining a few members of his father's household. They included Fritz Ponsonby, in spite of – or perhaps because of – Ponsonby's refusal to flatter his employer. The King regarded him as 'an unavoidable critic'

Sir Frederick ("Fritz") Ponsonby, Keeper of the Privy Purse to George V, auctions a painting by Winston Churchill at a charity fête at Balmoral in 1928.

(Ponsonby's own words), and the assistant private secretary and assistant keeper of the privy purse lost no opportunity to take George V down a peg if he thought the king was listening too closely to sycophants.[2] On one occasion in 1913, for example, he made up a four at real tennis with the King, Derek Keppel, the master of the household, and Keppel's deputy. Ponsonby and Keppel thrashed their opponents, at which the

King sulked and said they didn't understand the game, and they 'ought to send easy ones' – something which more pliant courtiers were happy to do. Ponsonby responded by sending exaggeratedly slow shots over the net, at which the King got cross and told him to play any way he liked. 'So I then proceeded to smash them at him and he sulked and wouldn't move.' The situation was only saved when they switched partners: after Ponsonby had given the King a swift tutorial in real tennis, they won their match. Ponsonby resolved to tell George's usual opponents that they must not 'kowtow to the king in this way'.[3]

By and large, the new king decided that if courtiers were going to behave in such an uncompromisingly familiar way towards George V, by the Grace of God, of the United Kingdom of Great Britain and Ireland and of the British Dominions beyond the Seas, King, Defender of the Faith, Emperor of India, he would prefer them to be old friends rather than old servants of his father and grandmother. Sir Henry Ewart was replaced as crown equerry by Captain the Hon. Sir Charles Wentworth-Fitzwilliam of the Royal Horse Guards, who had been master of the stables in George's household when he was Prince of Wales. The 61-year-old Arthur Bigge, who had started in royal service as assistant secretary to Henry Ponsonby in 1880, was invited to come in as joint private secretary with Sir Francis Knollys, who had held the post under Edward VII and retained it now.

Bigge, who was raised to the peerage as Baron Stamfordham in 1911 (although the King continued to call him 'Bigge'[4]), was sixteen years older than George V. He had served the King's grandmother for twenty years, and when he was ousted in 1901 by Knollys, who was Edward VII's own candidate, he was given the job of private secretary to the Prince of Wales. George quickly came to depend on him. 'I feel that I can always rely on you to tell me the truth however disagreeable and that you are entirely in my confidence,' he told Bigge in a New Year's Day letter of 1902. 'To a person in my position it is of enormous help to me. I thank you again from the bottom of my heart.'[5] For his part, the professional courtier worked hard to train the prince, making sure he took his duties seriously, even correcting his spelling and his writing style. 'What would have happened to me', George once said to him, 'if you had not been there to prepare and help me with my speeches? I can hardly write a letter of any importance without your assistance.'[6] If George lost his temper or was rude to his secretary, he was quick to repair the damage. 'I am a bad hand at saying what I feel,' he wrote on one occasion, 'but I thank God I have a friend like you.'[7]

Stamfordham.

G.R.I
June 1918

George V in June
1918, in the tent in
Buckingham Palace
Gardens that he used
as an office during the
war, attended by his
private secretary, Lord
Stamfordham.

Bigge was bald, with a luxuriant walrus moustache. Like his master, he was slightly built – both men were only about five feet six inches tall – and like him, he was motivated by a tremendous sense of duty and a belief in the Empire. As the main channel of communication between the King and his ministers, he steered a delicate path through some of the constitutional difficulties of the early years of the reign, although his undisguised Tory sympathies earned him the mistrust of successive Liberal leaders. He and Knollys – who was a Liberal – frequently gave the King conflicting advice, until in 1913 George V discovered that Knollys had put the Liberal interest before his duty to the crown and deliberately misled him, something Bigge would never do. Knollys was asked to resign, leaving Bigge as sole private secretary for most of the rest of the reign.

To return to George V's equerries: on his accession in 1910 the King appointed two soldiers and two sailors. The soldiers, Clive Wigram and

Charles Fitzmaurice, had both fought in the Boer War, and had served the King in various capacities when he was Prince of Wales. Fitzmaurice, a son of the Marquess of Lansdowne, had been appointed his equerry in 1909. 'Wiggy' had been on his staff during his visit to India in 1905–6, and was to spend the rest of his life as a courtier, serving the King's two sons and his granddaughter. He 'is simply a glutton for work, besides being a charming fellow,' said the King. 'I am indeed lucky in having found a man like him.'[8]

The naval officers, Charles Cust and Bryan Godfrey-Faussett, were old friends of the King. The three men were contemporaries – they were born within twenty months of each other – and had known each other since the 1870s, when George was serving in the navy with his late brother Eddie: Cust and the King had joined the service together in 1877, in fact. All three served together when George briefly captained the cruiser HMS *Melampus* in 1891. Cust and Godfrey-Faussett had been his

George, Prince of Wales, later George V, photographed in 1904 in one of the first Rolls-Royces. Charles Stewart Rolls is at the wheel, and the prince's equerry, Charles Cust, sits in the back seat (far left).

equerries when he was Prince of Wales. The two of them were devoted to their master. They both wept, overcome with emotion, as they knelt to kiss the new king's hand in 1910.

'I have grown up on the steps of the throne,' Cust once said.[9] His grandfather was equerry and master of the household to Prince Albert's uncle, Leopold of Saxe-Coburg-Saalfeld, and for nearly thirty years master of ceremonies to Queen Victoria. Cust himself spent thirty-eight years in George's service; he was remembered by the Duke of Windsor as 'my father's closest friend'.[10]

He could be as outspoken as Fritz Ponsonby when the mood took him: when Queen Alexandra refused point-blank to move out of Sandringham on Edward VII's death, and George was forced to make use of a cottage on the Sandringham estate, it was Cust who said how absurd it was that a huge house like Sandringham should be occupied by an old lady and her unmarried daughter (Princess Victoria), 'while tiny York Cottage should have to accommodate a married man with a family of six, more especially when that man happened to be the king'.[11] Princess Victoria swore she would never speak to Cust again, and the King told him 'he could not see what the devil it had got to do with him'; but he immediately forgave him.[12] Cust's strong point was that, unlike Fritz Ponsonby, he managed to combine candour with courtesy, straightforwardness with delightful manners.

Godfrey-Faussett was less candid, but just as courteous. Born in 1863 in Waterford, to parents who lacked money and influence, he was sent to sea when he was fourteen, serving as a cadet aboard the training ship HMS *Britannia*, which was where he first became friends with the future George V. Their paths crossed again throughout the 1890s, and when George became Prince of Wales in 1901 on the accession of his father, he appointed Godfrey-Faussett one of his equerries.

The appointment didn't mean giving up the navy, but it did mean abandoning hopes of a glittering naval career. Unlike the Army, which allowed military equerries to rise through the ranks as their turn for promotion came up, the Royal Navy kept a man at the rank he had achieved when he was seconded to royal service. So Godfrey-Faussett and Cust remained captains, on a naval captain's pay.

Godfrey-Faussett was always complaining of being hard up as an equerry, although his ideas of poverty were rather different from our own: he and his wife kept ten servants, for example, including a valet and a lady's maid. But marriage to a woman whose many virtues didn't include domestic economy, coupled with his own determination not to skimp on activities like the tables at Monte Carlo and the considerable expenses he incurred when he was in waiting, meant that money was often tight. (Until 1922, for instance, equerries were expected to pay for their own cartridges when they were shooting with the king.)

His employer knew it, and was generous. When in 1907 the Prince of Wales heard that Godfrey-Faussett was engaged to be married to Eugénie Dudley Ward, the niece of his friend Reggie Esher, he offered the couple the Mill House, a cottage next to a derelict windmill in Dersingham, on the Sandringham estate, at a nominal rent of £25 a year; and then he spent several thousands of pounds improving it. Shortly after the wedding Eugénie, known to everyone by her childhood name of 'Babs', fell ill with appendicitis and the equerry was struggling to pay her medical expenses. In his diary he wrote:

> The Prince left Marlborough House today with the King and, some time before he left, he gave me a letter and on the top he had written that I was not to open it until after he had started. When I did open it, I found it contained a most kind note saying he had been so sorry for me in my anxiety and worry about Babs, and he hoped I would accept the enclosed 'Little Gift which will anyway help to pay the doctor's bill'. The 'Little Gift' was a cheque for £100 … I think he is the kindest person in the world, and I told him so in the letter I wrote to him this evening.[13]

This kindness continued throughout Godfrey-Faussett's career as equerry to George V, which lasted until the latter's death in 1936. In 1913, after the birth of their second son and with Babs complaining that she had to spend long periods alone with the children (and the ten servants) while he was in waiting, he decided they could no longer live in bleak windswept Norfolk, and told the King he intended to leave the Mill House at Dersingham. George V gave him £500 to compensate him for the improvements he had carried out to the place. He offered him the rent-free use of the Ranger's Lodge in Hyde Park, a pleasant detached villa built in 1832. And then he said he didn't want the Godfrey-Faussetts to sever their connection with Sandringham, so he proposed paying the rent of the Mill House for them, on condition that they promised not to tell a soul.

The complement of four equerries dropped to two during the First World War, each serving one month on and one month off. Charles Fitzmaurice, a major in the 1st Royal Dragoons, was killed in action at Ypres in October 1914. Godfrey-Faussett went off to command a coastal patrol vessel in the North Sea, although he was already suffering from an unglamorous bout of haemorrhoids which would cut short his war and bring him home within the year. (The King showed more curiosity about his piles than about his departure for active service: Godfrey-Faussett recalled that his sovereign displayed 'a much more compelling interest in [his] distressing complaint and desired to know every intimate detail'.[14]) The number of equerries was restored to four after the war; and in 1927, when Cust and Godfrey-Faussett were both in their sixties and muttering about retirement, the king took Godfrey-Faussett to one side and said, 'I am going to be very good to you and appoint a fifth equerry, so that neither you nor Charles Cust need do any more winter months.'[15] They could work a couple of months in the summer, he said, and leave the other three equerries to do the rest.

First, last, and always among the equerries' duties was attendance on the monarch. Godfrey-Faussett accompanied George V and Queen Mary during their visit to India for the great Coronation Durbar at Delhi in 1911. (So did three shorthorn cows from Windsor, which were brought along on board HMS *Medina* to provide fresh milk: when one of them fell sick, no one quite knew how to treat the creature, so they poured a pint and a half of neat whisky down her throat. She recovered.) Cust was there in France in 1915 when the King's horse reared during an inspection of the Flying Corps and fell on top of him, breaking his pelvis. 'His colour was so bad two hours after', Cust wrote to Godfrey-Faussett, 'that we thought he was dying.'[16] When the King was being taken back to Boulogne aboard a hospital train and insisted on presenting a Victoria Cross to a sergeant in the Coldstream Guards who had held a position for twenty-four hours armed only with a few hand grenades, it was Cust who read out the citation as the sergeant knelt beside the hospital cot for his sovereign to decorate him.

There were the inevitable rivalries. Godfrey-Faussett was scheduled to be in waiting during the King's visit to the Western Front, but Fritz Ponsonby, who was placed in charge of the arrangements, decided that Cust should go instead, since Godfrey-Faussett had been away with his coastal patrol vessel for six months while Cust hadn't been away at all. Godfrey-Faussett was furious, taking it as an undeserved snub, and according to Ponsonby, 'poured out his lamentations' to the King.[17] George V found himself in an awkward situation, since he was fond of both men; he adopted the time-honoured solution of blaming Ponsonby.

An equerry accompanied the King whenever he travelled. He represented him at funerals. He took down letters and telegrams at the

King's dictation, and ensured that protocols were followed, that orders of precedence were observed, that cars were waiting. He bore the brunt of the King's temper: one day during the First World War when Godfrey-Faussett was kept on the telephone and arrived in the dining room after everyone else had started, he found nothing left for him, and rang the bell for a boiled egg. 'The king accused him of being a slave to his inside, of unpatriotic behaviour,' recalled a delighted Fritz Ponsonby, 'and even went so far as to hint that we should lose the war on account of his gluttony.'[18] And the equerries provided companionship of a kind, walking with their sovereign in the gardens of Buckingham Palace, shooting with him at Sandringham, becoming members of the family, while always remembering that they never quite could be.

Clive Wigram was often in waiting over Christmas, which the royal family spent at Sandringham, first in York Cottage and then after Queen Alexandra's death in 1925 at the 'Big House', as they all called Sandringham House. Wiggy's wife Nora, a member of a distinguished military family, was several times invited to join the party. She recalled a Christmas Eve tea party in the drawing room at York Cottage in 1917. There were six people present: the King and Queen, Clive and Nora, Lieutenant-Colonel Reginald Seymour, who had been appointed as an equerry the previous year, and Lady Catherine Coke, lady in waiting to the Queen. After tea – toast, biscuits, potato scones, jam and sponge cake – Queen Mary rang for a page and said, 'Tell the children we are ready, please,' at which, said Nora, 'there was an avalanche from all directions'.[19] Bertie (the future George VI), Mary, Henry and George arrived with their French mistress and tutor in tow, which makes it seem as though young children piled in from the nursery for their afternoon visit to their mamma and papa. In fact, Prince George, the youngest of the royal offspring, was already fifteen years old; Prince Henry was seventeen, Princess Mary twenty, and Bertie was twenty-two. (The twenty-three-year-old Prince of Wales was absent.) The entire party decamped to the billiard room, where everybody's presents were laid out in separate piles. There was something for everyone: a cigarette case for Reggie Seymour and a jade paper-cutter and a pair of sauceboats for Lady Catherine. Clive Wigram received two colour prints, one of the King and Queen, the other of the Prince of Wales. Nora was given an enamel brooch with a diamond 'G.M.' surmounted by a diamond crown. The Queen gave her husband a set of illustrated sporting books and a set of black pearl studs, while her own presents included lacquer boxes, jade ornaments and 'an old Stuart snuff-box'.[20] Princess Mary got a pair of tortoiseshell and diamond hairpins, an ermine muff and stole and 'a dreadful brilliant blue inkstand from Queen Alexandra', which is perhaps why Queen Mary chose her mother-in-law's present to herself, a pretty Chinese ornament. The three princes were given little pieces of jewellery and items of silver, a family tradition so that they would be well equipped when they married. 'It seemed so funny to see Princes Henry and George staggering off with silver toast-racks, salvers, tea-strainers etc!' Nora recalled.[21]

Christmases at Sandringham were happy family gatherings. They belie George V's reputation as a Victorian tyrant, which is largely based on his notorious pronouncement on child-rearing: 'My father was frightened of his mother; I was frightened of my father, and I am damned well going to see to it that my children are frightened of me.'[22] The king's biographer, Kenneth Rose, questioned whether he ever said those words, although Lady Elizabeth Bowes-Lyon, later queen consort to George VI, certainly believed the sentiment behind them. She once wrote that 'I was never afraid of him as his children were'.[23]

But while George V certainly liked to maintain the impression of an aloof, formidable figure, autocratic and remote from his subjects, the image of an ogre is hard to reconcile with these family celebrations at Sandringham. At another Christmas party to which the Wigrams were invited, in 1926, Nora remarked on the King's easy way with her own three young children (and also on the fact that the royal Christmas presents included ashtrays for all three). Everyone except the King wore party hats at the big dinner, which was held on Boxing Day; and afterwards everyone gathered in the ballroom, where the four princes and Bertie's wife Elizabeth sang rude music hall songs round the piano. Then the King turned on a gramophone and played selections from *La Traviata*, the 'Song of the Volga Boatmen' and finally, to make sure no one was dozing off, the National Anthem. Everyone leapt to their feet and he roared with laughter.

ALONG WITH HIS REPUTATION FOR ALOOFNESS, George V was always known as a king who loved the simple life, a man who was happiest at home with his close friends. That simplicity wasn't achieved without a great deal of effort on the part of those around him. 'My father's life was a masterpiece in the art of well-ordered, unostentatious, elegant living,' recalled Edward VIII. Everything he owned was the best, from his guns made by Purdey to his Fabergé cigarette case, and every detail of every moment of his life was perfectly managed, from the preparation of a shooting lunch in a tent at Sandringham – made 'with the same expert care by the chef as the fine banquets set before crowned heads at Windsor Castle or Buckingham Palace' – to the way the head gamekeeper approached with a game card after the morning's bag had been counted, which was 'as solemn and grave as that of an ambassador presenting his letters of credence'.[24] When the King and his guests processed into dinner at Windsor, a Guards string band hidden behind a grille in the dining room played 'God Save the King'. Cars were always waiting when and where they should be waiting; bands always played the right tunes; nothing ever went wrong. The secret behind this perfection, as an old courtier once explained to the Prince of Wales, was a system which involved having 'the equivalent of a man and a half for every job'.[25]

George V's year followed a fixed pattern. Christmas was spent at Sandringham, and he usually stayed there until the end of January for the last days of the pheasant season. Then he settled for six months in London, although he always moved to Windsor for several weeks at Easter and again in June for Ascot Week. He went down to the Isle of Wight at the end of July for the Cowes Week sailing regatta, then up to Balmoral in August and September for grouse shooting and the Highland games at Braemar, where the monarch was welcomed as chieftain of the Braemar Gathering. He was back in London in October, and off to Sandringham again for Christmas.

King George and Queen Mary had lived at Marlborough House during Edward VII's reign, but when they came to the throne George confirmed his grandmother's and father's choice of Buckingham Palace as the sovereign's main residence. The unveiling of the marble and gilt colossus that is Thomas Brock's Victoria Memorial in 1911 focused attention on the inadequacies of the ordinary piece of street architecture that now acted as a backdrop to the 2,300-ton memorial; and over a three-month period in the summer of 1913 the front of Buckingham Palace was entirely refaced, without even disturbing the glass in the windows, to designs by the stolid but uninspired architect Sir Aston Webb.*

George V took a keen interest in Webb's designs. He was responsible for the creation of the central balcony which over the past hundred years has become the single most famous stage on which the kings and queens

---

* The contractors, Leslie & Co., worked round the clock, employing 300 men during the day and 150 at night.

Buckingham Palace
in October 1913, as
Sir Aston Webb's
remodelling neared
completion.

of Great Britain have shown themselves to the world, insisting that space
was needed 'from time to time on occasions when the King and other
members of the royal family wish to show themselves to the people'.[26]
When the news of the Armistice began to spread on the morning of 11
November 1918, 5,000 people gathered in front of Buckingham Palace,

'the central point of the British Empire', said *The Times*.[27] It was on that balcony that the King appeared to them shortly after eleven o'clock, wearing the uniform of an admiral of the fleet, with Queen Mary beside him, bare headed and wearing a fur coat.

The inner workings of the palace remained arcane. The operational head, the man in charge of the legions of domestic staff, was Sir Derek Keppel, master of the household. Keppel, a son of the 7th Earl of Albemarle, had been appointed equerry to the Duke of York on the latter's marriage in 1893, and deputy master of the household when the Duke, by now Prince of Wales, came to the throne. Two years later he became master of the household, and he retained that post throughout the reigns of George V and his son Edward VIII. It was Keppel who stood beside Edward VIII as his father's coffin was lowered into the vault in St George's Chapel, Windsor, and handed the new king a silver bowl containing the symbolic earth for Edward to scatter over it as Archbishop Lang intoned, 'Earth to earth, ashes to ashes.' In his black frock coat, high collar and waxed white moustaches, Keppel was in effect the general manager of a large hotel, with a staff of around 120 minor officials, clerks, secretaries and menservants, and another eighty female cleaners and maids. This hotel had to feed not only the royal family but also the hundreds of men and women who ate there every day.

The royal chef, who for most of George V's reign was the Frenchman Henri Cedard, sat down in his office after lunch every day to compose the next day's menus, writing them out in a menu book which went for royal approval. Orders for everyday foodstuffs were sent from the chef's office to the department of the comptroller of supply, and the comptroller's staff telephoned out for them. Deliveries were made to the trade door in Buckingham Palace Road and taken straight to the kitchens, where a storeman noted each item in a ledger that was checked by the deputy comptroller every month. (The comptrollership was by now a purely political office; the real work of the department was carried out by the deputy.) A massive cold store held chickens, beef and lamb, grouse, pheasant and partridge in season. Fruit, vegetables and meats were regularly sent up from the royal gardens and farms at Sandringham, Balmoral and Windsor. Whatever the chef required for the day he had to record on a form which the storekeeper later gave in to the deputy comptroller's office for entering in a ledger, so that in theory every single item of food coming into the palace and being consumed was accounted for. Likewise, wines and champagne brought up from the royal cellars were checked in and out, although it was considered one of the perks of working in the palace that servants could help themselves to an occasional glass.[28]

The King's daily routine at Buckingham Palace didn't vary, any more than his yearly round from palace to palace. He was up early and working, before breakfasting with the Queen at 9 a.m. precisely. After breakfast he went to his business room and saw Arthur Bigge and the assistant secretaries. Then, after summoning other household officers as required, he held audiences. At 1 p.m. he went for a short walk in the gardens, accompanied by Charles Cust, or Clive Wigram, or whoever happened to be equerry in waiting, before taking lunch with the Queen and any invited guests at 1.30. The afternoons were usually taken up with official functions; tea, again with the Queen and invited guests, was at 5 p.m. There was more business until dinner, which was taken in the Chinese room and was a family affair, without members of the household present. Afterwards he might read or listen to the gramophone. Punctually at 11.10 each night he retired to bed.

The sequence of events at formal dinners was more strictly regulated. Edward VIII had vivid and uncomfortable memories of evenings spent at Windsor Castle during Ascot Week, when George V and Queen Mary usually entertained a dozen or so invited guests. Shortly before 8.30, the King and Queen and any other members of the family who were dining at the castle would set off towards the green drawing room, part of a suite created for George IV as part of Sir Jeffry Wyatville's remodelling of 1823–40. At the door they were met by Derek Keppel, who bowed and backed into the room, heralding their arrival to the other guests who were arranged in two quarter-circles, men on one side and women on the other. George, his sons and male members of the royal household wore the Windsor uniform, a tailcoat of dark blue with scarlet collar and cuffs, worn over a single-breasted white waistcoat and plain black trousers. The other men in the party wore black tailcoats and knee breeches. Women were more conventionally dressed in evening gowns and jewels.

Queen Mary moved along the men's line, shaking hands, while George V did the same with the women. Then whoever had been commanded to escort the Queen offered her his arm and led her to the table, where a Guards string band concealed behind a grille played 'God Save the King'. The band continued to play throughout the meal, out of sight in a small chamber, wearing their tightly buttoned tunics and, on a warm June evening, drenched in sweat.

Each course was served by liveried footmen in scarlet and pages in blue. The meal lasted no more than an hour, and when it was over the Queen would take the women back to the green drawing room, each one curtseying to the King as she left the royal presence. George V would spend twenty minutes with the men over coffee, port and liqueurs and then abruptly stand and lead them out to join the ladies. Punctually at eleven o'clock the company reassembled in its two quadrants, men on one side and women on the other; George and Mary wished them all good night, and the royal family left the room. The evening was over.

'Nothing was lacking but gaiety,' recalled Edward VIII, who as Prince of Wales found the abrupt and early ending to these entertainments particularly trying.[29] One night he and his brothers, determined 'to enliven the atmosphere for the younger members of the party', arranged for the Guards band to stay behind in the green drawing room and, after their parents had gone to bed, rolled back the carpets and held an impromptu dance. It was a failure: the musicians could only manage some outdated foxtrots. 'The ancient walls seemed to exude disapproval,' the prince remembered. 'We never tried it again.'[30]

At Sandringham and Balmoral, where the daily routine was governed by field sports, things were more relaxed. Guests and courtiers had lunch, tea and dinner with the King and Queen (breakfast was still a family-only affair), and poker was a favourite pastime. But that informality shouldn't be exaggerated: when the Queen rose after dinner to lead the women out, each one curtseyed to the King as she left, and he replied to each with a bow.

———————————•———————————

GEORGE V IS SOMETIMES REPRESENTED AS an emotionally repressed, unfeeling man, someone who cared more about killing game and racing his yacht than about his own children, whom he tyrannised like an ogre from a Victorian melodrama. He was certainly very fond of shooting, and he was very good at it. Bryan Godfrey-Faussett recalled seeing him at Powis Castle with four dead pheasants in the air at the same time; and George and the nineteen-year-old Prince of Wales were members of the shooting party of seven guns which held (and still holds) a British record: shooting on the Hall Barn estate near Beaconsfield on 18 December 1913, they killed 3,937 pheasants, three partridges, four rabbits and one 'other'. ('Perhaps we overdid it today,' the King said afterwards.) He and one of the equerries would sometimes go out alone on the marshes near Sandringham, and even then the death toll could be staggering: Godfrey-Faussett remembered one occasion when he and George V established a local record for variety, with a bag of 142 head of game which included pheasants, hares, rabbits, woodcock, snipe, mallard, widgeon, teal, pigeons 'and one lone moorhen'.[31] That same year, 1913, the King personally saw more than 80,000 head of game killed, and he himself fired over 40,000 cartridges.

As for ocean racing, the King's yacht *Britannia*, built for his father in 1892 and rigged as a racing cruiser in 1913 with groom in waiting Major Philip Hunloke as her racing master, was 'one of the objects dearest to King George's heart', according to an early biographer.[32] Refitted again in the early 1920s, *Britannia* became something of a legend in yachting circles. By 1924 she had won 164 first prizes in 323 starts; ten years later that tally had crept up to 231 firsts in 569 races. And the Sailor King didn't just own *Britannia*: he often took the helm himself, and nothing stopped him playing an active part in a race, so that on any number of occasions Major Hunloke was on edge as he waited to see his employer stunned or knocked overboard. Queen Mary, who didn't venture onto the water if she could help it, used to watch the races from the safety of the shore. 'The *Britannia* has just passed us,' she wrote in August 1925, 'and I saw the King looking very wet and uncomfortable in oilskins – what a way to enjoy oneself.'[33]

The King's other great passion was more sedentary. While he was still Duke of York, he began to take an interest in stamp-collecting, a schoolboy hobby which was just then emerging as a serious pastime. ('It is possibly a question whether the science should properly be called philately or timbrophily,' mused *The Athenaeum* in 1881.[34]) He was encouraged by his uncle Alfred, the Duke of Edinburgh, a keen collector himself and the honorary president of the Philatelic Society. In 1893 Prince Alfred introduced him to a solicitor and philatelist named John Tilleard, who was to serve as secretary to the Philatelic Society from 1894 to his death in 1913. Tilleard helped to manage the duke's growing collection, becoming philatelist to the King when George succeeded his father in 1910.*

George V didn't do things by half-measures. He once told Tilleard, 'I wish to have the best collection and not one of the best collections in England.'[35] To that end, he was prepared to spend enormous sums. In 1904, he paid £1,450 for a rare Mauritius twopenny blue, a world record price for a single postage stamp. The acquisition led to the famous story that the day after the sale, a courtier said, 'Did Your Royal Highness hear that some damned fool has just paid £1,450 for a single stamp?' 'I was that damned fool,' replied George.

The King spent three afternoons a week with his collection. Godfrey-Faussett read up on philately so that when he was in waiting he could talk sensibly about the subject, spending money that he couldn't afford

---

* In 1900 the impecunious Duke of Edinburgh sold his own collection to his brother Edward, then still Prince of Wales, who gave it to his son George.

on stamps. 'Look out you don't get ruined,' warned the King, before launching into an enthusiastic gossip about the fact that a pair of British Guiana two-cents on envelope had just fetched £5,250. 'Wonderful!'[36]

GEORGE V WAS FOND OF ANIMALS. He owned a parrot named Charlotte, an African grey which is variously said to have been acquired by him in Port Said in the 1880s, when he was in the navy, or more prosaically, given to him as a present by his sister Princess Victoria. Charlotte was allowed to roam freely over the breakfast table at Sandringham, pecking at hard-boiled eggs and defecating on the tablecloth, with the King discreetly hiding the mess beneath a mustard pot for fear of incurring his wife's wrath. If his young grandchildren showed signs of nervousness at Charlotte's approach, it drove the King into a rage: 'shouts of "Get that damn child away from me!" … made rather a strong impression on an awakening imagination,' recalled the Princess Royal's eldest son.[37] One of Charlotte's more presentable tricks was to perch on the King's shoulder while he went through his despatch boxes of government papers, squawking 'What about it? What about it?' She had her own table next to his desk in his business room at Buckingham Palace. The King telegraphed his staff when he was out of the country to check on her welfare. When he was sick with septicaemia in 1928–9 Charlotte was just as solicitous in return: kept away from his sickroom, 'she sulked and mourned until the time came again when she could once more be in her royal master's work-room as his constant daily companion', according to a press account at the time.[38] And when he lay dying in his bedroom at Sandringham, she kept vigil in the sitting room next door.

Charlotte wasn't the only parrot in the royal family. The Duke and Duchess of York undertook a tour of Australia in 1927, and returned to England with a white parrot as a present for their eldest daughter, the future Elizabeth II. It lived in the hall at the Yorks' London residence, 145 Piccadilly, where it talked and laughed 'in a manner that often creates a sensation when guests are in the house', gushed a journalist in 1929.[39]

Then there were the dogs. The royal family owned hordes of dogs. George V exhibited collies when he was younger, and bred and exhibited Labradors; in later years, he had a succession of cairn terriers (the last were Snip and Bob). So did the Prince of Wales, later Edward VIII, who was frequently photographed in the company of Cora, a cairn who travelled with him wherever he went. He bred from her, and presented one of her offspring to the little Princess Elizabeth, company for the white parrot and a chow she already owned named Brownie. The prince was also fond of a Welsh terrier presented to him by Welsh breeders when he was installed as Prince of Wales at Caernarvon Castle in 1911, and an Alsatian named Claus of Seale. By the mid-1930s the Duke and Duchess of York owned four golden Labradors and from 1933, a corgi with the rather grand kennel name of Rozavel Golden Eagle, the father of a royal dynasty of corgis that continues to thrive in the twenty-first century. Dookie, as he was called by the family, was prone to bite − another tradition which his descendants have maintained to this day. According to the young princesses' governess, he 'adored the taste of strange trousers'.[40]

George V's other three children all kept dogs. The Princess Royal had three cairn terriers (she also owned a Shetland pony and showed Barnevelder chickens and blue Beveren rabbits). The Duke of Gloucester liked Afghan hounds; the Duke of Kent, Alsatians.

Royal families have always had dogs. Charles II was fond of toy spaniels, and kept a black lurcher called Gypsy; his cousin, Prince Rupert, had greyhounds. Victoria and Albert had Landseer paint them surrounded by their pets − the greyhound Eos, and Skye terriers Islay, Cairnach and Dandie Dinmont. Victoria's King Charles spaniel, Dash, was her faithful companion for seven years; when Albert broke the news that he had died, it 'grieved me so much,' she wrote. 'I was so fond of the little fellow, and he was so attached to me.'[41] Edward VII had Caesar ('I belong to the King'), and Alexandra, a noted dog-lover, accumulated a canine menagerie at Sandringham, where her kennels were filled to overflowing with collies, borzois, dachshunds, fox terriers and spaniels. Journalists were occasionally given tours of Alexandra's kennels: articles appeared in *Country Life* and the *Lady's Realm* at the turn of the century, and Edwardian readers were informed that her two favourites, a pair of Japanese spaniels named Billy and Punchy, were habitually carried around under her arm and slept on silk cushions in her dressing room. The Queen made weekly visits to the others when she was at Sandringham. She was accompanied by her kennelman, Mr Brundson, and used to arrive wearing a white apron and equipped with baskets of bread to dish out as treats:

> The Queen opens the door of each kennel herself, and its occupants come rushing out at the sound of her voice; indeed, the previous

barking has shown that they know who is approaching even before she speaks. The scene is one of tremendous animation when all the dogs have been liberated, and deerhounds, wolfhounds, terriers, Newfoundlands, Spitz's, Bassets, and collies come jumping and barking around.[42]

By 1929, when the *Illustrated London News* carried an article on royal pets, the emphasis had shifted subtly from the dogs to their owners. The author of 'Our Royal Family as Animal-Lovers' wrote gushingly of how three-year-old Princess Elizabeth had 'a new doggy pet', a cairn terrier given to her by the Prince of Wales, 'who is, of course, the adored "Uncle David" of Princess Elizabeth'.[43] The piece ran through the entire royal family, listing their dogs and praising their successes as breeders. Snip, 'King George's special canine companion', had been 'a very unhappy little fellow' during the King's recent illness, but was happy again now by his master's side. The Princess Royal's rabbits, Prince George's Alsatians, the parrots of the King and the Duke of York – all came in for a mention. 'The Duchess of York's love for dogs dates back to her childhood days at Glamis, since when she has never been without a pet dog.'[44] In an accompanying photograph, a smiling 'Uncle David' looked out at the reader, wearing a flat cap and a Fair Isle jumper and brandishing one of his terriers above a caption proclaiming, 'With a cairn bred by himself: the Prince of Wales on holiday'.

Media stories that humanised the royal family are reminders that in an age of mass communications the King and his courtiers could not afford not to engage with the public. In 1917, when discontent about the conduct of the war was spilling over into mutterings about the role of the King and Queen, and there were fears among George V's close circle that his popularity was suffering, Charles Cust took Bryan Godfrey-Faussett to task for being rude to the press and complaining about press intrusion. 'Should we not readjust our sense of values and see whether we cannot use the press and photographers to the benefit of T.M's [Their Majesties]?' he asked his fellow equerry. 'Should we not all try to co-operate and encourage H.M. to step more before the public, and not hide his light under a bushel?'[45] Godfrey-Faussett agreed, but when the two men tried to manage the King's relationship with the media, they received short shrift from Arthur Bigge, who considered it no business of a royal equerry to modify policy. Even so, it was obvious that if George V ignored the media, the media would not ignore him. He had to appear more before the public.

And with the help and encouragement of his courtiers (and successive prime ministers) he did, achieving a remarkable balance between the contradictory claims on him from those who needed a reigning monarch to be distant from his people, above faction and politics, and those who would only accept a king who shared his people's hopes and cares. Edward VIII was full of admiration for his father's success:

> By the force of his own authentic example – the King himself in the role of the bearded paterfamilias, his devoted and queenly wife, their four grown sons and a daughter, not to mention the rising generation of grandchildren – he transformed the Crown as personified by the royal family into a model of the traditional family virtues, a model that was all the more genuine for its suspected but inconspicuous flaws.[46]

In 1923 John Reith, the managing director of the newly formed British Broadcasting Company, invited George V to deliver a wireless message to his subjects at Christmas or New Year. The King refused and, although the BBC broadcast his speeches on various ceremonial occasions in the 1920s, he continued to refuse until 1932, when a combined offensive by Reith, Prime Minister Ramsay MacDonald and Clive Wigram finally persuaded him. Shortly after 3.00 p.m. on Christmas Day of that year he broadcast a short speech which had been written for him by Rudyard Kipling, from a little room under the stairs at Sandringham. It began:

> Through one of the marvels of modern science, I am enabled, this Christmas Day, to speak to all my peoples throughout the Empire. I take it as a good omen that wireless should have reached its present perfection at a time when the Empire has been linked in closer union. For it offers us immense possibilities to make that union closer still.[47]

The broadcast was a great success. It brought the King into the homes of his subjects. He was addressing them personally when he told them that 'I speak from my home and from my heart to you all', and when he wished them a happy Christmas. *The Observer* announced that 'the annihilation of space is a new and a most momentous buttress of Imperial Britain', and predicted that it would not be long before the remotest subject would be able 'not only to hear the voice of the king, but to see his majesty in the act of utterance'.[48] The King himself was less enthusiastic, and decided he didn't want to repeat the experience. It ruined his Christmas, he said. Only when the secretary of state for the dominions, J. H. Thomas, showed him some of the appreciative letters that poured in from every corner of the Empire did he relent and agree to a Christmas message becoming a regular fixture.

Even more intriguing as an early example of the mass marketing of the monarchy were the silver jubilee celebrations three years later. On Monday 6 May 1935, the nation and the Empire marked the twenty-fifth anniversary of the King's accession to the throne. Congratulations poured in from all over the world. Pope Pius XI sent a telegram praising the King's 'enlightened and beneficent rule'; President Franklin Roosevelt told him: 'It is gratifying to contemplate the wise and steadfast influence which Your Majesty has exerted for a quarter of a century.'[49]

Less conventional, however, was the fact that the service of thanksgiving in St Paul's Cathedral was broadcast live by the BBC, and relayed across the world. Other countries' broadcasters were there to report on the ceremonies: 'I saw before me in flesh and blood the famous Yeomen of the Guard, with which we French are so familiar on tourist posters at home,' one French broadcaster told his audience. 'They really exist!'[50]

That evening the BBC broadcast live messages from all the Commonwealth leaders (except the official speaker of Newfoundland, which confounded the best efforts of the BBC's engineers: his loyal greetings had to be pre-recorded). There were contributions from India, South Africa, Southern Rhodesia; from Australia, New Zealand, Canada and Bermuda. Last to speak was Ramsay MacDonald, who after a reference to 'the economic destruction which is the inheritance left to our generation', praised George V for wearing a heavy crown with dignity and human understanding. 'His advisers have come and gone,' said MacDonald, 'but for him there has been no respite. Days have mounted into months, months into years, and he has had to endure, winning, however, the devotion of all who have been called to understand and serve him.'[51]

Then at eight o'clock came the King's speech, broadcast live from Buckingham Palace. It was relayed to theatres all over London. In the Connaught Rooms, where Rudyard Kipling was the speaker at the annual dinner of the Royal Society of St George, everyone stood up to listen to the broadcast. In towns and villages all over the country those who had wireless sets held open house. Pubs opened their windows so that people standing outside could listen as the King, coughing slightly and sounding old, told them that 'I dedicate myself anew to your service for the years that may still be given to me'.[52]

It was a sombre message that he gave that night, full of references to the Depression and the high unemployment rates. (No one was immune: even the palace had made drastic staff reductions.) 'My people and I have come through great trials and difficulties together,' said the King. 'They are not over.' Afterwards, Kipling's speech from the Royal Society of St George's banquet was broadcast; his subject was 'England and the English', and he ended with a rousing tribute to the King, whose sacrifice and devotion had come 'to create, to stiffen, and to inspire, the whole taken-for-granted fabric of sanity and silent discharge of duty, both in the island and throughout our Empire, on which our destiny depended'.[53] Then came community singing of national songs from Broadcasting House, and at 10.30 John Masefield, the poet laureate, read his Jubilee Ode: 'O God, vouchsafe him many years | With all the world as England's friend.'

The aftermath of this most public of public celebrations saw two of George V's longest-serving courtiers raised to the peerage. Fritz Ponsonby, who had served the King's father and grandmother over a period of forty years, became the 1st Baron Sysonby of Wonersh; and Clive Wigram, who had succeeded Arthur Bigge as the King's private secretary, became the 1st Baron Wigram of Clewer. It was touch and go as to whether the King would grant them their titles: he felt he couldn't ennoble Wigram without granting a similar honour to Ponsonby; but he didn't like Ponsonby, who continued to speak his mind and to irritate the King by doing so. Invited to a royal screening of *The Lives of a Bengal Lancer* at the Duke of Devonshire's Compton Place in Eastbourne, where the King was convalescing after catching a bad cold, Ponsonby remarked that although George told him he had brought very few servants down with him, when the screening began he looked round and counted forty-five of them. 'I wondered how many there would have been if the king had not expressed the wish to have a few.'[54] In the end, Wigram's plaintive cry that it was 'bad luck to be dispossessed of a heritage through the vagaries of a colleague' persuaded Ramsay MacDonald to lobby the King for a change of heart, and both old courtiers received their titles in the Jubilee Honours List of June 1935.[55]

Less than eight months later George V was dead of the lung disease which had dogged him for years, his end hastened by a cocktail of morphine and cocaine administered by his doctor, Lord Dawson. Bryan Godfrey-Faussett, who did not receive a title for his decades of service to his king (although he did get a knighthood), was heartbroken. Afterwards he asked to be left alone for a moment with his memories in the King's business room at Buckingham Palace. It was just the same as it always had been, except there was no Charlotte squawking on her perch by the desk, no cairn terrier barking a greeting. And no King, no 'dear little man', as the old equerry called him:

> How often in the last many years had I been in that room; sometimes sent for, sometimes without being asked; the king either at his desk, or sitting in his chair by the fire reading. While he talked I stood balancing first on one leg and then the other, often for a considerable time; and perhaps he would move on through the Audience Room to his Dressing Room – I following in his wake – to get ready for luncheon or for a walk in the garden … and sometimes I would be sworn at, though not often, and when I was, I usually deserved it. It is sad indeed to think it is all at an end.[56]

CHAPTER FIFTEEN

Secretaries

'THERE IS MUCH SPECULATION ABOUT THE NEW COURT,' wrote the American-born British politician Henry 'Chips' Channon in his diary for January 1936, a week after George V's death. 'Will the king keep his own entourage or take on his father's?'[1]

Edward VIII is the only British monarch to set out in print his thinking on how he shaped his new household. In *A King's Story*, the fascinating if self-justificatory memoir he published fifteen years after his abdication, he remembered how for the first six months of his reign he carried on with his father's somewhat elderly household team, as convention demanded. Both Sir Derek Keppel, master of the household, and Sir Bryan Godfrey-Faussett, the senior equerry, were seventy-three; Lord Wigram was sixty-three.

But Edward VIII, who was forty-one when he came to the throne, wanted younger men about him, men who had either been on his staff when he was Prince of Wales, or whom he had come to know over the

Clive Wigram (far right) beside a fallen elm in the grounds of Windsor Castle, 1916. Wigram's wife Norah stands beside him. The couple on the left is Sir John Fortescue, librarian at Windsor, and his wife Lady Winifred.

years. He was relaxed about most of the purely ceremonial appointments, which by now were being made by the government of the day, in this case a coalition national government led by Conservative prime minister Stanley Baldwin. And he turned for advice on some of the others to the Earl of Cromer, who had been George V's lord chamberlain and who agreed to stay on in the post.

But when it came to the most important posts in the twentieth-century royal household – the private secretary and the keeper of the privy purse – Edward VIII wanted men he knew and trusted. Lord Sysonby, who had been keeper since 1914, had died the previous year, and the duties of both the keeper and the private secretary had fallen to Wigram. Wiggy and the new king didn't like each other: Edward thought Wiggy belonged to the past, while Wiggy had no faith in Edward's judgement: 'He's mad. He's mad. We shall have to lock him up.'[2]

So in July 1936 Wiggy went. His place was taken by two men. Ulick Alexander was a decorated war hero who had been on the staff of the King's wayward youngest brother, Prince George, Duke of Kent. Edward first met him in South Africa in the 1920s. 'Major Alexander later on was associated with a South African mining interest and a large insurance company, and in addition looked after the affairs of my brother George,' he recalled. 'It was in this connection that I became impressed by his fine qualities.'[3] Alexander was appointed keeper of the privy purse.

The King's choice for private secretary was Sir Godfrey Thomas, a career diplomat who had acted as his private secretary for the past seventeen years; he had been instrumental in cultivating Edward's image when Prince of Wales as a new type of royal – informal, socially concerned, ready to flout convention and eager to look to the future rather than the past. The King's father had been a man of conservative tastes. In Edward's words, George V had disapproved of 'Soviet Russia, painted fingernails, women who smoked in public, cocktails, frivolous hats, American jazz, and the growing habit of going away for week-ends'.[4]

Edward could not have been more different. He wore a lounge suit on official engagements and flew his own aeroplane: when he bought a new De Havilland Puss Moth monoplane in 1930 the press commented that its closed cabin and spare seat would allow him to travel in 'ordinary dress' and be accompanied by his equerry.[5] He had his portrait painted wearing his polo kit. He was captain of three golf clubs, including the Royal and Ancient; the popular press noted that he was 'an excellent exponent of Jazz and the Tango'.[6] During the Depression he visited depressed coal-mining villages and working men's clubs, listening to the grievances of the unemployed and presiding over various job-creation initiatives.

Godfrey Thomas had many qualifications for the job of private secretary: a knowledge of languages, diplomatic skills, a dash of cynicism and, in Edward's words, 'a diffident manner that disguised perfect confidence in his ability to perform any task he undertook'.[7] He acted as Edward's press secretary, dealing with the media and issuing press releases. In fact, he helped to mould Edward's image as a popular playboy prince with a social conscience. But for some reason, when the new king asked him to continue as his private secretary, he said no; he would prefer to be an assistant secretary,

Edward later claimed this was down to modesty: 'he did not rate his own qualities quite so highly as I did',[8] Whatever the reason, Thomas suggested that Edward should offer the post to Alec Hardinge, who had served as equerry, assistant private secretary and assistant keeper of the privy purse to George V. Hardinge turned out to be an unfortunate choice.

So did Edward VIII's second assistant secretary. Alan Lascelles, known as 'Tommy', had an unusual career as a courtier. After a war in which he received both a Military Cross and a shell splinter in his right arm, he was appointed assistant private secretary to the Prince of Wales, working under Godfrey Thomas. For more than eight years he served 'the most attractive man I have ever met', as he confided to his diary after his first meeting with the Prince at St James's Palace in November 1920.[9] He accompanied him on overseas trips to America, Canada and east Africa; he wrote his speeches, answered press queries and generally did his best to help organise the prince's life.

But all the time he was growing more and more disillusioned with

Edward, Prince of Wales, with Alan 'Tommy' Lascelles, September 1924.

his employer's behaviour. One evening in Government House, Ottawa, at the end of the prince's 1927 Canadian trip, Lascelles asked Prime Minister Baldwin, who was with the royal party, if he could have a word. In a little sitting room at the end of a first-floor passage Lascelles sat Baldwin down and told him that the prince, 'in his unbridled pursuit of wine and women, and of whatever selfish whim occupied him at the moment, was going rapidly to the devil, and unless he mended his ways, would soon become no fit wearer of the British Crown'.[10] He went further, telling the prime minister that it might be best for the country if, in the course of one of the steeplechases he rode in, the prince were to break his neck. 'God forgive me, I have often thought the same,' replied Baldwin. Then he promised to have a straight talk with the prince when they got back to England.[11]

He didn't. The following year, while Lascelles was with the prince in east Africa, a cable arrived saying that George V was desperately ill (he had septicaemia) and urging the heir to the throne to come back to England immediately. The prince ignored the plea and spent the evening seducing a Mrs Barnes, wife of the local commissioner.

His callous attitude was too much for Lascelles. 'Sir,' he said to him, 'the King of England is dying; if that means nothing to you, it means a great deal to me.'[12] He resigned his post, giving the prince a good talking-to about his general behaviour before he went, and receiving this rather sad reply when the two men parted. 'Well, goodnight, Tommy, and thank you for the talk. I suppose the fact of the matter is that I'm quite the wrong sort of person to be Prince of Wales.'[13]

From 1931 to 1935 Lascelles was in Ottawa, serving as secretary to the governor-general of Canada. Back in England at the end of 1935, he was asked by Clive Wigram to join the King's household as assistant private secretary. At first he wasn't any too keen: the King was in poor health and if he died, Lascelles would find himself in the embarrassing position of working for the man he not only despised, but whose employment he had left so dramatically six years before. But Wigram reassured him that the King was in splendid health, with years left in him.

This was a lie, of course. Six weeks after Lascelles took up his post at Buckingham Palace, George V was dead and Edward VIII was on the throne of England.

As the disaster that was Edward VIII's 326-day reign careered towards its end, Hardinge and Lascelles found themselves at the heart of the abdication crisis. As the King saw it, their first duty was to him. As far as they were concerned, the King's first duty was to the country. These two positions were not compatible.

Edward's mistresses were an open secret at court and beyond it. For many years he had an on–off relationship with Freda Dudley Ward, the half-American wife of William Dudley Ward, a barrister who served as treasurer of the household to Edward VII and George V. The latter sneered at Freda, calling her 'Freda Loom' or 'the lace-maker's daughter', both references to her father's involvement in the Nottingham lace trade. Freda renovated houses and dabbled in interior decoration: she helped Edward to remodel Fort Belvedere, the strange concoction of towers and battlemented bays in Windsor Great Park that the prince begged from his father in 1929. 'What could you possibly want that queer old place for?' asked George V. 'Those damn week-ends, I suppose.'[14] It was Freda who advised on the decoration of the Fort, where the prince installed a new swimming pool and tennis court, central heating and a Turkish bath. But by the time he moved in he had also moved on, and begun a relationship with Thelma Furness, the wife of a shipping magnate and the daughter of an American diplomat. (Edward had a penchant for mistresses with American blood: when he said he wanted to introduce at Fort Belvedere 'many of the creature conveniences that I had sampled and enjoyed in the New World', those who knew him best must have smiled.[15]) Thelma openly acted as the prince's hostess at the Fort, greeting guests who came down for those damn weekends, presiding at his table. Jack Aird, the prince's equerry, was sometimes there, as was groom in waiting Gerald Trotter, a one-armed Boer War veteran who was devoted to Edward, habitually referring to him as 'My Master'.[16]

No one seemed to mind the arrangement. People who visited in Thelma's time often remarked on the relaxed way in which the prince entertained. The Fort was relatively small as country houses go, and there were rarely more than half a dozen guests. The prince would greet them personally at the door when they arrived, introducing them to their fellow-guests and then showing them up to their room. After cocktails and dinner, there might be cards, or desultory attempts at a jigsaw puzzle which was laid out on a long table in the drawing room. Thelma liked to dance, and a gramophone in the corner provided the music. The next day Edward was apt to appear in baggy plus-fours and a sweater, brandishing a billhook and inviting everyone to join him in clearing away the laurels.

'It's not exactly a command,' Trotter would tell them, 'but I've never known anyone to refuse.'[17] Work was never mentioned. 'There must be a tacit understanding in this place and in this company that he would deliberately put aside his official concerns,' recalled one guest, who spent the weekend with Thelma and the prince at Fort Belvedere in January 1932.[18]

That guest was an American, and her name was Wallis Simpson.

Edward's relationship with the wife of shipbroker Ernest Simpson began unexceptionally enough, in the early part of 1934. That January Thelma went to America to visit her sister Gloria. A few days before she sailed she had lunch at the Ritz with Wallis, an old friend, and asked her to look after the prince for her while she was away. 'It was later evident that Wallis took my advice all too literally,' wrote Thelma in her memoirs.[19] Within weeks, rumours were circulating, and Wallis was protesting to her aunt that 'it's all gossip about the prince. I'm not in the habit of taking my girl friends' beaux.'[20] But that was exactly what she did. When Thelma returned to England at the end of March the prince was unaccountably cool towards her. After a dinner at the Fort where she watched her lover flirting openly with Wallis, she confronted him that night in her bedroom:

> 'Darling,' I asked bluntly. 'Is it Wallis?'
> The prince's features froze. 'Don't be silly!' he said crisply. Then he walked out of the room, closing the door quietly behind him.
> I knew better. I left the Fort the following morning.[21]

The fact that the heir to the throne had a new mistress was no cause for distress to anyone, except Thelma (and, perhaps, Gerald Trotter – when he retired in 1936 it was rumoured that he had in fact been sacked because he kept up his friendship with Thelma). Over the next two years Mrs Simpson became a fixture in the prince's social circle. He introduced her to his friends and his family – his brothers and their wives, at least – and by April 1935 Chips Channon was confiding to his diary that 'she has already the air of a personage who walks into a room as though she almost expected to be curtsied to'.[22] According to Edward's own account, it was around this time that he began to consider the possibility of marriage, although since his intended was already married (and once divorced) he realised that the course of true love was unlikely to run smooth. However, accustomed as he was to getting his own way in most things, the prince seemed to have assumed a way would be found, even after he came to the throne in January 1936. Kingship didn't moderate his behaviour – he continued to preside over an alternative court at Fort Belvedere, dismissing those courtiers who disapproved of him as reactionaries. Channon was disgusted with the way that Alec Hardinge, although quite young – he was the same age as his master – had come to adopt traditional court mores, criticising Edward and his entourage: 'It is high time such dreary narrow-minded fogies were sacked.'[23]

Wallis filed for divorce in the summer of 1936, and a decree nisi was granted at Ipswich Assizes on 27 October. 'England keeps divorce of king's friend a secret' was the headline in the *Chicago Tribune*, which confidently predicted that the couple wouldn't marry:[24] 'the British middle-class morality will stand for discreet escapades of a bachelor monarch, but not for public defiance of conventions.'

Subsequent events were to prove that both marriage and the public defiance of conventions were in the King's mind by now, a fact that soon dawned on court and government. On the evening of 13 November, Edward returned to Fort Belvedere after two days spent with the fleet down at Portland, to find a letter from Hardinge marked 'Urgent and Confidential'. Hardinge informed Edward that it was only a matter of days before his intentions with regard to Wallis came out in the press; that the government was likely to resign if he didn't back down; and that there was no possibility of forming another. The letter ended:

> If Your Majesty will permit me to say so, there is only one step which holds out any prospect of avoiding this dangerous situation, and that is for Mrs Simpson to go abroad without further delay, and I would beg Your Majesty to give this proposal your earnest consideration before the position has become inevitable.[25]

The King was furious. Part of Hardinge's role was to advise him on his relationship with government, but Edward believed that his private secretary was in league with Stanley Baldwin's government – that he was putting the interests of the country before the interests of his king.

He was right. As battle lines were drawn over the affair, Hardinge had decided that his loyalties lay with the institution of the monarchy rather than with the monarch himself, and consulted with both Baldwin and the editor of *The Times*, Geoffrey Dawson, over what to do about Wallis. 'The King's private secretary is a solitary figure,' Edward later wrote, 'and ploughs a lonely furrow.'[26]

The power behind the throne: Tommy Lascelles in 1948.

Tommy Lascelles was equally hostile. He felt a real contempt for Edward VIII, whom he regarded as weak, venal, wilful and determined to put his own happiness first. He recalled hearing of a painful interview which the King had with Queen Mary at Marlborough House when the storm broke. The queen asked her son to reflect on the effect his actions would have on his family, the throne and the Empire:

> His only answer [wrote Lascelles] was, 'Can't you understand that nothing matters – nothing – except her happiness and mine?' That was the motto which, for some years past, had supplanted 'Ich Dien' [the motto of the Princes of Wales, 'I serve'] – and that was essentially the underlying principle of his brief reign.[27]

For Lascelles and Hardinge this was the simple, unforgivable crime. Years later, asked to reflect on the abdication, Lascelles produced a private and devastating critique of the character of the King:

> He had, in my opinion and in my experience, no comprehension of the ordinary axioms of rational, or ethical, behaviour; fundamental ideas of duty, dignity and self-sacrifice had no meaning for him, and so isolated was he in the world of his own desires that I do not think he ever felt affection – absolute, objective affection – for any living being, not excluding the members of his own family.[28]

Not surprisingly in the circumstances, Edward dispensed with the services of Hardinge and Lascelles in the final weeks of his reign. They remained in post, but he turned instead to his lord in waiting, Peregrine Brownlow, and his lawyer, Walter Monckton, whom he invited down to Windsor Castle a few days after receiving Hardinge's letter. (In the coming days, the King resorted to smuggling Monckton into Buckingham Palace to keep Hardinge and Lascelles from hearing about their meetings.) It was Brownlow who arrived in his Rolls-Royce at the Fort at dusk on 3 December to whisk Wallis Simpson away to France while the King made his decision to abdicate. It was Monckton who negotiated a financial settlement with the King's brother on Edward's behalf, and Monckton who prepared the first draft of the historic abdication speech, with its defiant confession that 'I have found it impossible to carry the heavy burden of responsibility and to discharge my duties as king as I would wish to do without the help and support of the woman I love.'[29]

When it was all over, Monckton managed to remain on friendly terms with the new regime. Not so Perry Brownlow. On 21 December, ten days after Edward VIII's brother Albert came to the throne as George VI, Brownlow was due to come into waiting. He received the customary card reminding him of the fact, but on the day, he was told that there was no need for him to appear at Buckingham Palace, since George VI was only meeting with the Archbishop of Canterbury that afternoon, and the meeting was an informal one at the King's old home, 145 Piccadilly. The following day a notice appeared in the Court Circular announcing that the Marquess of Dufferin and Ava had succeeded as lord in waiting. When Brownlow telephoned the palace for an explanation, he was told his name would never appear in the Court Circular again.

He demanded to speak to the lord chamberlain of the household, the Earl of Cromer. Cromer informed him that his resignation had been accepted, even though it had not been offered. 'Am I to be turned away like a dishonest servant with no notice, no warning, no thanks,' asked an outraged Brownlow, 'when all I did was to obey my master, the late king?'

'Yes,' said Cromer.[30]

⁎

THE EXTENT TO WHICH THE NEW REIGN meant triumph for the old guard at the palace rather depended on one's point of view. For Edward VIII, now the Duke of Windsor and simmering in exile in France, George VI was a younger version of George V, with the same outlook on life. For Edward's supporters, George VI's accession represented a defeat for the forces of progress. His decision to be styled King George, a deliberate reference to the happier, more stable reign of his father, was popular with the country, but it seemed to confirm fears that his presence on the throne represented a victory for the forces of reaction. His wife Queen Elizabeth, whose resentment at the way her brother-in-law had walked away and left her husband to pick up the pieces was well known, was accused of plotting to purge the court of anyone who might have been sympathetic to Edward. Others believed the retreat into the past was all the fault of Edward's household officers. 'It is those old courtiers, Wigram and Co. and above all Alec Hardinge, ever … the late King's … relentless foe,' wrote Chips Channon.[31]

To members of this old guard, though, King George VI and Queen Elizabeth proved distressingly modern. Bryan Godfrey-Faussett, now in his mid-seventies and already pained to see that many peers at the coronation wore their coronets at rather jaunty angles, was frankly appalled when he attended one of the new regime's first court balls: 'I saw many things which could not have happened in King George V's time: Ambrose's Dance Band: a crooner!!: sit-down suppers: smoking allowed everywhere except in the ball room: shades of King George IV!!'[32]

During World War II, the King would give a dance in Buckingham Palace's bow room once a fortnight. Officers from suitable regiments were invited as partners for the young princesses and their friends, and George VI and Queen Elizabeth – both of whom dearly loved dancing – usually joined in. One household official remembered seeing the King leading a conga, followed by his wife and daughters, their partners and their guests. Wearing a dinner jacket and black tie and laughing out loud, he led the line out and into the labyrinth of corridors, while the dance band played to an empty room. Eventually the dancers reappeared, slightly out of breath, to the sounds of 'Hi! Hi! Conga!'[33]

I N 1942 THE PUBLICATION OF ARTHUR PONSONBY'S BIOGRAPHY of his father, *Henry Ponsonby: His Life from His Letters*, caused a flurry of interest in the pivotal role of the private secretary to the sovereign. Much of it, admittedly, was directed at the light which the book shed on Queen Victoria. The *Manchester Guardian*'s reviewer pictured Sir Henry as constantly in attendance on an imperious, arbitrary and intolerant queen and decided that 'a more difficult and, one would think, a more disagreeable office could scarcely be found'. But here and there the book's appearance provoked musings on the role of the sovereign's secretary. What, exactly, did he *do*? What was his place in the constitution? And to whom was he accountable? One of the most thoughtful pieces came from the left-wing political theorist Harold Laski. In a review article simply called 'The King's Secretary' Laski set out the qualities that were required in a man whose position was, he said, one of 'dignified slavery':

> He must know all that is going on; he must be ready to advise upon all. But he must never so advise that he seems to influence the decision taken … Receiving a thousand secrets, he must discriminate between what may emerge and what shall remain obscure. And he has to steer his way through the complicated labyrinth of anxious politicians, jealous courtiers, the mass of continental royalties, each of whom is on the watch lest a right be withheld or a claim denied.[34]

The secretary to the sovereign, Laski went on, was there to advise and encourage and warn, without ever seeming to represent his own interests or to put those of the government above those of his employer. And the sovereign had to know that: once his or her confidence in a secretary was lost, there was no way back.

Alec Hardinge's relations with George VI, whom he went on to serve as private secretary after Edward VIII's abdication, were strained. Hardinge disagreed with Prime Minister Neville Chamberlain's policy of appeasement, unlike his employer, who complained that 'A.H. had always strong and unhelpful views'.[35] And he felt marginalised by George VI's practice of using his wife Queen Elizabeth as his confidante. In July 1943 Hardinge resigned as the King's private secretary, after seven years in the job. He was only forty-nine, but the story was put out that he had been advised to go by the royal doctors for the sake of his health.

The truth was more complicated. Although he was an able administrator he refused to delegate, and had a knack, unfortunate in any man, but doubly unfortunate in someone in his position, of upsetting people and not really caring that he had upset them. The politician and future prime minister Harold Macmillan accused him of being 'idle [which he wasn't], supercilious [which he was], without a spark of imagination or vitality'.[36] The Queen disliked him. The King wanted him gone, but couldn't bring himself to sack him. (In 1938, he suggested that Hardinge might like to become governor of Madras, but the secretary failed to take the hint.) According to Tommy Lascelles, Lord Clarendon, the lord chamberlain and the man who could have fired Hardinge, 'could not be trusted with negotiating a change of scullery maids, let alone of private secretaries'.[37] So nothing happened, and the discontent had rumbled on.

Until June 1943, when Hardinge accompanied George VI on a morale-boosting visit to the troops in north Africa and Malta. The trip was a success; but the King's secretary had taken the keys to the red despatch boxes which held government papers for the King's attention, so that for nearly two weeks the two assistant private secretaries left behind in England weren't able to deal with their contents. Lascelles was particularly furious and, when Hardinge returned and peremptorily dismissed his complaints, he announced that he was going to resign and added that Hardinge should go too. Then he told him why, at length.

Hardinge's response was to tender his own resignation to the King, who accepted it with enthusiasm. (When Lascelles suggested to George VI that he give Hardinge six months' leave to reflect on his position, the King replied, 'Certainly not – he might come back.'[38]) The end result was that Tommy Lascelles, as the senior of the two assistants, stepped into the post of private secretary.

Lascelles always maintained that he never aspired to Hardinge's job as private secretary, and perhaps he meant it. Tired out by four years of his second world war, and with no real flair for public life, he claimed, he wanted nothing better than to remain as assistant private secretary (APS) until 1947, when he would reach the age of sixty and retire to the country. Nevertheless, having precipitated Hardinge's departure he stepped into his shoes, to congratulations from everybody from the Archbishop of Canterbury to Admiral Mountbatten.

As APS to George VI, Lascelles had been upright, decent, efficient and urbane, with a soldier's capacity for action. In the crush after the 1937 coronation, when the crowds of guests trying to leave Westminster Abbey were jammed like sardines into the canvas tunnels which had been set up at the exit points, he drew his dress sword and slashed a doorway in the wall of one of them, through which he and his wife Joan managed to escape.[39] Knighted in June 1939 by a giggling George VI in the middle of the night aboard a train pulling into Buffalo, New York, in the course of a royal visit to the United States – 'I can fairly claim to be the first man to be dubbed in a train,' he wrote, 'and also the first Englishman to be so treated by his sovereign on American soil' – he also had a capacity for fun.[40] Playing charades at Balmoral in 1942 with the King and Queen and the two little princesses, he stole the show with his impression of a St Bernard dog, complete with an ice bucket slung round his neck to represent the brandy keg. He barked so much that he strained his vocal cords and couldn't talk next morning.

His duties weren't exactly onerous, even in wartime. As APS he made travel arrangements for the royal family, and travelled with them. He responded to telegrams and dealt with the press, applying a simple test to the frequent requests for an interview with, or an article about, the King and Queen – would it do more harm than good? Most, he felt, would do more harm, like the elderly author who wanted to publish details of long conversations he had had with the spirits of George V, Queen Alexandra and other members of the royal family.

But much of Lascelles's time was spent pursuing the leisurely life of a gentleman. In 1940, he and Joan moved out of the house they occupied at St James's Palace. He moved into Buckingham Palace while she went to live in the country, although she came up to town occasionally. 'Telegrams all day' reads a typical entry in his wartime journal. 'Joan dined with me at the Ritz, and we went to see the new Disney film, *Bambi*.'[41] He took a turn as a firewatcher on the roof of Buckingham Palace every Tuesday night, and sympathised with the female clerks at the palace when they complained that they couldn't find anywhere nearby to get a decent lunch.

That wasn't a problem with which he had to grapple. He was a regular at the Travellers' Club and Pratt's, both only a few minutes' walk from the palace; and in January 1943 he was elected to the Beefsteak, 'an unwarranted extravagance on my part, but, leading this sort of life, I get so sick of seeing only the same people at the Travellers or Pratt's that I must have a change'.[42] If the King and Queen went away without him he might watch the cricket at Lord's. ('Turf excellent, and no signs of any damage through enemy action.'[43]) There were brisk morning walks with the King along the river bank at Windsor, and games of bowls and croquet on a new lawn below the terrace there, which Lascelles had arranged to have laid.

In *The English Constitution* (1867), the journalist Walter Bagehot set out the three rights which the sovereign possessed in a constitutional monarchy: the right to be consulted, the right to encourage and the right to warn. The last two also belonged to the sovereign's private secretary, and an able and influential secretary like Tommy Lascelles might well take the first upon himself as well. Promotion to private secretary meant an increase in salary from £1,500 to £2,500 a year. It meant he could bring his family back from the country and install them in Winchester Tower at Windsor Castle, where they occupied a rather nice furnished flat that had been fitted out for the King and Queen in case bombs rendered Buckingham Palace uninhabitable. And it meant he could move from his small office at the palace into a more dignified apartment near the foot of the King's staircase, with the keys to the executive washroom, or at least, the Buckingham Palace equivalent: 'the plumbers (at my instigation) have rigged up a magnificent urinal in the private secretary's wash-place outside my room, which will be a great boon to me,' he noted in his diary.[44]

Promotion also meant more access to George VI. Proximity to power is itself power, as Lascelles found when the great and the good begged and bullied and wheedled to have the ear of the man who had the ear of the King. 'One of the amenities of my elevation is that I now get a chance of meeting the notabilities who call on H.M.,' he remarked ingenuously on 19 July 1943, two days after he formally took over from Hardinge.[45] That same day Prime Minister Winston Churchill invited him to lunch, and dinners at Downing Street with the War Cabinet, the chiefs of staff, visiting foreign dignitaries, became part of his routine.

So too did the demands of others. He was furious one night when his dinner at yet another of his clubs was interrupted by the Marquess of Londonderry, who demanded to know why he had been passed over for the chancellorship of the Garter. It was, as Lascelles remarked at the time, a monstrous question to ask the King's private secretary in front of other people. Slightly easier to deal with was the stream of letters from William Temple, the Archbishop of Canterbury, who in the spring of 1944 was anxious to know when Operation Overlord was to commence. This information, perhaps the war's most closely guarded secret, was necessary because Temple was eager to hold a day of prayer. He kept insisting that the military must fix a date for D-Day, so that it would not clash with Palm Sunday or Easter. 'He is, in some ways, most curiously out of touch with realities,' commented Lascelles.[46]

Lascelles exercised a discipline, formidable but always icily polite, over other senior courtiers and, as the occasion demanded, over government ministers. When Sidney Herbert, comptroller and private secretary to the King's sister-in-law, the Duchess of Kent, became embroiled in a heated political controversy with Sir Richard Acland in the correspondence columns of *The Times* over the latter's gift of his Killerton estate to the National Trust, Lascelles sent Herbert a stern letter telling him he had no business writing to *The Times* on such matters. And after Anthony Eden while foreign secretary got drunk at a state banquet and swore at the King's press secretary, it was Lascelles who

wrote to remonstrate with him and Lascelles who received a suitably contrite apology in return.

Nor was he afraid to tell George VI when he thought his master was about to do something foolish. In the run-up to D-Day, the King announced that he and Churchill were going to watch the invasion from one of the bombarding cruisers in the Channel. Neither man had thought through the implications of this – the impact on the course of the war if the cruiser went down with all hands, the impact on the ship's commander if he had to fight with his sovereign and his prime minister aboard. Lascelles shook the King by pointing out that if he was determined to go ahead, he had better advise the eighteen-year-old Princess Elizabeth on the choice of her first prime minister, 'in the event of her father and Winston being sent to the bottom of the English Channel'.[47]

That was enough to make George VI abandon the hare-brained plan. Churchill was harder to budge. In an awkward meeting in the map room at Downing Street between the King, Churchill and Admiral Sir Bertram

Tommy Lascelles (left), George VI and Major General Robert Laycock, Chief of Combined Operations, discuss the progress of the D-Day landings aboard HMS *Arethusa* in June 1944.

Ramsay, naval commander-in-chief of the Expeditionary Force, Lascelles relentlessly put forward arguments as to why Churchill should not go. It would be awkward if the King had to find a new prime minister in the middle of Operation Overlord; no minister of the crown could leave the country without the King's consent. Churchill paid no attention – at one point the King remarked, 'Tommy's face is getting longer and longer' – but on 3 June, just three days before the invasion, he finally gave in, after Lascelles first drafted a personal appeal to him from the King and then phoned him at Downing Street in the middle of the night to make even clearer the King's wishes on the matter. 'We have bested him,' he wrote in his diary the next day.[48]

The King's private secretary had not only to steer relations between sovereign and state; he was also there to advise the King on constitutional matters. Throughout 1943 and early 1944, for example, as Princess Elizabeth approached her eighteenth birthday, there was a move to give her the title of Princess of Wales in her own right. This would have been a new departure: previously the title went to the wife of the Prince of Wales, not to the daughter of the sovereign. Welsh ex-prime minister David Lloyd George supported the plan. So did some members of the cabinet (especially the Welsh ones), and Churchill himself. Lascelles dismissively wrote that the prime minister's 'pictorial imagination is no doubt fired by a vision of Princess Elizabeth looking charming on the steps of Carnarvon Castle, and blushingly acknowledging the loyal acclamations of a pan-Welsh Eisteddfod [the national festival of Welsh poetry and music that takes place every year].'[49] The *Manchester Guardian* reported in October 1943 that, with rather startling presumption, the North Wales Resorts Association 'at their annual meeting at Rhyl yesterday resolved that the question of creating the title of a Princess of Wales should be examined by the executive committee'.[50] The Scots jumped in to say that it would be historically inappropriate to confer the title on anyone other than the wife of the king's eldest son: Elizabeth should obviously be created Princess of Scotland.

But while it might have been a nice boost for morale, Lascelles was clear that it wouldn't do. Princess Elizabeth was the heir presumptive, not the heir apparent. It was possible (just) that the forty-three-year-old Queen might yet bear a son, who would leapfrog over both sisters to inherit the title of Prince of Wales and, eventually, the crown. Or the Queen might die, in which case George VI could remarry and father a Prince of Wales.

Lascelles sought to manage the story, having a quiet word over lunch with Robert Barrington-Ward, who had succeeded Geoffrey Dawson as editor of *The Times*; he also moved to have a draft statement prepared for the press stating that the King did not propose to change Princess Elizabeth's style and title for the time being. 'It is so much easier to do this before the waters have started to rise than to bury your head in the sand, and trust that the flood won't incommode you, which is the usual technique of the royal family in the face of such threatened agitations.'[51] When the statement was accepted, Churchill and the cabinet wanted it to come from Downing Street, but this wouldn't do for Lascelles. The announcement was made from Buckingham Palace, on 12 February 1944, to approving editorial comment from Barrington-Ward in *The Times*.

CHAPTER SIXTEEN

Gloriana

O N   A   C O L D   D A Y   I N   F E B R U A R Y   1 9 5 3, dozens of journalists congregated for a press conference at Church House, Westminster. They had come to hear Winston Churchill's minister of works, David Eccles, deliver a progress report on the preparations for the coronation of Elizabeth II.

George VI's death the previous year had taken almost everyone by surprise. The king was only fifty-six, and although he had been quite ill in 1951, he seemed to have come through: there was a day of national thanksgiving for his recovery on 9 December that year, and his cousin Princess Marie Louise was reported in the press as saying that 'His Majesty has made a wonderful recovery. In fact his own doctors say it was a miracle.'[1] No one but those doctors knew he was suffering from terminal lung cancer.

When he was found dead in his bed at Sandringham by his valet on the morning of 6 February 1952, Princess Elizabeth – now Queen Elizabeth II – and her husband Philip, Duke of Edinburgh were in Kenya on the first stage of a tour of Commonwealth nations. Elizabeth's private secretary, Martin Charteris, who was accompanying the couple, heard the news from a journalist at a hotel where he had gone to have lunch. He immediately phoned the duke's equerry, Lieutenant-Commander Michael Parker, who was with the duke and the Queen; and Parker told the duke. 'He looked as if you'd dropped half the world on him,' Parker later recalled. It was the duke who broke the news to his wife. When Charteris arrived fifteen minutes later at the Sagana Royal Lodge, where they were staying, he found the twenty-five-year-old queen 'very composed', he said, the 'absolute master of her fate'.[2]

I T   U S U A L L Y   T O O K   W E L L   O V E R   A   Y E A R to prepare for a coronation: more than thirteen months after his accession in George V's case. George VI's coronation had to wait only six months, but that was because preparations were already in hand for the coronation of his brother

Edward VIII, and courtiers decided to go ahead with the same date but a different king. Buckingham Palace announced the date of Elizabeth II's coronation, 2 June 1953, on 28 April 1952. 'The announcement so far in advance of the date', wrote the *Manchester Guardian*'s London correspondent on the following day, 'will be welcomed by all who have to make preparations for the event. Already the travel agencies and hotels are receiving inquiries and seats are being offered on what is assumed to be the processional route'.[3]

Now, with less than four months to go, David Eccles, who was dubbed 'the Abominable Showman' by his more conservative colleagues, was presenting to the world's press a series of enormous scale models which, as he proudly pointed out, had been carved and decorated by the Ministry of Works' architectural staff and made 'of odd bits of material – balsa wood, twigs, wire-wool, pins and so on'.[4] Pointing to each one in turn, he led the assembled journalists on a virtual tour out of the south gate of Buckingham Palace, past the Victoria Memorial, which was to be smothered in banks of velvety red pelargoniums set against blue spectator stands with pinkish-red undersides to their roofs, and down a miniature Mall.

It was the thousand-yard-long Mall, Eccles told them, which offered the best opportunity to create 'that blend of majesty and gaiety which so truly represents our Queen'; and it was to be dominated by four tubular steel arches capped with twenty-foot-high lions and unicorns designed by the sculptor James Woodford and made from steel tube and wire mesh. These rampant creatures faced each other, 'poised in the manner of old-time dancers'.[5] A princess's coronet would be suspended on gold wires from the centre of each arch, and polished aluminium spheres were to be threaded onto these wires, like 'drops of dew on strands of gossamer'.[6]

While the journalists were reeling from this flight of poetry, Eccles moved on to a large-scale model of The Mall with floodlighting in place: 'You can see on this model how we are going to light up The Mall after dark. I am hoping crowds of many thousands will take pleasure in gazing at the floodlit lions and unicorns standing guard over the illuminated coronets twinkling and floating in the night air.'[7] He went on to describe at length the different decorative schemes planned for various government buildings along the route, even listing the flowers which were currently being cultivated for use on the day, from azaleas and rhododendrons to delphiniums, chrysanthemums and gladioli. ('For the arrangement of the flowers I have the advantage of the advice of Mrs Constance Spry. She is here and will answer any questions which stump me.')[8] Keen to avoid accusations of extravagance in the midst of post-war austerity, he complained about how expensive big flags were, at £25–£30 each, including fixings.

But the excitement kept breaking through. These bits of painted balsa and wire wool signalled the approach of something awe-inspiring, something magical in the grey gloom of Britain in the early 1950s. 'How can I sum it up?' asked the Abominable Showman:

> Well, when someone asked what was the special fascination of the coronation he was told that all nice children pretend to believe in unicorns, golden coaches and fairy queens, and that the charm of the coronation is that you do not have to pretend … I go further. There is no make believe at all about this drama of church and state. It is a real and living part of the British constitution, which we have some reason to think is the best in the world.[9]

Eccles's Ministry of Works and its predecessors, the Office of Works and the King's Works, had been responsible for the maintenance and repair of royal residences and other crown property since the fourteenth century. Besides the building operations, the refits of royal lodgings and the requests for a design for anything from a doorcase to a country house, the Works was traditionally responsible for the theatricals that went hand in hand with royal occasions. It was the Works which decked out biers and coffins for state funerals in Westminster Abbey, built the stands for spectators at royal weddings, and fitted up the temporary seating when a peer of the realm stood trial in Westminster Hall. And it was the Works which created the necessary settings for coronations.

Which was how in February 1953 Eccles came to be outlining to the press the kinds of flowers that were going to be used to decorate the processional route when, on the morning of 2 June that same year, the young Elizabeth rode in her golden coach from Buckingham Palace to Westminster Abbey to be presented to her people, anointed with holy oil and crowned Elizabeth the Second, by the Grace of God of the United Kingdom of Great Britain and Northern Ireland and of Her Other Realms and Territories Queen, Head of the Commonwealth, Defender of the Faith.

The ministry's chief architect at the time was Eric Bedford. This heir to Inigo Jones and Christopher Wren, both of whom held the post

of surveyor of the King's Works, had joined the Ministry of Works in 1936, designing grain silos, communication centres and an abattoir in Guildford before becoming in 1950 the youngest chief architect the ministry had known, at the age of forty-one.

Bedford's main claim to fame lay in the future: in 1961, he was to design London's famous Post Office Tower. His work for the coronation was exciting, in a mildly Modern–Romantic Festival-of-Britain sort of way. It was Bedford who came up with the idea of the steel arches over the Mall with their dancing lions and unicorns; Bedford who was responsible for a temporary glass-fronted building added to the west end of Westminster Abbey, where arrivals could be marshalled before the coronation service began. Named the Annexe and flanked by ten heraldic beasts in plaster designed by James Woodford, it was described at the time as 'uncompromisingly "South Bank" in conception' (a reference to the new complex of buildings on the south bank of the Thames which were put up as part of the 1951 Festival of Britain) and criticised for its failure to make any concessions to the Gothic of the Abbey.[10] Nevertheless, even its critics acknowledged its charm as 'a modern version of one of

the royal tents on the Field of Cloth of Gold: light, bright, blazing with heraldic colour'.[11]

    Bedford, Eccles and their colleagues at the Ministry of Works shared

the responsibility of providing a suitable backdrop for the royal occasion with others. Hugh Casson, who had come to prominence as director of architecture for the Festival of Britain, was asked to advise the City of Westminster on its own coronation decorations. One of his suggestions was that at dawn on Coronation Day, posies of freshly gathered flowers be placed in the hands of the various statues that lined the route. Another idea was a pair of enormous aluminium venetian blinds decorated with coats of arms, which would hang at the bottom of Whitehall. A third, a proposal to paint Tudor roses on the tarmac of Regent Street, was turned down on the grounds that it would startle the horses.

A series of street committees also devised their own schemes and collaborated in a kind of crowd-sourced coronation. 'This has proved quite a test of community solidarity,' commented *The Observer*.[12] Some streets couldn't even organise a committee, let alone an array of celebratory decorations. Others couldn't agree on their areas of responsibility: three months before Coronation Day, for instance, Piccadilly and Mayfair were still in dispute over who was supposed to be decorating the area between the Ritz and Hyde Park Corner, which meant that neither was prepared to come up with a plan.

Then there were the big governmental and quasi-governmental committees, the gatherings of the great and the good. On 28 April 1952, Buckingham Palace announced the creation of a Coronation Commission 'to consider those aspects of the arrangements for the Coronation which are of common concern'.[13] Members of

Eric Bedford's Coronation Annexe under construction at Westminster Abbey, London, in preparation for the coronation.

the commission included the usual mix of distinguished figures, with a sprinkling of senior government ministers: Prime Minister Winston Churchill; the Labour leader, Clement Attlee; the Archbishop of Canterbury; and representatives from the leading Commonwealth countries. The commission was chaired by the thirty-year-old Duke of Edinburgh.

This was just the beginning. Over the coming months committees and councils and commissions spread faster than red-white-and-blue bunting. At its first meeting, the Coronation Commission set up a joint committee to consider any problems that might arise concerning the coronation. Weeks later a coronation committee of the Privy Council was established; it promptly appointed yet another committee to consider the preparations.

A Court of Claims was set up by proclamation in June 1952 to establish which of the Queen's subjects had the right to render special services on the day. The Duke of Newcastle, as lord of the manor of Worksop, was entitled to supply a glove for the sovereign's right hand and to support that hand when Elizabeth clasped the royal sceptre. Unfortunately, the duke had gone off to live in Rhodesia in 1948, and he showed no inclination to come back for the day. A request from the directors of the London and Fort George Land Company, the legal holders of Worksop Manor, that they be allowed collectively to support the Queen's right hand, was rejected.

Other claims were more successful. John Dymoke, a 26-year-old soldier from Lincolnshire, was given the privilege of carrying the Union standard into the abbey, since he was head of the Dymoke family and thus by right the thirty-fourth hereditary queen's champion. The champion's other role, appearing at the coronation banquet in Westminster Hall in white armour and on a white horse and throwing down his gauntlet three times as a challenge to anyone who disputed the new sovereign's right to rule, had been abandoned after George IV's coronation in 1821. This was perhaps more a matter of relief than regret to the bespectacled Captain Dymoke, one of whose forebears had fallen off his horse in the middle of the hall while flinging his glove about at James II's coronation in 1685. (There was a deathly silence, broken by a stifled giggle from Mary of Modena.)

The parts played by members of the Queen's household in all this were pivotal, although they were often played out in private. In the first months of her reign, Elizabeth II relied on the men and women who had served her father and mother. Tommy Lascelles was still private secretary.

Sir Piers Legh, who had been a courtier since 1919, when he joined the Prince of Wales's staff as an equerry, remained as master of the household, a post he had taken up in 1941. These men served on one or more of the various commissions and committees, reminding the other members – including, at times, the Duke of Edinburgh himself – of what the Queen's wishes were in this matter or that, and occasionally of what the Queen's wishes ought to be, whether she wished them or not.

The courtier in charge of making the day work was Bernard Marmaduke Fitzalan-Howard, 16th Duke of Norfolk and earl marshal and hereditary marshal of England. A stocky, round-faced army man who loved hunting, cricket and horse-racing and had little time for intellectual pursuits, Norfolk did at least have experience with organising coronations. He had organised George VI's in 1937, when he was still only twenty-eight; and on that occasion, he had shown he would stand no nonsense from anybody.

As Minister David Eccles put it, 'The earl marshal is the producer – I am the stage manager. He deals with persons – I (mainly) with things. I provide the seats in the Abbey: he decides who shall sit in them.'[14] In normal circumstances Norfolk would have chaired the Coronation Commission. It was at the Queen's request that he stood aside for the Duke of Edinburgh, who was a husband in search of a role, at sea in the midst of a vast ritual which centred on his wife and cast him as a supporting character.

But as the producer, it was Norfolk rather than the Duke of Edinburgh – or Prince Philip, as the press invariably but incorrectly called him (he wasn't created a prince of the United Kingdom until 1957) – who bore

As hereditary earl marshal, the 16th Duke of Norfolk was responsible for organising the coronation of Elizabeth II.

the brunt of criticisms which flew from Parliament, the press and the public. People complained that the processional route was too short. The cost of seats in government-erected stands along the route was too high, at £6 for a covered seat and £4 for an uncovered seat. Peers who still possessed coaches were anxious that they should be allowed to drive to the abbey in them.

The biggest bone of contention involved the media. The coronation processions of Edward VII in 1902 and George V in 1911 had both been filmed, but cameras had not been allowed inside the abbey. The want of footage was supplied, in the case of Edward VII's coronation, by a canny entrepreneur named Charles Urban who, after seeking advice on the finer points of the ceremony from officials in the royal household, sent photographs of the interior of the abbey and various costumes and accessories over to France, where the pioneering cinematographer Georges Méliès reconstructed the ceremony with a washhouse attendant as the King and a music hall singer as Queen Alexandra. Topped and tailed with actual footage of the King arriving at and leaving the abbey which was filmed by Urban on the day, *The Coronation of Edward VII* was premiered at the Alhambra, Leicester Square, within hours of the real coronation, to tremendous acclaim.[15]

Film of George VI's 1937 coronation had included parts of the actual service itself, which was also broadcast on radio. The procession was shown by the BBC's new television service, its first outside broadcast: the *Daily Mail* declared that 'when the King and Queen appeared the picture was so vivid that one felt this magical television is going to be one of the greatest of all modern inventions'.[16]

Fifteen years later, with private television ownership standing at around one in ten households, there was an assumption that of course the BBC would televise the coronation. But the young Queen Elizabeth was unhappy with the idea of showing the actual ceremony: it was an intrusion on a religious service which was also a quasi-mystical transfiguration. The Anointing, in which she was consecrated as sovereign by anointment with holy oil on her hands, breast and head, was said to date back to the tenth century BC when, in the words of 1 Kings 1:39, 'Zadok the priest took an horn of oil out of the tabernacle, and anointed Solomon.' It wasn't meant as public spectacle: it was a mystery, not something to be conducted under the harsh glare of floodlights. And, although no one admitted it, there was an element of danger in a live broadcast. Things had gone wrong at coronations before, and not only when the hereditary champion fell off his horse. At Victoria's coronation in 1838 Archbishop

Howley placed her ring on the wrong finger, and she had trouble getting it off, 'which I at last did with great pain'.[17] Then the octogenarian Baron Rolle tottered up to do homage, fell and, true to his name, rolled down the steps. At least if there were any mishaps during Elizabeth's coronation, they could and would be edited out of film footage: the earl marshal, the lord chamberlain and the Archbishop of Canterbury had the right to scrutinise all films of the event before they were released.

The Coronation Joint Committee agreed with the Queen and recommended to the Coronation Commission that on the day, no television cameras should be allowed east of the choir screen in Westminster Abbey. While viewers would be able to see the processions to and from the abbey, and even the guests who gathered in the nave, they would be excluded from the ceremony itself.

When the decision was announced to the public on 20 October 1952, there was an uproar. The Duke of Norfolk was pilloried in the press. Labour politicians attacked Churchill in the Commons, charging him with elitism and demanding that the ceremony be televised 'so that it can be viewed by many millions of Her Majesty's subjects instead of being limited to the favoured few in the abbey'.[18] The new chairman of the BBC, Sir Alexander Cadogan, who hadn't been consulted on the decision, stayed out of the fight: 'I think that we can leave it to an enraged public opinion to bring pressure on the Government,' he said.[19]

The 5th Marquess of Cholmondeley, Lord Great Chamberlain from 1952–1966.

He was right. Having originally agreed with the Queen, Winston Churchill began to worry about the public reaction. So did Elizabeth herself. Churchill still maintained that it would not be fitting that the ceremony 'should be presented as if it were a theatrical performance';

The carriage overseer polishes the Irish State Coach, which was used to carry Elizabeth II to state openings of parliament during the early part of her reign.

but after having informal meetings with Archbishop Fisher, Tommy Lascelles and the earl marshal, he suggested that the coronation joint committee might review its original decision.[20] Lascelles soon came up with a compromise. The cinema film of George VI's crowning had omitted the most sacred parts and, taking this as a precedent, the earl marshal announced on 9 December 1952 that television coverage could after all extend to parts of the service east of the screen. 'It is therefore hoped to make arrangements for the Recognition, the Crowning and the Homage to be included. The Anointing, the Communion Prayers and the Administration of the Sacrament would be excluded.'[21]

As the day came closer the earl marshal remained the public face of the coronation, while his wife Lavinia stood in for the Queen during dress rehearsals. By now, with Eric Bedford's annexe dominating the west front, the exterior of the abbey was all but unrecognisable. As for the interior, that had been transformed. The abbey had been closed for months so that monuments could be covered over for protection, and boarded floors put down. A railway line was laid the length of the building to make it easier to bring in the tons of scaffolding needed for extra seating, which was increased from the usual 2,500 to 7,000. Lighting, cabling for the public address system and positions for cameras all had to be installed. The 650-year-old Coronation Chair was cleaned by expert staff from the Ministry of Works, who took the opportunity to X-ray it. (The X-rays showed that the original colour scheme, dating from around 1300 and overpainted, consisted of an all-over coating of white-lead oil paint with red, green and gold decoration.)

The logistics of celebration were formidable. Down at Biggin Hill, an RAF station in Kent with a place in recent history as one of the command bases for the Battle of Britain, 168 jet fighters were being put through their paces for a coronation fly-past over Buckingham Palace. At parade grounds all over the country soldiers, sailors and airmen were being drilled. Some 11,651 of them would take part in the procession from the abbey back to the palace, under the command of Viscount Alanbrooke, who also had a place in recent history, as chief of the Imperial General Staff and thus the head of the British army during the Second World War. They included twenty-seven marching bands, detachments of Gurkhas, a dozen mounted British South Africa Police officers, the Yeomen of the Guard, four field marshals on horseback and seven admirals of the fleet. 'The processions will march at 112 paces a minute,' said the General Staff Orders. 'The pace will be 30 inches.' And, since there were limited numbers of latrines in the area, 'the maximum use must be made of the latrines in camp beforehand'.[22]

More than 20,000 policemen and women lined the route from 4 a.m. Those lucky guests who had been issued with tickets for the service were asked to be in their places between 6 a.m. and 8 a.m. The Queen, accompanied by the Duke of Edinburgh, was scheduled to enter the abbey at 11.15 a.m.

All over the country people begged, bought or borrowed TV sets. Sudbury prison in Derbyshire bought one specially so that the prisoners could watch. In Warrington, the local authority bought sets for its old people's residential homes. The BBC announced that on the day it would start broadcasting seventy-five minutes before programming began, so that everyone would have time to test their sets and make any adjustments to aerials.

And throughout, the earl marshal maintained a bluff composure. At one of the last big press conferences, he gave details of the grand procession in which the Queen, wearing a robe of crimson velvet trimmed with ermine and bordered with gold lace, was to walk. It would consist of about 260 people. Prince Philip would wear the full-dress uniform of an admiral of the fleet, under the crimson velvet robes of state of a royal duke. The archbishops of Canterbury and York would be wearing mitres for the first time at a coronation since before the days of George IV. The prime minister would be wearing his uniform of lord warden of the Cinque Ports, under his Garter mantle. And the earl marshal himself was going to wear a scarlet coat embroidered in gold, white knee breeches and stockings, and he would carry a baton of gold tipped with ebony.

But in case anyone might go away with the impression that the coronation had indeed become a mere 'theatrical performance', the Duke of Norfolk took the opportunity to remind journalists what the day was all about:

> Let us remember the spiritual significance of this solemn service. The heads of the Church, as is their duty, have asked the peoples to pray for her Majesty. My final word to you is to ask all the people throughout the great Commonwealth over which she reigns to think of the Queen on the night of June 1, and when they retire to ask God to bless and guide and keep her.[23]

On the day, everything and everyone behaved perfectly. The Queen 'was touching and quite perfect', wrote Chips Channon, who was there, 'while Prince Philip was like a medieval knight … I could have watched for ever.'[24] Everybody shouted 'God save the Queen' at the right moments, and in unison. When the time came for the anointing, the four Garter knights held a slightly wobbly canopy of cloth of gold over Elizabeth to hide her from view during what Laurence Olivier, in his hushed narration of the official film of the coronation, described in awed tones as 'the hallowing, the sacring … a moment so old, history can scarcely go deep enough to contain it'.[25] 'A moment too sacred for intrusion,' affirmed *The Times*.[26]

Westminster Abbey,
2 June 1953.

Huge crowds poured
into the Mall to
celebrate the coronation
of Queen Elizabeth
II. 'There is no make-
believe about this drama
of church and state. It is
a real and living part of
the British constitution.'

Queen Elizabeth the
Queen Mother, Prince
Charles and Princess
Margaret watching
the coronation at
Westminster Abbey. The
ceremony went on for
some time.

And this, the last great public gathering of the royal household in the twentieth century, was seen by more people than all the other British coronations in history put together. Millions watched as the master of the horse, the lord chamberlain, the lord steward acted out the parts set out for them by custom and practice. They saw Lord Woolton, chancellor of the Duchy of Lancaster, present the glove to his sovereign, having been appointed to the task after the directors of the London and Fort George Land Company failed in their bid for collective stardom. Viewers in France, the Netherlands and Germany watched live as Elizabeth II walked slowly through the abbey, her train carried by six ladies in waiting and her mistress of the robes, the Dowager Duchess of Devonshire. Canberra jets flew films of the BBC broadcast to Newfoundland, from where they were taken on to Montreal and New York so that viewers across the Atlantic could see how Gloriana and the New Elizabethans sought legitimacy in ancient tradition. Back in England, the proud father of a boy in the choir stopped peering at the grainy black and white images in the corner of his sitting room and telephoned the BBC to ask if they could adapt their coverage to show the choristers singing. In America, the networks were condemned for interrupting the ceremony to show advertisements from sponsors. 'Utterly disgraceful was NBC Video's interruption of the religious service in order to show a chimpanzee,' railed the *New York Times*. 'No apology can be adequate.'[27]

In the Paris villa of the American heiress Margaret Biddle, the Duke and Duchess of Windsor watched the live broadcast with a group of friends. Every now and then the duke explained some detail of the ceremony or named one of the characters on the screen. 'And those in the room with him heard that his voice, in the semi-darkness, was husky as if, at times, he found it difficult to talk.'[28]

CHAPTER SEVENTEEN

Affectionate Memoirs

THE EARLY YEARS OF ELIZABETH II'S REIGN were marked by a flurry of memoirs written by members and ex-members of the royal household, usually with help from ghost-writers. The first into this field of broken confidences appeared while her father, George VI, was still king, and in circumstances which are still something of a mystery. In 1949, Marion Crawford retired after sixteen years' service with the royal family as governess to the two princesses, Elizabeth and Margaret. That year 'Crawfie', as she was called by the family, was approached by an American mass-circulation magazine, the *Ladies' Home Journal*, with an offer for her memoirs of between $6,500 and $85,000, depending on whom you believe. Her husband, a bank manager who was always happy to make capital from her royal connections, urged her to take up the offer; but she went to Queen Elizabeth for advice.

The Queen's reply, given in a letter of 4 April 1949, was unequivocal:

> I do feel, most definitely, that you should not write and sign articles about the children, as people in positions of confidence with us must be utterly oyster. If you, the moment you finished teaching Margaret, started writing about her and Lilibet [the family's pet name for Elizabeth], well, we should never feel confidence in anyone again.[1]

The Queen did agree that Crawford could act as an adviser and be paid by the *Ladies' Home Journal*, as long as her name didn't appear. The need for her to obtain royal consent to any material she provided seems to have been taken for granted.

But the contract which Crawford signed contained a surprisingly vague clause which allowed for publication 'without Her Majesty's consent (possibly with only the consent of Princess Elizabeth, or no consent), and under your own name'.[2] During the summer of 1949 the ex-governess collaborated with a ghost-writer on her 'affectionate memoir'. It was shown to Queen Elizabeth, who was appalled and told the publishers of the *Ladies' Home Journal* that Crawford had gone off her head. That didn't stop them from publishing. The articles, which went

The Duchess of York
with her daughter
Elizabeth and their
nanny, Clara Knight.

into enormous and mawkish detail about her years bringing up Elizabeth
and Margaret, appeared in America under her name at the beginning of
1950 and, after *Woman's Own* bought the serialisation rights for £30,000,
in the United Kingdom as well. They were a sensational success. Later
that year the articles were turned into an equally popular book, *The Little
Princesses: The Intimate Story of HRH Princess Elizabeth and HRH Princess
Margaret by Their Governess*.

The Little Princesses is gossipy, but quite innocuous by today's standards.
When Crawford joined as governess the Duke and Duchess of York's
household at the Royal Lodge, Windsor, there was already a nanny, Clara
Knight, known as 'Alah', who had been nanny to the duchess. She was
helped by two sisters, Margaret and Ruby MacDonald, who were her
under-nurse and nursemaid. Both remained with the family. 'Bobo', as
Elizabeth called Margaret MacDonald, became the Queen's dresser and
one of her closest confidantes, serving her for sixty-seven years. Knight
and the MacDonald girls had charge of the children's health, their baths
and their clothes, while the governess looked after them from nine in the
morning until six in the evening and had charge of their education, with
occasional help from a French teacher.

The nursery secrets that Crawford revealed were hardly earth-shattering. Both children had a bad habit of biting their nails; Margaret had a bad habit of biting her sister. The governess shared details of the teenage princesses' bedroom furnishings: pink and fawn for Elizabeth, with flowered chintz and plain white furniture; salmon-pink and clutter for Margaret. She laughed over the poor state of the royal palaces: 'Life in a palace rather resembles camping in a museum. These historic places are so old, so tied up with tradition, that they are mostly dropping to bits.'[3]

At other times, though, she crossed a line. She speculated on whether the King and Queen were disappointed at not having a boy. She spoke of how embarrassed the King was when the girls showed him any affection: 'he was not a demonstrative man [and] Lilibet took after him'. She discussed at length Prince Philip's protracted courtship of Princess Elizabeth, and her parents' inability to decide if he would make a suitable husband for her. And she emphasised, in excruciating prose, her close relationship with the girls:

> One afternoon I was sitting in my room at Buckingham Palace. There came a gentle knock at the door and Princess Elizabeth put her head in. I invited her to have some tea.
>
> 'I have just come to tell you something, Crawfie,' she said after a pause. I waited.
>
> 'I'm having the old pram brought out!'
>
> I went to her side quickly and put my arms round her. 'I am so happy for you, darling,' I said. Then we kissed and wept a little.[4]

The broadsheet press was savage. Things like lessons, said one reviewer, 'did little enough to interrupt [Crawford's] life of happy importance'.[5] Described as 'Princess Elizabeth's close friend and confidante,' snarled another, 'she manifestly has clear views on how confidences should be treated'.[6] More significantly, Queen Elizabeth and her daughters were furious. They severed all contact with their old governess, who became a non-person within the royal circle, a traitor, a betrayer of confidences. On her retirement, George VI had given her a grace-and-favour house at Kensington Palace; she left it for her native Scotland in the autumn of 1950, ostracised and brought to the edge of a nervous breakdown. That didn't prevent her from following up the success of *The Little Princesses* with a succession of royal revelations, often serialised in magazines before appearing in book form. She wrote, or at least lent her name to, lives of Queen Mary in 1951, Queen Elizabeth II in 1952 and Princess Margaret in 1953, and gave her name to a regular column on royal affairs in *Woman's Own*. This column was always written six weeks ahead of time, a fact which was Crawford's undoing. The 16 June 1955 issue of *Woman's Own* carried a piece under her name describing the Trooping the Colour and Royal Ascot. Both events were cancelled at the last moment because of a rail strike. She retired to Aberdeen, where she died in 1988. The royal family did not send flowers.

After Crawford's *Little Princesses*, the next into the field was Gabriel Tschumi, the son of a professor of languages in Lausanne. Tschumi's cousin was one of Queen Victoria's dressers. It was through her influence that he was taken on at Buckingham Palace in 1898, as a sixteen-year-old kitchen apprentice under Victoria's *chef de cuisine*, Juste Menager. With a salary of £400 a year, Menager was more than just another royal servant: he had a London house of his own, and would arrive at the palace at eight o'clock each morning in a frock coat and top hat. (He also had his own line in foodstuffs – Menager's Pickle, Menager's Sauce and Menager's Chutney were to be obtained in all good grocers and stores.) He ran the royal kitchens well and the work was comparatively easy. Tschumi stayed on after his apprenticeship came to an end, and when Menager retired in 1910 Tschumi was made assistant to the new chef, Henri Cedard, remaining with the royal family for another twenty-two years. He was with George V when the King toured the Western Front in 1915, and put the big kitchen at the chateau which served as the royal headquarters to good use, war or no war. 'Quite a few high-ranking officers took me aside and wrung my hand with pleasure after they had dined with the King, saying they had forgotten what it was like to eat real meals.'[7] He helped to prepare the eight-course wedding breakfast for the Duke and Duchess of York in 1923: 'The truffle and tongue garnishing takes a long time to prepare artistically, but it can give a very pleasant colour scheme if arranged well.'[8]

After thirty-four years of unbroken service, Tschumi lost his job in the household economy drive that George V instituted during the Depression. Sir Derek Keppel, master of the household, mentioned his name to the Duke of Portland, who happened to be staying at Windsor for the Ascot races, and the upshot was that he went into service with the Portlands at Welbeck for the next ten years.

In *Royal Chef* (1954), Tschumi described his career in loving detail, helped, as he freely admitted, by Australian journalist Joan Powe. 'We felt', Tschumi said in his foreword, 'that an insight into that long-past style of royal life might be of value to those living in the new Elizabethan Age.'[9] At the end of 1947 Tschumi was invited to take on the post of chef to Queen Mary, and he remained in charge of the Marlborough House kitchens until retiring at the age of seventy in 1952, five months before the old queen's death. He and Powe devoted the final three chapters of *Royal Chef* to life with Queen Mary, something much more recent than 'that long-past style of royal life'.

The picture Tschumi painted was an old man's view of a world that was changing for the worse. He bemoaned the fact that every royal servant at Buckingham Palace was a member of the civil service trade union; that few of the families of old royal servants followed them into the royal household any more. They had no feeling for tradition, and 'the girls who would automatically have followed their fathers or brothers in royal service were now more interested in jobs in factories or offices'.[10] He still managed at Marlborough House, though, with the help of a cook, Mrs Picken, three kitchenmaids and a scullery man. These five helped Tschumi to prepare meals for Queen Mary and any of the royal family who visited her, and for her sixty-odd members of staff. They had a modern kitchen to work in, which helped a lot. There was a large electric refrigerator, and huge new gas ranges. 'Everything was shining and neat, with plenty of storage space and a special section for the food which was served to Queen Mary herself,' recalled the royal chef. 'Into this cabinet went many of the gifts of food the queen received from admirers and well-wishers from all over the world, as well as the delicacies I prepared at times to tempt her appetite.'[11]

The British public loved this level of detail. They loved to read that Queen Mary's breakfast tray was sent up to her sitting room at nine o'clock sharp each morning; that it held coffee, toast, butter, marmalade and a little fresh fruit, except during the winter months, when instead of the coffee she had hot milk, in a tall glass and slightly sweetened.[12] Or that the Duke and Duchess of Gloucester were very fond of 'a cheese savoury, *Quiche de Lorrain*', and that when the Duke of Windsor visited Marlborough House he liked cold grouse served with a plain green salad.[13] It made readers feel that the royal family was just like them. And if they cared to continue the parallel by eating the same food as the royals, Tschumi helpfully provided some recipes as an appendix. They included chicken mousse ('Queen Mary's Favourite Invalid Food') and *Jambon froid à la gelée*, which was 'made for Queen Mary with tinned ham from Australia'. Quite where most of Tschumi's readers would acquire the eight grouse which were the main ingredient of *Grouse à la Balmoral* is harder to say.

Members of the royal household had produced behind-the-scenes memoirs before this. In 1896, 'One of Her Majesty's Servants' published a series of articles on 'The Private Life of the Queen'. The anonymous author, while claiming to be 'inspired by a desire born of sincere admiration, to pay in some way the tribute of a humble servitor to his Royal mistress',[14] dwelt at intrusive length on what the Queen liked to eat and drink: she was particularly fond of potatoes and chocolate sponges, apparently. And he devoted an entire chapter to 'the Queen's fads and fancies'. She hated cats and clergymen who preached in surplices, and was fussy about her tableware:

> No gold plate is ever taken to Osborne or Balmoral, and when she takes breakfast *en plein air* at Frogmore, as she does so often, woe betide the forgetful person who should serve her table with the gold she uses only in her own dining-room at the Castle, or who should omit to place alongside the quaintly-modelled 'cock-and-hen' egg cups the peculiar salt cellar in blackened silver that Lady Alice Stanley once gave her Royal friend, and which the Queen at once said was always to be used under those circumstances.[15]

The articles were followed up in 1901 by *The Private Life of Edward VII by a Member of the Royal Household*, which, judging from the fact that the author refers to Edward throughout as the Prince of Wales, was in preparation for some time before his accession to the throne. It was less intimate than its predecessor, apart from the occasional knowing aside: 'The younger years of the Prince of Wales were not devoid of the frailties of youth.'[16] In 1913, with its royal subject decently dead, the wonderful royal motor expert Charles Stamper published his *What I Know: Reminiscences of Five Years' Personal Attendance upon His Late Majesty King Edward the Seventh*. There was also a smattering of books by retired policemen who might devote a chapter or two of their autobiographies to their time on duty with the royal family. Thereafter, memoirs by members of the household all but disappeared until Marion Crawford's *The Little Princesses*. There was a tacit agreement that the private lives of the royal family were off limits, at least so long as they were still alive. Fritz Ponsonby's *Recollections of Three Reigns* (Victoria, Edward VII and George V) was warmly received when it appeared in 1951. But when the Duke of Windsor (the former Edward VIII) published his self-justificatory *A King's Story* in the same year, it received mixed reviews in Britain. The *Sunday Times* was cautious, saying that 'though many will think the publication of these memoirs premature, they cannot be dismissed as either commonplace or offensive'.[17] *The Spectator*, on the other hand, was unimpressed, declaring it 'a great pity' that the duke decided to publish, and roundly condemning him both for marrying 'Mr Simpson's wife' and for his resolve 'to drag every detail of this old unhappy affair to light again when it had been well forgotten'.[18]

The dawn of the New Elizabethan Age whetted the public's appetite for more, and more revealing, information about Gloriana and her court. There were endless photo-spreads on the Queen at various events, attending a screening of Walt Disney's *Rob Roy*, or at the Goodwood races, or reviewing a Royal River Pageant on the Thames (complete with historical tableaux representing Vikings, the signing of the Magna Carta and inevitably, Queen Elizabeth I and Sir Francis Drake). When the Queen and the Duke of Edinburgh embarked on a six-month tour of the Commonwealth in November 1953, readers lapped up photographs of the royal suite aboard the Shaw Savill liner *Gothic*, which was to carry them part of the way: they saw the Queen's day cabin, painted in off-white with pale turquoise curtains, with chairs in unglazed chintz; the mahogany writing desk used by Queen Victoria aboard the royal yacht *Victoria and Albert*, and now installed in the Duke's own day cabin; the royal ante-room which had been converted into 'a portable cinema'.[19] The *Illustrated London News* carried a full-colour, double-page cutaway picture of the *Gothic*, showing every furnished inch of the royal accommodation, right down to the positions of the separate bathrooms used by the Queen and her husband.

Not everyone was enthusiastic about this new tendency to lay bare the innermost workings of the royal household, to strip away the mystery and leave behind the washing-up. And when it came to kiss-and-tell memoirs from former members of the household, no matter how innocuous they might be, critics condemned what one reviewer called 'the garrulity of these chatterboxes', and urged the royal family's advisers to exert themselves rather more enthusiastically to preserve the details of their employers' private lives.[20]

There was no doubt that 'worthy menials [who] assume the airs of authorship', to quote the same reviewer, were on the increase in the 1950s. In 1956 Frederick Gorst, who had been a royal footman during the reign of Edward VII, published his autobiography, *Of Carriages and Kings*, although at least Gorst confined his memories to a past which was respectably distant. The same year saw the appearance of *Fit for a King: A Book of Intimate Memoirs* by Frederick Corbitt, deputy comptroller of supply at Buckingham Palace: 'likely to tickle thousands of palates,' said the *Sunday Express*.[21] Corbitt entered royal service in 1932, and left

Frederick Corbitt's ID card, giving him access to Buckingham Palace and Windsor Castle as deputy comptroller of supply in the royal household.

it shortly before the publication of his book – a wise move, one feels. He wrote at length about the mechanics of supplying the palace and the feeding habits of the sovereigns under whom he served. The Queen Mother, his readers learned, was fond of a grilled herring. Her daughter liked freshly killed trout; and both queens were partial to young broad beans, new peas, and new potatoes just out of the ground.

"'P.P.' – as Prince Philip, the Duke of Edinburgh, is always known among his friends and staff – ' came in for criticism for his determination to modernise the workings of Buckingham Palace, which was seen by palace staff as intolerable interference in household matters. P.P. went into every one of the 600-odd rooms at the palace, Corbitt claimed, asking every one of the men and women on the staff exactly what he or she was doing, and why.[22] He tried and failed to introduce a cafeteria system for the servants, and wanted to set up an in-house laundry and an in-house bakery to save money. Both were old and expensive ideas, said Corbitt. 'It seemed he would be much happier with all these things being done on the spot, where he could control them himself.'[23]

Mildly intrusive, massively voyeuristic, Corbitt's memoir showed the shape of things to come in the New Elizabethan Age. It contained an assumption of intimacy, a knowingness, a conviction that the private lives of the royal family were somehow public property. But there was

Overleaf: Public interest in the royal family soared in the wake of Elizabeth II's accession to the throne. When the queen and Prince Philip sailed for New Zealand aboard the S.S. *Gothic* in November 1953, the *Illustrated London News* gave its readers a chance to view their sleeping arrangements, and even the location of their separate bathrooms.

ROYAL DAY CABINS
(SITUATED AT AFTER END
OF PROMENADE DECK);
AND
ROYAL SLEEPING
CABINS
(SITUATED AT AFTER END OF
BOAT AND GAMES DECK).

POSITION OF ROYAL
SLEEPING CABINS.

POSITION OF
ROYAL DAY CABINS.

DUKE OF EDINBURGH'S
SLEEPING CABIN.

DUKE OF EDINBURGH'S
BATH ROOM.

H.M. THE QUEEN'S
BATH ROOM.

LEVEL OF BOAT AND GAMES DECK.

DUKE OF EDINBURGH'S DAY CABIN.

H.M.
THE QUEEN'S
SLEEPING

VERANDAH.

VESTIBULE.

No. 4 CARGO
HATCH TRUNK.

H.M. THE QUEEN'S
DAY CABIN.

B
AND
D

VERANDAH.

PROMENADE DECK.

BRIDGE DECK.

ROYAL BARGE
STOWED OVER HATCH.

SHELTER
DECK.

THE ROYAL SUITE IN S.S. GOTHIC: VIEWS OF THE INTERIOR OF THE LINER, SHOWING T

On November 27 H.M. the Queen and H.R.H. the Duke of Edinburgh were to embark at Kingston, Jamaica, in the Shaw Savill liner S.S. *Gothic* for their journey to New Zealand, where they are due to arrive on December 23. The Royal apartments in S.S. *Gothic* are situated on three decks, the day cabins being at the after-end of the Promenade deck, and the sleeping-cabins and bathrooms on the deck above—that is, at the after-end of the Boat deck. The

Royal ante-room and dining-cabin are at the forward end of the Bridge deck, no temporarily as the Saloon deck. As will be seen from our diagrammatic drawing, the day cabin is on the starboard side and the Duke of Edinburgh's cabin is on the with a vestibule connecting the two apartments. The cabins are decorated in ligh the Queen's having off-white walls and turquoise curtains. The Duke's day cabin

DRAWN BY OUR SPECIAL ARTIST

S.S. "GOTHIC"

POSITION OF ROYAL ANTE-ROOM AND DINING CABIN.

GOTHIC

ROYAL ANTE-ROOM AND ROYAL DINING CABIN.

(SITUATED AT THE FORWARD END OF BRIDGE DECK.)

ANTE-ROOM FOR OFFICERS, RETINUE AND PRESS.

ENTRANCE

MESS FOR OFFICERS, RETINUE AND PRESS.

ROYAL ANTE-ROOM.

No 2 CARGO HATCH

SHELTER DECK.

PROMENADE DECK.

ENTRANCE

ROYAL DINING CABIN

VESTIBULE.

BRIDGE DECK.

LEVEL OF PROMENADE DECK.

G H DAVIS 1953

...MODATION PREPARED FOR HER MAJESTY'S JOURNEY TO NEW ZEALAND AND AUSTRALIA.

...desk used by Queen Victoria in the Royal yacht *Victoria and Albert*. Aft of the Royal ...ins the existing Verandah Café has been adapted as a verandah for the Royal travellers; ...ains a large record-player which can be seen against the forward wall. The Royal ...g-cabins and the two bathrooms which are placed between them can be seen in our ...g with the after-walls diagrammatically cut away to show the interiors. The Royal ...A., WITH OFFICIAL CO-OPERATION.

ante-room at the forward end of the Bridge or Saloon deck has numerous windows looking forward over the ship's bows. Just aft of the ante-room, on the starboard side of the same deck, is the large Royal dining-cabin, with its magnificent table at which the Queen will entertain her official guests. It will be noticed that the Royal barge is stowed on the after-end of the Shelter deck; it is shown in our drawing without its tarpaulin cover.

'Another Royal
Romance': Group
Captain Peter Townsend
and Princess Margaret.

more. The American edition of *Fit for a King* contained a few minor variations on the British text – and one major one, in the form of an extra chapter. Coming after a discussion of Edward VIII and Wallis Simpson, this additional chapter was titled 'Another Royal Romance: Princess Margaret and Peter Townsend'.

The relationship between the Queen's sister and a decorated Battle of Britain pilot was common knowledge in Britain by the time *Fit for a King* was published. Group Captain Townsend had been appointed equerry to George VI in 1944, one of a number of young war heroes to join the household, and having served for a brief spell as deputy master of the household, he was appointed an equerry to Elizabeth II when she came to the throne. He was married with two sons (George VI stood godfather to the younger), and for a while he and his wife lived in a grace-and-favour cottage in Windsor Great Park. But the marriage failed. Townsend fell in love with the royal family, it was said, while his wife fell in love with a baronet – and he was granted a divorce in an undefended petition in 1952.[24]

It is hard to say exactly when he and Princess Margaret, who was fifteen years his junior, first became attracted to each other. There was speculation about a romance between the two in the foreign press as early as September 1948, when Townsend was one of the party accompanying Margaret to Amsterdam to represent her father at Crown Princess Juliana's inauguration as queen of the Netherlands, her first important royal engagement. But the idea that a princess who was the third in line to the throne after her sister should enter into a serious relationship with her father's equerry, and a decidedly middle-class equerry at that, seemed absurd. The last princesses to fall for royal equerries had been George III's daughters Augusta, Amelia and Sophia. None of those relationships had ended happily – and their lovers were bachelors. The notion that a princess should be romantically attached to a married man was unthinkable.

According to Christopher Warwick, Princess Margaret's official biographer, Townsend declared himself to Margaret in 1951, a year before his divorce. After George VI's death in 1952, he was appointed comptroller of the Queen Mother's household at Clarence House, where the princess was living with her mother. He is thought to have proposed to her in April 1953, in the crimson drawing room at Windsor Castle.

And now their troubles began in earnest. The Queen, whose consent to Margaret's marriage was required under the Royal Marriages Act of 1772, refused it – at least, she asked the couple to wait for a year. (Without her sister's consent, Margaret's only option was to wait until she was twenty-five, when she would no longer need it, although she would still need formal approval from both Houses of Parliament.) The Queen's private secretary, Tommy Lascelles, was implacably opposed to the marriage: he advised Elizabeth that Townsend should be removed from his post as comptroller of the Queen Mother's household and packed off abroad somewhere. The Queen refused, but she did agree that the group captain should transfer from Clarence House to become her own equerry.

At the coronation that June, reporters noticed the proprietorial way in which the princess flicked a piece of fluff from Townsend's uniform. 'That little flick of her hand did it all right,' recalled Townsend. 'After that, the storm broke.'[25] The next day papers in America and Europe began to speculate openly about an engagement. Lascelles drove down to Chartwell, Prime Minister Churchill's country house in Kent, to discuss the situation with him, and the *Sunday People* ran a story which, although it masqueraded as an attack on the rumours circulating in the foreign press, was in effect a public outing of the couple: 'It is quite unthinkable that a royal princess, third in line to the throne, should even contemplate a marriage with a man who has been through the divorce courts.'[26] Lascelles was adamant that Townsend had to go, and four weeks later, while Margaret was on a tour of Rhodesia, he was posted with immediate effect to Brussels as air attaché at the British embassy.

The American press screamed that 'Princess Meg's' suitor had been 'banished', 'exiled' by her own sister. In Britain, the *Daily Mirror* ran a poll of its readers, ninety-seven per cent of whom thought the pair should be allowed to marry. Reading of it, Noël Coward confided to his diary that the public interest was 'incredibly vulgar'. Could nothing be done, he asked, 'to stop these tasteless, illiterate minds from smearing our Royal Family with their sanctimonious rubbish?'[27]

Two years later, with Margaret past her twenty-fifth birthday and Townsend back in Britain, public interest in the romance reached a climax. Ranged on one side were those who saw them as heroic lovers, defying convention; on the other were the constitutionalists and the traditionalists, who could not brook the idea that a member of the royal family might marry a man whose wife was still living. It became clear that the government, now headed by Sir Anthony Eden as prime minister (a man who had divorced his wife in 1950 and married Churchill's niece two years later) would not consent to Margaret's marriage: her only option was to renounce her right to the throne and become a commoner. That October, as the couple wrestled with the dilemma in which they – or rather she – was placed, dining together at the homes of friends, meeting at house parties in the country, they were hounded by literally hundreds of journalists. Townsend arrived one evening at the borrowed flat in Lowndes Square, Belgravia, to find himself surrounded by pressmen: 'You don't know what a state the newspapers are in about this,' one journalist told him. 'You don't know what a state I'm in,' he replied.[28]

On 31 October, the BBC interrupted its normal programming to read a brief statement from Princess Margaret. She had admitted defeat: 'I would like it to be known that I have decided not to marry Group Captain Townsend … mindful of the Church's teaching that Christian marriage is indissoluble, and conscious of my duty to the Commonwealth, I have resolved to put these considerations before any others.'[29] Eden wanted her to omit the reference to the indissolubility of marriage, but she refused. In an approving editorial the next day, *The Times* declared that she had done her duty to God, to her sister and to the Church of England, while criticising the fact that over recent weeks she had 'been made the victim of an unmannerly curiosity such as no one of any rank should be made to endure' – a sentiment echoed by most of the British press, without a trace of irony.[30] The *Manchester Guardian* produced a bizarre piece on Townsend which even today reads like an obituary: 'Group-Captain Peter Townsend, CVO, DSO, DFC, was born in Rangoon on November 22, 1914, the second son of the late Lieutenant-Colonel E. C. Townsend of the Indian Civil Service', and so on.[31]

This was the state of things when Frederick Corbitt included a chapter on the romance in the US edition of his *Fit for a King*. In spite of the massive press intrusion into the lives of an equerry and a princess, there was still a line to be drawn when it came to eye-witness accounts of their relationship – in Britain, at least. Not so in America. 'There has never been any doubt in my mind that these two young people were in love,' wrote Corbitt.[32] (Townsend was forty.) He offered some rather odd titbits of reminiscence: during his last years at Buckingham Palace, Townsend was often to be found alone reading his Bible, apparently. Princess Margaret always pronounced that name, 'Peter', with a 'special quality of affection'.[33] Corbitt had heard all the rumours in the servants' hall, the stewards' room and the officials' mess, he declared, but seeing them together at Balmoral in 1952, he knew those rumours were right.

'The Princess seemed to be smiling at me as if to say, "You understand."'[34] Of course she did.*

That one member (or recently retired member) of the royal household was able to discuss, in print, the emotional life of another recently retired member of the household and his relationship with a princess still seems inappropriate today. More significantly, the intrusion into the personal lives of the royal family heralded the grainy snapshots and prurient digging of a thousand paparazzi and tabloid journalists, an absence of deference which decayed into something more unpleasant, something that ended with the death of a princess in the Pont de l'Alma road tunnel in Paris one August night in 1997.

As for Princess Margaret, she was the most modern member of the modern royal family. Her marriage in 1960 to the photographer Anthony Armstrong-Jones was the first royal wedding to be televised; their divorce, eighteen years later, was the first royal divorce since Henry VIII.

———————

BUCKINGHAM PALACE'S RESPONSE TO THE SPATE OF revelations by household staff was to reinforce royal disapproval with civil penalties. In January 1955 Commander Richard Colville, the Queen's press secretary, wrote to the Press Council to condemn the fact that a small number of 'those persons who, by virtue of their work or other circumstances, are brought into contact with the Sovereign or members of the Royal Family', had chosen to break the Queen's trust in them.[35] He announced that all those who entered service in the royal household now had a clause on communicating with the press inserted into their terms of employment. It read:

> You are not permitted to publish any incident or conversation which may be within your knowledge by reason of your employment in the royal service, nor may you give to any person, either verbally or in writing, any information regarding her Majesty or any member of the Royal Family, which might be communicated to the press.[36]

Commander Colville, a naval officer whom the Queen had inherited from her father, was unswerving in his conviction that the royal family deserved a private life, and implacable in his determination

---

* Princess Margaret always blamed Tommy Lascelles for wrecking her relationship with Townsend. Years later, when she caught sight of the old man in the street, she shouted to her chauffeur, 'Run the brute down!'

Prince Charles taking part in the tug o' war at his school sports day. Richard Colville reported that the prince's parents were 'disturbed' at press interest.

to control the flow of information about them. Colville was constantly doing battle with the press right up until his retirement in 1968. As his obituary in *The Times* put it, 'his forthrightness and uncompromising personality meant that his tenure of office was never entirely free from friction'.[37] He was a regular fixture at meetings of the Press Council in the late 1950s, complaining that the Queen was disturbed by intrusive press interest. She was going to have to give up attending the Duke of Edinburgh's polo matches at Windsor because of the publicity, he told members of the council in 1957. She considered that her children's inoculations were a private matter, not something for the press. She and her husband were 'disturbed' – a favourite Colville expression – by the publicity surrounding the nine-year-old Prince Charles's participation in school sports.

Occasionally, Colville's brief, bland statements to the press dealt with more serious matters. In February 1957, he was forced to issue a denial that the Queen's marriage was in trouble. 'It is quite untrue that there is any rift between the Queen and the Duke of Edinburgh.'[38] The rumour, which began with a report by a London staff reporter for the American *Baltimore Sun*, was tied in with a story that the duke's private secretary had resigned his post after it emerged that he had separated from his wife.

As stories like this flew round the globe, and the British press steadily lost its reticence to relay what the rest of the world was reporting about the royal family, the response of the press to Colville's routine denials and complaints of a 'disturbed' sovereign was to say that of course royal news should at all times be handled with discretion, but to point out that if 'the quality and the supply of news and guidance from the Press Secretariat' could be improved, that would help relations between Fleet Street and the palace.[39] In other words, if only Colville had been a little freer with royal news, the press wouldn't have had to pounce on every titbit of gossip.

This is the version of Commander Colville's career which has come to be accepted by historians and royal biographers. By so severely restricting press access to royal news, the story goes, he actually made things worse for the royal family. It isn't entirely fair: Colville, like the other senior members of the household in the 1950s – Tommy Lascelles and his successor as private secretary to the Queen, Michael Adeane – wasn't just an employee. He had the values of a traditional courtier, and he was driven by loyalty, by a desire to protect at all costs the Queen and the monarchy. And he had to contend with a public whose respect for their sovereign was evolving rapidly into an adoration – Elizabeth II was perhaps the most popular monarch in British history – coupled rather dangerously with a conviction that her private life belonged to them.

In the summer of 1957 a small-circulation monthly, the *National and English Review*, carried an article on 'The Monarchy Today' by its editor, John Grigg, Lord Altrincham. Driven by what Altrincham later described as a general approach in the media which ranged 'from gushy adulation to Shinto-style worship', intensified by the 'secular religiosity' of the coronation, he criticised the Queen's advisers as being 'almost without exception people of the "tweedy" sort'.[40]

But Altrincham went further. He complained about the way in which Elizabeth II presented herself in public, saying her voice was 'a pain in the neck' and that 'the personality conveyed by the utterances which are put into her mouth is that of a priggish schoolgirl, captain of the hockey team, a prefect, and a recent candidate for confirmation'.[41]

There was uproar. Altrincham was attacked in the press, condemned by the Archbishop of Canterbury, banned by the BBC. 'The attacks on our monarchy must cease' was daubed on the road outside his house in yellow paint, in letters a foot high. Borough councillors in the town of Altrincham issued a statement dissociating their town from his views. Reproaches came from all over the world. Australia said the article 'is so personal it becomes vulgar'.[42] The Vatican observed that the criticisms were an insult, 'especially as a lady is involved'.[43] An Italian royalist challenged him to a duel. A member of a group called the League of Empire Loyalists punched him in the face in the street. When his assailant was brought before the bench the next day, the chief Metropolitan magistrate fined him for a breach of the peace while commenting that 'ninety-five per cent of the population of this country were disgusted' by Altrincham's article.[44]

In August 1997, to mark the fortieth anniversary of his article's appearance, Altrincham (now plain John Grigg, having renounced his title in 1963) looked back at the furore. He was largely unrepentant, arguing that his remarks had been aimed at the Queen's household, which, he said, was still largely staffed at its higher levels 'by white members of the landed and professional classes', who failed adequately to reflect the character of the Commonwealth, 'or even that of an ethnically mixed Britain'.[45] He wrote that 'a key figure in the royal household' arranged to meet him at the house of a mutual friend a few days after the row broke out, greeting him with the words, 'This is the best thing that has happened to Buckingham Palace in my time.'[46]

So much had changed in those forty years. 'Now,' Altrincham reflected ruefully, 'it is open season for anybody to say anything about members of the royal family, and to treat the monarchy itself with rudeness or contempt.'[47] Richard Colville had been succeeded as the Queen's press secretary in 1968 by an Australian, William Heseltine, who within a year of taking up his post brokered a behind-the-scenes TV documentary, *Royal Family*, which showed the Queen, Prince Philip and their children behaving like people instead of symbols. Prince Charles and Princess Anne sat round the table with their parents, just the four of them. The Queen laughed and told stories and behaved like an ordinary mortal. It has never been shown since its first airing in 1969, allegedly because the Queen thought the film made her family look too ordinary. A monarchy without mystique is no monarchy at all.

THE INTRODUCTION OF SERVICE CONTRACTS to replace the traditional ties of loyalty that bound members of the household to the royal family, or at least to reinforce them, was only partially successful. For one thing, it was impossible to prevent elderly ex-courtiers from being indiscreet: in 1995 the octogenarian Lord Charteris, who as Martin Charteris had been private secretary to the Queen between 1972 and

1977, told a journalist that Prince Andrew's wife, Sarah, was 'vulgar, vulgar, vulgar, and that is that'.[48]

More serious was the deliberate flouting of the rules. In 1960, shortly before Princess Margaret's marriage to Anthony Armstrong-Jones, David John Payne, who had worked for her as a footman at Clarence House for about a year, left her employment – for 'private reasons', he said. When the first instalment of his memoirs, *My Life with Princess Margaret*, appeared in a Paris newspaper later that year, the Queen Mother took out an injunction preventing the twenty-eight-year-old Payne from being a party to the publication of any information regarding the royal family, on the grounds that it would be a breach of his obligations under his service agreement. Payne stalled for months, failing to provide a defence while in the meantime *My Life* was serialised in an American magazine and then came out in America in book form. Eventually in June 1961, when it was rather too late, Payne apologised to the court and expressed his 'deep and sincere regret at what had taken place, and for any inconvenience caused to the Queen Mother or to other members of the Royal Household'.[49]

Payne ran down Anthony Armstrong-Jones, whom the footman clearly thought not good enough for 'my princess', as he referred to his employer throughout his oleaginous memoir. He sneered at 'Tony' for committing the unpardonable sin, as a dinner guest, of smiling at the staff when they served the food: 'I knew he felt out of his depth in that company,' said the footman.[50] And like Frederick Corbitt, he was quite overcome with the romance of Margaret's doomed love for Peter Townsend. He described how she kept three photographs of him by her bedside, and when the group captain visited Clarence House for tea with the princess and her mother in 1958, Payne lingered over every unlikely detail. Margaret ran to him as he entered her sitting room, apparently, and kissed him firmly, full on the lips:

> They lingered over this kiss, neither wanting to draw back … At last they parted and Margaret leaned back, taking his hands but keeping them still on her waist. Only then, for the first time that afternoon, did she speak. 'Oh Peter…' was all she said. And I was close enough to hear the sigh in her voice.[51]

On her marriage to 'Tony', himself an iconic emblem of the Swinging Sixties, the sighing princess and her groom moved into a new home in the Clock Court at Kensington Palace. They had a staff of eight: Margaret's dresser, Ruby Gordon, who had been with her since she was a child; the butler, Thomas Cronin, an under-butler and a footman; the

Princess Margaret holds court on Mustique, 1972.

housekeeper, Nora Foley; and a chef, a kitchenmaid and a chauffeur. Cronin didn't last: three weeks after the move to Kensington Palace he walked out, declaring that Armstrong-Jones was making it impossible for him to do his job properly, ordering him to account for every penny spent and cutting back on everything from the wine served at table to the cutlery in the servants' hall. Cronin went off to be a 'super-butler' at a Florida beach resort, before coming back to England to marry a widow who ran a hotel in St John's Wood. At least he didn't write a book.

Public interest in the private life of Princess Margaret never waned, as the star-crossed lover of the 1950s turned into the rebellious socialite of the 1960s. Her life was more exciting, edgier, less *dutiful*, than that of her sister. Nor did that interest subside in later years, when her marriage to Armstrong-Jones was on the rocks and she retreated to Mustique, her island in the sun with her young lover, Roddy Llewellyn. There were no more book-length breaches of confidence from her household staff, but the British reading public didn't need them: her own friends were always ready to provide the gossip columnists with juicy titbits, while their memoirs were littered with instances of her autocratic putdowns and louche behaviour. One of the more unusual social occasions was recorded by Katherine Tynan in her biography of her husband, the theatre critic Kenneth Tynan, as she recounted holding a dinner party for Margaret and Tony. The other guests were the playwright Harold Pinter and his wife, actress Vivien Merchant; and the comedian Peter Cook and his wife, Wendy. Merchant snubbed the princess, they all got drunk together, and after dinner Kenneth Tynan showed them homoerotic pornographic movies. Pinter fell down the stairs on the way out.[52]

THE QUEEN MOTHER'S HOUSEHOLD ran on rather more conventional lines, but even here the public had an insatiable appetite for news. Colin Burgess, a Guards officer who did a two-year tour of duty as equerry to the Queen Mother in the mid-1990s (and who, ironically enough, published his own account of his life in royal service after her death) was convinced that junior employees at Clarence House were always willing to sell stories to the press. 'I suspect that most of the junior butlers and some of the cooks were on the payroll of at least one Fleet Street newspaper,' he recalled.[53]

The senior members of the Clarence House household, the 'home team', as Burgess called them, were led in the 1990s by Sir Alistair Aird

(Eton and Sandhurst), who had joined the household as an equerry in 1960 and risen to become her comptroller in 1974 and then her private secretary in 1993, holding both posts until her death in 2002. Aird ran things at Clarence House, but he was also the man who arbitrated on etiquette and protocol. He 'knew all the rules concerning how to address people and how to write letters correctly, that sort of thing,' recalled the young equerry. And at twenty-six, Burgess seemed very young indeed in the Clarence House milieu: the Queen Mother was ninety-four when he arrived; Aird was sixty-three; and his predecessor in the post of private secretary, Lieutenant-Colonel Sir Martin Gilliat, had been eighty when he died, still in harness. The treasurer of the household, Sir Ralph Anstruther (who also held the post of hereditary carver to the Queen, although this didn't involve much carving), was seventy-three. The Queen Mother's trusted steward and page of the backstairs, the bouffant-haired William Tallon, known affectionately as 'Backstairs Billy', was fifty-nine; his life-partner Reginald Wilcock, the deputy steward and page of the presence, was sixty. The night-time protection officer was in his seventies (and armed). Many of these old courtiers had served for most of their lives, although Margaret Rhodes, the Queen Mother's confidante and niece (and hence the Queen's first cousin), was first appointed as one of her women of the bedchamber in 1991 at the age of sixty-six. When another of the women of the bedchamber, who was about to celebrate her eightieth birthday, suggested that perhaps it was time to retire, the Queen Mother (then ninety-eight) wouldn't hear of it. 'You'll find that you feel marvellous after you're eighty,' she said.[54] 'Our rather elderly entourage was very well briefed on how to behave before we went out to meet the public,' recalled Rhodes, 'and the private secretary would warn us about any potential trouble spots, like tricky stairs and steps.'[55]

The Clarence House routine was relatively sedate by this time. When there were no visitors, lunch would be taken in a corner of the drawing room or, in fine summer weather, out in the garden. The Queen Mother usually ate with one of her ladies in waiting and two men from the 'home team'. Contrary to popular myth, her alcohol consumption was steady rather than excessive. Rhodes was adamant that it never varied: a gin and Dubonnet before lunch, followed by 'some wine' with the meal; a dry Martini before dinner, and a glass of champagne, after which she would sit down and watch television. Burgess suggested a more flexible regime – an occasional glass of port after lunch; one or two Martinis, which it was his job to mix, before dinner; and one or two glasses of Veuve Clicquot with. 'She was a devoted drinker,' he declared, going on to say that for official engagements, he would sometimes take a bottle of Dubonnet with him in case it wasn't available at the venue.[56] He struggled to keep up with the Queen Mother and the older members of the home team, sometimes retreating to his office after a heavy lunch, where he pulled out his two desk drawers so that he could rest his arms in them while he slept with his head on the desk.

There were the inevitable tensions and internecine feuding within the Queen Mother's household. Tallon and Wilcock could be touchy if they felt they had been slighted in any way, or if they hadn't been consulted over some arrangement or other. Burgess quickly found out that issuing orders to other members of staff, even when they were well below him in the hierarchy, did not yield happy results. When early in his royal career he peremptorily told a chauffeur to have a car ready to collect the Queen Mother 'at eight forty-five prompt, ready to leave', the chauffeur simply said, 'No.' Aird had to take the equerry aside and explain. 'Look, you can't speak like that to the chauffeur; he is a very emotional person … you just have to approach it in a very nice kind of conversational way.'[57] But although they occasionally squabbled among themselves, the members of the Clarence House home team were united in one thing – a fierce, almost feudal devotion to their mistress.

The same held true for the Queen. Courtiers rarely broke ranks, and the glimpses they occasionally gave of everyday life at Buckingham Palace or Windsor or Balmoral were usually quite amiable: Margaret Rhodes described how during the preparations for a big state banquet every one of the 150 place settings would be measured with a ruler to ensure a perfect fit, with the Queen personally inspecting the entire table afterwards. (Margaret also noted how live music from a regimental band accompanied the meal, recalling that when President Mugabe of Zimbabwe was a guest, the tunes included 'If I Ruled the World'.) There were exceptions: Guy Hunting, who arrived at Buckingham Palace as a teenager in 1961 to take up a post as silver pantry assistant, at a salary of £3 10s. a week plus seven shillings board wages, caused something of a stir in 2002 when he published a memoir, *Adventures of a Gentleman's Gentleman*, which went into detail about his frequent homosexual encounters below stairs while in the Queen's service.

But when it came to hearing all about scenes behind the throne, the public's interest focused on the royal children and particularly on their marital difficulties. Princess Anne's nineteen-year marriage to fellow-equestrian Mark Phillips ended in divorce in 1992; in the same year she married naval officer Timothy Laurence, who had served as the Queen's

equerry from 1986 to 1989. Also in 1992 Prince Andrew separated from his wife of ten years, Sarah Ferguson; their marriage was dissolved in 1996. And then there was Charles and Diana.

In August 1992 the *National Enquirer* in America and *The Sun* in Britain both published extracts from a taped conversation said to have been accidentally recorded by two different amateur radio enthusiasts several years earlier. In the tape, the Princess of Wales could be heard speaking from Sandringham, where she was spending Christmas, to a car-dealer, James Gilbey. The pair had been friends for years, and it was clear that they were now more than friends. Gilbey – who called the princess 'Squidgy', leading the British press to nickname the release of the tape 'Squidgygate' – repeatedly told her he loved her, while she railed against her marriage and her in-laws. 'It's just so desperate … I can't stand the confines of this marriage … Bloody hell, after all I've done for this fucking family.'[58]

Squidgygate came hard on the heels of Andrew Morton's bestselling

The public face of the British monarchy: Queen Elizabeth II, the Duke of Edinburgh and Prince Andrew attend the first day of Royal Ascot in 2005.

biography, *Diana: Her True Story*, which revealed that the princess suffered from bulimia and had attempted suicide several times. It was initially dismissed as sensationalism, with Buckingham Palace issuing a statement claiming that Diana did not cooperate with the biography in any way, but it later emerged that she had, in fact, secretly collaborated with Morton. The book painted an unflattering picture of the royal family: Prince Charles was cold and unfaithful; the Queen blamed the fact that the Waleses' marriage was clearly failing on her daughter-in-law's instability. The couple's household had split into rival camps: an unnamed courtier told Morton, 'You very quickly learn to choose whose side you are on – his or hers. There is no middle course.'[59] As each camp battled it out in a proxy war, deliberately scheduling a high-profile public appearance by 'their' royal on the same day as the other, repeatedly failing to keep the other side informed of their movements, matters became impossible. In 1992 the prince's comptroller suddenly resigned: Charles blamed his wife for making life too difficult for him, but staff on both sides of the so-called 'War of the Waleses' were sure the departure was due to the atmosphere of mistrust and non-cooperation. The release of the Squidgygate tapes was blamed on the prince's people; and when a second tape surfaced weeks later, this time containing a sexually explicit conversation between the Prince of Wales and his lover, Camilla Parker-Bowles, it was assumed by some, at least, that this was a retaliatory strike by the princess's side, an attempt to mitigate the damage done to her reputation. (It should also be said that the release of both recordings has been blamed by the more conspiratorially minded on the arcane workings of the British intelligence services.) On 9 December 1992 the British prime minister, John Major, announced to the House of Commons that 'with regret, the Prince and Princess of Wales have decided to separate ... The Queen and the Duke of Edinburgh, though saddened, understand and sympathise with the difficulties that have led to this decision.'[60] MPs listened in total silence, broken only by a gasp as Major said there was no reason why the Princess of Wales shouldn't be crowned queen in due course. The Buckingham Palace statement announcing the separation of the Prince and Princess of Wales assured the public that the couple had no plans to divorce. But divorce they did, four years later.

As if the collapse of three of her children's marriages and the embarrassment of having the intimate personal details of the heir to the throne and the future queen of England aired around the world were not enough, on 20 November 1992 a disastrous fire broke out at Windsor Castle. Caused by a spotlight being too close to a curtain in the Queen's

Paul Burrell, footman
to Elizabeth II and later
butler to Diana, Princess
of Wales. Burrell's *A
Royal Duty* was one
of many memoirs by
members of the royal
household to appear
in the wake of Diana's
death.

private chapel, it spread through the state apartments, causing damage which would cost £36.5 million to repair. '1992 is not a year on which I shall look back with undiluted pleasure,' said the Queen in a speech four days later at London's Guildhall to mark the fortieth anniversary of her accession to the throne, famously speaking of it as her 'annus horribilis'.[61] Her broadcast Christmas message a few weeks later, after the formal separation had been announced, also struck a personal note. 'Like many other families, we have lived through some difficult days this year,' she said. 'As some of you may have heard me observe, it has, indeed, been a sombre year.'[62]

It's All to Do with the Training

O N THE NIGHT OF 31 AUGUST 1997 Diana, Princess of Wales, died in a car crash in a Paris underpass, along with her lover, Dodi Fayed, and their driver Henri Paul. Only Diana's bodyguard, Trevor Rees-Jones, survived.

As we reach that royal death, the past collides with memory, and history, which has no place in the present, comes to an end in a welter of judgement. In the sorry story of the Prince and Princess of Wales's failing relationship and its sad aftermath, confidentiality was one of the first casualties, as members of their household raced to tell all. The two leading protagonists had already appeared on national television to discuss details of their private lives in a way that must have made Tommy Lascelles and Richard Colville turn in their graves. The Prince of Wales told the world that he had been unfaithful to his wife, in a 1994 interview with Jonathan Dimbleby, and the following year Diana famously said, in the course of a heart-wrenching but carefully choreographed interview for the BBC, that 'there were three of us in this marriage, so it was a bit crowded'.[1]

Now a flood of memoirs appeared, from the princess's housekeeper, her butler, her personal protection officer, her private secretary. Worse, the public's grief for a stranger, its demand to see grief expressed, its assumption that the royal family must bare its soul like the contestants on some second-rate reality show, all but brought down the monarchy in that summer of 1997. For the Queen to be forced, as she was, to appear live on TV simply to acknowledge that she was sorry Diana died, that she admired and respected her, that she was speaking 'from my heart' when she paid tribute to her ex-daughter-in-law, shows how far the balance of power between sovereign and people has shifted. Gloriana must be a people's queen. She and her children and grandchildren must smile for the cameras whether they choose to or not. Diana's therapist, Stephen Twigg, once asked her, 'Do we want the royal family to be revered because of their position or in a modern society do we want to admire them because of the way they cope with traumas and tribulations of everyday life and learn from them in the process?'[2] The answer is that,

impossibly, they must be both. Above all, it seems, they must be whatever we want them to be.

The royal household has moved with the times in happier ways. Its website, www.royal.uk, 'the home of the Royal Family', declares that

> we are a truly diverse organisation – not just in the range of people who work here, but also in the careers that we offer. Alongside the roles you may expect, you'll find everything from HR, Finance and IT professionals to Engineers, Curators and Chefs. They all work as one towards a shared and unique purpose.[3]

In the twenty-first century, the *Domus Regie Magnificencie* and the *Domus Providencie* of Edward IV's Black Book have given way to a modern, streamlined household. Where the knight marshal once kept order within twelve miles of the sovereign's person, now a director for security liaison coordinates and implements all security plans and procedures related to the royal household. Kitchen staff once slept in corners. Now Buckingham Palace boasts a staff gym, swimming pool, squash court and tennis court, with discounted membership to fitness facilities elsewhere in the country. There is a choir, a book club, a 24-hour confidential counselling service for staff.

A digital engagement team manages the monarchy website and social media channels. It forms part of Royal Communications, a branch of the private secretary's office. The Court Circular, the official record of royal engagements established by George III, is available online. Vacancies at Buckingham Palace are regularly advertised on the royal website. The royal family's Instagram account, @theroyalfamily, has nearly 800,000 followers. Their Twitter account, @RoyalFamily, has over three million.

These days, the Queen's private secretary is the single most important courtier in the household. The spiritual heir of Arthur Bigge and Tommy Lascelles advises on constitutional matters and liaises with government ministers. He steers his employer through media crises and drafts her speeches. And it is always a 'he' – a woman has never been appointed, although there have been several female assistant private secretaries.

It goes without saying that Queen Elizabeth I would not recognise her namesake's daily routine; but nor would she recognise the degree of professionalisation which goes into organising it in the twenty-first century. The Tudor queen might feel more at home with the bouts of back-stabbing that are said to erupt periodically between courtiers: one source at Clarence House recently likened the Prince of Wales's

Elizabeth II, photographed by Cecil Beaton at Buckingham Palace in 1968.

household to Hilary Mantel's *Wolf Hall*, such were the internecine battles that went on there.

Yet in spite of all the changes, there is still a lord chamberlain, a lord steward, a master of horse, as there was in Elizabeth I's day. There are still women of the bedchamber and a keeper of the privy purse and a mistress of the robes. The digital engagement team and its counterparts elsewhere in the royal household haven't entirely ousted the traditions and rituals that mark out the monarchy as different. They exist alongside them in a synthesis between past and present, partners in time with ghosts in powdered wigs and livery.

Walk through the state rooms at Windsor or Buckingham Palace and those ghosts are there at your shoulder. Listen, and you may hear them whispering in their sovereign's ear.

BIBLIOGRAPHY

Airlie, Mabell, Countess of, *Thatched with Gold: The Memoirs of Mabell, Countess of Airlie*, London: Hutchinson (1962).

Anand, Sushila, *Indian Sahib: Queen Victoria's Dear Abdul*, London: Gerald Duckworth (1996).

Ansell, Jacqueline, 'The Seal of Social Approval: Or "How Girls Are Presented at Court"', *Court Historian*, vol. 4, no. 2 (1999), 151–60.

Arnold, Janet (ed.), '*Lost from Her Majesties Back': Items of Clothing and Jewels Lost or Given Away by Queen Elizabeth I*, London: Costume Society (1980).

Aronson, Theo, *Royal Subjects: A Biographer's Encounters*, London: Sidgwick & Jackson (2000).

Aylmer, G. E., *The King's Servants: The Civil Service of Charles I, 1625–1642*, London: Routledge & Kegan Paul (1961).

Barclay, Andrew, 'Charles II's Failed Restoration: Administrative Reform below Stairs, 1660–4', in Cruickshanks, Eveline (ed.), *The Stuart Courts*, 2nd edition, Stroud: History Press (2009).

Barclay, Andrew, 'The Impact of James II on the Departments of the Royal Household', unpublished PhD thesis, Darwin College, Cambridge (1993).

[Bayley, P.,] *A Queen's Appeal*, London: Robert Stodart (1820).

Beattie, J. M., 'The Court of George I and English Politics, 1717–1720', *English Historical Review*, vol. 81, no. 318 (1966), 26–37.

Beattie, J. M., *The English Court in the Reign of George I*, Cambridge: Cambridge University Press (1967).

Bergeron, David M., 'Creating Entertainments for Prince Henry's Creation (1610)', *Comparative Drama*, vol. 42, no. 4 (2008), 433–49.

Birch, Thomas, *The Life of Henry, Prince of Wales, Eldest Son of King James I* (1760).

Blencowe, R. W. (ed.), *The Sydney Papers, Consisting of a Journal of the Earl of Leicester, and Original Letters by Algernon Sidney*, London: John Murray (1825).

Bloch, Michael (ed.), *Wallis and Edward: Letters 1931–1937*, New York: Summit (1986).

Bloomfield, Georgiana, Baroness, *Reminiscences of Court and Diplomatic Life*, London: Kegan Paul, Trench (1883).

Bogdanor, Vernon, *The Monarchy and the Constitution*, Oxford: Clarendon Press (1995).

Botonaki, Effie, 'The Audience of the Jacobean Masque, with a Reference to *The Tempest*', *Gramma: Journal of Theory and Criticism*, vol. 15 (2007), 67–86.

Bradford, Sarah, *Elizabeth: A Biography of Her Majesty the Queen*, ebook edition, London: Penguin (2002).

Bradford, Sarah, *George VI*, ebook edition, London: Penguin (2002).

Bray, William, 'An Account of the Revenue, the Expences, the Jewels, &c. of Prince Henry', *Archaeologia*, vol. 15 (1806), 13–26.

Brazier, Rodney, 'Royal Incapacity and Constitutional Continuity: The Regent and Counsellors of State', *Cambridge Law Journal*, vol. 64, no. 2 (2005), 352–87.

Broughton, Mrs Vernon Delves (ed.), *Court and Private Life in the Time of Queen Charlotte*, 2 vols, London: Richard Bentley (1887).

Brown, Craig, *Ma'am Darling: 99 Glimpses of Princess Margaret*, ebook edition, London: 4th Estate (2017).

Brown, Rawdon et al. (eds), *Calendar of State Papers Relating to English Affairs in the Archives of Venice*, 38 vols, HMSO (1864–1947).

Bucholz, R. O., *The Augustan Court: Queen Anne and the Decline of Court Culture,* Stanford, CA: Stanford University Press (1993).

Bucholz, R. O., 'Going to Court in 1700: A Visitor's Guide', *Court Historian*, vol. 5, no. 3 (2000), 181–215.

Bucholz, R. O. (ed.), *Office-Holders in Modern Britain, vol. 11 (revised): Court Officers, 1660–1837*, University of London (2006).

Bülow, Gottfried von (ed.), 'Journey through England and Scotland Made by Lupold von Wedel in the Years 1584 and 1585', *Transactions of the Royal Historical Society*, vol. 9 (1895), 223–70.

Burgess, Colin, *Behind Palace Doors: My Service as the Queen Mother's Equerry*, ebook edition, London: John Blake (2007).

Burnet, Gilbert, *Bishop Burnet's History of His Own Time*, 6 vols, London: A. Millar (1753).

Burney, Frances, *The Diary and Letters of Madame D'Arblay (Frances Burney)*, ed. W. C. Ward, 3 vols, London: Vizetelly (1890–1).

Burrell, Paul, *A Royal Duty*, London: Michael Joseph (2003).

Burton, Thomas, *Diary of Thomas Burton Esq., Member in the Parliaments of Oliver and Richard Cromwell, from 1656 to 1659*, 4 vols., ed. John Towill Rutt, London: Henry Colburn (1828).

Bury, Lady Charlotte, *The Diary of a Lady-in-Waiting*, ed. A. Francis Steuart, 2 vols, London: John Lane (1908).

The Ceremonial of the Coronation of His Most Sacred Majesty King George II: And of His Royal Consort Queen Caroline, Dublin: S. Powell (1727).

Chaloner, Sir Thomas, *A Shorte Discourse of the Most Rare and Excellent Vertue of Nitre*, London: Gerald Dewes (1584).

Chamberlain, John, *Letters of John Chamberlain*, ed. Norman Egbert McClure, 2 vols, Philadelphia: American Philosophical Society (1939).

Channon, Sir Henry 'Chips', *Chips: The Diaries of Sir Henry Channon*, ed. Robert Rhodes James, London: Weidenfeld & Nicolson (1967).

Chase, Malcolm, *1820: Disorder and Stability in the United Kingdom*, Manchester: Manchester University Press (2013).

Childe-Pemberton, William S., *The Romance of Princess Amelia, Daughter of George III*, London: G. Bell (1910).

Cole, Mary Hill, *The Portable Queen: Elizabeth I and the Politics of Ceremony*, Amherst: University of Massachusetts Press (1999).

Collins, Arthur, *The Life of that Great Statesman William Cecil, Lord Burghley*, London (1732).

Colvin, H. M. (ed.), *The History of the King's Works, vol. 3: 1485–1660, part 1*, London: HMSO (1975).

Corbitt, F. J., *Fit for a King: A Book of Intimate Memoirs*, London: Odhams Press (1956).

Corbitt, F. J., *My Twenty Years in Buckingham Palace: A Book of Intimate Memoirs*, New York: David McKay (1956).

Cox, J. Charles, *The Cost of the Royal Household, Royal Annuities, and Crown Lands*, 5th edition, Derby: W. & W. Pike (1871).

Cox, Montague H. and G. Topham Forrest (eds), *Survey of London, vol. 14: St Margaret, Westminster, Part III: Whitehall II*, London County Council (1931).

Cox, Montague H. and Philip Norman (eds), *Survey of London, vol. 13: St Margaret, Westminster, Part II: Whitehall I*, London County Council (1930).

Coxe, William, *Memoirs of the Life and Administration of Sir Robert Walpole*, 3 vols, London (1798).

Crawford, Marion, *The Little Princesses: The Story of the Queen's Childhood, by Her Nanny*, ebook edition, London: Orion (2011).

Creevey, Thomas, *The Creevey Papers*, ed. Sir Herbert Maxwell, 2 vols, London: John Murray (1904).

Croft, Pauline, 'The Parliamentary Installation of Henry, Prince of Wales', *Historical Research*, vol. 65, no. 157 (1992), 177–93.

Croker, John Wilson (ed.), *Letters to and from Henrietta, Countess of Suffolk, and Her Second Husband, the Hon. George Berkeley, 1712–1767*, 2 vols, London: John Murray (1824).

Dalrymple, Sir John, *Memoirs of Great Britain and Ireland*, 4 vols (1773).

Dasent, John Roche et al. (eds), *Acts of the Privy Council of England*, 46 vols, HMSO (1890–1964).

Day, John, *The Ile of Guls* ([1606] 1831).

Dekker, Thomas, *1603, the Wonderfull Yeare: Wherein Is Shewed the Picture of London Lying Sicke of the Plague*, London: Thomas Creede (1603).

Delany, Mary, *Letters from Mrs Delany … to Mrs Frances Hamilton*, 3rd edition, London: Longman, Hurst, Rees, Orme & Brown (1821).

Delany, Mary, *Mrs Delany at Court and among the Wits: Being the Record of a Great Lady of Genius in the Art of Living*, ed. R. Brimley Johnson, London: Stanley Paul (1925).

Dickens, Charles, the Younger, 'The Boy Jones', *All the Year Round*, 5 July 1884.

Doran, John, *The History of Court Fools*, London: Richard Bentley (1858).

Douce, Francis, 'Copy of an Original Manuscript, Containing Orders Made by Henry Prince of Wales, Respecting His Household, in 1610', *Archaeologia*, vol. 14 (1803), 249–61.

Dungavell, Ian, 'The Architectural Career of Sir Aston Webb (1849–1930)', unpublished PhD thesis, University of London (1999).

Erasmus, Desiderius, *In Praise of Folly*, London (1876).

Evelyn, John, *Memoirs of John Evelyn*, ed. William Bray, 4 vols, London: Frederick Warne (1879).

Finet, John, *Ceremonies of Charles I: The Note Books of John Finet, Master of Ceremonies, 1628–1641*, ed. Albert J. Loomie, New York: Fordham University Press (1987).

Finet, John, *Finetti Philoxenis: Some Choice Observations of Sir John Finett Knight*, London (1656).

Firth, C. H. and R. S. Rait, *Acts and Ordinances of the Interregnum, 1642–1660*, London: HMSO (1911).

'A Foreign Resident', *Society in the New Reign*, London: T. Fisher Unwin (1904).

Fortescue, Sir John, *The Governance of England: Otherwise Called the Difference between and Absolute and a Limited Monarchy*, Oxford: Clarendon Press (1885).

Fulford, R. (ed.), *Darling Child: The Private Correspondence of Queen Victoria and the Crown Princess of Prussia, 1871–1878*, London: Evans (1976).

Furdell, Elizabeth Lane, 'The Medical Personnel at the Court of Queen Anne', *The Historian*, vol. 48, no. 3 (1986), 412–29.

Furnivall, Frederick J. (ed.), *Harrison's Description of England in Shakspere's Youth*, London: New Shakespeare Society (1877).

The Genuine Book: An Inquiry, or Delicate Investigation into the Conduct of Her Royal Highness the Princess of Wales, London: R. Edwards (1813).

George, Prince of Wales, *Correspondence of George, Prince of Wales*, ed. A. Aspinall, 8 vols, New York: Oxford University Press (1963–71).

Georgian Papers Online, Royal Collection Trust, http://gpp.royalcollection.org.uk

Gibbs, G. C., 'George I (1660–1727), King of Great Britain and Ireland and Elector of Hanover', *Oxford Dictionary of National Biography*, Oxford: Oxford University Press (2009).

Glover, George, *The Arrivall and Intertainements of the Embassador, Alkaid Jaurar Ben Abdella, with His Associate, Mr Robert Blake*, London: I. Okes (1637).

Godfrey-Faussett, George, *Royal Servant, Family Friend: The Life and Times of Naval Equerry Captain Sir Bryan Godfrey Faussett R.N.*, Shoreham-by-Sea: Bernard Durnford (2004).

Goldring, Elizabeth et al. (eds), *John Nichols's 'The Progresses and Public Processions of Queen Elizabeth I': A New Edition of the Early Modern Sources*, 5 vols, Oxford: Oxford University Press (2014).

Gordon, Peter and Denis Lawton, *Royal Education: Past, Present and Future*, London: Frank Cass (1999).

Gore, John, *King George V: A Personal Memoir*, London: John Murray (1941).

Gorst, Frederick, *Of Carriages and Kings*, London: W. H. Allen (1956).

Green, Mary Anne Everett (ed.), *Calendar of State Papers, Domestic: Interregnum*, 13 vols, London: HMSO (1875–86).

Green, Mary Anne Everett (ed.), *Calendar of State Papers, Domestic: James I*, 4 vols, London: HMSO (1857–9).

Greig, James (ed.), *The Diaries of a Duchess: Extracts from the Diaries of the First Duchess of Northumberland (1716–1776)*, London: Hodder & Stoughton (1926).

Greig, James (ed.), *The Farington Diary*, 8 vols, London: Hutchinson (1922–8).

Greville, Charles C. F., *The Greville Memoirs (Second Part): A Journal of the Reign of Queen Victoria from 1837 to 1852*, ed. Henry Reeve, 3 vols, London: Longmans, Green (1885).

Greville, Robert Fulke, *The Diaries of Colonel the Hon. Robert Fulke Greville, Equerry to His Majesty King George III*, ed. F. McKno Bladon, London: Bodley Head (1930).

Grigg, John, 'Punched, Abused, Challenged', *The Spectator*, 16 August 1997, 13.

Groot, Jerome de, 'Space, Patronage, Procedure: The Court at Oxford, 1642–46', *English Historical Review*, vol. 117, no. 474 (2002), 1204–27.

Grose, Francis et al., *The Antiquarian Repertory: A Miscellaneous Assemblage of Topography, History, Biography, Customs, and Manners*, 4 vols, London: Edward Jeffery (1807).

Hadlow, Janice, *The Strangest Family: The Private Lives of George III, Queen Charlotte and the Hanoverians*, ebook edition, London: William Collins (2014).

Haile, Martin, *Queen Mary of Modena: Her Life and Letters*, London: J. M. Dent (1905).

Hardie, Frank, *The Political Influence of the British Monarchy, 1868–1952*, London: B. T. Batsford (1970).

Harris, Frances, '"The Honourable Sisterhood": Queen Anne's Maids of Honour', Electronic *British Library Journal* (1993), http://www.bl.uk/eblj/1993articles/article13.html

Harris, Wilson, 'The Uncrowned King', *The Spectator*, 7 September 1951, 5.

Hart-Davis, Duff (ed.), *In Royal Service: The Letters and Journals of Sir Alan Lascelles, vol. 2: 1920–1936*, London: Hamish Hamilton (1988).

Hart-Davis, Duff (ed.), *King's Counsellor: Abdication and War – the Diaries of Sir Alan Lascelles*, London: Weidenfeld & Nicolson (2006).

Haslam, M. T., 'The Willis Family and George III', *History of Psychiatry*, vol. 8, no. 32 (1997), 539–53.

[Hawkins, John], *The Life and Death of Our Late Most Incomparable and Heroique Prince, Henry Prince of Wales*, London: Nathaniel Butter (1641).

Hayward, Maria, 'Symbols of Majesty: Cloths of Estate at the Court of Henry VIII', *Furniture History*, vol. 41 (2005), 1–11.

Herbert, A. P., 'Here comes the Queen!', *Life*, 27 April 1953, 92–104.

Hervey, John, Lord Hervey, *Lord Hervey's Memoirs*, ed. Romney Sedgwick, London: William Kimber (1952).

Hervey, John, Lord Hervey, *Some Materials towards Memoirs of the Reign of George II*, ed. Romney Sedgwick, 3 vols, London: Eyre & Spottiswoode (1931).

Hulse, Lynn, 'Hingeston, John', *Grove Music Online*, Oxford: Oxford University Press (2001), http://www.oxfordmusiconline.com/grovemusic/view/10.1093/gmo/9781561592630.001.0001/omo-9781561592630-e-0000013060 (accessed 15 February 2018).

Hunting, Guy, *Adventures of a Gentleman's Gentleman: The Queen, Noel Coward and I*, London: John Blake (2002).

Hutchinson, Lucy, *Memoirs of the Life of Colonel Hutchinson*, London: Everyman ([1806] 1936).

Hyde, Edward, Earl of Clarendon, *The History of the Rebellion and Civil Wars in England, Begun in the Year 1641*, 6 vols, ed. W. Dunn Macray, Oxford: Clarendon Press (1888).

Hyde, Edward, Earl of Clarendon, *The Life of Edward Earl of Clarendon, Lord High Chancellor of England*, new edition, 3 vols, Oxford: Clarendon Press (1827).

James I, *Basilikon Doron: Or His Majestys Instructions to His Dearest Sonne, Henry the Prince*, London: Roxburghe Club ([1599] 1887).

'Janus', 'A Spectator's Notebook', *The Spectator*, 19 April 1951, 5.

Jephson, P. D., *Shadows of a Princess: Diana, Princess of Wales 1987–1996*, London: HarperCollins (2000).

Jerrold, Clare, *The Early Court of Queen Victoria*, New York: G. P. Putnam's Sons (1912).

Jerrold, Clare, *The Married Life of Queen Victoria*, New York: G. P. Putnam's Sons (1913).

Jesse, John Heneage, *Memoirs of the Court of England from the Revolution in 1688 to the Death of George the Second*, 3 vols, Richard Bentley (1843).

Journal of the House of Commons, vols 1–10, London: HMSO (1802).

[Judge, Jasper Tomsett], *Sketches of Her Majesty's Household: Forming a Guide to Situations in the Sovereign's Domestic Establishment*, London: William Strange (1848).

Kenney, E. J., review of Michael von Albrecht, *A History of Roman Literature from Livius Andronicus to Boethius with Special Regard to Its Influence on World Literature*, *Bryn Mawr Classical Review*, 98.2.4 (1998).

Knight, Cornelia, *The Autobiography of Miss Cornelia Knight, Lady Companion to the Princess Charlotte of Wales*, 2 vols, London: W. H. Allen (1861).

Knowler, William (ed.), *The Earl of Strafforde's Letters and Dispatches*, 2 vols, Dublin: Robert Owen (1740).

Kuhn, William M., 'Queen Victoria's Civil List: What Did She Do with It?', *Historical Journal*, vol. 36, no. 3 (1993), 645–65.

Langtry, Lillie, *The Days I Knew*, New York: George H. Doran (1925).

Laski, Harold, 'The King's Secretary', *Fortnightly Review*, vol. 152, new series (July–December 1942), 389–93.

Law, Ernest, *The History of Hampton Court Palace*, 2nd edition, 3 vols, London: George Bell (1898).

Lefkowitz, Murray, 'Masque', *Grove Music Online*, Oxford: Oxford University Press (2001), http://www.oxfordmusiconline.com/grovemusic/view/10.1093/gmo/9781561592630.001.0001/omo-9781561592630-e-0000017996 (accessed 16 February 2018).

Levy, Martin J., 'Fitzherbert [née Smythe; other married name Weld], Maria Anne (1756–1837), Unlawful Wife of George IV by a Marriage Invalid under the Royal Marriages Act of 1772', *Oxford Dictionary of National Biography*, Oxford: Oxford University Press (2004).

Lewalski, Barbara Kiefer, 'Anne of Denmark and the Subversions of Masquing', *Criticism*, vol. 35, no. 3 (1993), 341–55.

Lindquist, Eric, 'The Failure of the Great Contract', *Journal of Modern History*, vol. 57, no. 4 (1985), 617–51.

Lindquist, Eric N., 'The King, the People and the House of Commons: The Problem of Early Jacobean Purveyance', *Historical Journal*, vol. 31, no. 3 (1988), 549–70.

Lindsay, Ivan, *The History of Loot and Stolen Art, from Antiquity until the Present Day*, 2nd edition, London: Unicorn Press (2014).

Little, Patrick (ed.), *Oliver Cromwell: New Perspectives*, ebook edition, Basingstoke: Palgrave Macmillan (2009).

Liverpool Financial Reform Association, 'The Royal Household: A Model to Parliament and the Nation', *Financial Reform Tracts*, New Series, no. 14 (1856).

Llewellyn, Sacha, 'George III and the Windsor Uniform', *Court Historian*, vol. 1, no. 2 (1996), 12–16.

Lloyd, H. E., *George IV: Memoirs of his Life and Reign, Interspersed with Numerous Personal Anecdotes*, London: Treuttel & Würtz / Treuttel Jun. & Richter (1830).

Lodge, Edmund (ed.), *Illustrations of British History, Biography and Manners, in the Reigns of Henry VIII, Mary, Elizabeth and James I*, 2nd edition, 3 vols, London: John Chidley (1838).

Lower, Sir William (trans.), *A Relation in Form of Journal, of the Voiage and Residence Which the Most Excellent and Most Mighty Prince Charls the II King of Great Britain, &c. Hath made in Holland, from the 25 of May, to the 2 of June, 1660*, The Hague (1660).

Ludlow, Edmund, *The Memoirs of Edmund Ludlow, Lieutenant-General of the Horse in the Army of the Commonwealth of England, 1625–1672*, ed. C. H. Firth, 2 vols, Oxford: Clarendon Press (1894).

Lyttelton, Sarah, Lady, *Correspondence of Sarah Spencer, Lady Lyttelton, 1787–1870*, ed. Mrs Hugh Wyndham, London: John Murray (1912).

MacAlpine, Ida and Richard Hunter, *George III and the Mad-Business*, London: Penguin Press (1969).

Macnaghten, Sir Melville L., *Days of My Years*, London: Edward Arnold (1914).

'The Man in the Moon', *A Tragi-Comedy, Called New-Market-Fayre, or a Parliament Out-Cry: Of State-Commodities, Set to Sale* (1649).

'The Man in the Moon', *The Second Part of the Tragi-Comedy, Called New-Market-Fayre, or Mrs Parliaments New Figaryes* (1649).

Manchester Guardian.

Marlborough, Sarah, Duchess of, *An Account of the Conduct of the Dowager Duchess of Marlborough: From Her First Coming to Court, to the Year 1710*, London (1742).

Marlborough, Sarah, Duchess of, *Letters of Sarah, Duchess of Marlborough*, London: John Murray (1875).

Marlborough, Sarah, Duchess of, *Private Correspondence of Sarah, Duchess of Marlborough, Illustrative of the Court and Times of Queen Anne*, 2 vols, London: Henry Colburn (1838).

Marschner, Joanna, 'Baths and Bathing at the Early Georgian Court', *Furniture History*, vol. 31 (1995), 23–8.

Martin, Sir Theodore, *The Life of His Royal Highness the Prince Consort*, 7th edition, 5 vols, London: Smith, Elder (1880).

Matson, John, *Sandringham Days: The Domestic Life of the Royal Family in Norfolk, 1862–1952*, ebook edition, Stroud: History Press (2011).

Melikan, R. A., 'Pains and Penalties Procedure: How the House of Lords "Tried" Queen Caroline', *Parliamentary History*, vol. 20, no. 3 (2001), 311–32.

Melville, Sir James, *Memoirs of His Own Life*, ed. T. Thomson, Edinburgh: Bannatyne Club (1827).

'A Member of the Aristocracy', *Manners and Rules of Good Society*, 23rd edition, London: Frederick Warne (1898).

'A Member of the Royal Household', *The Private Life of King Edward VII*, New York: D. Appleton (1901).

'A Member of the Royal Household', *The Private Life of the Queen*, New York: D. Appleton (1897).

Merton, Charlotte Isabelle, 'The Women Who Served Queen Mary and Queen Elizabeth: Ladies, Gentlewomen and Maids of the Privy Chamber, 1553–1603', unpublished PhD thesis, Trinity College, Cambridge (1992).

Michael, Wolfgang, *England under George I: The Beginnings of the Hanoverian Dynasty*, 2 vols, London: Macmillan (1936–9).

Middleton, Thomas G., 'Our Royal Family as Animal-Lovers: Their Pets', *Illustrated London News*, 28 December 1929, 1146.

Millar, Oliver, 'The Inventories and Valuations of the King's Goods, 1649–1651', *Walpole Society*, vol. 43 (1970–2).

Monmouth, Robert, Earl of, *Memoirs of Robert Carey, Earl of Monmouth*, ed. G. H. Powell, London: Alexander Moring (1905).

Montagu, Lady Mary Wortley, *The Letters and Works of Lady Mary Wortley Montagu*, ed. W. M. Thomas, 3rd edition, 2 vols, London: Henry G. Bohn (1861).

Montague, E. N. and W. A. Turner, 'The Residence of Sir Julius Caesar Adelmare in Mitcham', *Surrey Archaeological Collections*, vol. 67 (1970), 85–94.

Morrill, John, 'Cromwell, Oliver (1599–1658), Lord Protector of England, Scotland, and Ireland', *Oxford Dictionary of National Biography*, Oxford: Oxford University Press (2004).

Morton, Andrew, *Diana: Her True Story – In Her Own Words*, revised edition, London: Michael O'Mara (1997).

Nichols, John (ed.), *A Collection of Ordinances and Regulations for the Government of the Royal Household, Made in Divers Reigns*, London: Society of Antiquaries (1790).

Nichols, John, *The Progresses and Public Processions of Queen Elizabeth I: Among Which Are Interspersed Other Solemnities, Public Expenditures, and Remarkable Events, during the Reign of That Illustrious Princess*, new edition, 3 vols, London: Society of Antiquaries (1823).

Nichols, John, *The Progresses, Processions, and Magnificent Festivities, of King James the First, His Royal Consort, Family, and Court*, 4 vols, London: Society of Antiquaries (1828).

Nicolas, Sir Harris, *Memoirs of the Life and Times of Sir Christopher Hatton KG, Vice-Chamberlain and Lord Chancellor to Queen Elizabeth*, London: Richard Bentley (1847).

Orrell, John, 'The Agent of Savoy at the Somerset Masque', *Review of English Studies*, New Series, vol. 28, no. 111 (1977), 301–5.

Pearce, Charles E., *The Amazing Duchess: Being the Romantic History of Elizabeth Chudleigh*, 2 vols, New York: Brentano's (1911).

Peel, Sir Robert, *Sir Robert Peel: From His Private Papers*, ed. by C. S. Parker, 2nd edition, 3 vols, London: John Murray (1899).

Pepys, Samuel, *The Diary of Samuel Pepys*, ed. Robert Latham and William Matthews, 11 vols, London: HarperCollins (2000).

Peters, Timothy J. and Allan Beveridge, 'The Madness of King George III: A Psychiatric Re-assessment', *History of Psychiatry*, vol. 21, no. 1 (2010), 20–37.

A Pill to Purge State-Melancholy: Or, a Collection of Excellent New Ballads, 3rd edition (1716).

Plumb, J. H., *The First Four Georges*, London: B. T. Batsford (1956).

Ponsonby, Arthur, *Henry Ponsonby, Queen Victoria's Private Secretary: His Life from His Letters*, London: Macmillan (1942).

Ponsonby, Sir Frederick, *Recollections of Three Reigns*, London: Eyre & Spottiswoode (1951).

Price, Daniel, *Prince Henry His First Anniversary*, Oxford (1613).

Pritchard, Allan, 'George Wither and the Sale of the Estate of Charles I', *Modern Philology*, vol. 77, no. 4 (1980), 370–81.

Pyne, W. H., *The History of the Royal Residences: Of Windsor Castle, St James's Palace, Carlton House, Kensington Palace, Hampton Court, Buckingham House, and Frogmore*, 3 vols, London (1819).

Queen Victoria's Journals online, RA VIC/MAIN/QVJ (W), http://www.queen victoriasjournals.org/home.do

Ravelhofer, Barbara, *The Early Stuart Masque: Dance, Costume, and Music*, Oxford: Oxford University Press (2006).

Report from the Committee Appointed to Examine the Physicians Who Have Attended His Majesty, during His Illness, Touching the Present State of His Majesty's Health, London (1789).

Rhodes, Margaret, *The Final Curtsey: A Royal Memoir by the Queen's Cousin*, ebook edition, London: Umbria Press / Edinburgh: Birlinn (2012).

Richards, Jeffrey, 'The Coronation of Queen Elizabeth II and Film', *The Court Historian*, vol. 9, no. 1, (2004), 69–79.

Ridley, Jane, *Bertie: A Life of Edward VII*, ebook edition, London: Vintage (2013).

Roberts, Michael (ed.), 'Swedish Diplomats at Cromwell's Court, 1655-1656: the Missions of Peter Julius Coyet and Christer Bonde', *Camden Fourth Series*, vol. 36 (1988).

Rose, Kenneth, *King George V*, London: Weidenfeld & Nicolson (1983).

Royal Commission on Historical Manuscripts, *Calendar of the Manuscripts of the Marquess of Ormonde*, New Series, vols 3, 6–7, London: HMSO (1904, 1911).

Royal Commission on Historical Manuscripts, *Calendar of the Manuscripts of the Most Hon. the Marquess of Salisbury*, vols. 11, 15, 16, London: HMSO (1906, 1930, 1933).

Royal Commission on Historical Manuscripts, *Fifth Report of the Royal Commission on Historical Manuscripts*, London: HMSO (1876).

Royal Commission on Historical Manuscripts, *The Manuscripts of the Earl Cowper*, vols 1–3, London: HMSO (1888).

Royal Commission on Historical Manuscripts, *Manuscripts of the Earl of Egmont: Diary of the First Earl of Egmont*, vol. 2, London: HMSO (1923).

Royal Commission on Historical Manuscripts, *The Manuscripts of the Marquis of Bath*, vol. 4, London: HMSO (1908).

Royal Commission on Historical Manuscripts, *Report on the Manuscripts of His Grace the Duke of Portland*, vols 5–6, London: HMSO (1899).

Rushworth, John, *Historical Collections of Private Passages of State, Weighty Matters in Law, Proceedings in Five Parliaments, Beginning the Sixteenth Year of King James, Anno 1618, and Ending the Fifth Year of King Charls, Anno 1629*, 8 vols, London (1721).

Scott, Jennifer, *The Royal Portrait: Image and Impact*, London: Royal Collection (2010).

Seddon, P. R., 'Household Reforms in the Reign of James I', *Bulletin of the Institute of Historical Research*, vol. 53, no. 127 (1980), 44–55.

The Several Declarations, Together with the Several Depositions Made in Council … Concerning the Birth of the Prince of Wales, London (1688).

Shannon, Andrea, '"Uncouth languages to a Princes ears": Archibald Armstrong, Court Jester, and Early Stuart Politics', *Sixteenth Century Journal*, vol. 42, no. 1 (2011), 99–112.

Shefrin, Jill, *Such Constant Affectionate Care: Lady Charlotte Finch, Royal Governess, and the Children of George III*, Los Angeles: Cotsen Occasional Press (2003).

Sherwood, Roy, *The Court of Oliver Cromwell*, Cambridge: Willingham Press ([1977] 1989).

Sillitoe, Peter, '"And afterward to his palace of Westminster, there to solace himself": Rediscovering the Progresses of Charles I', *Yearbook of English Studies*, vol. 44 (2014), 87–102.

Smith, E. A., *George IV*, New Haven, CT, and London: Yale University Press (1999).

Smith, Hannah, 'The Court in England, 1714–1760: A Declining Political Institution?', *History*, vol. 90, no. 297 (2005), 23–41.

Smith, Hannah and Stephen Taylor, 'Hephaestion and Alexander: Lord Hervey, Frederick, Prince of Wales, and the Royal Favourite in England in the 1730s', *English Historical Review*, vol. 124, no. 507 (2009), 283–312.

Somerset, Anne, *Queen Anne: The Politics of Passion*, London: HarperPress (2012).

Southworth, John, *Fools and Jesters at the English Court*, ebook edition, Stroud: History Press (2011).

Spall, Richard Francis, Jr, 'The Bedchamber Crisis and the Hastings Scandal: Morals, Politics, and the Press at the Beginning of Victoria's Reign', *Canadian Journal of History*, vol. 22, no. 1 (1987), 19–39.

Spedding, James (ed.), *The Letters and Life of Francis Bacon*, 7 vols, London: Longman, Green, Longman & Roberts (1861–74).

Stamper, C. W., *What I Know: Reminiscences of Five Years' Personal Attendance upon His Late Majesty King Edward the Seventh*, London: Mills & Boon (1913).

Stockmar, Baron E. von, *Memoirs of Baron Stockmar*, 2 vols, London: Longmans, Green (1872).

Stow, John and Edmund Howes, *The Annales, or, a Generall Chronicle of England, Begun by John Stow: Continued and Augmented with Matters Forraigne and Domestique, Ancient and Moderne, unto the End of This Present Yeere, 1631*, London: Richard Meighen (1631).

Strong, Roy, *Henry Prince of Wales and England's Lost Renaissance*, London: Thames & Hudson (1986).

Stuart, Denis, *Dear Duchess: Millicent Duchess of Sutherland, 1867–1955*, London: Victor Gollancz (1982).

Sutton, James M., 'The Decorative Program at Elizabethan Theobalds: Educating an Heir and Promoting a Dynasty', *Studies in the Decorative Arts*, vol. 7, no. 1 (1999–2000), 33–64.

Taylor, John, *The Praise, Antiquity, and Commodity, of Beggery, Beggers and Begging*, London (1621).

Taylor, Noreen, 'Saying What Everyone Thinks', *The Spectator*, 7 January 1995, 14.

Thackeray, W. M., *Thackeray's Lectures: 'The English Humorists' and 'The Four Georges'*, New York: Harper & Brothers (1867).

Thoms, William J. (ed.), *Anecdotes and Traditions Illustrative of Early English History and Literature*, London: Camden Society (1839).

Thurley, Simon, *Houses of Power: The Places that Shaped the Tudor World*, London: Bantam Press (2017).

Thurley, Simon, *Whitehall Palace: An Architectural History of the Royal Apartments, 1240–1690*, New Haven, CT, and London: Yale University Press (1999).

Thurley, Simon, *The Whitehall Palace Plan of 1670*, London: London Topographical Society (1998).

Thurloe, John, *A Collection of the State Papers of John Thurloe, Esq., Secretary First to the Council of State, and Afterwards to Oliver and Richard Cromwell*, ed. Thomas Birch, 7 vols, London (1742).

Tinniswood, Adrian, *The Long Weekend: Life in the English Country House between the Wars*, London: Jonathan Cape (2016).

Townsend, Peter, *Time and Chance: An Autobiography*, London: BCA (1978).

Tracts of the Liverpool Financial Reform Association, London: 'Standard of Freedom' Office (1851).

The Trial at Large of Her Majesty Caroline Amelia Elizabeth, Queen of Great Britain, in the House of Lords, on Charges of Adulterous Intercourse, 2 vols, London: T. Kelly (1821).

The Trial of Queen Caroline, 3 vols, New York: James Cockcroft (1874).

Tschumi, Gabriel, *Royal Chef: Recollections of Life in Royal Households from Queen Victoria to Queen Mary*, London: William Kimber (1954).

Vanderbilt, Gloria and Thelma, Lady Furness, *Double Exposure: A Twin Autobiography*, New York: David McKay (1958).

Waldstein, Baron, *The Diary of Baron Waldstein, a Traveller in Elizabethan England*, ed. G. W. Groos, London: Thames & Hudson (1981).

Walker, Clement, *Anarchia Anglicana: Or, the History of Independency, the Second Part, Being a Continuation of Relations and Observations Historicall and Politique upon This Present Parliament, Begun Anno 16. Caroli Primi*, London (1649).

Walpole, Horace (ed.), *Paul Hentzner's Travels in England during the Reign of Queen Elizabeth*, London: E. Jeffery (1797).

Warwick, Christopher, *Princess Margaret: A Life of Contrasts*, ebook edition, André Deutsch (2002).

Watts, Isaac, *An Ode on the Coronation of Their Majesties King George II and Queen Caroline*, London: J. Robert (1727).

Weiser, Brian, *Charles II and the Politics of Access*, Woodbridge: Boydell Press (2003).

[Weldon, Sir Anthony], *The Court and Character of King James*, London: John Wright (1651).

Wilson, John Harold, *Nell Gwyn, Royal Mistress*, New York: Pellegrini & Cudahy (1952).

Windsor, Edward, Duke of, *A King's Story: The Memoirs of HRH the Duke of Windsor KG*, London: Cassell (1951).

Wood, Anthony à, *Athenae Oxonienses: An Exact History of All the Writers and Bishops Who Have Had Their Education in the University of Oxford*, 3rd edition, 3 vols, London: Rivington (1813–20).

Woodworth, Allegra, 'Purveyance for the Royal Household in the Reign of Queen Elizabeth', *Transactions of the American Philosophical Society*, vol. 35, no. 1 (1945), 1–89.

Wrighte, T., 'Particulars of the Expence of the Royal Household in the Reigns of Henry VI, Henry VIII, Queen Elizabeth, &c', *Archaeologia*, vol. 12 (1796), 80–8.

Wynne, Sonya, 'The Mistresses of Charles II and Restoration Court Politics', in Eveline Cruickshanks (ed.), *The Stuart Courts*, 2nd edition, ebook edition, Stroud: History Press (2009).

ENDNOTES

INTRODUCTION
Appearing between pages 1 and 10

1. Nichols, *Collection of Ordinances*, 120.
2. Ibid., 28.
3. Ibid., 28.
4. Colvin, *History of the King's Works*, 2.
5. Fortescue, *Governance of England*, 125.

CHAPTER I
Progress
Appearing between pages 11 and 33

1. Goldring et al., *John Nichols's 'The Progresses and Public Processions of Queen Elizabeth I'*, II, 254.
2. Ibid., II, 254.
3. Nichols, *Progresses and Public Processions*, I, 444.
4. Goldring et al., *John Nichols's 'The Progresses and Public Processions of Queen Elizabeth I'*, II, 259.
5. Ibid., II, 248, 249.
6. Ibid., II, 295.
7. Ibid., II, 248, 245.
8. British Library, Harleian MS 6395, f. 36v.
9. Goldring et al., *John Nichols's 'The Progresses and Public Processions of Queen Elizabeth I'*, II, 39.
10. Ibid., II, 40.
11. Ibid., II, 200.
12. Montague and Turner, 'Residence of Sir Julius Caesar Adelmare', 85.
13. Dasent, *Acts of the Privy Council of England*, IX, 13.
14. Nicolas, *Memoirs of the Life and Times of Sir Christopher Hatton*, 126.
15. Royal Commission on Historical Manuscripts (RCHM), *Calendar of the Manuscripts of the Most Hon. the Marquess of Salisbury*, XI, 184, Lord Admiral and Sir Robert Cecil to Earl of Lincoln, 30 April 1601.
16. Nichols, *Collection of Ordinances*, 293.
17. 'Modern History Sourcebook: William Harrison (1534–1593): *Description of England*, 1577 (from Holinshed's Chronicles)', Fordham University website, http://sourcebooks.fordham.edu/MOD/1577harrison-england.asp (accessed 16 February 2018).
18. Collins, *Life of That Great Statesman William Cecil, Lord Burghley*, 37.
19. Ibid., 41.

20. Cole, *Portable Queen*, 55, 57.
21. Woodworth, 'Purveyance for the Royal Household', 73.
22. British Library, Lansdowne Manuscripts, 21, 63, 'Reformations to be made to diminish the great expenses of the queen's household, with marginal observations by Lord Burghley, July 1576.
23. PRO LS 13/280 no. 307, quoted in Seddon, 'Household Reforms', 54.
24. Walpole, *Paul Hentzner's Travels*, 24.
25. Ibid., 22.
26. Waldstein, *Diary*, 43.
27. Ibid., 51.
28. Thurley, *Houses of Power*, 383.
29. Thoms, *Anecdotes and Traditions*, 71.
30. RCHM, *Manuscripts of the Marquess of Bath*, 186.
31. Quoted in Thurley, *Houses of Power*, 386.
32. Lodge, *Illustrations of British History*, II, 97.
33. Ibid., II, 97.
34. Arnold, 'Lost from Her Majesties Back', 75.
35. Ibid., 76.
36. Ibid., 77.
37. Ibid., 9.
38. Waldstein, *Diary*, 73.
39. Bülow, 'Journey through England and Scotland', 257.
40. Walpole, *Paul Hentzner's Travels*, 34.
41. Ibid., 35.
42. Melville, *Memoirs*, 123–4.
43. Woodworth, 'Purveyance for the Royal Household', 15, quoting 1592 Lansdowne MSS 73, no. 34.
44. Nichols, *Collection of Ordinances*, 281.
45. Ibid., 287.
46. Ibid., 293.
47. Ibid., 293.
48. British Library, Lansdowne Manuscripts, 21, 64, 'Remedies to be used for reformation of expenses in some of the particular offices of the household, 1576'.
49. British Library, Lansdowne Manuscripts, 21, 65, 'General causes of the extraordinary charges in the queen's household, 1576'.
50. British Library, Lansdowne Manuscripts, 21, 62, 'Lord Burghley's account of the cause of increase of expenses in the Queen's household, July, 1576'.
51. British Library, Lansdowne Manuscripts, 21, 63, 'Reformations to Be Made to Diminish the Great Expenses of the Queen's Household.'
52. Ibid.

CHAPTER 2
Behind the Masque
Appearing between pages 34 and 55

1. Dekker, *1603, the Wonderfull Yeare*, unpaginated.
2. Stow and Howes, *Annales*, 815.
3. Monmouth, *Memoirs of Robert Carey, Earl of Monmouth*, 79.
4. Nichols, *Progresses, Processions, and Magnificent Festivities*, I, 195.
5. Lodge, *Illustrations of British History*, III, 34.
6. Letters of Philip Gawdy, 158, quoted in Lindquist, 'The King, the People and the Early House of Commons', 562.
7. Nichols, *Collection of Ordinances*, 300.
8. Ibid., 304.
9. Spedding, *Letters and Life of Francis Bacon*, III, 183.
10. In Lindquist, 'Failure of the Great Contract', 625, quoting speeches to the Commons on 13 March and 14 November 1610.
11. Price, *Prince Henry His First Anniversary*, 4.
12. Quoted in Birch, *Life of Henry, Prince of Wales*, 369.
13. Brown et al., *Calendar of State Papers*, X, 514.
14. PRO SP 14/43/108.
15. Quoted in Croft, 'Parliamentary Installation of Henry, Prince of Wales', 178.
16. [Hawkins], *Life and Death of Our Late Most Incomparable and Heroique Prince*, 193–4. Although this early biography (existing in manuscript by 1613) is said to be by Sir Charles Cornwallis, Roy Strong puts forward a convincing case for its authorship by John Hawkins, who may have been one of the gunners of the Tower (Strong, *Henry Prince of Wales*, 227).
17. Ibid., 194.
18. *Oxford Dictionary of National Biography*.
19. Chaloner, *Shorte Discourse*, 8.
20. Douce, 'Copy of an Original Manuscript', 250.
21. Ibid., 261.
22. Ibid., 259.
23. Ibid., 260.
24. Ibid., 259.
25. Ibid., 259.
26. Strong, *Henry Prince of Wales*, 76, quoting Georges Ascoli, *La Grande-Bretagne devant l'opinion française au XVIIe siècle*, Paris: Librairie universitaire J. Gamber (1930), 27.
27. Douce, 'Copy of an Original Manuscript', 254.
28. [Hawkins], *Life and Death of Our Late Most Incomparable and Heroique Prince*, 39.
29. Ibid., 44.
30. Ibid., 47.
31. Ibid., 51.
32. Ibid., 55.
33. Ibid., 73.
34. Nichols, *Progresses, Processions, and Magnificent Festivities*, I, 301.
35. Ibid., I, 312.
36. Ibid., I, 314.
37. Quoted in Law, *History of Hampton Court Palace*, II, 24.
38. Nichols, *Progresses, Processions, and Magnificent Festivities*, I, 485.
39. Ibid., I, 486.
40. Ibid., I, 487.
41. Brown, *Calendar of State Papers*, X, 207.
42. Quoted in Lewalski, 'Anne of Denmark', 352, n. 19.
43. Nichols, *Progresses, Processions, and Magnificent Festivities*, I, 473.
44. Ibid., I, 473.
45. Chamberlain, *Letters*, I, 198.
46. Privy Council to James I, December 1604, RCHM, *Manuscripts of the Marquess of Salisbury*, XVI, 389.
47. Lewalski, 'Anne of Denmark', 349.
48. Nichols, *Progresses, Processions, and Magnificent Festivities*, I, 166.
49. Brown, *Calendar of State Papers*, XI, 86.
50. Nichols, *Progresses, Processions, and Magnificent Festivities*, II, 216.
51. This passage draws heavily on Lefkowitz, 'Masque'.
52. Brown, *Calendar of State Papers*, XI, 222.
53. Quoted in Ravelhofer, *Early Stuart Masque*, 76.
54. Finet, *Ceremonies of Charles I*, 272.
55. Cox and Norman (eds), *Survey of London*, vol. 13, 116.
56. Brown, *Calendar of State Papers*, XI, 220.
57. Despatch from Giovanni Battista Gabaleoni, the agent of Savoy, in Orrell, 'Agent of Savoy', 304. In fairness, I should point out that Gabaleoni was having a feud with the Florentine agent at James I's court, and was all too eager to describe in loving detail the woeful inadequacies of the Florentine de Servi.
58. Carleton to John Chamberlain, 7 January 1605, quoted in Botonaki, 'Audience of the Jacobean Masque', 74.
59. Nathaniel Brent to Carleton, quoted in Green, *Calendar of State Papers: James I*, II, 512.
60. Brown, *Calendar of State Papers*, XV, 117.
61. Cox and Norman (eds), *Survey of London*, vol. 13, 119.

CHAPTER 3
Diplomats and Fools
Appearing between pages 57 and 69

1. Finet, *Ceremonies of Charles I*, 22.
2. Ibid., 22.
3. Nichols, *Progresses, Processions, and Magnificent Festivities*, II, 538.
4. Ibid., II, 549.
5. Finet, *Finetti Philoxenis*, 3.
6. Ibid., 4.
7. Ibid., 8.
8. Ibid., 9.
9. Rushworth, *Historical Collections*, II, 257.
10. Finet, *Ceremonies of Charles I*, 233.
11. Ibid., 233.
12. Ibid., 234.
13. Knowler, *Earl of Strafforde's Letters and Dispatches*, II, 124.
14. Glover, *Arrivall and Intertainements*, 33.
15. Finet, *Ceremonies of Charles I*, 249.
16. Ibid., 223.
17. Chamberlain, *Letters*, II, 131.
18. Ibid., II, 131.
19. [Weldon], *Court and Character of King James*, 84–5.
20. Ibid., 85.
21. Erasmus, *In Praise of Folly*.
22. Day, *Ile of Guls*, 7.
23. Shannon, '"Uncouth Language to a Prince's Ears"', 101.
24. Southworth, *Fools and Jesters*, ch. 15.
25. John Taylor, Epistle Dedicatory.
26. Rushworth, *Historical Collections*, II, 470–1.
27. Doran, *History of Court Fools*, 210.

CHAPTER 4
A Court without a King
Appearing between pages 71 and 87

1. Hyde, *History of the Rebellion*, VI, 37.
2. British Library, Harleian MS 6851, f. 117 r–v, quoted in Groot, 'Space, Patronage, Procedure', 1218–19.
3. Ibid., 1219.
4. Wood, *Athenae Oxonienses*, 1238.
5. *Journal of the House of Commons*, V, 468.
6. Ibid., VI, 119.
7. Death warrant of Charles I; see http://www.nationalarchives.gov.uk/pathways/citizenship/rise_parliament/transcripts/charles_warrant.htm (accessed 16 February 2018).
8. Green (ed.), *Calendar of State Papers: Interregnum*, I, 10.
9. Millar, 'Inventories and Valuations', 255.
10. Hutchinson, *Memoirs of the Life of Colonel Hutchinson*, 292.
11. Lindsay, *History of Loot*, 95.
12. Millar, 'Inventories and Valuations', 122, 344.
13. Green (ed.), *Calendar of State Papers: Interregnum*, I, 295.
14. Blencowe, *Sydney Papers*, 96.
15. 'Man in the Moon', *A Tragi-Comedy*, 4.
16. Green (ed.), *Calendar of State Papers: Interregnum*, I, 262.
17. Ibid., I, 501.
18. Walker, Anarchia Anglicana, 186.
19. Green (ed.), *Calendar of State Papers: Interregnum*, VI, 279.
20. 'December 1653: The Government of the Commonwealth of England, Scotland and Ireland, and the Dominions thereunto belonging', in Firth and Rait (eds), *Acts and Ordinances*, 813–22, available at http://www.british-history.ac.uk/no-series/acts-ordinances-interregnum/pp813-822 (accessed 16 February 2018).
21. *Journal of the House of Commons*, VII, 404.
22. Ludlow, *Memoirs of Edmund Ludlow*, II, 379.
23. Sherwood, *Court of Oliver Cromwell*, 41.
24. Morrill, 'Cromwell, Oliver'.
25. Andrew Barclay in Little, *Oliver Cromwell*, ch 8.
26. Burton, *Diary of Thomas Burton*, II, 522.
27. *Weekly Intelligencer*, no. 223 (14–21 March 1653), 179.
28. A point made by Andrew Barclay in his excellent essay, 'The Lord Protector and his Court', in Little, *Oliver Cromwell*. I have drawn heavily on Dr Barclay's essay in the paragraph that follows.
29. Hulse, 'Hingeston, John'.
30. Quoted in Sherwood, *Court of Oliver Cromwell*, 138.
31. G. Ayloff to John Langley, 17 November 1657, in RCHM, *Fifth Report*, 183.
32. William Dugdale to John Langley, 14 November 1657, ibid., 177.
33. Thurloe, *Collection of the State Papers*, II, 257.
34. Roberts, 'Swedish Diplomats', 51.
35. Ibid., 114.
36. Ibid., 120.
37. Burton, *Diary of Thomas Burton*, II, 517.
38. Ibid., II, 520.
39. Ibid., II, 522.
40. *Publick Intelligencer*, no. 152 (22–29 November 1658), 22.
41. Ibid., 21.

CHAPTER 5
We Have Called You Gods
Appearing between pages 88 and 104

1. Hyde, *Life of Edward Earl of Clarendon*, I, 365.
2. Pepys, *Diary*, VIII, 499.

3. Hyde, *Life of Edward Earl of Clarendon*, I, 365.
4. 'Chronological Survey 1660–1837: The Later Stuart Household, 1660-1714', in Bucholz (ed.), *Office-Holders in Modern Britain*, lxxvi–xcviii.
5. Hyde, *Life of Edward Earl of Clarendon*, I, 367.
6. LS 13/252 ff. 110, 111r–v.
7. Earl of Anglesey to the Duke of Ormonde, 22 August 1663, RCHM, *Calendar of the Manuscripts of the Marquess of Ormonde*, III, 78.
8. Lower, *Relation in Form of Journal*, 74.
9. *Mercurius Publicus*, 28 June 1660.
10. *Parliamentary Intelligencer*, 2–9 July 1660.
11. Ibid.
12. Evelyn, *Memoirs*, II, 430.
13. Waldstein, *Diary*, 79.
14. James I, *Basilikon Doron*, 152.
15. Quoted in Weiser, *Charles II and the Politics of Access*, 17.
16. Pepys, *Diary*, V, 4.
17. Quoted in Thurley, *Whitehall Palace Plan*, 19.
18. PRO LC5/12, 232.
19. 'The Household below Stairs: Knight Marshal 1660–1837', in Bucholz (ed.), *Office-Holders in Modern Britain*, 518–21.
20. PRO LC 5/140, 248–9, quoted in Weiser, *Charles II and the Politics of Access*, 38.
21. Nichols, *Collection of Ordinances*, 358.
22. Ibid., 361.
23. Law, *History of Hampton Court Palace*, II, 228, quoting *Secret History of Charles II*, I, 447.
24. Anthony Wood, quoted in Kenney, review of Albrecht, *History of Roman Literature*.
25. Pepys, *Diary*, IX, 24.
26. Quoted in Wynne, 'Mistresses of Charles II'.
27. Wilson, *Nell Gwyn*, 197.
28. Burnet, *Bishop Burnet's History*, II, 281.
29. Ibid.,, II, 281.

CHAPTER 6
The Catholic King
Appearing between pages 105 and 115

1. Quoted in Barclay, 'Impact of James II', 116–17.
2. Quoted ibid., 60.
3. Evelyn, *Memoirs*, II, 450.
4. Quoted in Barclay, 'Impact of James II', 60.
5. Ibid., 63.
6. Evelyn, *Memoirs*, II, 212.
7. Barclay, 'Impact of James II', 105.
8. Evelyn, *Memoirs*, III, 31.
9. Burnet, *Bishop Burnet's History*, II, 381
10. Ibid., II, 381
11. Evelyn, *Memoirs*, III, 31.
12. *Several Declarations*, 17.

CHAPTER 7
Mrs Morley and Mrs Freeman
Appearing between pages 116 and 135

1. Marlborough, *Account of the Conduct*, 14.
2. Ibid., 9.
3. Somerset, *Queen Anne*, 49.
4. Marlborough, *Account of the Conduct*, 26.
5. Ibid., 27.
6. Ibid., 28.
7. Somerset, *Queen Anne*, 133.
8. Ibid., 134.
9. Marlborough, *Account of the Conduct*, 110.
10. Ibid., 122.
11. Ibid., 291.
12. Ibid., 127.
13. Pyne, *History of the Royal Residences*, II, 23.
14. Thurley, *Whitehall Palace*, 143.
15. Burnet, *Bishop Burnet's History*, III, 117.
16. Dalrymple, *Memoirs*, II, 150.
17. Law, *History of Hampton Court Palace*, III, 171.
18. Ibid., III, 180.
19. Somerset, *Queen Anne*, 43.
20. Quoted in Harris, '"Honourable Sisterhood"', 187.
21. Ibid.,188.
22. Croker (ed.), *Letters to and from Henrietta, Countess of Suffolk*, I, 292–3.
23. Marlborough, *Account of the Conduct*, 182.
24. Quoted in Smith and Taylor, 'Hephaestion and Alexander', 303.
25. Somerset, *Queen Anne*, 329.
26. *Pill to Purge State-Melancholy*, 35.
27. Somerset, *Queen Anne*, 362.
28. Marlborough, *Account of the Conduct*, 223.
29. Somerset, *Queen Anne*, 389.
30. Ibid., 391.
31. Marlborough, *Private Correspondence*, I, 295–9.
32. Somerset, *Queen Anne*, 417.
33. Marlborough, *Account of the Conduct*, 83.
34. Ibid., 289.
35. Ibid., 288.

CHAPTER 8
Happy Families
Appearing between pages 136 and 155

1. Beattie, 'Court of George I', 27.
2. Ibid., 27.
3. Montagu, *Letters and Works*, I, 127.
4. Quoted in Jesse, *Memoirs of the Court of England*, II, 333.

5. Hervey, *Some Materials*, I, 66.
6. Beattie, 'Court of George I', 27.
7. Coxe, *Memoirs of the Life and Administration of Sir Robert Walpole*, II, 60.
8. RCHM, *Manuscripts of the Earl Cowper*, III, 186.
9. Beattie, 'Court of George I', 31.
10. Ibid., 32.
11. RCHM, *Report on the Manuscripts of His Grace the Duke of Portland*, V, 549.
12. Gibbs, 'George I'.
13. *Ceremonial of the Coronation*, 37.
14. Isaac Watts, *Ode on the Coronation*, 4.
15. Quoted in Pearce, *Amazing Duchess*, I, 45-6.
16. Hervey, *Lord Hervey's Memoirs*, 64.
17. Thackeray, *Thackeray's Lectures*, 370.
18. Hervey, *Lord Hervey's Memoirs*, 50.
19. Ibid., 187.
20. Ibid., 201.
21. Ibid., 249.
22. Ibid., 262.
23. Ibid., 308.
24. Ibid., 264.
25. Ibid., 186.
26. Pearce, *Amazing Duchess*, I, 66.
27. Hervey, *Lord Hervey's Memoirs*, 275.
28. Ibid., 275.
29. Ibid., 276.
30. Ibid., 278.
31. Ibid., 280.
32. RCHM, *Manuscripts of the Earl of Egmont*, II, 426.
33. Hervey, *Lord Hervey's Memoirs*, 291.
34. RCHM, *Manuscripts of the Earl of Egmont*, II, 429.
35. Ibid., II, 432.
36. Hervey, *Lord Hervey's Memoirs*, 301–2.
37. Ibid., 302.
38. RCHM, *Manuscripts of the Earl of Egmont*, II, 436.
39. Warrant of appointment for the Right Honourable Lady Charlotte Finch as governess in ordinary to the Prince of Wales, 13 August 1762, Royal Collection Trust, GEO/ADD/15/437, http://gpp.royalcollection.org.uk/GetMultimedia.ashx?db=Catalog&type=default&fname=GEO_ADD_15_0437.pdf (accessed 19 February 2018).
40. Quoted in Shefrin, *Such Constant Affectionate Care*, 49.
41. Letter from Queen Charlotte to Lady Charlotte Finch, Royal Collection Trust, GEO/ADD/15/8154, http://gpp.royalcollection.org.uk/GetMultimedia.ashx?db=Catalog&type=default&fname=GEO_ADD_15_8154.pdf (accessed 19 February 2018).
42. Letter from Lady Charlotte Finch to Queen Charlotte, 31 October 1774, Royal Collection Trust, GEO/ADD/15/8155, Royal Collection Trust, GEO/ADD/15/8154 (accessed 19 February 2018).
43. Ibid.
44. Ibid.
45. Delany, *Mrs Delany at Court*, 274.
46. Broughton, *Court and Private Life*, I, 155.
47. Ibid., I, 133.
48. Burney, *Diary and Letters of Madame D'Arblay*, I, 444.
49. Delany, *Letters*, 63.
50. Ibid., 63.
51. George, Prince of Wales, *Correspondence*, I, 5.

CHAPTER 9
An Agitation of Spirits
Appearing between pages 156 and 173

1. Greville, *Diaries*, 79
2. Peters and Beveridge. 'Madness of King George III', 24.
3. Burney, *Diary and Letters of Madame D'Arblay*, II, 229.
4. Peters and Beveridge. 'Madness of King George III', 24.
5. Greville, *Diaries*, 105.
6. Peters and Beveridge. 'Madness of King George III', 24.
7. Ibid., 24.
8. Greville, *Diaries*, 133.
9. Broughton, *Court and Private Life*, II, 13.
10. Burney, *Diary and Letters of Madame D'Arblay*, II, 266.
11. Greville, *Diaries*, 108.
12. Ibid., 113.
13. *The Times*, 15 December 1788, 3; *The Times*, 17 December 1788, 3.
14. *The Times*, 9 December 1788, 4.
15. Plumb, *First Four Georges*, 139.
16. Macalpine and Hunter's theory was aired in articles in the *British Medical Journal* and the *Proceedings of the Royal Society of Medicine* before appearing in their *George III and the Mad-Business*.
17. Peters and Beveridge, 'Madness of King George III'.
18. 'Mental Health Treatment: Dr Francis Willis', Lincs to the Past website, https://www.lincstothepast.com/Download/1347 (accessed 19 February 2018).
19. George, Prince of Wales, *Correspondence*, I, 406–7.
20. Greville, *Diaries*, 119.
21. Ibid., 119.
22. Ibid., 120.
23. Ibid., 122.
24. Ibid., 129.
25. Ibid., 141.

26. Ibid., 149.
27. Ibid., 151.
28. George, Prince of Wales, *Correspondence*, I, 405.
29. *The Times*, 8 December 1788, 2.
30. *The Times*, 12 December 1788, 3.
31. Greville, *Diaries*, 136.
32. Ibid., 149.
33. *Report from the Committee*, 15.
34. Ibid., 16.
35. Ibid., 63.
36. Ibid., 78.
37. Brazier, 'Royal Incapacity'.
38. George, Prince of Wales, *Correspondence*, I, 429.
39. Ibid., I, 437.
40. Greville, *Diaries*, 126.
41. *Report from the Committee*, 52.
42. Greville, *Diaries*, 187.
43. Ibid., 217.
44. Ibid., 250.
45. George, Prince of Wales, *Correspondence*, 496.
46. Burney, *Diary and Letters of Madame D'Arblay*, II, 303. The poem was actually composed by Fanny Burney at the Queen's request.

CHAPTER 10
Regent
Appearing between pages 174 and 193

1. Haslam, 'Willis Family', 547.
2. Knight, *Autobiography*, I, 175.
3. Childe-Pemberton, *Romance of Princess Amelia*, 227.
4. Ibid., 261.
5. Ibid., 307.
6. Hadlow, *Strangest Family*, ch.14.
7. *The Times*, 1 November 1810, 2.
8. *Cobbett's Political Register*, 14 November 1810, 921.
9. Peters and Beveridge, 'The Madness of King George III', 30.
10. Hadlow, *Strangest Family*, ch.14.
11. *The Times*, 16 November 1810, 2.
12. Peters and Beveridge, 'The Madness of King George III', 30.
13. Ibid., 31.
14. *The Times*, 24 January 1811, 3.
15. *Cobbett's Political Register*, XIX, 371. November 1810, 921.
16. Lloyd, *George IV*, 146.
17. Smith, *George IV*, 35.
18. George, Prince of Wales, *Correspondence*, I, 197.
19. Quoted in Levy, 'Fitzherbert, Maria Anne'.
20. George, Prince of Wales, *Correspondence*, I, 231.
21. Ibid., I, 234.
22. Ibid., I, 229.
23. Ibid., I, 231.
24. Greig, *Farington Diary*, VII, 22.
25. George, Prince of Wales, *Correspondence*, VIII, 52.
26. *Bury and Norwich Post: Or, Suffolk, Norfolk, Essex, Cambridge, and Ely Advertiser*, 19 June 1811.
27. Lloyd, *George IV*, 290–1.
28. *Morning Post*, 21 June 1811.
29. Lloyd, *George IV*, 292.
30. *Morning Post*, 24 June 1811.
31. *Morning Post*, 26 June 1811.
32. Ibid.
33. *Morning Post*, 28 June 1811.
34. *Hampshire Telegraph and Sussex Chronicle*, 1 July 1811.
35. 'Chronological Survey 1660–1837: The Later Hanoverian Household, 1760–1837', in Bucholz, *Office-Holders in Modern Britain*, cv–cxxxii.
36. *Genuine Book*, Appendix A5, deposition of William Cole.
37. Chase, *1820*, 144.
38. *The Times*, 7 June 1820, 3.
39. [Bayley], *Queen's Appeal*, 79.
40. Melikan, 'Pains and Penalties Procedure', 311.
41. *Trial at Large*, I, 3.
42. Ibid., I, 28.
43. Ibid., I, 273.
44. Ibid., I, 583.
45. *Trial of Queen Caroline*, III, 473.
46. *The Times*, 13 November 1820, 3.
47. *The Observer*, 3 December 1820, 3.
48. Ibid., 3.
49. *The Times*, 20 July 1821, 3.

CHAPTER 11
The Respectable Household
Appearing between pages 194 and 218

1. *The Times*, 30 September 1831, 3.
2. Creevey, *Creevey Papers*, II, 307.
3. *The Observer*, 2 July 1837.
4. Queen Victoria's Journals, 13 July 1837.
5. Dickens the Younger, 'Boy Jones', 235.
6. *The Standard*, 15 December 1838.
7. Queen Victoria's Journals, 3 December 1840.
8. Ibid., 2 February 1839.
9. Jerrold, *Early Court*, 259.
10. *Annual Register*, vol. 81 (1839), 471, 469.
11. Ibid., 464.
12. *The Times*, 11 March 1839, 5. In fact Miss Davys ('a very nice girl, though not at all pretty', according to Victoria (Queen Victoria's Journals, 13 July 1837)) didn't leave the household until the end of July,

and she mysteriously managed to keep her title and her £300 p.a. salary for another five years.

13. *The Examiner*, 24 March 1839, 3.
14. Jerrold, *Early Court*, 273.
15. Ibid., 261.
16. Greville, *Greville Memoirs*, I, 172.
17. Stuart, *Dear Duchess*, 57.
18. Peel, *Sir Robert Peel*, II, 392.
19. Queen Victoria's Journals, 9 May 1839.
20. Ibid., 9 May 1839.
21. Ibid., 11 May 1839.
22. Spall, 'Bedchamber Crisis', 36.
23. Ibid., 38.
24. Jerrold, *Early Court*, 282.
25. Ibid., 281.
26. 'Elizabeth Lindsay, Ellen Lindsay, James Lindsay: Theft – Stealing from Master, Theft – Receiving, 10 June 1844' (t18440610-1557), Proceedings of the Old Bailey website, http://www.oldbaileyonline.org/browse.jsp?div=t18440610-1557 (accessed 19 February 2018).
27. Ibid.
28. *The Examiner*, 15 June 1844.
29. Stockmar, *Memoirs*, II, 116–17.
30. Ibid., II, 121–2.
31. Ibid., II, 122.
32. Ibid., II, 126.
33. Jerrold, *Early Court*, 375.
34. Martin, *Life of His Royal Highness the Prince Consort*, I, 160.
35. Queen Victoria's Journals, 18 July 1851.
36. Martin, *Life of His Royal Highness the Prince Consort*, II, 383.
37. Kuhn, 'Queen Victoria's Civil List'.
38. [Judge], *Sketches of Her Majesty's Household*, 143.
39. *Tracts of the Liverpool Financial Reform Association*, Tract 1, 15.
40. Ibid., 16.
41. Liverpool Financial Reform Association, 'Royal Household', 13.
42. Ibid., 19.
43. Ibid., 29–30.
44. Bloomfield, *Reminiscences*, 64.
45. Queen Victoria's Journals, 1 December 1840.
46. Ibid., 15 December 1840, 4 April 1841.
47. Ibid., 2 December 1841.
48. Lyttelton, *Correspondence*, 326.
49. Queen Victoria's Journals, 6 April 1841.
50. Ibid., 17 April 1841.
51. Lyttelton, *Correspondence*, 401.
52. Bloomfield, *Reminiscences*, 31.
53. Gordon and Lawton, *Royal Education*, 155.
54. Ibid., 156.
55. Fulford (ed.), *Darling Child*, 202.
56. Queen Victoria's Journals, 15 October 1844.

57. Ibid., 8 September 1848.
58. Greville, *Greville Memoirs*, III, 296.
59. Ibid., III, 296.

CHAPTER 12
After Albert
Appearing between pages 219 and 236

1. Queen Victoria's Journals, 8 November 1861.
2. Quoted in Ridley, *Bertie*, ch. 4.
3. Queen Victoria's Journals, 22 November 1861.
4. Ibid., 30 November 1861, 4 December 1861.
5. Ibid., 1 December 1861.
6. Ibid., 2 December 1861.
7. Ibid., 4 December 1861.
8. Ibid., 7 December 1861.
9. 'The last hours of Prince Albert', *Daily Dispatch*, 31 January 1865.
10. Queen Victoria's Journals, 11 December 1861.
11. Martin, *Life of His Royal Highness the Prince Consort*, V, 437.
12. Queen Victoria's Journals, 13 December 1861.
13. Martin, *Life of His Royal Highness the Prince Consort*, V, 439.
14. *The Observer*, 23 December 1861, 5.
15. Ibid.
16. Quoted in Ridley, *Bertie*, ch. 4.
17. Ponsonby, *Henry Ponsonby*, 119.
18. Ibid., 116.
19. Ibid., 64.
20. Ibid., 36.
21. Queen Victoria's Journals, 1 April 1870.
22. Ponsonby, *Henry Ponsonby*, 133–4.
23. Ibid., 48.
24. Ibid., 50.
25. Ibid., 46.
26. Ibid., 45.
27. Ibid., 372.
28. Ibid., 128.
29. Ibid., 126.
30. Ponsonby, *Recollections of Three Reigns*, 96.
31. Ponsonby, *Henry Ponsonby*, 128.
32. Queen Victoria's Journals, 23 June 1887.
33. Ibid., 11 August 1888.
34. *The Times*, 6 November 1893, 6.
35. Queen Victoria's Journals, 18 November 1893.
36. Ponsonby, *Henry Ponsonby*, 131.
37. Ibid., 131.
38. Ibid., 131–2.
39. Ponsonby, *Recollections of Three Reigns*, 15–16.
40. Ibid., 15.
41. BL MSS Eur F 84 126a, Sir Frederick Ponsonby to 'Babs', 27 April 1897.
42. Ibid.

43. Anand, *Indian Sahib*, 102.
44. Kuhn, 'Queen Victoria's Civil List', 662.
45. Civil List Notes, February 1901, National Archive, CAB 37/56/19, 15.
46. Queen Victoria's Journals, 16 July 1900.

CHAPTER 13
Court Circular
Appearing between pages 237 and 250

1. *London Post with Intelligence Foreign and Domestick*, 18–20 October 1699, 2.
2. Queen Victoria's Journals, 19 July 1837.
3. *The Times*, 12 February 1902, 11.
4. Ibid., 11.
5. Ibid., 11.
6. *The Times*, 23 November 1791, 2.
7. *The Times*, 10 June 1825, 3.
8. 'Member of the Aristocracy', *Manners and Rules*, 68.
9. Ibid., 69.
10. Airlie, *Thatched with Gold*, 106.
11. Queen Victoria's Journals, 25 February 1898.
12. Langtry, *Days I Knew*, 107.
13. Queen Victoria's Journals, 10 May 1898.
14. Ansell, 'Seal of Social Approval', 156.
15. *London Gazette*, 9 January 1906, 187.
16. 'Member of the Aristocracy', *Manners and Rules*, 76.
17. Gorst, *Of Carriages and Kings*, 193.
18. Ibid., 194.
19. 'Foreign Resident', *Society in the New Reign*, 12.
20. Ibid., 12.
21. Ibid., 113.
22. Stamper, *What I Know*, 1.
23. Ibid., 27.
24. Ibid., 186.
25. Ibid., 109.
26. Ibid., 124–5.
27. Macnaghten, *Days of My Years*, 83.
28. *The Times*, 11 November 1907, 9.
29. Ridley, *Bertie*, ch. 27.

CHAPTER 14
That Dear Little Man
Appearing between pages 251 and 274

1. 'The Stables: Equerries 1660–1837', in Bucholz (ed.), *Office-Holders in Modern Britain*, 607–11.
2. Ponsonby, *Recollections of Three Reigns*, 279.
3. Rose, *King George V*, 147.
4. Gore, *King George V*, 275.
5. Ibid., 175.
6. Ibid., 220.
7. Ibid., 221.
8. Matson, *Sandringham Days*, ch.11.

9. Rose, *King George V*, 64.
10. Windsor, *King's Story*, 243.
11. Ponsonby, *Recollections of Three Reigns*, 279.
12. Ibid., 279.
13. Godfrey-Faussett, *Royal Servant*, 153.
14. Ibid., 210.
15. Ibid., 296.
16. Ibid., 228.
17. Ponsonby, *Recollections of Three Reigns*, 314.
18. Ibid., 329.
19. Matson, *Sandringham Days*, ch.11.
20. Ibid.
21. Ibid.
22. Rose, *King George V*, 57.
23. Matson, *Sandringham Days*, ch.11.
24. Windsor, *King's Story*, 183.
25. Ibid., 184.
26. Quoted in Dungavell, 'Architectural Career of Sir Aston Webb', 279.
27. *The Times*, 12 November 1918, 11.
28. This passage is adapted from my *Long Weekend*.
29. Windsor, *King's Story*, 186.
30. This passage is adapted from my *Long Weekend*.
31. Godfrey-Faussett, *Royal Servant*, 172.
32. Gore, *King George V*, 327.
33. Quoted in Rose, *King George V*, 322.
34. 'Philately', *Oxford English Dictionary Online*, Oxford: Oxford University Press (2018).
35. 'A Magnificent Collection: Introduction', Smithsonian National Postal Museum website, https://postalmuseum.si.edu/queen's/introduction.html (accessed 19 February 2018).
36. Rose, *King George V*, 316.
37. Bradford, *Elizabeth*, ch. 2.
38. Middleton, 'Our Royal Family'.
39. Ibid.
40. Crawford, *Little Princesses*, ch. 4.
41. Queen Victoria's Journals, 24 December 1840.
42. 'The Dogs of Alexandra of Denmark: A Tour of the Kennels at Sandringham', Mimi Matthews website, 29 April 2016, https://www.mimimatthews.com/2016/04/29/the-dogs-of-alexandra-of-denmark-a-tour-of-the-kennels-at-sandringham/ (accessed 19 February 2018).
43. Middleton, 'Our Royal Family'.
44. Ibid.
45. Godfrey-Faussett, *Royal Servant*, 250.
46. Windsor, *King's Story*, 279.
47. 'The First Christmas Speech', History of Government blog, 24 April 2013, https://history.blog.gov.uk/2013/04/24/the-first-christmas-speech/ (accessed 19 February 2018).
48. *The Observer*, 25 December 1932, 9.
49. *Manchester Guardian*, 7 May 1935, 18.

50. Ibid., 18.
51. Ibid., 16.
52. *The Times*, 7 May 1935, 16.
53. Ibid., 9.
54. Ponsonby, *Recollections of Three Reigns*, 356.
55. Rose, King *George V*, 397.
56. Godfrey-Faussett, *Royal Servant*, 317.

CHAPTER 15
Secretaries
Appearing between pages 275 and 291

1. Channon, *Chips*, 56.
2. Hart-Davis (ed.), *King's Counsellor*, 108.
3. Windsor, *King's Story*, 303.
4. Ibid., 187.
5. 'The Prince of Wales as airman', *Illustrated London News*, 2 August 1930, 197.
6. 'When the princes travel by liner', *Illustrated London News*, 9 May 1931, 780.
7. Windsor, *King's Story*, 134.
8. Ibid., 304.
9. Hart-Davis (ed.), *In Royal Service*, 1.
10. Hart-Davis (ed.), *King's Counsellor*, 104.
11. Ibid., 104.
12. Ibid., 105.
13. Ibid., 105.
14. Windsor, *King's Story*, 235.
15. Ibid., 237.
16. Vanderbilt and Furness, *Double Exposure*, 305.
17. Bloch (ed.), *Wallis and Edward*, 75.
18. Ibid., 74.
19. Vanderbilt and Furness, *Double Exposure*, 206.
20. Bloch, *Wallis and Edward*, 116.
21. Vanderbilt and Furness, *Double Exposure*, 314.
22. Channon, *Chips*, 30.
23. Ibid., 46.
24. *Chicago Tribune*, 18 October 1936, 2.
25. Windsor, *King's Story*, 326.
26. *The Times*, 29 November 1955, 9.
27. Hart-Davis (ed.), *King and Counsellor*, 108.
28. Ibid., 109.
29. 'Edward VIII Abdicates the Throne', History Place website, http://www.historyplace.com/speeches/edward.htm (accessed 19 February 2018).
30. Channon, *Chips*, 103.
31. Ibid., 104.
32. Godfrey-Faussett, *Royal Servant*, 321.
33. Corbitt, *My Twenty Years*, 188–9.
34. Laski, 'King's Secretary', 390.
35. Quoted in Bogdanor, *Monarchy and the Constitution*, 214.
36. Quoted in Hart-Davis (ed.), *King's Counsellor*, fn. 138.
37. Ibid., 139.
38. Ibid., 140.

39. Ibid., 103.
40. Ibid., 10.
41. Ibid., 51.
42. Ibid., 92.
43. Ibid., 29.
44. Ibid., 160.
45. Ibid., 161.
46. Ibid., 204.
47. Ibid., 224.
48. Ibid., 229.
49. Ibid., 195.
50. *Manchester Guardian*, 21 October 1943, 2.
51. Hart-Davis (ed.), *King's Counsellor*, 194.

CHAPTER 16
Gloriana
Appearing between pages 292 and 309

1. *The Times*, 3 December 1951, 6.
2. Sarah Bradford, *George VI: The Dutiful King*, 609.
3. *Manchester Guardian*, 29 April 1952, 7.
4. 'Coronation Preparations: Speech by the Minister of Works, the Rt Hon. David Eccles MP, at Church House, Westminster, Tuesday February 17th 1953', 1, available at http://media.bufvc.ac.uk/newsonscreen2/BPN/44258/NoS_44258_other.pdf (accessed 20 February 2018).
5. Ibid., 2.
6. Ibid., 2.
7. Ibid., 3.
8. Ibid., 8.
9. Ibid., 8.
10. *The Observer*, 1 March 1953, 5.
11. Ibid., 5.
12. Ibid., 5.
13. *Manchester Guardian*, 2 June 1953, 7.
14. Quoted in Herbert, 'Here comes the Queen!', 98.
15. Richards, 'Coronation of Queen Elizabeth II', 69–70.
16. 'The Story of BBC Television: Television Out and About', History of the BBC, BBC website, http://www.bbc.co.uk/historyofthebbc/research/general/tvstory8 (accessed 20 February 2018).
17. Queen Victoria's Journals, 28 June 1838.
18. *Manchester Guardian*, 29 October 1952, 1.
19. Bradford, *Elizabeth*, ch 7.
20. *The Times*, 29 October 1952, 4.
21. 'Coronation – Television', cabinet minute, 12 November 1952, National Archives, CAB 129/57/6.
22. 'Orders for Processions to and from Westminster Abbey', 1953, 8, 55, National Archives, MEPO 4/141.
23. *The Times*, 13 May 1953, 5.
24. Channon, *Chips*, 476.

25. *A Queen Is Crowned*, Rank Organisation (1953).
26. *The Times*, 3 June 1953, 12.
27. *Manchester Guardian*, 8 June 1953, 1.
28. *Manchester Guardian*, 3 June 1953, 3.

CHAPTER 17
Affectionate Memoirs
Appearing between pages 310 and 335

1. *Daily Record*, 24 June 2000, 20–1.
2. Ibid, 20–1.
3. Crawford, *Little Princesses*, ch. 4.
4. *The Spectator*, 12 October 1951, 4.
5. *The Observer*, 28 January 1951, 7.
6. *The Spectator*, 12 October 1951, 4.
7. Tschumi, *Royal Chef*, 139.
8. Ibid., 155.
9. Ibid., 6.
10. Ibid., 169.
11. Ibid., 172.
12. Ibid., 173.
13. Ibid., 179.
14. 'Member of the Royal Household', *Private Life of the Queen*, v.
15. Ibid., 114.
16. 'Member of the Royal Household', *Private Life of King Edward VII*, vi.
17. *Sunday Times*, 30 September 1951, 3.
18. 'Janus', 'A Spectator's Notebook'; Harris, 'Uncrowned King'.
19. *Illustrated London News*, 14 November 1953, 769.
20. *The Observer*, 21 February 1954, 9.
21. Advertisement, *The Observer*, 21 October 1956, 16.
22. Corbitt, *Fit for a King*, 188.
23. Ibid., 192.
24. This passage owes much to Christopher Warwick's excellent biography, *Princess Margaret: A Life of Contrasts*.
25. Warwick, *Princess Margaret*, ch. 9.
26. Ibid..
27. Ibid.
28. Ibid., ch. 10.
29. *The Times*, 1 November 1955, 8.
30. Ibid., 9.
31. *Manchester Guardian*, 1 November 1955, 3.
32. Corbitt, *My Twenty Years*, 228.
33. Ibid., 229.
34. Ibid., 231.
35. *Manchester Guardian*, 26 January 1955, 4.
36. Ibid., 4.
37. *The Times*, 17 June 1975, 16.
38. *Manchester Guardian*, 11 February 1957, 1.
39. *Manchester Guardian*, 22 January 1958, 1.
40. Grigg, 'Punched, Abused, Challenged'.
41. *Manchester Guardian*, 5 August 1957, 4.
42. *The Times*, 7 August 1957, 6.
43. Ibid., 6.
44. Grigg, 'Punched, Abused, Challenged'.
45. Ibid.
46. Ibid.
47. Ibid.
48. Taylor, 'Saying What Everyone Thinks'.
49. *The Guardian*, 29 June 1961.
50. Brown, *Ma'am Darling*, ch. 37. This is a wonderful book.
51. Ibid., ch. 29.
52. Ibid., ch. 53.
53. Burgess, *Behind Palace Doors*, p. 36.
54. Rhodes, *Final Curtsey*, ch. 8.
55. Ibid.
56. Burgess, *Behind Palace Doors*, p. 11.
57. Ibid., p. 18.
58. 'The Infamous "Squidgygate" Transcript', http://www.geocities.ws/rickanddarvagossip/diana_gilbey.html (accessed 20 February 2018).
59. Morton, *Diana*, 191.
60. *The Times*, 10 December 1992, 1.
61. 'A Speech by the Queen on the 40th Anniversary of Her Accession (Annus Horribilis Speech', Royal Family website, 24 November 1992, https://www.royal.uk/annus-horribilis-speech (accessed 20 February 2018)).
62. 'The Queen's Christmas Message 1992', https://www.sim64.co.uk/queens-speech-1992.html (accessed 20 February 2018).

POSTSCRIPT
'It's All to Do with the Training'
Appearing between pages 337 and 340

1. 'The Panorama Interview', http://www.bbc.co.uk/news/special/politics97/diana/panorama.html (accessed 20 February 2018).
2. Morton, *Diana*, 307.
3. 'Inside the Royal Household', Royal Family website, https://www.royal.uk/inside-the-royal-household (accessed 20 February 2018).

Getty Images; pp. 318-9 © Illustrated London News / Mary Evans Picture Library; p. 320 ANL/Daily Sketch/REX/Shutterstock; p. 325 Hulton Deutsch / Contributor via Getty Images; p. 329 © Lichfield / Contributor via Getty Images; p. 333 Tim Graham / Contributor via Getty Images; p. 338 © Victoria and Albert Museum, London

The author and publishers have made every effort to trace and contact copyright holders. The publishers will be pleased to correct any mistakes or omissions in future editions.